Novels by John Hawkes

JOHN HAWKES

Adventures in the Alaskan Skin Trade

SIMON AND SCHUSTER

NEW YORK

This novel is a work of fiction. Names, characters, places and incidents either are the product of the author's imagination or are used fictitiously. Any resemblance to actual events or locales or persons, living or dead, is entirely coincidental.

Copyright © 1985 by John Hawkes
All rights reserved
including the right of reproduction
in whole or in part in any form
Published by Simon and Schuster
A Division of Simon & Schuster, Inc.
Simon & Schuster Building
Rockefeller Center
1230 Avenue of the Americas
New York, New York 10020
SIMON AND SCHUSTER and colophon are registered trademarks
of Simon & Schuster, Inc.
Designed by Irving Perkins Associates
Manufactured in the United States of America
10 9 8 7 6 5 4 3 2 1
Library of Congress Cataloging in Publication Data
Hawkes, John, date.
    Adventures in the Alaskan skin trade.

    I. Title.
PS3558.A82A63   1985   813'.54   85-11795
ISBN: 0-671-47304-2

For Sophie

Adventures in the Alaskan Skin Trade

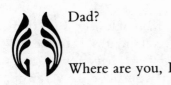 Dad?

Where are you, Dad?

To the north. To the west. To the far north and the receding west. Where the seas are black and the fish dead. Where the rivers flow and the mountains rise. Where the fog drifts and the rain falls. Where the birds fly off course and the caribou limps and the wolverine hunts itself along the water's edge. Where the wind sings and the log rots and moss grows on glaciers. Where the sun is cold and the white bear grins on his bed of ice that turns and floats on the salty currents through the night. To the north that is mine. To the west that is mine. To the bones and teeth and pinnacles and silence of the north and the west that are mine, Sunny, still mine.

Westward ho!

2 —

I do not speak French. I dislike travel. I am afraid of horses. But soon I shall leave Alaska. In a week or month or several months, I shall leave Alaska. I shall make my way by air to France, where I have never been, and I shall find myself a boy of twenty—every woman on the verge of thirty-nine deserves at last a French boy of twenty—and from my young boy, who shall be a stable-hand, I shall learn to speak French and ride horses. I shall find repose in France. I shall find the elegance I have never known, and forgive my father, and love my French boy in some village famous for its wine and the breeding and riding of horses.

Tomorrow, or the next day, or in a week or month or several months, I shall reach for my Winchester and lift it down from its rack of antlers, and cradling my loaded Winchester I shall leave my cabin—the second of the only two luxury log cabins in Alaska—and stroll down the path through the ferns and pines to the lake, where I shall stand for a moment surveying the lake, the glacier on its far side, the nearby float, the gasoline pump on the edge of the float, the small green and white airplane tethered in the drizzle at the end of the float. I shall watch the drizzle putting cold steam on the sides of my airplane and dotting the water around the pontoons as if fish were rising to the surface to eat or drink, though I have never caught a fish in this dark lake that is my landing field. I shall stand there cradling my rifle and smelling gasoline and staring at my fur-rimmed goggles hanging behind the windshield of my plane. Once more I shall watch this small airplane drifting to and fro on its moorings, and I shall see the soot on its cowling, the traces of rust on the pontoons, the drizzle weighting down its wings, the goggles rocking gently behind the yellowed plexiglass.

Then, carefully, I shall lift the rifle and brace myself with one foot forward and one back, and lean toward the plane and fire once into the nearest pontoon and once into the other. Then two shots more. Then two more. The shots will carry out across the lake to the cliffs of ice and fade. If I wait, sitting on the thick wet planking of the float, I shall see the pontoons sinking, the fuselage tipping downwards, the tail rising, the airplane sinking to one side and going down, until only the tip of the rudder shows above the black waters. But I shall have no need to contemplate the slow disappearance of the airplane with my goggles and the old flying jacket still inside. Instead I shall merely lean the Winchester against the fuel pump, run my hand through my head of dark wet hair, slap a wet hip and stroll away, leaving the Cessna half under water and my cabin unlocked.

I shall abandon the Alaska-Yukon Gamelands, which is the trailer park containing my luxury log cabin; I shall leave behind the nine females and the nine Mastodon mobile homes of our establishment and quit Alaska forever and go to France. Fields of battle, war monuments, vineyards, chateaux, horses, lover, the elegant terrain of my father's past—I shall drink it to the last ruby drop, Sunny in her tight jeans and tee shirt with a fleur-de-lis stenciled between her fulsome breasts.

No bra. Dark glasses. A French accent. An Alaskan woman feeling good in her skin in France.

3 —

My father took my mother and me to Alaska shortly after the stock market crash of 1929. He needn't have left Connecticut, then or ever, though that year his youngest brother, the darling of the Deauville boys as he was known to everyone acquainted with the family, shot himself on the tennis courts one early morning, and my father's two closest friends, one an amateur landscape painter and the other a drinker who wanted to eliminate industrial smokestacks through the use of small economical machines that would blow waste gases higher into the air than the tallest unsightly smokestack could carry them, both killed themselves within the week. The painter thrust his head through an unfinished canvas and, wearing his rent canvas like a sumptuous ruff, shot himself in the temple. The inventor rowed out to his sailboat three mornings later and tied a length of line from his neck to a spare anchor, and eased himself over the side as the sun came up on the still water. The painter was a bachelor. The inventor left behind a young tight-skinned wife and an only son, a weeping little boy who at the age of eight was three years my senior and my favorite playmate, and also left behind a last half-drunk quart of whiskey on the kitchen table.

But such dashed dreams did not drive my father to Alaska. The ruin that overtook many of those around him merely created a climate suitable to his own inventiveness. Not an excuse—he was too cheerful and noble and youthful ever to need excuses for what he did—but merely a climate that made appropriate the idea when, thanks to a chance meeting with a friend, it came to mind. He was charming, he was tall, his handsomeness depended in part on his shy smile. He needed direction. He needed some vastness to smile upon. He had the potential for being an agreeable and even heroic adventurer. It was not long after the rash of suicides that he heard of Alaska. He may have begun to think that it was unseemly to continue living with his wife and child in his father's world of tennis courts and stables—his father was a breeder of blooded horses and was French by birth—which was not far by shaded lanes from his dead friend's studio or from the blue waters where his other friend had kept his trim sailboat. But if so, that sense of unseemliness at being husband and father in the childhood home he still adored, with its horses and open cars and two surviving horse-drawn carriages, never became any great concern for him. Actually my father had only one regret about Alaska, which was precisely that he did not wish to leave the Deauville estate or leave behind the handsome black-haired matriarch who was his beloved mother. The brother who committed suicide may have been the family's darling, but my father was his mother's favorite son. At any rate his cheer and determination did not fail; uprooting wife and daughter was swiftly and deftly done; his last kiss he gave to his mother.

When we drove to the local railway station in one of the open cars piled high with luggage, my father wore a stylish tan fedora and a tailored camel's hair overcoat; my mother wore a green long-skirted suit and a green felt Scottish hat and was weeping; while I was dressed in a sailor coat and cap and leather leggings, though I was a girl. Seated on my father's lap in the sun and wind and noise, I felt that I myself was the chauffeur of that large and shiny vehicle instead of the silent, goggled man who grimly held the wheel beside us.

At that moment my father's handsome face was flushed with joy.

Years later, when I was stepping down onto the pontoon of the Cessna, suddenly I thought of my long-lost friend, the inventor's little son with his poor face shaped like a peanut and wet and pink from crying. By that time my mother had been dead for years, my father had disappeared, and I, not he, had become the adventurer.

4 ——

My father told us that in Alaska he was going to find vast fields of gold or exotic metal, or unnameable forms of splendid treasure, though the truth was that he really went to Alaska in search of a totem pole. A friend in Washington had told him that there existed somewhere in Alaska a totem pole carved by Indians who had been so moved by a missionary's tale of the President who had freed the slaves that they had carved a totem pole surmounted by Lincoln, stovepipe hat and all. It was the totem pole that had lured my father to Alaska. For my father, Alaska and Lincoln on the totem pole were synonymous. At least my father discovered the wooden Lincoln, if nothing else.

5 ——

Once, when I was still a child, he told me that there had been a time when the palm tree had flourished in Alaska. Nothing pleased him so much as the notion of palm trees growing on the sites of present glaciers in a warm sun that has long since been displaced by rain, in all its endless varieties, and by wind and snow and darkness. Not even the totem pole so took his fancy. As if the missing palm trees lent a tropical cast to our brutally northern clime, or made this cruel territory in any way attractive to gentler sensibilities like his and mine. But he was that kind of adventurer—gentle, optimistic, inventive, never ruthless. He was an artist in the life of adventure. The rarity of the adventure itself was far more important to him than the riches he was forever promising my mother and me. In his worst agonies he never lost the light of adventure—in his eyes, in his smile.

It was up to me to discover ruthlessness, and I quickly did. Until

my mid-girlhood I loved all this monumental waste of nature as did
my father. Then, luckily for me, I discovered its true hatefulness, and
began to succeed where my father only grandly failed. At an early age
I knew that woman, not Alaska, is the last frontier. I have made the
most of it. In sex I have found my father's gold mine. And there are
no palm trees at Gamelands.

6 —

For a month now I have not been my own woman—my vigor, my
tough body, my tough mind notwithstanding. For four long weeks,
or since my decision to leave Alaska, my father has been calling to
me—in dreams. And in those dreams I have gone to him, returned to
him, found him again, heeded his call. It's worse than palm trees. Much
worse.

I start up with a groaning sound though I am still asleep. Naked and
groaning I drag myself from satin sheets and Hudson Bay blankets, in
a log cabin fitted out with fancy furniture, tape decks, a shortwave
radio, and in the cold and darkness smelling of pine and cedar, perfume
and wood smoke, I pull on my jeans and woolen shirt and unlaced
boots. Then I am on my way to the glacier trail, where I'll find him.
Behind me the mobile homes are like sleeping whales; in a world
without light the Cessna glows, shines, is an enormous winged insect
dipped in phosphorus. The trail around the edge of the lake is rimmed
with thin glass that cracks and crunches beneath my boots. He is ahead
of me, inside the glacier, the King of the North in his tomb.
    Sunny, he calls. Sunny.
    I hear him. I think of him. Again it comes to me that Hamlet must
have been a woman, since what father would return from the dead
except to his daughter? I smile to myself and pick up my pace.
    I thrust my hands into my hip pockets. I walk with long strides
and a heavy tread. The lake, which I cannot see, is cold enough to
freeze in, and bottomless; the firs and pines are laced together with

cobwebs and rivulets of frozen sap. I am walking on beds of mosquitoes too cold to rise in this hell for nature lovers where the timber
is unfit for cutting and the land impassable to trail bikes and snow-
mobiles.

What kind of father lures his sleeping daughter into such a morning?

What woman, even a mechanically minded woman, can ignore the
love of a phantasm?

The ascent is over rock, across rock, up rock, and on the glacier trail
above the lake I am transformed, become in a breath a supple athlete
hot in her perspiration, cold in the rain, quickened by steep angles and
rising heights. Steadily I climb and swiftly; along the way and in my
sudden eagerness I have discarded shirt and boots, am bare-chested,
barefooted, a mannish maenad drawing closer, ever closer, to her phantasm.

The height is in my brain, my blood. I dislodge pebbles, climb with
my hands, find sure and painless footing with my bare feet.

In my sleep I am climbing the glacier trail and pausing, thoughtlessly
rubbing my wet breasts, pushing on.

Where are you, I call. But I know full well where he is, and I am
nearly there. The rain is like oil on my nakedness. My feet are warm,
soft, unbloodied, though now I am stalking him across the lunar ice—
eagerly, against my will. I skirt small crevasses, glide across the treacherous ice, which is a chaos of wrinkles, ridges, little knife-sharp points
like the tips of inverted icicles that crack and shatter beneath my bare
feet, and still I am immune to the torturous surface, the dangerous way,
the perilous height that only piques my recklessness.

But now I stop, I quiver, I stand at the edge of my destination—the
black crevasse. There is a slush of light around me, but hardly enough
to distinguish air from ice, ice from rock, blackness of the wide crevasse
from the night's shadows.

Then I look down. Straight down. One moment I am an impatient,
half-blind, reckless woman peering across a crevasse wider than a Yukon cargo sled with sixteen dogs driven in full flight, and the next
moment I am staring down one hundred feet or more into the space
between two perpendicular walls of clearest glass, and not into darkness.
On the surface there is only the half-light, the drizzle, not the slightest
illumination rising from the chasm; yet below me in the depths of the
ice the sun is flooding his lair.

I look down. And all the way to the bottom of that crevasse the ice
is not glacial. Not at all. Even in my dream I know that glacial ice is

black, dark blue, dark green, a solidity of folds and cracks, sutures, striations, a massing of unnaturalness, a vast injury of dark seas frozen and turned into the color and density of hopelessness. But at my feet those nether icy regions of the sun are a catacomb of glass; the chasm is a fierce brightness cut into walls of light.

I look down. I will not slip or suddenly fling myself into that deep vastness of warm light in the cold millennia. My head is bent, my mouth filled with the taste of night; I am as easy in my stance as if I were leaning against Lincoln's totem pole in the rain. I am poised, relaxed, calmly horrified, whatever. And my name—nickname actually—is the joke of the dream. Sunny discovering the buried sun. Sunny as clear in her head as ever. Sunny standing at the edge of death. Dad in the depths.

Where are you, Dad?

Down there, of course. The king in his tomb.

And there he is. The King of the North. There at the bottom of the black crevasse in the brightest light, wielding his long whip over toppled sled and tangled dogs, there he stands, taller than ever, hood of his squirrel-skin parka thrown back, flaps of his wolf-fur hat boyishly upraised, eyes agleam, long face pink with his exertions, pink with the pleasures of the north, brows and lashes and hair at the tips of his ears all white and rimed with frost. He is strong, brave, laughing, as tall as a wooden Lincoln. His feet are apart, his arm is raised, the whip sings, the tangled dogs are fighting, drawing blood. There he stands in the golden light of his last voyage, his spilled cargo.

A Yukon cargo sled and its load of little sacks filled with gold dust lies at his feet. The sacks have burst, are empty, and man, dogs, wrecked sled are covered in a film of gold; in the sunstruck air the cloud of golden dust is a sheen, a haze, and magnifies and makes all the clearer his blue eyes, pink face, the bloodied fang, the wrecked sled.

The lead dog, a handsome brute, clamps his jaws into a white and furry flank. Half the team lies dead. The survivors fight in harness, engorge themselves, climb end on end atop each other, feast on the red and slimy shreds and ribbons of their fellows.

He stays his arm. He watches. He surveys what is his—this glorious and hopeless cannibalism—and laughs, throws down his whip, removes his fur cap, flings it aside. His hands are bare. The last dog is dying.

Then—and he is proud, still valiant—then he looks up at me.

He rears back, throws back his head, looks up, and there before my eyes he freezes. One long pink cheek turns black, hangs down, the right hand blackens. He loses three black fingers from the right hand. Still he looks up at me and laughs. Then he raises his right arm. Slowly he lifts it high above his head, and now the thick black hair is white with frost, the happy eyes are lit with pain, on the last black frozen finger of the right hand the Deauville family ring is a lump of gold.

Then he waves.

Hello? Farewell?

Does he think I'll pity him? I don't.

Does he think I'll forgive him? But I don't.

In the light and ice the phantasm, the King of the North, makes his appeal, and now I refuse it. And abruptly, in that instant, the bright light turns to blackness and he is gone.

Then I am sitting up awake and wet, hot and cold, hugging to myself my nudity and breathing in the scent of the evergreens beyond the open window, listening to the flights of mosquitoes that swell the dawn.

Who's more contemptible, I ask myself, shaking my head and slapping my substantial arms and breasts and thighs—the King of the North or his daughter?

7 —

The Deauville family is all but extinct. Once there were nine brothers, including my grandfather, who, in Chantilly, in France, rode to the hounds with their own father in the lead, and in their time no finer men rode out in red coats and white britches or blew higher, clearer notes on their brass horns. They were gallant, frolicsome men; their horses were fiery, high-spirited, large-boned, deep in the chest.

The Deauville chateau was small, for the richness of the life it housed, a gray and mustard-colored edifice of chimneys, conical black slate roofs on supple turrets, and gates of black iron and polished brass. The stable and the chateau were as one: on occasion the nine brothers and the Old Gentleman, as their father was called, took their meals in the stables; the Old Gentleman insisted that they keep their nine saddles, nine bridles, nine pairs of boots and nine velvet-covered caps and brass

horns on display in the main hall of the chateau, despite the inconve-
nience. The Deauvilles bred and raised elegant blooded horses and
children who were always male. A mysterious woman, with whom
the Old Gentleman took up, began their ruin, though the old man and
his long-suffering wife and the mysterious woman all lived long enough
to cast their blight of elegance on my own father when, as a boy, he
participated in a Deauville family reunion in France.

The ninth son, my grandfather, came to America with an entourage
of young French maids, young French grooms, and several mares and
a stallion from the original Deauville estate. In Connecticut he bought
open land, built house and stables, married a woman as tall and handsome as himself, a young matriarchal person born and raised in Ireland.
She was of the gentry and expected nothing less than love and faith-
fulness in marriage. My grandfather, though an aristocrat, was bent on
creating and corrupting family lines, a process dependent initially on
the young maids, who were replaced, even into my own lifetime, by
such a variety of women as to put the original mysterious woman to
shame. There was nothing mysterious about my grandfather's women,
while his wife, of stately carriage and long thick black hair, was as
proud and long-suffering as her predecessor, my great-grandmother in
Chantilly. My grandfather, while running rampant and ravaged as he
was by satyriasis, nonetheless fathered, in his turn and in wedlock, four
sons, of whom my own father was the second.

The Deauville family, already splintered in a sense, was finally brought
still closer to ruin. The oldest son died in 1918 in the Great Air War in
France; the youngest shot himself behind the wheel of his open Stutz
Bearcat, which one early morning he drove onto the tennis court and
parked at a sudden crazy angle for the fatal event; the next-to-youngest
abandoned his heritage to spend his life selling box cameras in every
state except his native Connecticut; my father had a chance meeting
with a friend from Washington and set off with my mother and me for
Alaska. Even then my grandfather was chasing more women than ever,
and with more vigor than ever.

Now the Deauville family is all but extinct. I am the last of the line
and not a man but a woman. When I die—long years in the future, I
assume, and of course in France—the Deauville family name, which
is pronounced "dough-veal," will die as well. It is a family name that
deserves extinction. It was a family of men, a family of confusion, a
family in which women were at best only prized like horses, a conglomerate of men who did not know that between innocence and sa-

tyriasis there's little to choose, or who could not find it in themselves to bridge extremes. The question is what brought about the family ruin: the innocence that flowered in my father or the satyriasis that surged through the lives of my grandfather and great-grandfather? But they are one and the same, those false flourishes of manhood, and it is up to me to discover how and why it happens that lust and innocence are only two faces in the same pool, and to forgive if I can the Alaskan adventurer as I have long since forgiven the old womanizer in all his gleeful and crafty pursuit of women.

It is not for nothing that I have pursued a career in the oldest profession in the world, as they say, or have made a business, and a spankingly successful one at that, out of the only thing more important to men than money. Dream itself is the source of all ruin. And perhaps I'm wrong. Perhaps my grandfather was not a dreamer. Perhaps there is only one handsome, hateful face in the pool.

8 —

Shortly after my birth in 1925, when my father was already forty-five years old, I was carried to a small stone chapel near the Deauville family home in Connecticut. At the insistence of my grandmother, and over the protestations of my mother, which were so mildly and softly voiced that they were dismissed by all concerned including my father, who was well aware of the justice and sensibility of his wife's desires but was unswervingly loyal to his mother's every wish or whim, no matter how unreasonable, I was christened Jacqueline Burne Deauville. So from the outset I was defined, as was my father, by the combination of the Deauville family name and my grandmother's Irish maiden name, my mother's own maiden name of Flowers being forever denied her daughter from that first and last sprinkling of the blessed waters—first and last since I was my parents' only child, and a girl at that. My mother, whose given name was Cecily, called me Jackie and spent her poor wronged life clinging to music and femininity. For my father, on the other hand, who invented new names for friends, acquaintances, and loved ones, and even for himself, I was Sunny from the hapless, rainy day of my birth, while for him my mother was always Sissy, a nickname she wanly bore and helplessly detested throughout the eleven sad and baffling years of her marriage. She died abruptly one Saturday afternoon in Alaska when I was ten.

My father was christened John Burne Deauville, but from his earliest boyhood was known as Jack, until, a few months prior to going to Alaska, he renicknamed himself Uncle Jake. Thanks to my father my three uncles were inescapably known as Billy Boy (the youngest), Doc (the camera salesman), and Granny (the oldest, who was shot down in France in 1917 and was in fact grandmotherly in his patient, extravagant love for his three brothers).

My father, then, was Uncle Jake. I was not allowed to call him Father. I was never allowed to call him Dad. Especially was I never allowed to call him Dad. But if my father was to be blamed for humorously renaming the unoffending population of his little world, and most of all denying to his daughter what was rightfully hers—the name appropriate to that man who was her sole spell-caster—how much more was I to be blamed, since I too called my mother Sissy. For all the years of my girlhood I was not aware of how my father wronged me, or of how he and I both wronged my mother. How happily I cried out Uncle Jake! or Sissy! when the rains fell and I grew up an Alaskan.

My father could not have understood his thralldom over wife and daughter or have known how he denied us. No man was larger, kinder, handsomer, braver, or more admired than Uncle Jake. Yet despite his glamour and courage that's all he was: Uncle Jake.

He could not have known.

Sometimes I think that the only redeeming fact in my father's life was that he too was involved with a mysterious woman—a French woman who singled him out for her own in the Great War. She might have been his ruin then and there and spared us all. But she was not.

In me my grandmother's strong but selfish spirit lives on as ruthless determination and good sense. In me my mother's femininity lives on as my secret self. In me her flesh lives on, though my flesh is shaped by sex, to sex, and hers was not.

I owe you nothing, Uncle Jake.

9 —

Of the nine other females presently working at the Alaska-Yukon Gamelands, seven are transient girls: Jenny, Elaine, Marie and Joan, Liz, Susan, and another self-nicknamer who insists that we call her Freckles, though her face is clearer than a china doll's and her only freckles lie in a faint little strawberry cloud between her shoulders. These girls are young; they enjoy using lotions and washing themselves with scented soaps. They are ordinary-looking girls who strip down to the bare flesh without self-consciousness. One by one they drifted up to Alaska for fun and money and, for more than a year now, have been content to live and work at Gamelands. There were other girls before them.

I befriend and comfort and counsel Jenny and Elaine and Liz and the rest but I do not mother them. In fact I don't spend much time with our transient girls, don't take much interest in them except professionally. The Alaska-Yukon Gamelands is a safe and ever-surprising place for those who work in it and those who come looking for the last frontier.

I don't mean that the transient girls are children. Not at all. They range in age from seventeen to twenty. They have their hurts, blemishes, bad days, spites, jokes. They are not special, no different from anyone else, and I know full well how Joan's father died in the machinery of a rusty harrow and how Jenny came to be known as the Little Whore from Idaho. I know them, I respect them all. Sympathy, fairness, good management is what they need from me, not mothering. What I need from them are happy steadies, a full count of men who are faithful to what we offer (girls, women, fetishism, the comforts and surprises of technology in the wilderness) and a substantial number of first-timers, the ever-replenishing line of men and boys who come to us and like what they find, find what they need, and come back to us. And that's what we have at Gamelands, thanks by and large to the transients.

Spooky Ruth and Thelma, on the other hand, are different. They are mature women, professionals, Alaskan. They are regulars; they are my friends; they helped me found the Alaska-Yukon Gamelands. Together we are three women of the same age and similar interests. Thelma is a marksman, a sex photographer, a female stud. Spooky Ruth is clairvoyant. She tells our Willies, as we call them, what they want to know, and her most hurtful truths are worth as much to the Willies as the juice of the forbidden fruit or what we have on tape. She's shy about her clairvoyance, and sometimes it fails. But it's Spooky Ruth who has contributed most in body and mind to Gamelands' reputation. The forgotten past, the secret future, as well as the fluids of the flesh, the music of the flesh recorded in a Mastodon mobile home equipped as no place they've ever seen, and played back—what more could our Willies want? It was Spooky Ruth who told me that I'm going to leave Alaska. Hers was the prophecy, mine the decision.

And me? "Heed hedonism," that's my motto. Heed hedonism, be true to your skills, drive your bargains well. I like men, even the smell of their sweat, their urine. I'm something of a man myself, or have my share of the masculine component, as they say, and dress like a man and stand alone. But underneath my thick woolen shirt of dark blue and dark green checks I wear an imitation French half-bra; and underneath my thick cord pants (tawny gold, smooth in the seat, worn tucked into my high-laced boots) I wear a see-through imitation French bikini of bright flesh-tinted silky nylon nipped with little bows and sporting three rosebuds in the crotch. The lingerie catalogue is a close companion to my maps and flight manuals. It pleases me to know the surprise that awaits the man who fumbles with my stiff buttons, and pulls aside or down my outer male garb—if I allow him to. Rough clothing, an unruly patch of pubic hair, a flounce of imitation silk, hot buttocks, and a clear head, widely known but rarely discovered, ripe for taking but rarely given—that's Sunny Deauville, or the woman behind the myths of Woman. I do in fact heed hedonism, and help others to do the same, out here with nine entertaining, instructive, desirable girls and women at the Alaska-Yukon Gamelands.

In the midst of us there stands a tall totem pole freshly painted in bright colors.

10 —

We are located eight miles from town on a good road of crushed gravel and in a flat half-acre hewn from purple pines that are centuries in diameter and taller than the tallest masts of the old whalers that sailed through the Bering Sea to the Arctic. The lake, my aquatic landing field, is only a short distance through the pines and evergreens; through those dark green and purple depths the soiled whiteness of the glacier's face is visible, and it is the glacier, as much as the girls and women awaiting them at Gamelands, that brings the pink of boyish pleasure into the faces of the men and youths who come out to us. Most men are more at ease with a glacier across a lake than alone with an Elaine, say, or a Jenny who is unmistakably about to take off her clothes. But the enticements we offer are hot and cold, near and far, small and vast, public and picturesque, private and pornographic. Our famous posters of an elk's antlers and black-stockinged leg are prominently displayed in shop windows and the lobbies of the two local banks and three motels and at the front desk of the old Baranof Hotel, where I stayed as a child. Everyone knows that the Alaska-Yukon Gamelands is not for fishing, hunting, or the innocent study of wildlife. But they also know about the Cessna and my abilities as guide and pilot, and that I'm available to anyone looking for outdoor as well as indoor sport.

Our large parking lot for their cars and motorcycles is equipped with trash receptacles and is fenced in with long, thick cedar rails darkly stained. A red wooden arrow points the way discreetly down a path through the trees. The path, which is a soft, deep ribbon of pine needles for those not too agitated to notice, winds a short way through the smells and shadows of the woods and then abruptly stops, having brought the urgent visitor to the edge of our clearing where he faces an archway of two tall, thick cedar poles spanned by a fifteen-foot crescent of blond pine wood with *Gamelands* burned by a fiery iron in a large and flowery script across all the curving surface of that great slab of wood. The urgent visitor enters our astounding space as we intend him to. He walks through our archway because the totem pole, taller than any, agleam with fresh paint, stands beyond the arch like the post behind the wicket in some giants' game of Alaskan croquet. Our Willie is drawn to the totem pole; he wants to approach it facing the angry beaks and spread pairs of wings. So he walks through the archway and stands before the totem pole in homage. He can't help himself. The totem pole speaks to him as does the glacier.

What then does he see, our shy or eager Willie? A quarter-acre of crushed quartz; nine Mastodon mobile homes the size and shape of jet plane fuselages, rainbow painted and randomly positioned inside the three walls of trees; a drinking fountain; two log cabins larger than the mobile homes. The cabin on his right is mine, and is identified by a large wooden sign that says, quite simply, *Private*. In front of the other cabin is a larger wooden sign that says, *Welcome—Men Only*. The *Men Only* is meant to inspire amusement, curiosity, a dash of pride. At any rate our Willies have the courage to enter, and step or stomp onto the veranda, push open the heavy wooden door of what is in fact our combination bar, snack room, reception lounge. The posters on the wall are life-sized: Willie grins or blushes. Among other Willies, he sits on one of the leather and aluminum chairs or cream-colored calfskin couches as deep and soft as snow, and reads quickly from one of the magazines heaped on the low glass tables, and has trouble turning the pages or wets his lips in pleasure. If he reaches for a different sort of magazine he fails. They're all the same. Perhaps he has never seen such magazines, certainly has never seen such a profusion of them and so casually spread about, smart and shocking sisters to all the waiting-room periodicals he has perused indifferently in moments of pain, boredom, anxiety. The anxiety he feels now—if so he does—is akin to elation.

"You better try the shower first," says Marie or Elaine or Liz, giving him a squeeze on the upper thigh and winking. "Come on, we'll soap each other." And down the hall they go to our hot and scented facilities tiled in blue tiles and emerald green and lit by skylights. "After," she says, "there's the sauna," and together they disappear into the steam where the laughter rings and the slapping of wet flesh adds agreeable tones to the music piped even there.

That's the beginning. Or just the beginning. Ours is an ultra-artificial settlement that guarantees sex twenty-four hours a day, sex in all seasons. In former times, long before Uncle Jake Deauville ventured north, there came the first flood of white women who, as the old-timers said, were not wives, not sisters. They inspired new ideas, as the old-timers said. Their clothing was known as feminine frippery. A portrait (head and shoulders) of one of their unnamed numbers hangs in a large gilded frame over the Gamelands bar. I look like her, she and I look like Amelia Earhart. I enjoy the resemblance. I don't condescend to feminine frippery. None of us do.

And who stands atop the totem pole, Uncle Jake? Is it the freer of the slaves frocked in black? I wish that for a moment you could be here, like any other Willie, and see for yourself.

11—

Sex is my favorite word. It's a nice word, a cute word, a tiny green snake stiff in the mouth. It clips sibilance in the middle so that the little rush of air left to expire behind the teeth, in the pink pocket between plump tongue and shiny palate, becomes the most seductive sound there is, for those with an ear. It is anything but a mere hiss, since the air of it is regulated in pronunciation as by a valve, is a precise deposit and the same with every saying of the word. And yet it lingers, that air, that little wind that could not flow were the tongue not engorged with shapeliness, bedded to teeth, and its duration varies infinitely each time this word, my word, is voiced. Sex, the word, goes its way without euphony, flees from euphony, is sweetness without music, which is best of all. Not big with blood, not round, lacking the inwardness of the sigh, the body of a word like passion, how could it be more unexpected for what it means, what it arouses? And isn't sex the heart of the unexpected? It's so short, that word, so small, with its vowel that hardly deserves the name, is so purely of the mouth that it cannot be said without invoking the ear. The smallness and closeness of the ear is drawn to that sound as to no other. No sooner does anyone say it—sex—than you want to put your ear to his mouth. Or hers. Actually it's a word best heard when spoken by one young girl to another. But whether said by girl, man, woman, boy, still no word so thrusts me to the edge of the cliff, so to speak, except perhaps its second cousin and runner-up, which is sucks.

Those were the words—sex and sucks—that my father spent his life avoiding. The one I never heard pass from his lips, for the other he would go to endless lengths to find a substitute, was a master of euphemism when it came to suck or sucks. Honor forbids absolutely the hard wet words that invoke, of necessity, the soft. Even the word soft gave him trouble.

Honor lies at the root of ruin—or did for my father.

But we at Gamelands talk to our Willies, pay attention to what they say, teach them new words, old words, are good at listening, are liberal with our use of taboo words, taboo expressions, are experts at demonstrating how sex the word is not just a dry term from a high school textbook but makes the jaw snap, sets the lips for kissing.

Gamelands is garlanded in rhythm. We talk as well as perform our sex.

12 —

The first entry in my mother's journal reads: "Juneau, Alaska. August 17, 1930. Last night cried myself to sleep as usual."

She was born in 1900 and hence was a mere thirty years old when she penned this line, while Uncle Jake was fifty and I was five. In 1924 they met, played tennis, married. She had a sweet wide smile, hair like mine, a small willowy body that was typical of the happy female athlete and which should have driven the men wild, as they said in her time, but which did not. Dimly she understood that she had no beaus, as her sisters would say, dimly understood that her lack of admiring beaus had something to do with her sisters, who kept her at home at the piano or caring for their gentle father whom she dearly loved. Those sisters shouldered her aside at social functions they could not prevent her from attending, and brusquely made off with any young man who so much as glanced at my mother. Generally she was content to stay at home reading aloud to the dying father or spending long hours at the piano and making her nimble fingers fly, as she liked to say. But she understood, at least dimly, that somehow she had earned the ever-lasting disdain and disapproval of her sisters, who did all they could to keep her in seclusion and to make her feel inferior. She spent as much time as she could, to no avail, trying to earn their forgiveness for wrongs no one would specify, to acquit herself of the accusation that was never voiced. They were ten years her senior, those relentless sisters, who in earnest began their silent persecutions when my mother, at the age of nine, was stricken with an illness which left her without hair. The governess tried each day to conceal the child's baldness with a broad silk ribbon tied atop her head in a great floppy bow. It was then, at the height of her first humiliation, that those two sisters smiled— openly but as if behind their hands. My mother's hair grew back even-tually and was a heavier, shinier chestnut than ever, though cut rather short. But she knew she had been stricken. Dimly she had understood those smiles.

By the time my mother was twenty-four—ever brightly pleased that her age and the year coincided, and despite her miseries convinced that in birth she had been singled out for astral protection—there was one restriction she would not brook, one prohibition she would not accept: she refused to give up her tennis. Dances, picnics, walking out with young men, canoeing in silvery and dusky light—let the denial be complete but for her tennis. She was small, her muscles were resilient, shapely, she had a driving serve, she was too good at the game she loved to give it up though her father was dying and her sisters said that she must abandon her tennis and remain in the house and help care for him.

The Flowers summer home was near Deauville Farms. On a Saturday afternoon in mid-July of 1924 my mother appeared as a contestant in a tennis match at one of two local country clubs, which she had not on previous summers visited either as guest or tennis player. My father, who enjoyed the game himself, was on hand to watch the women's singles.

Four pairs of short-skirted women provided my father with all the entertainment he might have desired before my mother and her partner stepped onto the court. My father saw at once my mother's dilemma.

The day was cool for July, the sky was the blue of honest eyes, the small grandstand was filled with appreciative spectators in yachting costumes or print gowns. The ivy on the clubhouse wall was a green confection. So far the women's singles had been exemplary of female tennis players at their best, and spirits were high, the breeze fresh, the light a pinkish hue. But at the first sight of my mother, then only a pretty stranger laboring under some odd discomfiture apparently unnoticed by everyone except my father, and at first sight of her partner, a redheaded woman curiously confident, my father knew immediately what was wrong and why my mother looked to him downcast. So all the more he admired the wide smile, the small and willowy figure, the various signs by which he knew that she was swift, determined, exceptionally talented at tennis.

My father was six feet and four inches tall, unmarried at the age of forty-four, and was dressed like the other men in the crowd in white flannel trousers, soft white shirt, blue blazer. His black hair was parted in the middle. The Deauville features—long and heavy jaw, high forehead, fine aquiline nose—were redolent with summery color and good cheer. He had been enjoying himself. He had been smiling. He liked to watch women playing tennis.

Now he frowned. Clay courts, he said to himself. Clay courts.

He meant that the courts at this particular country club were grass, which the young woman with the chestnut hair must not have known in advance of the competition, and that the poor young woman was used to a different kind of court, one made of clay. All this my father knew because of the young woman's shoes. They had smooth rubber soles, those small white shoes, appropriate to clay, not grass. On grass you needed a different kind of shoe, with soles that would provide good purchase. My father saw it all. He frowned. He leaned forward uncomfortably. His heart went out to the pretty woman, not much more than a girl, so justifiably distressed and so alone in this crowd in her discomfort. He knew that only he and the redheaded opponent were aware of the young woman's problem. Clearly the opponent intended to use what she knew to ultimate advantage. What my father knew, had seen in an instant, caused him to experience, suddenly, totally unfamiliar longings of the deepest kind. He wanted nothing less than to stop the game before it began and to carry her off to safety. But he could not.

The young woman with the hopeless problem won the serve. She took her position, stopped smiling, infused her narrow shoulders with the ultimate twisting gesture of tennis players on the attack, sent up the new white ball, then swung, bore down upon it with all the speed and power of a man. But her footing was not secure. Her serve was not perfect, and the expressionless redheaded opponent, using what appeared to be a minimum of effort, smashed back the ball with a velocity belied by her reserve, even disinterest, and her lanky form. The smaller woman, admirably opposite from her opponent in that from this first instant of play she was cheerfully putting all she had into her game, leapt to return the ball, surprise and dismay flickering across the pretty heart-shaped face. She was already aware, obviously, of exactly what the afternoon held in store for her, play by play, and lurched slightly and netted the ball. The stillness of the crowd was more of embarrassment than rapt attention; already the little willowy player with the chestnut hair was perspiring, biting her lip, squaring the narrow shoulders, though her face revealed the saddest kind of girlish puzzlement.

My father leaned forward lovingly and watched. He saw that around one slender wrist she wore a little ivory elephant on a green ribbon— a good luck charm which, on this bright afternoon, was bound to fail. The smile, he saw, was wider, somewhat crooked, helpless. She was trim, he noted again, an open, vulnerable person of rare sweetness, nonetheless capable, under better circumstances, of playing tennis skillfully, unsentimentally, aggressively, to win. Again my father's heart went out to her. He himself was perspiring. Distinctly he heard someone coughing, someone shifting his feet.

Twice more she served, each time with that faint fluttering of imbalance and awkwardness approaching panic. She persevered. The flush in her cheeks was shell-pink in color. She lost both points.

Clearly her confident opponent was watching, waiting, pretense or no pretense of being bored at finding the advantage so strongly hers. Now it was the redheaded woman's serve, and my father concentrated, the small woman he was championing assumed the ready expectant stance of the defender—feet wide, knees bent, torso forward, chin up, the racket horizontal between the right hand that gripped the handle and the left hand that lightly held the head.

The serve, when it came, was surprisingly gentle, a slow ball placed impassively close to the small woman clearly mobilized in an attitude of good sportsmanship. She managed to return the ball, which brought a sigh of pleasure from the crowd. Hardly had she recovered herself when back came the ball, lobbed just out of reach so that once more she ran several steps, returned the ball, barely catching her balance and showing her look of strain, puzzlement, desperation. Whereupon the lanky opponent, in one swift effortless gesture, placed the ball with calculated cruelty in that corner of the court opposite from that into which the smaller woman had been driven, and where now, lurching visibly, she attempted to maintain her footing and change directions. She went after the speeding ball valiantly and swung, missed by three lengths of the racket, fell to one knee, flung out her poor free arm for balance.

Quietly the opponent waited, hitching the waistband of her short white skirt, shifting her feet, glancing at the golden weather vane atop the clubhouse cupola, until the smaller woman, winded, distraught, managed to stand up, collect herself, assume the ready. The poor knee was stained with the green of the grass, her racket was trembling in her hands. My father groaned. The crowd was suddenly filled with coughers.

The opponent, whose long shapely legs at this moment evoked in my father a sudden and severe sensation of anger—he had observed her lanky golden legs against his will—now brushed back a shank of the fiery hair, a splendid orange mane as my father admitted to himself. Then taking her time, glancing head to foot at the woman trembling in disarray across the net, she served for the second time, still gently, and, with her tactics now crude, nearly insulting, entrapped and entangled the smaller woman in a lengthy volley which my father thought would never end. He watched the jerking, the slipping, the ungainly little movements for the sake of balance, the slow destruction of the smaller woman's coordination. Again the redhead drew back her arm, fired, placed the blistering ball impossibly beyond the small woman's reach, knowing that she would take the bait, as indeed she did, speeding like an inept ice skater across the cool greenness after the white ball which even as she lunged was changing direction away from her. She swung, missed, began to fall; and still in dreadful, awkward motion, she prevented herself from going down only by running well off the court and sliding to a dejected stop.

For one extremely unpleasant moment my father found himself on the side of the redheaded woman: he saw her bringing her little improperly shod victim to the swift end she deserved, knew what it would be to hold that tall, passive woman in his arms that very night in the outdoor dance lit by colored lanterns. Then he recovered himself, felt proper shame, felt again his surge of longing for the pretty creature distraught, already thrice defeated, and deservedly so in the eyes of everyone in that now disapproving crowd except himself.

He waited. A swallow dipped low over the green court. It would never end. Now my father was in fact urging on the woman with the big bones, the flaming hair, the calculated passivity—but only to end the match, to get it over with, to spare his small, disheveled but heroic friend, as he now thought of her.

Ready. Collected. Or as collected as she could possibly be. Waiting. Shadows descending. Spectators stirring like bits of paper in the wind. Expectancy. Despair. And again the serve. The serve. But gone the deceptive gentleness, the crafty vindictive volleying. Now, deliberately, still expressionless, though with just the faintest hint of malice in all the sinews of her body, now the opponent tossed up the ball and in one deft stroke drove it across the net and toward the small person who, painfully startled, lunged from her crouch, skidded, swung at the ball, missed, went down. Yes, down she went, asprawl, legs and racket in the air, white skirt upflung around her waist, white bottom of the tennis shorts smeared in the green of the hateful grass, and eyes wide, the poor mouth locked in its blind smile, left arm pathetically extended but failing to break the fall. The impact was audible. Everyone heard it; no one was able to look away from the little victim where she sprawled—helpless, inert, full in the light of her humiliation.

The redheaded woman crossed her ankles, dangled her racket, waited. Until at last the smaller woman regained her breath and picked herself up, retrieved her racket, and made her way to the net, where the redheaded woman stood waiting to shake her hand. The little victim smiled. The winner did not. Then the smaller woman, her white skirt streaked with green, eyes bright with unshed tears, fled from the court.

My father watched her leave. He wanted to rush after her, pick her up in his arms, carry her off, since only saving by a white knight, as he now thought of himself, could possibly atone for such a complete defeat. But even at forty-four he was shy and slow to move, and so for the moment lost her. But at least his heart, as he now knew, was set on her.

And that very afternoon, while still at the country club, and in his own way and at his own pace, my father commenced his courtship. He learned that there were three sisters, an old governess, though the girls were grown, and a father who was thought to be dying. He learned that their summer home was an easy drive from Deauville Farms down

back lanes shaded by weeping willow trees and bordered by white
fences. He then made up his mind and left, before the next game began.
That night he did not attend the dance at the country club as he might
have, but stayed home, went to bed early, passed most of the night
hours in serious, wakeful contemplation in the way his wheel, as he
thought of it, had turned. Once it occurred to him as he lay there in
the summer darkness vaguely listening to a little owl in a tree near his
open window that the tall redheaded victor was probably dancing that
very moment at the country club. At last he fell into his usual untroubled
sleep.

There was a circular gravel driveway in front of the Flowers summer
home, a driveway that made a considerable circle around an immense
planting of asters and petunias, and the following late afternoon the
two older Flowers sisters, seated together on the wide veranda facing
the driveway and the lovely round of the garden, watched as an extremely large open automobile, white lacquered and bound in brass
and driven by a man whom they knew at once was eligible, entered
their premises, approached them loudly but at the slowest possible
speed. They put down their books, their fans, their daring cigarettes.
Avidly they watched the nearing visitor. The great car rumbled closer,
the driver, who was of course my father seated happily behind the
steering wheel of his brother's Stutz Bearcat, presented to the two
women a visage of startling and wonderful allure. The car, like an
imposing locomotive, swung grandly into the circle around the flowers.
With a single movement the two women stood up, each thinking that
he had come for her. In happiness they smiled their selfish smiles, those
two already brushed by the wing of spinsterhood, and stepped forward,
each preparing to greet the visitor, whoever he may be, and to drive
off with him. But then dismay, disappointment, incomprehension, because the obviously emboldened man behind the wheel did not drive
up to the veranda, in noise and brightness, and stop and park his great
vehicle, and climb the wide steps and reach for the hand of one of
them, but instead merely continued on around the circle, without pausing, without slackening pace. Around he went, and again, and again,
making five slow mysterious circles in all, while the two women,
slighted and with no understanding at all of his behavior, tossed their
heads and flounced back to their books and fans and cigarettes.

Around and around, five times, he drove, and then slowly drove
away in the direction from which he had come, without so much as a
smile or wave of the hand. The sisters could not speak for anger; they

did not understand at all such eccentric trespassing. But the youngest sister, peering from behind a curtain in a darkened upstairs window, understood at once, with the intensest pleasure, and raptly watched the sportive, stately machine going round and round—for her. He did not have to look up at her window. He did not have to wave. She knew by some instinct of those who are long suppressed and unjustly blamed that the solemn man driving his fine machine at a speed no greater than that of a walk, when clearly it was capable of traveling at ninety miles an hour or more, must have been present at yesterday's tournament (hadn't she in fact caught sight of him among the spectators?), must have seen at once to the heart of her, seen behind the horrible performance (oh, those now detested shoes!) to the best of her that had been so keenly forged in a lifetime of injustice. So he had come at last to one who had never until that moment even hoped for a saviour. She dropped the curtain, listened intently to the silence he had left behind, then returned to the care of her now gently smiling father. He too had intuited what was happening and squeezed her hand.

For three weeks the stranger continued the first unvarying stage of his courtship—appearing every afternoon, driving five times around the flowers, then going off as he had come, certain that she had been watching and that she appreciated to the full his shyness and what he meant to convey to her behind the unusualness and humor of his approach. Then at the end of three weeks he stopped, alighted, climbed to the veranda hotly quitted by the two older sisters and where the youngest waited, unashamed of her wide smile, and already dressed casually, attractively for driving. He took her off for an hour of exuberant high speed down country lanes intended for the horse and carriage and not this roaring white machine now fast and reckless with the release, the abandon of this happy pair who could not talk for the noise. But they laughed together in all the safety and privacy of what my father, at least, considered to be their nuptial car, though it belonged to Billy Boy, his youngest brother. Day after day my father appeared in the white car. Day after day they sped together through the shade and the green fields where the frightened mares ran with their foals and the larks took flight.

Then they broadened their activities. They ate chocolates together. They walked down the lanes where they had driven. They spent a certain amount of time each day in the sickroom. They went to dances, not at the country club where they had met but at the other country club where the Flowers family had its membership. And above all they played tennis—on the courts of Deauville Farms, which were made of clay. Red clay. He gave no quarter, she always won, swooping and darting, crying out in her pleasure, and winning still more his affection with her driving serve. So they were together, the tall man and short young woman. Still, however, there was no talk of marriage. The older sisters said that the couple looked like father and daughter and would never marry. But they only smiled, the presently oldest Deauville boy and the youngest of the Flowers girls, and went back to the tennis courts.

On impulse they decided to return for an evening at that country club which they had not visited since the day of the debacle, which is how my father referred to it. The club was having its last dance of the season. They decided, reasonably enough, to attend it in vindication and celebration both, which is what they did.

She wore a light green gown that matched the ribbon on her wrist; he wore dress clothes suitable for summer. They said good night to her father, who squeezed the hand of his favorite girl, kissed her cheek when she leaned down, shook the hand of handsome Jack Deauville, as he was still called, bonded them once more in that soft benediction shared only by the three of them, then let them go. That evening the sisters were lurking about the long low house but were not to be seen.

The white car. A cloak around her shoulders. An August moon. Her head resting against his upper arm while he drove.

The five-piece orchestra of the club might have been playing on the deck of a cruise ship in the tropics. My father was a good dancer. His partner loved knowing how well she followed him, how well she complemented his sort of grace, which, in a large man, is like no other. At eleven o'clock they participated in a game on the dance floor and won a prize. At midnight they danced the last dance, when the music had become the strains of sweet sleep. Then they drank champagne on the terrace and left.

The night had turned cold and my father found himself driving not recklessly but faster than he should. The heat from the engine warmed their legs, the noise of the engine was louder than it had ever been and shook them everlastingly awake and sent its din blasting and dying across the black countryside through which they raced. Still she had no premonition and nestled against him in the cold air, the heat of the engine, the noise that had not yet destroyed the lingering music. The night had been hers. Never before had she spent an entire evening in his arms, and still she was rippling, tingling at the thought that this night he had refused to let her dance with any other man—and many had asked. How high could she soar?

Her father's house, when they came upon it loudly out of the night, was like a ship in distress, a great ship foundering in a black sea. Every light in that house was on.

The gravel scattered. They parked and raced inside. The two sisters, wearing white aprons and carrying bowls and towels, barred their way. The doctor was in their father's room, they said, and had left firm instructions: not one visitor, not one interruption. You are too late, they said, and this is the price. He called for you. You were not here. Now you had best wait downstairs with Nanny.

They obeyed. She was distraught, his face was white, in the instant the green frock and elegant dress clothes grew wrinkled, shapeless on the bodies of their wearers. She turned. He caught her arm. The smell of her innocent perfume and his cold cologne mingled with the smell of carbolic acid. There was not a sound, for all the lights that blazed. And they obeyed, obeyed the sisters who waited until the youngest and her beau were well down the stairs before returning to their father's room.

Logic? Illogic?

But they obeyed without question, improbably, too stunned, too stricken with grief and guilt, too innocent to detect the lie. Down they went alone, excluded, crushed, and waited with the old governess who wept and comforted the youngest sister as best she could. The youngest sister drooped in agony; her companion of the evening stood by helplessly, with his dress suit jacket hanging open and his back to the cold fireplace. Once he turned and looked for a long while at the portrait above the mantel. It was a portrait in oils of the face of the woman who had died giving birth to her youngest child. But now no face was to be seen above the mantel; the portrait was nothing but a large black oval in the unnatural light.

At three-thirty in the morning they heard the slow footsteps of a single person on the staircase, and a moment later the old family doctor, with satchel and square beard, paused on his way to the front door, glanced into the room. Slowly he entered, set down the satchel, despite his weariness conveyed surprise.

"You're here," he said, and opened his arms to her. "But he asked for you. He was waiting for your return. And now," he said in a still softer voice, "now it's too late." The doctor glanced with significance at the Deauville heir.

But the doctor's glance roused my father. The lie burst upon him. He read the doctor's rage; he shook once, mightily, then controlled himself. He buttoned his jacket, approached the doctor, and waited while the doctor relinquished the youngest daughter into his own arms and against his chest. He held her, gathered her up against him, spoke once to the governess. Then the doctor and he and Sissy, as he had been calling her for most of the summer, quit the house.

My father took her home to his mother. The next day he returned for the governess. In one month, exactly, Sissy and my father were married in the stone chapel where eleven months later I was christened. Those in attendance were my disapproving grandfather, my matriarchal Irish grandmother, Doc and Billy Boy, and the governess. Sissy was dressed in white. On her left wrist she wore the tiny ivory elephant on the green ribbon, and around her throat a black choker. Through her despair her joy was evident to all.

Orphaned child, charmed bride. White knight, saviour.

For nearly six years Sissy lived a precarious, elated, unreal life as the guest, which is what she really was, of her Irish mother-in-law and as the bride, ever the bride, of the matriarchal woman's favorite son. Every evening her proud husband presented her with flowers. Happily she nursed her daughter, watched her grow, sat at her mother-in-law's piano, basked in the love of the old governess, avoided as much as possible her father-in-law, awaited each day's shyly proffered flowers. Her tennis game improved, if that was possible; she enjoyed her daily practice sessions with Billy Boy which prepared her for Saturdays and Sundays on the court with her husband, with whom no other man could compete.

Then abruptly the fabric was torn as by age, by blades, and hung in shreds. The governess died, the Stutz Bearcat stood one morning with its gruesome occupant on the tennis court that she had come to think of as her own, and in mid-May of 1930 she found herself in Alaska.

"Last night cried myself to sleep as usual."

13 —

Luckily for him my father was unaware that she kept a journal. But I've read that journal, and more than once, and know firsthand from those poor pages which she shared with no one the truth that my father never gleaned: namely that the dead flower, as she called herself in the journal, was in life a person of courage, though she was ignorant of her strength, her courage. At any rate his were the risks, hers the suffering.

14 —

It had a prow of iron, a salt-encrusted hull, our dark ship making its slow way out of the dawn, this S.S. *Alaska* bearing its small band of unwary travelers north to the night.

It was 6 A.M. on Sunday, May 11, 1930, our fifth day at sea and last full day before docking at Juneau. (Population 2,800 plus 900 Siwash Indians.) Most of the travelers were on deck as bidden, since yesterday evening it had been announced that in ten hours the ship would detour somewhat from its course in order that those who had never seen a glacier might do so now. Tony, the skipper, as my father called him (Uncle Jake had a way of achieving instantaneous intimacy—another of his favorite words—with those in positions of authority, and was himself a nautical person, thanks to his naval duties in the Great War), had urged everyone to rise early and be on hand to see the sight, and most had obeyed.

At 6 A.M. the rainy darkness smelled of salt tides and the vast cold atmosphere that shrouds black reefs, uninhabited shores, wrecks at sea. The wooden starboard rail, where near the bows our small band waited, was wet to the touch, and the iron plates beneath our feet shook and trembled to the beat of the engines that were buried far below us and were straining, ever straining, to push us on through oceanic treachery, swift cross currents, sullen swells at a speed of approximately eight miles per hour. The ship was a monster making monumental efforts merely to crawl. Occasionally the wet and foggy dawn smelled of diesel fumes or of some hot breath of cooking loosed from vent or open hatchway; we were moving, not moving, there was nothing to see, shivering as we were at the starboard rail and waiting for the mouth of the world to yawn and display its marvel.

Everyone not appropriately dressed for the vigil went below and returned with coats, jackets, hats, ship's blankets, which they draped about their shoulders or over their heads like survivors on a drifting hulk. Everyone, that is, except Uncle Jake, who was immune to the cold, generally indifferent to wind, snow, rain, and now stood tallest among those at the rail and wearing his gray double-breasted suit and white shirt, blue polka-dotted tie, crisp white handkerchief in the suit-coat breast pocket. No hat, no raincoat, no blanket for my father. He had made his toilet at 5 A.M. and his dark hair was parted in the middle and stiff and shining with brushing and the cream he applied each dawn. With a large hand cupping my shoulder he held me to him protectively; on his other side Sissy clung to his arm, though the ship was as steady as a barrel and there was no risk of being lost in that little crowd. My head came to Uncle Jake's mid-thigh; with my left arm I encircled his enormous leg, happily, rhythmically, to the laboring pulse of the old engines. Near me a great white life preserver was affixed to the rail. It was slick with the fog and intermittent rain, in black paint it announced itself: *S.S. Alaska*.

"There," said Uncle Jake to the group at large, "Tony has changed course. Do you feel it? Twenty degrees to starboard. And he's reduced speed. We've entered Taku Bay. The light will come up in about five minutes and then Tony will give us the spectacle of our lives."

He spoke as if he were a ship's officer, as if he were a frequent traveler on this ship, as if he were old friends with the ship's skipper and had done all this and seen all this before—which I thought he had. Now he released my shoulder and rested his large warm hand atop the sailor hat on my head. I squeezed his leg. From the bridge far behind us came the faint brassy sound of a bell—distant, mechanical, impersonal. Sea water was smashing irregularly against the sides of the ship. I freed myself from Uncle Jake and stepped around him, took Sissy's hand in mine and leaned against her.

"Darling," she said, "are you warm enough?"

I was.

And was I not like my father? Size and gender aside, I was his replica. I had become the sit-in drummer of the three-piece ship's orchestra, with Uncle Jake had sat at Tony's table when the seas were high and thick and all the rest of them were below in their berths, with Uncle Jake had visited Tony on the bridge and steered the ship. Sailors in wet undershirts and blue threadbare pants were forever hoisting me onto their shoulders; I had smiled at the greasy men in the engine room; I was the wireless operator's friend and had worn his headset, tapped out messages in code; hand-in-hand had strolled on wet decks with the purser and was the favorite of the cook, second officer, chief engineer. The ship was Uncle Jake's and mine as well. And I was first to fire drills, which frightened Sissy, and first to meals, where I, not Sissy, sat to Tony's right (on three thick books from the ship's library), and first to see the porpoises or anything else of interest that hove into sight. I was the girl mascot of the old *Alaska* and knew it well.

"Now," said Uncle Jake suddenly and still to the group at large, "here's the light. . . ."

At that moment the fog lifted, the day broke, like a white continent the fog rose up from where it had lain pressed to the sea and hovered above us, grew translucent, admitted to the panorama disclosed to us a dead but welcome light that was without heat, without brightness, as if there were no sun at all above the fog. But at least it was all spread visibly before us, and even this first daylight, receptive to nothing but impending rain, was preferable to the blackness in which that handful of passengers had been standing, waiting: the broad mouth of Taku Bay was already behind us; the rocky, untimbered reaches of land were in the distance to the left. To the right, off the starboard bow, rocking gently on the long swells and so close that we might have run it down had not the fog lifted and the ship slowed, the surprise of an Indian fishing boat with a man and woman side by side in the stern and holding mugs of coffee. And dead ahead, a half-mile distant, the gray-white face of Taku Glacier.

"Now there," said a short, fat man standing close to us, "now there's a glacier!" And he put his hands on his hips and smiled as the others joined in to share his awe, his elation, and for the first time on the voyage began using their cameras though the light was poor.

"It's Taku Glacier," said my father. "In the old days they used to cross glaciers like that on horseback."

"And look at those people in that little boat," said the fat man. "We have an escort!"

"They're Siwash Indians," said Uncle Jake, "from Juneau. They're about two hundred miles from their usual fishing grounds. They're after cod."

The S.S. *Alaska* was aimed directly for the center of the icy wall and slowly, ponderously went forward, black iron drawn dangerously to sullied ice. Again the bell sounded, the engines slowed, the ship continued on toward the ice which loomed larger, revealed jagged vertical fissures in its face, small chunks and slabs bobbing where the wall of ice met the dark sea.

The Indian stared up at us, then tossed the remains of his coffee over the side, bent down, started his own dismal little gasoline engine, began to follow us in toward the ice. A gull that had been sitting on the roof of the pilothouse rose and sailed off, swooping and crying through the flat dawn. The Indian woman stooped and went out of sight into the dark and smoky hovel of the cabin. From the tall, narrow, rusty smokestack that jutted above the pilothouse came a thin trail of bright blue exhaust. The little boat listed, sat low in the water, was smothered in heaps of netting, coils of frayed rope, rusted chain, seaweed.

"I think we're wanted on the bridge," said Uncle Jake, now speaking softly and only to Sissy and me, instead of to the group at large. "Tony wants us up there. He has a treat for Sunny."

And so saying he smiled at Sissy and me, disengaged himself from clinging wife and clinging child, and, on long sea legs, walked aft in the direction of the iron stairway that led up to the bridge. We followed, Sissy holding me by the wrist, I tugging and straining after the promised treat.

Across the stairway, hanging from a wet chain, was a wooden sign that said *No Admittance*. Uncle Jake unhooked it, led the way up.

The bridge was open to spray and gales, sleet and rain, and it was here that stood the ship's skipper to supervise the intricacies of docking, say, or to direct his crew whenever the safety of the ship and all aboard her was jeopardized, or whenever the ship was involved in any maneuver that was not merely run-of-the-mill, such as the one now underway. But we ascended to the bridge, met Tony (who was wearing a slicker over his white uniform), surveyed the forward portion of the ship, the passengers down there in the bows, the vista of the wide bay empty except for ourselves and the anomalous fishing boat, and the suddenly towering glacier.

"Oh Jake," cried Sissy, clutching the chest-high iron skirt that enclosed the bridge on three sides. "Oh Jake, it's much too close! We'll crash!"

He smiled, shook hands with Tony, lifted me into his arms so that I could see.

"Sissy," he murmured, laughing, "there's no danger. And isn't it a splendid spectacle?"

Then Tony, the captain of the S.S. *Alaska,* put his hand on her shoulder. "Good morning, Sissy," he said quietly. "You know, we do this on every northbound trip. You needn't worry." Then, hand still on her shoulder, he turned toward the open door of the ship's pilot-house, and in his soft voice spoke to one of the men inside. "Hard astern," he said, and the man rapidly worked some levers, rang the brass bell.

High in my father's arms, absently flattening his hard black shiny hair with both my hands, high above them all I stared at the immensity of the rising glacier. I glanced down at the panic on Sissy's heart-shaped face, I craned to see into the pilothouse when Tony gave his order. When I looked again at the shaggy whiteness, I saw that it was higher than the masts of the S.S. *Alaska,* and that off to the port at the ocean's edge there was a dark cave as big as the *Alaska* herself, and that the cave was growing larger and more darkly blue even as I looked at it. All around us the black water was making whirlpools because the direction of our propellers had been reversed, and I saw that there was now a large clawlike bird skimming the peaks of gray ice, and felt Uncle Jake's pleasure through the hands and arms that held me so high. In his arms I thought that Uncle Jake and I were alone in marveling at what we saw.

"Stop engines," Tony said over his shoulder, and the shuddering ceased, the churning in the water ceased, through the abrupt silence came the sounds of spoons and kettles in the galley and the popping of the fishing boat's gas engine, louder than ever. We were motionless before the glacier and had not even begun to drift. The little boat to starboard was still rocking and pitching in the echo of our thundering halt and the Indian was staring up at Tony. I smelled tar and thick white leaded paint, salt on the cold wet air, Uncle Jake's cologne, the stench from the fishing boat below us. Dead ahead the bird was hovering over the great wall of ice.

"All right, Jake," said Tony, "time for the show. Sunny may do the honors."

"Oh Jake," said Sissy, "please, can't you put her down?"

But Uncle Jake merely smiled—I felt his smile with my fingers—and still carrying me on high stepped over to the narrowly protruding roof of the pilothouse.

"Sunny," he said, twisting so that he could turn up to me his blue eyes, his faintly colored face, his aquiline nose, his sensuous and smiling lips, "do you see that lanyard hanging down there from the roof of the pilothouse? Pull hard on it and don't let go until I give you two good squeezes."

I nodded, reached out, took hold of the red handle dangling at the end of the short length of rope and then tugged down as hard as I could with both hands and clung to it, held the red handle down with my weight.

It was the ship's whistle of course, and that blast of sound cried out for help, shrieked danger, sent its long imperious bellow of dissonance resounding for miles. Stays, guy wires, deck plates, the entirety of the S.S. *Alaska* was vibrating to the powerful off-key note it was sounding. We were inside the sound, inside some terrible gathering of lighthouses with foghorns chorusing all together in the midst of a storm. Ships might have been colliding all around us; catastrophe was booming. The basso blast consumed the very atmosphere. On it went, unvarying, stretching my arms, tearing the shocked smile loose from my small face, knocking my sailor hat to the deck. In the instant Sissy was all but toppled, and only Tony's strong arm saved her. Below us the passengers were crouching, wrists to ears, and the little Indian boat was foundering in the weight of the noise. But we hung on, Uncle Jake and I, and I knew that I alone was the cause of the electric whistle's withering, ungainly noise and that soundlessly Uncle Jake was laughing. Together we reveled, he and I, inside the vast paralysis of that deep dreadful voice which is heard only at sea and which I alone pulled down upon us.

Then he squeezed me twice and I let go of the rope.

It stopped. It left behind a silence more majestic, more painful, more deafening than the sound it had made only moments before. And in that silence, suddenly, we heard an answering crack, a lofty splintering, a deep sound of breakage so abrupt, so loud, that it might have been caused by the largest of electric bolts driving straight down through the layers of gray mist above us, but was in answer, of course, to the terrible tremors of the ship's whistle. All eyes were open. Everyone was watching. And there to the accompaniment of that loud crack, there before us and for all to see, one great icy crag of the glacier trembled, split away from that high white barrier, fell forward, dropped, and slowly plunged into the black and waiting sea. The spray rose, the tip of that immense torn tooth reappeared from the cold depths to which it had sunk; the long low cave off to port was suddenly no more to be seen, filled as it was with the black waters displaced by the girth and length of the sharply pointed tooth of ice extracted there, before our eyes, from the assaulted face of the glacier.

Below us, and forward, in the bows, the passengers began to clap.

"It was a big one, Tony," said my father. "Wasn't it beautiful, Sissy? Sunny was surely the author of grand havoc."

"Well, it pleases the tourists," said Tony.

"But this was out of the ordinary," said my father. "This was a spectacle for Sunny."

Then in the silence and desolation of Taku Bay there came a small and angry piping: below us, to starboard, the Indian was holding his boat's horn to his mouth and blowing on the tinny, reedy horn repeatedly, while shaking his free fist at Tony. The Indian had let go of the wheel, the fishing boat was swinging in aimless circles, and atop its pilothouse sat the angular black bird that had been skimming the glacier.

"Quarter speed ahead," said Tony, tightening his hold on Sissy and glancing down at the Indian who, standing amidst rusty hooks and tangled netting and fish heads slick with blood and slime, was still blowing his horn and shaking his fist.

"Hard to port," said Tony in his soft and mild voice, and again we were rumbling, turning, gathering the momentum that would put us back on course. Behind us Taku Bay was already filled once more with the densest fog, and there was nothing to see.

In the middle of that night, the last night of our voyage, since we were among the six passengers disembarking at Juneau and the ship was due at Juneau at 6 A.M. on the morning of May 12, I dreamt that the wind rose, that the darkness was filled with stars, that the seas became willful, more willful, causing the ship to climb, fall, climb again through crackling and tumbling fields of floating ice.

And I dreamt that side by side in the very prow of the ship, Uncle Jake and I stood barefooted in pajamas and hallooing through our cupped hands at a ghostly mountain of ice lying dead in our path. We were dancing up and down and hugging each other with every shard of ice we sent rushing and shattering into the sea with the force of our voices. I heard the ice crumbling, saw the stars descending, clapped as Uncle Jake pulled loose the enormous life preserver and, in all his grand benevolence, tossed it down to the Indians trapped on a listing block of ice in the tumult.

My sea legs were as good as Uncle Jake's, the perilous night itself imparted to our clear cries a tone so strong and lyrical that it might have been shaped by the brass of the ancient Deauville hunting horns. He picked me up, he dangled me over the side so that I could wave to the Indians; behind us there was not a light to be seen anywhere on the dark and tossing ship—no riding lights to locate us for other ships, no lights in the lounge or cabin windows, and yet faint bursts of sparks and phosphorescence were skimming through the wires and around the tops of the smokestacks like crowns of fire and across all of the black wet surface of our ship in the night. My little skull was a lighthouse. I was deafened by the noise I myself was making, and now Uncle Jake was singing to the glacier, destroying it before we crashed into it head on.

Then I awoke. We were in fact still rising, falling, wallowing, and even as I slipped to my knees in my top bunk and pressed my face and chest to the porthole, a wave crested, unfurled, and flung itself against the glass. I shivered happily, safe behind the thick glass and in the blue light that lit the cabin. Again we wallowed, the porthole was again submerged, and happily I breathed in the smells of heavy linen, fresh paint, warm blankets, brine. I pressed myself to the porthole like a starfish, lost my balance, fell back, rolled to my side and looked over the perilous edge of my high bunk. There on the other side of the narrow cabin sat my father, fully dressed on the edge of the bottom bunk where Sissy lay sleeping. She had not awakened, could not know how rough it was, yet there sat Uncle Jake beside her, drawing the bedclothes about her shoulders, stroking her hair, tucking her in as he might have tucked me in.

We rolled, we burrowed into the bed of the deep sea, I hung on and watched my father until I heard someone tapping on the cabin door. Uncle Jake stood up, braced himself, opened the door onto the red and yellow light of the corridor, and from Jim, our steward—for it was he—received a plate covered by a heavily starched white napkin. They whispered a few words, lurched suddenly—I heard Jim laugh—and then my father gave him a coin and closed the door.

Beneath our bunks the life jackets were stored like chunks of gray wood. Most of our luggage was already packed and strapped and, out in the corridor where it was piled ready for our debarkation, slid and toppled to the rhythm of the willful seas—as I had heard and seen before the door was closed. Sissy's green robe swayed from the hook where it hung. Down we rolled, up we came, there was a sudden impact, we stopped dead in a trough, then came the painful recovery in slow motion, and again, safely, we began to make headway against the storm.

In three easy strides Uncle Jake was across the cabin and standing beside my bunk, plate in hand, his head just level with mine where I leaned over the low protective rail of the bunk and reached out to him. In the blue light, which shone for the sake of emergency and thus keyed me up for the gravest danger and yet persuaded me all the more of our safety, my father's hair was groomed, his shoulders square, his features more relaxed and comforting than ever, as if in the deadly cast of the blue light it was his life that shone forth.

He gave me the plate, smiled, covered my head once with a warm hand that was so large that it held me as if my head had been a mere softball in his gentle grip, then returned to Sissy's bunk and sat beside her, drew up the blanket, wedged a pillow between her slender figure and the bulkhead.

It was a sandwich. A chicken sandwich. He must have arranged much earlier with Jim to bring me a chicken salad sandwich at the height of the gale, knowing how I would fill my little mouth with soft white bread, golden crusts, cold lettuce, mayonnaise that could not have been creamier, the firm wet cubes of chicken flavored with all the succulence of a secret childhood meal at the height of a gale. And there I lay, propped on an elbow, bracing myself with naked foot, knee, elbow, and savoring, as he knew I would, my plump white sandwich while the cabin reeled and the porthole ran with water and the wind howled. The storm drove my face into the sandwich, smeared soft butter and softer mayonnaise on my lips, my nose, my eyebrows, my cheeks, which I wiped with the back of my hand, which I then licked. Chewing turned into rumination and slow bliss. I was my father's replica, my father's child, I carried the taste of the treasured sandwich back to the bottom, down to the dreamless sleep of my peace and pleasure.

Then: "Rise and shine, Sunny!" I heard him say and woke again, awoke at once, in an instant transformed myself from the child curled in the deepest sleep to the child upright and kneeling amidst the tossed-off covers and quick and bright with the event which I knew was nearly upon us—arrival at last.

"Down you come!" he said. "We'll dock in about half an hour."

"Good morning, darling," Sissy said. "We're almost there!"

The plain white narrow cabin was filled with sunlight and there was no wind, the seas were calm. For the first time since we had started north by ship the fog and rain, lowering mists, and sudden squalls had given way at dawn, at the dawning of this day, to the sun, which we had forgotten. Now in the warmth and brightness Uncle Jake was at his most composed and yet as eager as I was, obviously, for the event we three had awaited from the start of our shipboard journey. A new home, a landscape unlike any we had ever seen, the prospects of the last frontier, as he called it—it was all contained in the press of his fawn-colored suit, the tightly knotted red and white polka-dotted tie, the camel's hair coat which Sissy was holding ready in her arms along with my sailor coat and her own light green wrap with the silver buttons. In the sunlight Sissy was as content and eager as Uncle Jake and me and wore her dark green Scottish highlander's hat (with the dark ribbons down her neck) at a trim and jaunty angle.

For a final time I pressed myself to the salt-encrusted porthole, looked out upon the unexpected light, the unexpected flatness of the sea on which we were moving at what appeared to be a speed we had never attained until now in our final hours. Then I leapt into my father's arms and he swung me down. Sissy, still holding the coats, and cheerier than at any time since the rainy midnight when we had left the S.S. *Alaska*'s home port back in the States, as Uncle Jake called our native country which we had left behind us, perhaps forever, knelt down and hugged me and with her thin shapely fingers played a little tune on my spine, put her cheek against my cheek and made her wordless sounds of approval, adoration.

"You smell like mayonnaise," she said and laughed, the breath of her speech warming my smooth cheek. "Midnight snack? Uncle Jake's been spoiling you again?"

I nodded, I kissed her, she drew away, she looked at me with her most engaging expression: chin slightly raised, eyes serene and quick, a personal yet faraway look as if in the distance she saw some vista no one else could see, a crescent of promise which she might happily pursue and possibly attain, alone.

Quickly I dressed, watched by the two of them, who were already dressed (by now Uncle Jake had donned his fedora), my haste suddenly and oddly prompted not only by the adventure that was now at hand but by the faint sensation that I might be left behind, though even then I knew full well that I was the myth of our trio, the myth of their lives, the embodiment of the myth of the only child, and a girl as well.

"On deck everyone!" said Uncle Jake, and Sissy gave us each our coats, we quitted the cabin, gongs were sounding fore and aft. Jim, the steward, had removed our heap of luggage from the narrow corridor to the deck where the passengers' gangway was already in place for lowering.

In single file, with Uncle Jake in the lead, briskly we climbed to the upper deck where we could best watch our arrival, best see the first signs of this new place to which Uncle Jake had brought us. Standing together at the rail, holding each other's hands, bodies touching, for some odd reason we three were alone to survey the panorama spread before us, to look upon the green world slowly approaching. No other passengers, no members of the crew, only ourselves to stand together in that clear light, and to smell the air that was fresh at last, and to look to our fullest satisfaction out toward the landfall that would soon be ours. Uncle Jake squeezed my hand, and I knew that he was squeezing Sissy's; the sun came down, the deck was dry, a steady gentle wind was in our faces.

"In a moment," said Uncle Jake, and for the first time his voice was sober, more sober than I'd ever heard it, "in a moment we'll see Juneau—dead ahead."

"But it's lovely, Jake," said Sissy, though my father—tall and stalwart and with eyes on the lookout and chin jutting—appeared not to have heard her voice, not even to see the sparkling picturesque panorama before us but instead the unrolling scenes of all his future exploits in Alaska.

"Besides ourselves," he said and as if to himself, "only Fitzgibbon and his friends are getting off at Juneau. And the Fitzgibbon party will only stay for a month. A month of hunting. Then they go back."

"But it's not at all what I expected, Jake," Sissy said, swinging one carefree arm in a half-circle, "it's thrilling. It's lovely. And you're the real hunter. Oh, you'll have a lot more than a month of hunting, Jake. We're here. I'm glad we're here."

With those words she must have pressed more lightheartedly against him, because though he did not reply to her, still he lifted his chin, looked with more interest in the direction in which she pointed, allowed the boyish good nature to return again to the strength, the firmness, the trustworthiness of the handsome face. Again he rested a hand atop my head and I knew all was well.

We were proceeding up a wide corridor of rocky, tree-lined coast and small inlets, and on either side of us the green and black land was coming closer. There were shining rocks, gulls on rocks, fish leaping. Then suddenly the ship turned, and through an all-but-invisible opening into what appeared to be the land itself we entered our channel, a sort of immense inverted funnel of still calmer waters reflecting the cool and rushing light, and there, at the narrowest tip of the funnel, was Juneau. Twice Tony blew the ship's whistle, and the little town lay in the bright sunlight in the distance.

"Mountains!" exclaimed Sissy. "Oh Jake, I hadn't expected mountains!"

He smiled. He stood taller. He was beginning to repossess a wild, natural world which until now, this moment, he had never seen but only dreamed, imagined. Clearly the sights he had dreamed into being now pleased him.

Gongs were sounding, bells, and now the deckhands were all around us and hard at work with ropes, with chains, and in my excitement it seemed quite natural that they did not wave to me, or recognize us, or call out comradely greetings to Uncle Jake. We were no longer Uncle Jake and Sunny but only two passengers who were leaving the ship for good in this place where the S.S. *Alaska* would remain in port for only an hour. At that moment Uncle Jake picked me up once more, held me sitting in the crook of his right arm, put his left arm around Sissy's shoulders. She leaned to his arm, to his side, from my perch I leaned to the splendid view I commanded.

"Those mountains," said Uncle Jake, "are Mount Juneau and Mount Roberts. The one on the far left is nameless. The top of the highest, there in the center, is nearly five thousand feet from sea level. Shall we climb it, Sunny?"

I nodded, laughed, and closer it all came, more swiftly, the trio of mountains, the remnants of the abandoned town of Douglas to our left, and to the right a heap of black slag from the Alaska-Juneau Gold

Mine, and now docks, fishing boats, several pontoon airplanes tied to a float.

Up rose the mountains, still closer they came. The lower slopes of the left-hand mountain were covered with swatches of dead timber and a few wooden rust-colored buildings that were the remains of the abandoned Treadwell Mine; Mount Roberts, to the right, was handsomely green, gentler, and bore up her side a blinding column of tin roofs that were the exterior emblems of all the tunneling and burrowing that went on inside the mountain, thanks to the operations of what was then the largest low-grade gold mine in the world. Straight ahead was Mount Juneau, with black skirts, sharp peaks, long gray noble scars left down the sides of her by avalanches. And even now, in mid-May, all three mountains were crested with ribbons and pockets and ridges of white snow—unattainable, not for skiers, pure whiteness deposited on those lofty heights as if by the cold sun itself.

Half speed. Quarter speed. The slow turning of winches. Tony on the bridge above us, tar and oil softening all around us where the sun was warm. The crew was bustling. Some gulls were landing on the water. Two men were watching our slow approach from a long pier empty except for themselves, a loading shed, a half-dozen Indians lounging near one end of the shed. A car started up somewhere beyond the pier. And drifting through the sunlight the sudden smells of wood, potatoes frying in iron skillets, the fat wet masses of seaweed wrapped like thick golden bandages about the crooked pilings that held up the pier.

"Oh Jake," Sissy said, pleasure and the spirit of adventure ringing softly in her sweet voice, "it's wonderful. It's all so different. Those strange buildings and the beautiful mountains. But Jake," she said, looking about her, shading her eyes, searching in the distance, "where is the town? When shall we come to Juneau?"

"Why, Sissy," he said, and laughed, bounced me a bit in my perch, shook Sissy's shoulder good-naturedly, "we're here! That's Juneau! Right there! We'll be docking in just a minute or two. And do you see that tall building about four blocks from the docking shed? That's the Baranof Hotel. Our hotel. Another few minutes and we'll be in our room. The journey's over, Sissy. We've arrived!"

How, I wondered in my childish exhilaration and ignorance, could she not have seen the town? It lay before us in plain sight, it had been perfectly visible at the base of the largest mountain even when we were still out in the channel. I had known it was Juneau when it first came into view, why didn't she? The little cluster of buildings to the left of us on the far side of the harbor could not possibly be Juneau: the houses had caved in, the windows were black and glassless specks, pieces of old machinery as high as the broken roofs stood unaccountably in empty streets. I could see not a person, not a dog in that little place from which the reddish wooden structures climbed partway up the empty slope. That place was hardly Juneau. Whereas there were men on the dock we were now drifting toward (with engines rumbling and pulling astern) and beyond the tall gray wooden hotel there was clearly visible a wooden church with a Russian spire. There were curtains in the windows of all the unpainted wooden houses spread like a field of gray strawberries from the foot of the mountain down to the docks where the Indians tied up their boats. And what of the airplanes that looked like shiny wooden ducks in the water? and what of the black letters stenciled boldly across the sloping roof of our loading shed: *Alaska Steamship Company?* What was it all if not Juneau, just as my father had said?

"Well," said Uncle Jake, noting the group of silent and slouching Indians, "the poor fellow in Taku Bay must have called ahead and told them we were coming. They don't look very happy to see us. But why should they? The Indians up here are badly treated. I tell you, Sissy, I feel strongly about the Alaskan Indians. I'm going to help them out whenever I can. I'm going to have one of them for a friend. But, look there, Sunny, we're docking!"

And as if he had heard what Uncle Jake had said, the young crew member who had been waiting and smoking in the bow dropped his cigarette over the side, straightened up, taking his foot from the gunwale, and with one swift and sudden motion tossed into the air the coil of rope he had been holding. Out it sailed, that rope with the lead weight on the end of it, and for a moment the rope hung suspended in the clear air (yellow, supple, yet also taut), and then the weight clove to the perfection of the sailor's aim and landed, with a hard noise I could plainly hear, at exactly the proper distance from the dockhand.

"There," said Uncle Jake, "we're attached to shore, we're no longer at sea," and suddenly he dropped me to my feet, removed his tan fedora, took Sissy in his arms and kissed her. "Now," he said, "now we go below to the gangway and go ashore."

Steam rose from the donkey engine, the ship's winches turned, winding in the dripping hawsers, and drew them tight, and sideways we moved until, with not the slightest sensation of collision, all the slow weight of the ship rested against the pilings of the pier. Yet still we moved, slowly, imperceptibly, and the entire pier began to shift, to groan, to buckle, while the dockhands waited and the Indians lolled or squatted in the sunlight, as if the pier weren't being silently and steadily crushed, as if no ship from the Southland loomed before them. Then we backed off, and I too squatted, peered down through the rail, stared into the black sea refuse beneath the pier, happily sniffing the fumes from that dark space where flowed and collected the bilge of the town and the pulpy sludge of the sea. From openings in the ship's side came thick splashing curls of water; behind an open porthole far below me someone was singing.

At the gangway, where our voluminous luggage was heaped high, we met the Fitzgibbon party and I saw that once again Uncle Jake was momentarily dismayed because it appeared that the three hunters had journeyed north with only new tents, new packs, and a shockingly large number of obviously new big-game rifles in hard, highly polished leather cases.

"Good luck!" said Uncle Jake, but Fitzgibbon and his friends were too bad-tempered in the dawn hour or too preoccupied counting their rifles to reply.

Then Tony appeared in his fresh white uniform and gold braid and shook my father's hand; and again, since generally it took little to restore my father's faith in himself, again Uncle Jake was husband, parent, head of the family, and proud to be a chechaqua (pronounced chee-chalk-a and meaning newcomer to the Alaskan Territory) instead of a transient hunter who drank whiskey (my father did not approve of drinking) and was probably a bad shot as well.

"Thanks," he said to Tony. And then, followed by me, Sissy, Jim with the first load of our luggage, in that order, down the steep gangway went Uncle Jake, nodding to the Indians, who looked away, and once more taking off his hat in a handsome gesture of self-welcome. The long pier smelled like a leveled forest; on the staved-in boat the barnacles were golden nuggets; when the old dog rose to meet us, I saw that she had what looked like a large black circle painted around one of her pink eyes.

"This old bull terrier," said Uncle Jake, versed already in the lore of Juneau, "this old bull terrier is Patsy Ann. She greets every arriving ship, no matter what hour of the day or night, and is always on hand before the ship's in sight and before the ship's whistle sounds. No one understands the mystery of Patsy Ann. No one knows who she's looking for. But she's Juneau's mascot and the pride of the town and famous up and down the coast of Alaska."

Jim carried down the last of our luggage, above us a skid of cargo swung high from the hold of the ship, and here we were at last, three Deauvilles beside a lifetime's luggage (the shiny leather cases, the bright black steamer trunk with brass handles) on the long gray, nearly empty pier with the town of Juneau piled around us in the clear light, the warm sun. Behind the uppermost houses the evergreens rose like crooked fingers, the angle of the electric wires drew the eye upwards to dense forest and naked rock, to the timberline, to the snow atop Mount Juneau. A man in a nightshirt was leaning from a window in the Baranof Hotel and shading his eyes and watching us. One of the Indians was flipping his knife at a scrap of paper lying at his feet on one of the massive wooden planks of the dock. Another car engine started up.

"Where is he, Patsy Ann?" said Uncle Jake for Sissy's amusement. "Where's your master? On the next ship?"

Sissy then made a little gasping sound, glanced swiftly to her left, to her right, taking in all that there was to see of Juneau, and then, looking down at me where happily I sat on the largest and most deeply golden of the suitcases, and suddenly squatting like one of the Indians and holding out a limpid, graceful hand to the old dog: "Oh, the poor thing," she said in her clear, sweet-natured voice, "the poor thing...."

Before our eyes the aged and sickly-looking town mascot gave way to her depths of dejection. In her pink eyes and dusty white coat and her steady, labored scrutiny of us, in all this she conveyed the full aura of her mournful air. She sank into herself, sank visibly into her sadness. She watched us. She looked at us with her small pink eyes, one peering out from the black circle, and in her woe was a faint sad trace of accusation: the fault was ours, we too were merely strangers, she had not come slowly down to the docks this morning for us. Not for us.

Then hearing the Fitzgibbon party clattering down the gangway with Jim and two other stewards bearing all their tents and guns, abruptly the old bull terrier perked up, trembled, and rippling and twisting in rekindled anticipation, off she lumbered to greet her second disappointment of the morning, bony head and stumpy tail wagging.

"Good girl!" called Uncle Jake. "Good girl!"

Slowly my mother climbed to her feet, set straight her jaunty Scottish cap, stood waiting.

May 12, 1930. 6:45 A.M. Arrival.

• • •

Later, from our dark and musty room in the Baranof Hotel (twin beds, a cot for me, one window, the luggage) we heard a single deep loud blast of a ship's whistle and, still later, after we had breakfasted on steak and eggs in a place called Doug's and had walked the town, and had allowed ourselves to return hand-in-hand to the hot pier, we found ourselves alone at the water's edge and saw that the pier was empty and that the S.S. *Alaska* was gone from sight. Would it ever again steam up that empty channel?

15 —

Uncle Jake Deauville was a legendary resident of Juneau for somewhat more than a decade. Yet in all that time he never knew what most male visitors to the Baranof joked about before they were even off the boat: namely, that the old hotel, with its spittoons, linoleum-covered floors, moose head and girlie calendar above the registration desk, was, naturally enough, the main place of business for that handful of women who, back in 1930 in Juneau, Alaska, advertised themselves as being neither wives nor sisters. Though none of us could have detected their influence at the time, these were the selfsame women who, during my first childhood days in the Baranof Hotel (as history proved), determined and inspired my future life in Alaska.

Even now I think of them, unknown progenitors who planted in the unwitting child the seeds of their calling, and it pleases me to think that the Alaska-Yukon Gamelands is the final flourishing of their brief hours in those hired beds. I wish they could have known what was to come of their labors; I wish that they might sign on today, to use the nautical vernacular of Uncle Jake, at Gamelands, and in lavish plenty work with the ever-thankful woman the long-lost child has become.

Today, after nearly thirty-five years, the Baranof Hotel still stands and is more or less as it was, except for superficial refurbishing and the women. Nowadays the brightly lighted lobby is bereft of women except for legitimate lady travelers and a married manicurist; nowadays the only sign of feminine frippery remaining in the lobby of what used to be a dank and antiquated stopping place for a nearly all-male clientele is the shapely black-stockinged leg pictured along with the elk's antlers on our poster prominently displayed at the main desk. Our old-fashioned poster is an invitation to sex, to love and lust as we say, in modernist splendor; there's no longer any old-fashioned illicit love and lust in the modern Baranof. Gamelands, after all, is a monopoly.

But in the spring of 1930 a handful of women worked out of the Baranof. They gossiped with the desk clerk, wore mail-order slacks and blouses and lipstick of deep shades of red, were good pool players, but with salesmen or muckers on their off-shift from the mine feigned girlish ineptitude at the table in the rear of the lobby. Occasionally, during the week we spent in the Baranof Hotel, one of them approached the tall easterner and his little girl, and was inevitably surprised and puzzled by my father's politeness, grand manner, willingness to talk at length and personally to a strange woman while failing utterly to recognize her signals, her intention, the obvious burden of her forwardness. There he would stand, talking about Sissy, who was always resting in our room upstairs, about me, as he rested his hand on my head, about Deauville Farms and our trip on the S.S. *Alaska,* about Chantilly and his older brother buried in France and the totem pole whose fame had spread down to the States and as far as the nation's capital—all this until at last his listener, whose entire repertory of enticement had been repeatedly ignored by my father in the course of his agreeable monologue, would smile, touch his arm, and take embarrassed and irritated leave of us to the bar, where, beer in hand, she would slowly and grimly regain her self-esteem.

If Uncle Jake had understood what she was or what she wanted he would not have believed her; if he had been able to detect at all the scent of her provocation he would have pitied her and perhaps said something to the management; if she had persisted, so that even he could not have mistaken the invitation she was attempting to thrust upon him, he would have quit the hotel—reluctantly, politely, with restrained severity, brows knit and nostrils flaring, unable to comprehend or accept the hotel's betrayal of his trust and judgment. But Uncle Jake was deaf to sexual messages, immune to emissions of sexual stimulation, and thought that the Baranof Hotel was a place of comfort and good repute, a classic of northwest public lodgings comparable, in its way, to some small and highly recommended hotel in a resort town in

France. He liked the Baranof, approved of it, though he did not smoke, drink, or play pool, and considered it an appropriate place to leave Sissy while he took me off on his errands. Somehow he managed to take no notice of the calendar above the reception desk.

But if Uncle Jake was not the man to be seduced by strange women, he became enamored quickly enough with certain new acquaintances who were men. Which is to say that my father spent on male friendships, especially new friendships, the kind of obsessive energy that most of the men around him spent on liaisons with women. My father did not approve of single men who pursued women; he did not like his friends to discuss women; he refused to listen to what he called off-color stories. He detested married men who confessed to eying other women. Skirt-chasing, as my father called it, which was generally no more than a sudden flickering of candor on a friend's face, provided the main grounds for breaking off most of his friendships with those same men to whom, until the betrayal, he had been devoted. In his lifetime my father did in fact break off most of his friendships except for those otherwise destroyed. Betrayal by others was the backbone of his morality, the dark god in his heaven, the demon in his Elysian fields of justice, and he suffered it through his lifetime, on every hand, unremittingly. His own father was his nemesis and worst offender.

Frank Morley was the perfect friend. Frank Morley, of Juneau, Alaska, via some equally small town in Colorado, was, as it turned out, one of my father's last two faithful friends. The other was Sitka Charley.

Frank Morley, whom my father met on the very day of our arrival in Juneau, was a pure man. He was fifty-eight at the time and as tall as my father though stoop-shouldered, a winning attribute to Uncle Jake whose own upright carriage incurred the admiration of all who saw him, men and women alike, yet embarrassed him constantly. Indoors and out Frank Morley was always dressed the same in a black hat of broadish brim, a black vest, a collarless gray shirt, dark wool trousers that rode high in the waist and short in the leg, exposing the soft black spinster shoes laced well above the ankles, and wide suspenders the color of tobacco juice faded in a wintry sun. He had long jowls, sad eyes, skin that had become as soft as a woman's despite his years of hunting, prospecting, enduring seasons of misery in tent cities. Across his breast on a gold chain he wore an elk's tooth in a gold socket. He did not drink, rarely talked, never thought about any woman dead or

alive or represented by photographer or artist, though he did smoke
home-rolled cigarettes. He survived all the challenges my father could
devise for testing or straining friendship; he became my affectionate
protector when Sissy died and then my sole guardian when we, Frank
Morley and I, finally accepted the unavoidable fact that Uncle Jake had
disappeared for good.

Frank Morley was garbed in homely masculinity, and yet was as
gentle and passive, as supportive and vulnerable as any woman might
have been. He frequented the lobby of the Baranof Hotel to smoke and
read back issues of Stateside magazines and never once was he sugges-
tively approached by one of those women who tried to turn my father's
head. Frank Morley's disinclination was unmistakable. Respectfully they
kept away.

Sitka Charley was just as loyal a friend to my father as Frank Morley,
but less important, because he was young and an Indian. He was a
mixture of foster son and handyman and boon companion to Frank
Morley, who, in the days of Sitka Charley's boyhood, had befriended
the orphaned full-blooded Siwash Indian youth and taught him how
to work in Guns & Locks & Clothes, Frank Morley's store. Sitka
Charley was similar to his mentor Frank Morley (few words, no women
white or native). He could be trusted with money; he could read and
occupied himself for long periods with Frank Morley's books; he handled the merchandise in Guns & Locks & Clothes with the same
luminous respect with which his forebears had first accepted rifles
and thin blankets in exchange for their daughters. Even as a boy he
had shown himself to be a silent and solitary artisan of far greater gifts
than most of his fellows in using the tools of the carver, and now, in
May of 1930, his long knives and broad leather belts were featured
in the window of Guns & Locks & Clothes and brought Frank Morley the highest prices. The knives had ivory animals for handles and
on the belts were depicted ferns and fish and streams and trees in bright
colors. In his mid-twenties, in size and color and features no different
from the publicly derided Siwash men and boys who kept to the water-
front and lived in shacks on pilings (he was thin, dark, not large,
expressionless and hence off-putting to white strangers), Sitka Charley
knew full well his privilege: to live with Frank Morley in their sanctuary
above Guns & Locks & Clothes and to be as favored by a white man
as any Siwash had ever been. There were those in Juneau who did not
approve of Sitka Charley or trust him. Nonetheless Frank Morley
worked with him, ate with him, hunted and fished with him, allowed

him to sleep in Frank Morley's own loft above the store.

When Uncle Jake and I entered Guns & Locks & Clothes early on the afternoon of May 12, 1930, Sitka Charley's allegiance to Frank Morley was instantaneously split as by a ragged and furious golden bolt. Uncle Jake was younger, taller, thanks to his upright carriage, broader in the shoulders and stronger and livelier of features than Frank Morley, and, in his tie and business suit and camel's hair coat—he had already given up the fedora and was bareheaded—was from the east, a fact which both Frank Morley and Sitka Charley knew at once but which only Frank Morley could have put into words. With his powerful yet boyish and lanky physique, with his black hair parted in the middle, with his pink complexion and the bluest eyes Frank Morley or Sitka Charley had ever seen, Uncle Jake strode into Guns & Locks & Clothes that early afternoon like a god, an apparition, a male figurehead on the prow of a ghost ship. In the instant he became a fast friend of Frank Morley and a sort of second prince for Sitka Charley.

My father responded instantly to the two men inside the store as they did to him and the bonds were forged. That day Frank Morley and Sitka Charley were to my father as were the women of the Baranof Hotel to me; together the middle-aged proprietor of Guns & Locks & Clothes and the young Siwash Indian determined, like two Fates, the future of my father's life in Alaska. Frank Morley and Sitka Charley and my father were a trio spiritually united throughout my father's legendary decade in the last frontier.

No union of the flesh was firmer.

The ship was gone but the desolation left in its wake was not mine. The town of Juneau consisted mainly of a few steep streets and wooden houses built on tree stumps, along with the docking area stained daily by the empty sea, and yet I saw it through my father's eyes and eagerly, lavishing on every stump and plank my own design. The smells of strangers lingered in the furnishings, the thin walls, the loose wallpaper, the dusty comforts of the Baranof Hotel, but it was my first hotel and I the only child among its guests; its appeal to my vanity was exceeded only by its appeal to Uncle Jake's. As for Guns & Locks & Clothes, which was directly across the street from the Baranof, it was an establishment for men, a domain of masculine provisioning, an enterprise for outfitting men, and so from the first it shocked me with the allure of the purely alien. There was no such store for women.

No man could come north, no man could stop in Juneau without passing through the caverns of Frank Morley's store. And entering Guns & Locks & Clothes in the early afternoon of May 12, 1930, was to enter the dark caves of male endeavor, male dauntlessness, a space and darkness so serene and severe, so stocked with the necessities of survival, exploration, and conquest of the natural elements that it brooked no woman, denied that anything had come from Adam's rib except another crack shot, as Uncle Jake later phrased it to Sissy—yet suddenly there I was, where I did not belong, amidst the dark shadows of male certitude, where no woman ventured and which, presumably, no woman could ever know, let alone a small child. I clung to Uncle Jake's hand rapturously in the underworld of the purely alien.

We walked beneath the giant replica of a key suspended above the door and stepped inside. A bell tinkled when we entered the mysterious gloom of hunting lodge or old whaling ship's interior filled with the smell of Union Leader, Frank Morley's tobacco, and of the fur and hides of animals. Frank Morley, introducing himself at once, rose from his old high-backed rocking chair near the iron stove still softly aglow even in mid-May and came forward and extended his hand. It was not at all Frank Morley's habit to offer to shake the hand of every customer who entered Guns & Locks & Clothes, but in this case and on this day he did so, and just as naturally Uncle Jake returned the greeting and introduced himself and me as well, while young Sitka Charley slowly approached us from the darkness in the rear of the store. He was not included in the introductions or conversations that afternoon, but he was there. He did Frank Morley's bidding, he watched every move of his mentor and the strange visitor from the east, and he listened to them, stayed close to them, now and then stared intently at the stranger's child.

"Frank Morley," said the gentle, stoop-shouldered, shawled and hatted figure without whom no industry could be undertaken, no serious expedition launched, and in the pronouncing of his name was the first to welcome Uncle Jake officially to Alaska.

"Jake Deauville," said my father, full in the sun through the dusty window at his back and wearing unbuttoned his sensuous and smartly styled camel's hair coat, which was the first and last such garment that Frank Morley ever saw, and which was partly how he recognized my father for the man he was—a man, that is, of moral bearing who nonetheless could on occasion dress himself not for purpose but for the distant lights of fashion. "And this," said my father, propelling me forward by the shoulder and displaying me, "this is Sunny."

Frank Morley nodded and allowed himself to reach down and gently, with soft and leathery thumb and forefinger, pinch my cheek.

"Just arrived?" Frank Morley asked.

"On the morning boat," said my father in a cheerfully boastful tone that shared with Frank Morley what both men already knew, which was that my father's arrival in Alaska was fortuitous, noteworthy, fated, and not at all like the comings and goings of other men.

"Here for long?" Frank Morley asked, casually as if in true ignorance, which he was not, and as if their comradeship had not just the moment before been forged by the smithies of the far north. "Or just passing through?"

"Here to stay," Uncle Jake answered, and I too shared the import of that brief declaration, spoken so as to reveal even to me the immensity of my father's satisfaction at that which distinguished him from most men who stepped ashore at Juneau.

Frank Morley nodded, then turned and led us to shelves and piles and racks of sundry goods and clothing, though my father had made no mention of purchases, had given no indication of what, if anything, he might want or need. And yet Frank Morley went down the aisles, opened cartons, went wordlessly to ancient caches and from all the nooks and crannies and glass showcases of Guns & Locks & Clothes assembled a vast array of northland furbishings worthy of and, down to the last item, essential to the man in the camel's hair coat, who was democratic as well as debonair, as Frank Morley had known at once.

White suits of long winter underwear, and woolen shirts, and a mackinaw coat, and the parka of silky squirrel fur and the wolfskin cap that was like a bishop's mitre, and heavy gloves and gum boots, as my father came to call his shoepacks, and ax, hatchet, knives, tent, sleeping bag, packboard, and thread, needles, blue bandannas—Frank Morley harvested it all, to my father's delight, and the objects gleamed and the size of each article of clothing was correct. Absolutely correct. It was uncanny, as Uncle Jake said later when he tried on his purchases for Sissy and me in our room at the Baranof, uncanny how Frank Morley had known in advance and to intimate degree his new friend's weight and dimensions and preferences, even though they did not in fact discuss such matters. It was then that Uncle Jake made it clear to Sissy that Frank Morley was now the friend of our family. It made no difference, said Uncle Jake, that Frank Morley came from a different walk of life from ourselves. He was our friend.

But Frank Morley had saved the best to last, and if my father's boyish happiness had been surprisingly inflated by the great store of goods that Frank Morley had already bestowed upon the easterner, now that same happiness gave way abruptly to a state of seriousness which exemplifies, for a man, his greatest good, greatest contentment, since this seriousness is self-importance in its purest form and is in fact a kind of secreted elation of far greater weight and moment than those emotions felt by the mere receiver of unexpected gifts—and all this because Frank Morley had kept the best to the last and took us now to the guns.

It was the sight of rows and racks of silent and brightly oiled rifles, new and used, and of whole families of long-barreled revolvers with wooden handles large enough to accommodate the graceful meaty hand of Uncle Jake, that now induced in Uncle Jake his sensations of seriousness so latent with intoxication. The guns shone in the gloom, they hung, they stood, they waited to be taken up, they constituted an entire arsenal of manliness. We walked among them, stopped, were reverent, walked on, with Sitka Charley observing my father's mien in admiration. Those guns with their walnut stocks were polished and their bright blue barrels signaled feats of skill and courage on terrains of struggle. There were lever-action rifles and bolt-action rifles and shotguns which were no concern of ours even though Uncle Jake had never in his life done any shooting except at clay pigeons with a sixteen-gauge shotgun which Sissy herself might have handled with ease. As we walked their ranks and attended on Frank Morley's grave decision, Uncle Jake knew that one of those big-game rifles was already his. Of course Frank Morley had already made his decision, had chosen the rifle before they had spoken their names or shaken hands. But which would it be? And had it not already altered and enhanced his character? Uncle Jake speculated, he studied the guns, he was cloaked in seriousness, he was a man who was being singled out by another man and, in a matter of consequence, set apart—even from such exalted men as Robert Fitzgibbon, whose guns and equipment, my father knew, had been purchased in a vast and chandeliered and thickly carpeted store in an eastern city.

Frank Morley stopped. We stopped. Sitka Charley drew close to watch. And then like some humbled Joseph the Provider Frank Morley reached out and from a separate rack on the wall took down the rifle that was my father's own. For an instant Frank Morley held it, hefted it, appreciated for a last time its weight and balance, and then put it carefully into my father's hands.

"It's a .405 Winchester," Frank Morley said. "The only one in the store. It's no good for any sort of distance, but at short range it'll stop a bear better than anything made in the States or Europe. It's what you need."

In silence Uncle Jake held athwart his breast the heavy short-barreled Four-Hundred-and-Five, as he called it thereafter, and for an instant gun and camel's hair coat vied for possession of the man. Then the fingers on the big hands tightened and the gun won out. The leather strap hung in an inverted arc, a chip of bright light shone from the tip of the sight at the end of the barrel in which the black and ominous bore was larger in diameter than Uncle Jake's thumb.

"Go ahead," said Frank Morley. "Try it. But watch out for the kick."

With the long soft skirts of his tailored coat loose and flaring, and the red silk polka-dotted tie an unmistakable emblem of the Deauville Farms he had forsworn and left behind forever, and the Deauville family ring agleam on his finger, slowly Uncle Jake obeyed Frank Morley and placed his feet one before the other and took a breath and raised the gun, which now that we could see it fully and to best advantage, was obviously the most menacing hunting rifle of them all. Still more slowly, with the deliberation of the true marksman, he nestled the heavily cushioned stock into his right shoulder and, leaning sharply forward from the waist so as not to be thrown off balance when he fired, steadied himself, tracked his target, took careful aim. Then he squeezed the trigger.

Surely he had sighted the Fitzgibbon bear in Guns & Locks & Clothes, had waited amidst mukluks and mackinaws and union suits with buttoned flaps in the seats until the brute creature, nearly eight feet tall on its hind legs, was all but upon him. The bear was crashing and towering toward him in massive and malignant readiness to kill, and then, holding his own, calmly, calculating his deadly trajectory, he had fired and had dropped the snarling Fitzgibbon bear in a breath.

"Good shot!" said Frank Morley, chuckling and shaking his head and looking upon his newfound friend and hunter with a warmth of admiration which he, Frank Morley, had not felt since his own arrival, as a youth, in the Territory.

"It's a beauty," said Uncle Jake. "But it packs a wallop!" And he laughed and lowered the Four-Hundred-and-Five and handed it to Sitka Charley, who, himself admiring the imaginary shot, secured the mammoth rifle in its case of white canvas and burnished leather. "And now," said Uncle Jake, once more seizing my shoulder and giving me another turn or two, "now for Sunny!"

Frank Morley nodded, Sitka Charley went off immediately to the dustiest shelves in the depths of the store while Uncle Jake leaned down and removed my sailor hat, my coat, my leggings. Frank Morley watched impassively, with the gentlest interest, as Uncle Jake stripped me down to my white underpants and skimpy nakedness. When Sitka Charley returned to us laden with my Klondike clothing, Uncle Jake dressed me again in thick woolen socks, a lumberjack's red shirt scaled down to fit the small boy I was fast becoming, and in tawny corduroy britches that tucked into little high leather boots which Uncle Jake himself laced up to my knees. Three grown men, and one my father, silently attending me naked, newly dressed; large men surrounding me, standing close to me, hands in hip pockets (Sitka Charley) or rolling a cigarette (Frank Morley) or fumbling with my buttons (Uncle Jake), waiting upon me with a respect and benign curiosity I had not known before, dark figures ministering to my transformation, though of course it was only Uncle Jake who put hands upon me, as Sitka Charley passed him each article of new apparel while Frank Morley smoked and fixed on me his shy concentration. Thus I was specially and unusually treated in darkness and amidst the sweet smells of Union Leader, and though everything about my stooping or squatting father gave sanction to our brief tableau, since his was the authority of the male parent while I was so young as to have no gender, still for that moment I knew they were watching, and as I pulled up my socks or raised one thin bare leg to the proffered britches, with my hands on Uncle Jake's shoulders and frowning in my childish pleasure, I could not have been more aware that I was the center of their quiet regard, as if I were some small Diana with slightly awkward men for handmaidens.

"Done," said Uncle Jake and got to his feet and stepped back, surveying me where I stood proudly in the pool of my discarded clothing. Never had his approval of me been so strong.

"Well, you've made an old man happy," murmured Frank Morley, smiling and shaking his head.

"Soon," said Uncle Jake, "we'll teach her to shoot."

At those words Frank Morley gave another significant glance in the direction of Sitka Charley, who once more understood Frank Morley's wishes and did his bidding. The young Indian, in tight denim pants bound to his hips by a broad belt carved and painted, stepped to one of the glass cases, reached inside, rejoined us and handed Frank Morley the object he had removed from the case. In his turn Frank Morley handed this object to my father, who held it, admired it, then gave it to me.

It was a knife in a scabbard. The ivory handle was carved to represent a bear on his hind legs; the blade was a thin crescent of steel; into the blond leather of the scabbard the artisan had carved another standing bear holding in his claws a fish. From my father I took that knife and held it, studied it, removed the blade from the scabbard.

"Careful, Sunny," my father said. "It's sharp."

Slowly I returned the knife to its scabbard and gratefully, in both hands, clutched my gift and looked up into each of their faces.

"Tomorrow Sitka Charley will make her a belt," said Frank Morley. "The ones we have are too large."

I saw the dark young face, the slim and retiring figure, and I understood that the knife was the work of Sitka Charley and somehow I understood that all along his had been the mute scrutiny, his the mute concern for me, his the unallowed presence that had most aroused in me the allure of the alien. I tried to thank him in the way I pressed his gift to my shirtfront and looked at him.

"Jake!" exclaimed Sissy when he paraded me into our room at the Baranof, "what have you done to her! My little pioneer," she said and hugged me to her, laughing, stroking my hair. When Uncle Jake came back from the lavatory down the hall where he had retired to dress, and stood before us costumed for the life to come, he was the full-blown portentous image of what I was but the amusing mockery. She looked upon him keenly, worshipfully, despite her grief.

16 —

I still own Sitka Charley's knife. Sitka Charley still lives in Juneau—faithful, more remote than ever, lithe at sixty. Occasionally he comes out to Gamelands, from time to time I visit his loft above what used to be Guns & Locks & Clothes. He has a boat, he fishes. He owns the Four-Hundred-and-Five.

Sunny's Indian.

17 —

There was no reason for Uncle Jake to join Rex Ainsworth's rescue mission, no reason to leave us, Sissy and me, a mere ten days after our arrival in Juneau and to fly off with Rex Ainsworth for the sake of Robert Fitzgibbon and his friends. There was no more reason for Uncle Jake to leave in Rex Ainsworth's plane on an afternoon of scattered fog and steady drizzle than there was for his journey to Alaska in the first place—that precipitous nomadic northward venturing from which there was no turning back. No reason or just as much, since Uncle Jake had little or no belief in cause and effect, or did not admit to the effects he had caused, or did not perceive the causes that drove him on, or lived outside the ordinary orbit of cause and effect. He made sense, he did not make sense. He honored his own will, he submitted to whim; he was steadfast and dictatorial, a chance word from friend or stranger could change everything. He claimed to be the foe of reason when he thought of it. And yet he was in fact predictable, and buried deep in the chaos of his vanity and good intentions there lay an intelligibility of sorts, a dark center of meaning that was understandable and which even he could not entirely avoid.

He had never fired a rifle at any living creature large or small, had had little experience with bandages or setting bones. Yet off he went with Rex Ainsworth, carrying with him a wooden medicine chest and the Four-Hundred-and-Five. Why not a doctor? Why not a guide? Why not some longtime male resident of Juneau for whom the hot droppings of an Alaskan brown bear would have significance? Why not the local government nurse with her Red Cross pin and black satchel? Why Uncle Jake? Why this first senseless feeding of his vainglory?

Frank Morley had no reason for doing so, but it was Frank Morley who caused Uncle Jake to climb into Rex Ainsworth's Fairchild that afternoon and vanish.

Sissy survived her first night in the Baranof Hotel despite her initial grief at arriving. In the days of rain that followed she continued to play the part of the good sport, as she now thought of herself, reverting to her role in the ancient tennis match still not forgotten. She read in our darkened room or chatted with one of the women in the lobby and remained as innocent as Uncle Jake. And she showed nothing of the despondency she felt when Frank Morley and Uncle Jake led us up to the one-story, three-room wooden house that Frank Morley had found for us on the uppermost edge of town. They told her it had a splendid view, as indeed it did, since from that height the view down the channel up which the S.S. *Alaska* had sailed a little more than a week before was broad, full, unobstructed; any time she wished she could glance down the long watery way on which the S.S. *Alaska* had disappeared. But Sissy was lonely and afraid of heights. They told her that as one of the last houses above the town our new home had privacy and the authenticity of a rustic location and so it had. There was a great half-naked fir rising above the roof and the last tenants had left hardy fernlike plants growing in tin cans wired to the railing of the narrow porch. Sissy was afraid of isolation and afraid of bears; she had wanted only to live in a large eastern city in a safe and spacious apartment when the time came for Uncle Jake to take us from Deauville Farms to a place of our own. Now she was doomed to live in fear of marauding bears. Yet it was she who tied her hair in one of Uncle Jake's new blue bandannas and swept, dusted, scrubbed, she who found used furniture and persuaded a fat and early-morning beer drinker to bring us new propane tanks in his rusty truck. And she it was who insisted that the only bedroom in the house must go to me and that she and Uncle Jake could sleep happily enough in the living room on the already much-used foldaway bed she had proudly bought. It was narrow, uncomfortable, and much too short for Uncle Jake, and on all the mornings of my early childhood, whenever he was not absent from Juneau, Uncle Jake's large white feet hung far over the end of what he called the contraption. In addition to the contraption our living room contained some wooden orange crates used as end tables, a cushioned rocking chair for Uncle Jake, inspired by Frank Morley's, and Sissy's slowly growing collection of Alaskan trinkets, which hung on the walls.

In blue bandanna and old sweater and attractive slacks, singing to herself and washing the insides of windows streaked on the outside with intermittent rain, thus Sissy greeted Frank Morley and Uncle Jake on the midmorning when they climbed our hill to give her the bad news about Robert Fitzgibbon and his friends. We heard the familiar voices suddenly low and serious; Sissy was happily surprised. And in they came, Frank Morley wearing his black hat and old canvas hunting coat, Uncle Jake his double-breasted business suit and tan reversible, and at once their solemnity brought the pain of apprehension to Sissy's face. She was loyal; she had accompanied Uncle Jake to Alaska; she had not complained about the wooden house or Juneau. We were all safe and she was adding her own decorative flair to the home Frank Morley had found for us—and she could not imagine what could possibly be wrong.

"What is it?" she said, dropping the wet cloth into the sudsy bucket, and looking to Frank Morley and then to Uncle Jake, who frowned and did not meet her eye.

"Fitzgibbon," Frank Morley said.

"Fitzgibbon?"

"They're in trouble," Frank Morley said, glancing down at Sissy with all the moroseness he could muster.

"Well," said Sissy, "I don't understand."

"They put out distress signals," Frank Morley said. "Chippy Smith was flying over the area where they were supposed to be and saw the signals. He got me on the shortwave as soon as he did."

"Chippy is a bush pilot," said Uncle Jake. "He's good but reckless."

"But Fitzgibbon has nothing to do with us," said Sissy, addressing herself to Frank Morley and, for the first time in her life, ignoring Uncle Jake.

"Oh yes," said Frank Morley. "It's serious."

"I still don't understand," said Sissy.

They paused. Frank Morley pulled out his pouch and papers but rolled no cigarette. Uncle Jake studied the bare floor, the dead wood-burning stove with its tin pipe disappearing through the wall, the bundle of gauzy curtains which Sissy had yet to hang. Like Sissy and Frank Morley he did not acknowledge my presence though I was seated on one of the orange crates in the middle of the floor with my boots newly oiled and my red shirt as bright as the day they had put it on me in Guns & Locks & Clothes. I was enjoying the novelty of being ignored and the novelty of bad news and of Sissy and Uncle Jake and Frank Morley quarreling.

"Well," said Uncle Jake, "I'm going."

"What do you mean?" asked Sissy. "Where are you going?" She faltered, beginning to admit to consciousness what Uncle Jake had had all the while in store for her, and which she knew he would never himself admit to consciousness: that she was not going to understand what was happening, ever, and that she was here in Juneau only to suffer, which no one but herself could know. The drizzle fell, I smiled, the two men waited.

"Tell me," she said then. "What do you mean?"

"They need help," said Uncle Jake quickly. "They need to be rescued. Rex Ainsworth is the most reputable pilot in town, despite that name of his." Uncle Jake smiled but darkened at once, at once resumed his burden. "Rex has agreed to fly, despite the weather. I'm going along."

"You?"

He nodded.

"But why? Why you? Oh Jake, you mustn't."

"Frank says I must."

Then she turned to our new family friend and quivered. "Frank Morley," she said, "what are you trying to do to us?"

He shuffled, put away the makings, as he called them, and for Sissy's sake allowed the sadness of the situation to show on his face. "Rex has a basket stretcher," he said slowly. "After taking out four seats to make way for the stretcher, he'll still have room for a passenger. He needs a man like Jake to go along."

"That's right," said Uncle Jake quickly. "We've just come from the docks. I've met Rex, he's already taking the seats out of the Fairchild. I've agreed to go." And then: "Don't worry," he said, "Frank's here. You can count on Frank."

They glanced at each other, those two, and then at me, finally, and wiped the rain from their faces. The fog that was rising off the sea and

descending down the slopes of the mountains shrouded our house; with
one hand Sissy made a gesture as if to push back her hair, which was
already tied up in the blue bandanna, and raised her heart-shaped face.
In an instant she accepted the entire chain of senseless and fearsome
episodes of which this was but the first, and in the same instant regained
the full flush of her loyalty to Uncle Jake.

"Well," she said, smiling and looking up at Uncle Jake with the trust
and forgiveness he had depended on, "when are you going?"

"Right now," he said quickly, and in a second glance shared with
Frank Morley his relief and pleasure. "Rex is waiting. As soon as I'm
ready we'll take off."

"Now?" she asked and faltered, recovered, raised to him her wide
smile, pure brow.

He nodded.

"While you're dressing," she said then after a long pause, "I'll make
some coffee."

She touched his arm, she wiped the dampness from the lapel of the
reversible; then the two of them disappeared, she to the stove, he to
my bedroom, where he packed his knapsack and changed his clothes.
Frank Morley sat down in the rocker and took me up on his lap. We
smelled the coffee which Sissy had already learned to make like a camper,
tossing egg shells into the black and boiling pot of grounds, and we
heard Uncle Jake hurrying and readying himself behind the closed door
of the room that was mine. In Frank Morley's wet hunting coat and
woolen pants I smelled the cold steam of secret forests, the rank bare
life of the tundra, and wriggled still deeper into the wilderness that
cloaked his stiff and gentle person.

"Oh Jake," said Sissy when he at last emerged, "you look wonderful!" And the black and green checked shirt was brighter, and the
britches shinier, and the thick boots more oily, and his entire figure
more rugged here in our nearly empty house than when he had first
appeared to us, so garbed in newness, in the Baranof Hotel. He laughed,
he drank his coffee, he slung his gear onto his back and seized the Four-
Hundred-and-Five and led the way out of our house and down the hill
to the docks and the waiting Rex Ainsworth.

Frank Morley walked in a stooped and manly fashion at Uncle Jake's
side. Sissy and I trailed after them down the wooden sidewalk, past
Guns & Locks & Clothes and the ever-watchful Sitka Charley and into
the oppressive depths of the fog that smelled of gasoline and dead fish.

We congregated on the rocking float to which the yellow Fairchild was tied and where Rex Ainsworth waited, Sissy hugging herself and I standing with feet apart in miniature imitation of the lanky sailor Uncle Jake had been in the Great War. We smiled at Rex Ainsworth. He nodded. He reached for Uncle Jake's gun and gear and, stepping onto the pontoon of the old and often-repaired airplane, he stowed it away. Then he turned significantly to Uncle Jake and held wide the flimsy door while Uncle Jake shook Frank Morley's hand and patted Sissy on the shoulder and me on the head.

The old Fairchild frightened Sissy, as well it might, with recent patches on the thin fabric of its fuselage and wires dangling from its high wing and black and oily engine. But Rex Ainsworth was not at all what Sissy had expected and from the first he had inspired in her sudden waves of trust, waves of relief. He was as tall as Uncle Jake, as silent as Frank Morley, and as unlike a pilot of an airplane as she could have imagined. No goggles or coveralls or fur-lined boots or fur-collared leather jacket for Rex Ainsworth. Nothing to suggest the horrors of, say, Chippy Smith, whom Sissy had of course already envisioned. No bravado, arrogance, or foolhardiness in this quiet, intelligent man who was about to carry off our Uncle Jake. To the contrary, Rex Ainsworth was, if anything, more dignified than his passenger and a shade taller. He wore no hat and was dressed in a black business suit and white shirt and dark blue tie. He belonged in a bank, as Sissy thought, and not in the pilot's seat of an ancient airplane. His eyes were clear, he was serious. Sissy knew that she could trust the man she loved to Rex, as she now thought of him, if she was fated to trust that man to anyone, as she knew she was.

Together, like two brothers, they climbed up into the plane. The engine puffed, exploded, the wooden propeller began to turn. Above us, beneath the wobbling wing and behind the small and shadowed windows, there they sat together side by side as in some dim photograph or as if they were already thousands of feet into fog, wind, wet air. Uncle Jake was waving, Rex Ainsworth was sitting sharply upright and might have been reading a book.

They pulled away. We lost them, white knight and priestly pilot. Frank Morley continued to wave his black hat in wide arcs until the sound of the engine disappeared above us, while Sissy wept to herself and invisible gulls cried and called to each other in the surrounding fog. The seats Rex Ainsworth had removed from the Fairchild huddled beneath a tarpaulin at the end of the float like four corpses clutching their knees.

18 —

Rex Ainsworth well deserved my awe and Sissy's trust. He was no Frank Morley, was in fact too similar to Uncle Jake ever to become a friend of our family. But for a decade, whenever Uncle Jake required the swiftness and expediency of flight instead of the longer-range possibilities of ship or boat, inevitably he called on Rex Ainsworth, who, in all that time, piloted Uncle Jake about with hardly a mishap. And it was not long before Rex Ainsworth began to carry me as well as Uncle Jake aloft in the Fairchild, to Sissy's great dismay, and to propel me as firmly toward the sky as had the unwitting women of the Baranof Hotel started me off toward sex. I rode with him, I flew his Fairchild; before my fifteenth birthday I was one of those who, under Uncle Jake's direction, retrieved his body from the Fairchild's wreckage.

Together Uncle Jake and Frank Morley created the legends of Rex Ainsworth. But even without their stories about his courage, his exploits, his civilized manner, he was bound one day to crash and crash he did. But not before he gave a silver cast to my young desires and taught me a purely pragmatic view of flying. Rex Ainsworth was not romantic, despite the stories of Frank Morley and Uncle Jake. And neither am I.

19 —

Each afternoon Frank Morley paid us the visit Uncle Jake had promised; he slumped in the rocking chair and smoked and told Sissy there was no danger and tried to help her rally. Then on the fourth day he arrived with heavy breath and his shoulders less stooped than usual and reported that Rex Ainsworth had just returned. Within the hour Rex Ainsworth had landed on rough water and in almost no visibility, had barely missed a piling which beyond a doubt would have caused the Fairchild to explode at the moment of contact, and had docked, had discharged his passenger—the fat member of the Fitzgibbon party whom Uncle Jake had finally strapped into the basket stretcher—and was even now restoring the missing seats to the cabin of the plane.

Thanks to the ministrations of Uncle Jake and the courage of Rex Ainsworth, the injured man, who had been mauled and crushed by a seventeen-hundred-pound Alaskan brown bear and given up for dead, would live, and even now was undergoing surgery in the government hospital downtown. In another half-hour or so, Frank Morley said, Rex Ainsworth was starting back for the others in the Fitzgibbon party and for Uncle Jake, who had proven himself the hero of Rex's rescue mission, as Frank Morley had predicted.

Sissy heard him out in horror, but smiling, hand to cheek, eyes bright. The aromas of coffee and Union Leader filled the house. Suddenly the noise of the Fairchild's engine at full throttle passed directly overhead and shook walls, floor, windows, the iron stove, and then was abruptly stilled. Frank Morley, generally despondent, no matter his good nature and words of optimism, looked at Sissy from under his beetling brows and nodded. Sissy in her turn was also encouraged. We had our family friend and so far no accident had befallen Uncle Jake, who would soon arrive triumphant back in Juneau.

That night the wind rose, the rain fell, the rain sounded like nailheads on the tarpaper affixed to our roof of thin planking, and throughout the dark hours Sissy paced, on guard, valiant, wet with fear, alert for the sounds of the lowering bear which, she was convinced, would come to us seeking shelter from the storm or, for no reason she could understand, to menace those who had been left behind at the edge of town in the house which she could not possibly barricade. There was no Frank Morley to comfort Sissy when she was afraid of bears.

"He's back!" declared Frank Morley, wheezing from the exertions of climbing our steep hill at the fastest pace he could manage. "Just got back, not a half-hour ago!"

"And safe?" asked Sissy. "He's all right?"

"You'll see," said Frank Morley, smiling a rare smile between the drooping jowls. "He got the bear!"

Sissy had waited. Sissy had washed windows in the rain, had struggled with the demons none of us would ever see, had done her best to prolong Frank Morley's visits with hunter's coffee and homemade cakes, and now she was prepared for Uncle Jake's arrival. She had lighted the oven in the kitchen stove, braving burns or worse since Uncle Jake had not yet had the old and faulty oven repaired, though it was clearly dangerous, and stuffed the frozen turkey which she had bought for the occasion and had already thawed, as though by premonition, and set four places at the makeshift table. From the ice chest she removed four bottles of ginger ale, which was Uncle Jake's favorite beverage, as he called it, and which he could drink all night when telling stories, and arranged them in a festive clump in the table's center. Then she stepped among the fir trees behind the house and happily, in haste, smoked half of one of her precious cigarettes, since from the moment of Uncle Jake's departure she had become a secret smoker and was to keep at least that pleasure to herself for the rest of her short life, unbeknownst to him.

"He's here!" I cried and flung myself into the arms of Uncle Jake while Sissy and Frank Morley stood back together, sharing their silent veneration of the man who had so violently changed—"Oh, how he's changed!" whispered Sissy under her breath—only to have become more vigorously than ever the self he was.

"Sissy!" he said. His shirt was torn, his boots scuffed, his britches stained with sap and blood of the dead bear. He was bearded, his black hair was unkempt, he smelled of iodine and dying fires. He stood in his favorite sailor stance, feet wide apart, and his eyes were clearly fevered with all he had seen, and around him lay his rifle, his gear by now well broken in, and, tied in heavy ropes, a great mound that was the head and hide of the bear he had killed.

"Jake," whispered Sissy. "How are you, Jake?"

He swung me down then and went to her, embraced her, pressed against the short and slender length of Sissy all the transformed solidity of he who had cooked over open fires and slept on the ground.

"It was terrible," he said. "Appalling. Fitzgibbon should be whipped or jailed."

"Poor Jake," Sissy whispered.

"One of them, Harry Harrison, was nearly dead when Rex and I arrived, and Johnson, their guide, was blue with agony. The camp was a shambles, Johnson was delirious and Harrison unconscious, and there was Fitzgibbon—when I found him—drunk as a lord. He would have drowned on his own vomit if I hadn't appeared on the scene. Even the bear wouldn't touch him, with that breath of his. He's down in Billy's Bar right now getting soused."

"Ah," said Frank Morley, "I thought as much. Everyone had doubts about Fitzgibbon."

"A full case of whiskey," said Uncle Jake. "A case of whiskey! You know what happens when you bring liquor into a hunting camp."

They listened, they drew him to the rocking chair, Sissy and Frank Morley, and sat him down with me on his lap, and gave him a glass of ginger ale and begged him to talk. Beyond our circle the wet air was darkening and from the shrouded harbor below came the cries of the gulls.

"It was outrageous," said Uncle Jake, drinking off the ginger ale and holding out his glass for more, and passing the back of his weathered hand before his eyes and beginning to laugh, since the more catastrophic the story he told the more he laughed, which was a mannerism he had acquired in his shy youth.

"Start from the beginning," said Sissy, kneeling close enough to the muddy boots to touch them while Frank Morley pulled up a chair and eased down and made himself comfortable, rounding his back and clasping his hands, leaning into the long story that was sure to come. He smoked, tipping his ashes into a chipped saucer, and the turkey roasted and Uncle Jake held forth.

"In the first place," he said, squeezing me and rolling the golden ginger ale in the tilted glass, "when we took off we couldn't see. Not a thing," he said and laughed. "If the S.S. *Alaska* had been out there in the fog we might have smashed right into her broadside or ripped off her bridge, Tony and all," he continued, laughing more loudly so as to smooth the waters of horror with his own amusement. "It was rough, there were downdrafts, we weren't fifty feet in the air when the wind began chopping at us like crossed swords. I thought we were going down then and there and we would have if it hadn't been for Rex and that sixth sense of his. But up we went. We climbed, battered every step of the way. And storms? Why, it was just one storm after another, and nothing to see except the occasional cliff jutting suddenly out of the rain and fog and so close that in the instant I could see our impact, hear it—but Rex never batted an eye and with that elegant hand of his lightly gripping the joystick, which is what they call it, Sissy, though for the life of me I don't know why, he managed to keep us on course. If I had been prone to airsickness, which of course I'm not, I would have lost Rex's respect once and for all in those first ten minutes up there. But I was fit as a fiddle and I knew he was glad I was along.

"I suppose Rex was navigating by the stars. He must have been able to see the stars through the daylight, the rain, the fog, the black clouds, must have been able to chart our way by the stars since not once did he look at the little mapboard strapped to his thigh. We bounced, we fell, we couldn't talk for the noise of that engine, and I didn't have the slightest idea of where we were or when we'd arrive. But Rex knew. After that trip I'd fly anywhere with Rex. I tell you Chippy Smith can't hold a candle to Rex. I'm certain of it, without ever having met the man.

"Then down we went. One moment we were careening along up there at five thousand feet, according to Rex's altimeter, which he ignored and which I studied the whole way like the clock of doom, swooping and jerking this way and that in the old Fairchild that reminded me of Granny and might have been Granny's heavenly coffin and ours too, as I thought of it, and then in the next moment we were going down. Rex banked us. He simply put the Fairchild on her side and banked us—and steeply. Why, those wings were vertical, absolutely vertical, and even as we were going down, falling to a quick and shattering death for all I knew, I was thinking that no one could handle an airplane as Rex Ainsworth could. The farther we fell the faster my admiration for that man mounted. If he had made a miscalculation, as I knew he couldn't, and had plunged us to a fate like Granny's, at least no death could have been happier, for me at least. I can tell you that."

He paused, he laughed, he rolled my head against his chest. He drank down another glass. He waited, and in his silence Sissy and Frank

Morley stirred uncomfortably, as he had known they would.

"Jake," said Sissy, "you mustn't say such things." But he was there, he was home in all his soiled and tousled splendor, and the girlish satisfaction of Sissy's voice belied her remonstrance.

"Oh," said Uncle Jake, hiding half my head in his hand, "it gets worse. It gets much worse. I've never seen anything like what was waiting for us in Fitzgibbon's camp. There is no punishment fit for Fitzgibbon. None. They hadn't been in camp five minutes when he began to drink. From the bottle! From the mouth of the bottle! He was sick in Rex Ainsworth's plane; not once in his life had he fired a rifle or scrubbed himself in the pure and freezing waters of a creek. He didn't know how to make a fire or read a compass. Why, he didn't even tie up poor Johnson's leg! He left Johnson to apply his own tourniquet, despite the pain. And he abandoned Harry Harrison to His Unholiness, as I dubbed Fitzgibbon's bear the moment I first heard of him. Of course it was a big bear. One of the biggest on record, wasn't it, Frank?"

Frank Morley nodded, frowned, shifted, leaned still further into the force of the tale.

"Seventeen hundred pounds," said Uncle Jake. "And eight feet tall on his hind legs. With a mind like a man's. And a heart you couldn't stop. And all seventeen hundred pounds pumping with the blood of cruelty and wallowing in the fat of destruction and wrapped and hooded in the fur of savagery. That bear was enough to frighten anyone. But Fitzgibbon wasn't just afraid. He was dishonorable. It's too bad the bear didn't get Fitzgibbon instead of poor Harry Harrison—"

"Jake," said Sissy, still in tones of tenderest reproach, and leaned forward and placed a timid hand against one of his booted calves. But he ignored her, staring into the wreckage of the Fitzgibbon camp and stroking my head, my cheek, my shoulders, and talking on. By now no one cared about the turkey, including Sissy herself.

"Well," said Uncle Jake, "we landed. Rex brought us in so low that the pontoons cut a path through the tops of the pines like scythes through wheat, and then at the last minute he dropped us down. That lake above Icy Inlet is too short for the Fairchild, and each time Rex landed on it or took off the lake shrank another hundred yards or so. It was perilous, even for a man like Rex.

"No one stepped out of the woods to meet us. No one called, though they couldn't have missed the Fairchild's engine. We drifted in to a little strip of beach and climbed out, made the Fairchild fast, unloaded the medicine chest and basket stretcher. I removed the Four-Hundred-and-Five from its case right then and there and slung it onto my shoulder. I told Rex he ought to wait with the plane and let me go ahead alone and find them, but he wouldn't hear of it, despite the fact that he was dressed improperly for the woods. We carried the medicine chest between us; I carried the stretcher under my left arm, it was that light. The rain had stopped but those woods were saturated underfoot and overhead, I can tell you. Dark and dripping. And slippery? Those deadfalls were covered with a skin of slime. Every few minutes I shouted, but there was no answer. I don't know how Rex did it, but he got through all that tangle as smoothly as he flew his plane. He was as good in the woods as in the air, and I told him so.

"Then we found their camp in a clearing, or what was left of it. And I can tell you what was waiting for us in that clearing: devastation! Or not mere devastation but a kind of unnatural wreckage in which some hot breath of pure malevolence was still fluttering. The tents were down, brand-new shirts and pants and drawers and boots and hunting caps were strewn about as if the entire Fitzgibbon party had been stripped naked by perversity itself—as if perversity had gone on a rampage and torn off their clothes and then for the sport of it had flung all that apparel around the camp they had tried to make for themselves in the clearing. Sacks of dried apricots and swollen beans, enough to feed twenty men instead of four, had been slashed open and scattered among the clothes and ashes as if by the grim reaper. A bare slab of bacon—it must have weighed eighteen pounds if it weighed an ounce—was lying on a heap of trampled canvas that had been a tent, and half that slab of bacon was so crushed and torn and flattened that some mastodon from the age of ice might have stamped on it, chewed it, toyed with it, tossed it aside. And Fitzgibbon's shower, as it proved to be—can you imagine bringing a portable shower to Alaska?—even this remarkable contrivance had been sideswiped and left for dead, flexible pipes and tank and nozzle half hanging from the branch where Fitzgibbon himself had fastened his machine for bathing. It was sickening to come upon the remnants of Fitzgibbon's vanity and dishonor; more sickening to find it plundered; and worst of all to see his empty bottles gleaming out of the wreckage like deadly gems in offal. And to top the whole thing, the entire conglomerate of ruin had been tramped down endlessly, ruthlessly, as we saw at once, because the prints were everywhere, the clawed prints as long and fat as a Virginia ham. Why, he had even trampled his own leavings, that bear Fitzgibbon had come all this way to hunt.

"If excrement is sickening, and I believe it is, then that bear's excrement was enough to turn the stomach of a saint. His droppings were a sure sign of his immensity, his wrath, his perseverance, as was the mad dance of those prints of his. And that bear was even worse than I thought, as I was soon to learn.

"I lost no time in unslinging the Four-Hundred-and-Five, I can tell you, and putting off the safety and holding it in both hands at the ready, more for the protection of Rex Ainsworth than myself. I was determined to protect Rex from that marauding bear at any cost.

"And Fitzgibbon? And Johnson? And Harry Harrison and the other fellow? Hiding! They were all hiding! At least Fitzgibbon and his drinking partner—for that's what he was of course—were hiding like the pair of cowards that they were, since poor Harrison was unconscious and Johnson in too much pain to consider hiding from the animal that one of them, Fitzgibbon or the other, should have shot the first time he appeared in camp. We found them, Rex and I, in fact we nearly stumbled over Fitzgibbon and his spineless pal where they had half buried themselves in their sleeping bags in the roots of a dead spruce. We smelled them before we saw them; the whiskey they'd drunk and the whiskey they'd sloshed around themselves in panic smelled to high heaven and, I can tell you, destroyed the very breath of nature where those poor devils lay in their stupor. We left them and pushed on until we found Johnson and Harrison under the canvas lean-to that Johnson had been able to rig up professionally despite the pain. I was dismayed to see that they too were lying in a host of bottles, though Johnson's efforts to ease his pain with whiskey could hardly be called drunkenness, and from the first it was plain to see that he was sober, thick speech or no thick speech. Johnson's rifle was by his side—you sold it to him, didn't you, Frank?—so I could leave Rex tending the two of them while I returned for the medicine chest and stretcher which we had left back at the camp they'd all abandoned.

"By dusk we had set up a proper tent and started a good blaze and given Johnson enough morphine to relieve him of his need for Fitzgibbon's whiskey. With the old Four-Hundred-and-Five propped within handy reach against a windfall, I knelt and worked on Johnson and then on Harrison for at least an hour—grimly and more than liberal with the iodine, which stained poor Johnson redder than his own blood and at least put an end to the smell of the whiskey which is one of the most offensive smells I know of.

"Harrison was nearly dead. Johnson had done his best, of course, but Johnson could hardly crawl and was struggling against delirium the whole time. Nonetheless it was Johnson who had plucked Harrison from the ruins, so to speak, though Harrison would have been better left unmoved, were it not for His Unholiness and though Johnson had no recollection of dragging or carrying Harrison so far from where the bear had left him. But Johnson's a man of character, and somehow he managed to relocate Harrison and raise the lean-to and put out the distress signals and generally to prepare a tidy makeshift camp in which the two of them might survive—if Harrison didn't bleed to death in the night or catch pneumonia.

"I can tell you, Harry was a broken man under all the blankets and bits of clothing Johnson had used to staunch the blood. Or like a mummy under all that bloody cloth that Johnson had somehow packed around him. He was raked, he was crushed, the scalp had been torn from the back of his head in a single stroke. Why, I snagged my fingers on the tips of poor Harrison's broken ribs that protruded like ivory shards through the poor fellow's fat. But I cleaned, dressed the wounds, taped him, sewed him up, doused him even more than Johnson with the iodine. Rex complimented me on that performance.

"We spent the first night awake at the fire, Rex and I, with the Four-Hundred-and-Five across my knees and Rex still unperturbed in his dark suit and one of Johnson's blankets draped across his shoulders. And we could hear him: even in the dark of night that bear attacked the empty camp. Through the rain and darkness and sighing branches we could hear him, faintly, far off, throwing things about and for the hundredth time trampling down the shambles he had already made of Fitzgibbon's camp. Unnatural? There was nothing more unnatural than Fitzgibbon's bear, I can tell you.

"The next morning Harrison was still breathing and Johnson had revived enough to drink a cup of coffee—I thought of you, Sissy, when I made it, and it was skookum as Johnson and Rex both said—and to tell us how the whole catastrophe occurred.

"There they were, on the morning of their first day in camp, with their new tents nicely pitched and all their bright gear arranged, including an elaborate gasoline stove Fitzgibbon had brought along with the shower. Everything was in order, Fitzgibbon was only mildly drunk, they were discussing how they were going to get their bear. It had stopped raining and their spirits were high as kites, as Johnson said.

"Now Johnson was born on the trail and grew up with wolves. He had all the earmarks of an Indian, though there was not a drop of Indian blood in his veins, as he himself insisted, and in Johnson Fitzgibbon could not have hired a guide more assiduous and canny. Of course Johnson had spotted Fitzgibbon for what he was from the start: a rich, spoiled, egotistical amateur sportsman without one shred of moral fiber in his being. There could be no man more dangerous in the woods, and Johnson knew it. Nonetheless Johnson agreed to be their guide— for money. He had never been promised a larger fee, and he accepted, though he had already caught a whiff of Fitzgibbon's breath. So Johnson was under a cloud of bad luck from the start and knew it. And then on that first morning there occurred what never should have occurred in the case of a man like Johnson, skilled and practiced and sensible as he surely was. Why, Johnson had chopped ten thousand cords of wood if he had ever notched a tree on a trail. He knew timber like the back of his hand and always put safety first. And yet he slipped—on that first morning. Even as he raised the ax he knew that he was going to slip, and that he himself was the instrument of his own bad luck.

"Fitzgibbon had brought along a brand-new ax, a splendid tool of considerable weight and perfect balance. Its handle was a long and gentle curve of the whitest oak, its head of the shiniest steel. And sharp? Why, the blade of that ax could quarter a hair, as Johnson said.

"And there was Johnson at the edge of camp and all set to chop a pile of green wood he had cut and stacked at dusk the day before, when they arrived. It was just the luck he deserved for joining Fitzgibbon in the first place—to have cut a stack of firewood when the light was poor and then slip with the ax at dawn when he was fresh, in the best of spirits, and the light clear. But he knew it was going to happen as soon as he raised the ax but couldn't stop.

"It happened all right.

"Up he swung Fitzgibbon's ax and brought it down—in a glancing blow so that the blade slipped off the log and clean as a whistle split poor Johnson's kneecap instead of the log. He watched it a moment, the great and razor-sharp ax blade buried in the round of his precious bone and gleaming, and then he cried out and fell. One of the best guides in Alaska, and there he was, stretched out in pain and humiliation with the bloodied ax beside him.

"Fitzgibbon cursed.

"And that was the signal, that combination of the curse and cry, because it was then that the largest Alaskan brown bear Johnson had ever seen emerged from among the dripping trees and lumbered into the very center of the new campsite, and slowly rose up on his stumpy hind legs like a wrestler. Johnson tried to regain his feet and reach for his rifle, but he knew he was losing consciousness and could do no more than hold the spurting kneecap together and watch as the mammoth and wary bear had his way with them.

"They began to fall all over each other, Fitzgibbon and his drinking partner, while Harry Harrison, thinking to save the day, snatched up Johnson's rifle and turned on the bear, despite Johnson's moaning protestations and Fitzgibbon's curses, and fired point-blank at his towering target.

"I don't know what came over Harrison, a chubby and cheerful fellow who should not have allowed himself to become a pawn in Fitzgibbon's nightmare, who should not have taken it upon himself to defend that hopeless crowd when he must have known that he himself was just as inept as the rest of them, and who should have known enough to remain still and leave the Fitzgibbon bear, which is now the Deauville bear, to his own devices. But perhaps Harry was trying to set an example, or expected Fitzgibbon and his insipid pal to join him in taking up their arms. Perhaps he was trying to protect the injured Johnson, who was passing out. At any rate Harry acted on impulse, on his own poor judgment—and fired point-blank at the bear and in a single shot brought down the catastrophe that the moaning Johnson had set off.

"At the sound of the shot Fitzgibbon shouted, his drinking partner screamed, and then as one they fled, those spineless fellows, leaving Harry at the mercy of the bear and Johnson to bleed to death, for all they knew. As for Harry, at that moment he understood what he had done in the height of rashness, and in his bewilderment threw down his gun—as if by throwing away the gun he could deny the catastrophe that he himself had caused.

"Well, Johnson said it was a dreadful sight. In fading consciousness and in pain as pure as a diamond he saw it all and thought that he had become a dying witness to a scene of dread.

"Harry made no attempt to run but simply stood there, looking wildly about him for the saving miracle, which never came, of course, until the bear cuffed him, knocked him down, waited, rolled him over a few times—by now Harry was weeping like a child—then picked him up, tore the shirt and most of the flesh from his right side and shoulders, and then hugged him, cracking a good six ribs or so, and tossed him aside. Harry screamed at the first incision of the claws, then fainted. And as he fought not to follow suit, Johnson watched while in slow motion, and deliberately, the enraged animal proceeded to destroy the camp, item by item, yard by yard. At one point, Johnson said, the fuming bear was so close to him that his hot odor all but smothered him to death. He could see the bloodied claws, the tiny eyes, the coat of dark fur thicker and shaggier than the bulky coats those young men wear to their football games back home. The earth shook, deep in his throat the bear appeared to be talking to himself or strangling on the fury he could not contain. And the terrible thing, as Johnson said, was that through the entire siege, the entire time of methodical destruction, the poor beast kept twisting his head and snapping his jaws, tossing the great head this way and that in a sort of baffled frenzy, despite his willful action, as though the creature had been mortally wounded or at least stung to vengeance by Harry's shot— whereas Harry had missed him even at point-blank range.

"The last thing Johnson saw before his light went out, as he put it, was the bear taking a good crack at Fitzgibbon's shower before dropping to all fours and nuzzling the prostrate Harrison, which was too much for Johnson, who finally, and at that moment, swooned like a girl.

"Well," said Uncle Jake into the gathering dusk and steadily increasing rain, as Sissy leaned her head against his knee and Frank Morley cleared his throat and waited, "well, you know the rest. Since I was perfectly willing to wait alone with Harrison until he was well enough to fly, and was perfectly capable of putting up with the slowly sobering Fitzgibbon and his pal, I urged Rex to return without me. At least Rex might have come back alone with Johnson. But Johnson refused to leave until the bear was dead, and Rex declared that he would stay until the end, and there was no arguing with Rex. I agreed, we allowed Fitzgibbon and his insipid friend to join us in Johnson's camp, though there was little conversation between ourselves and them, I can tell you that.

"So for three days I nursed Harry Harrison as well as any woman might have. During the hours he slept, I returned to the original campsite and cleaned it up, cleared away Fitzgibbon's refuse, noticing each time I did fresh signs of the bear. And in between my visits, when the others watched me changing Harry's dressings or we sat around listening to Johnson's catalogue of misadventures in a lifetime of hunting

trips, none of which equaled this one, as he said repeatedly, every now
and again we would hear the bear—growling, clawing, searching vainly
for his victim or for some scrap of the missing ruin that drew the poor
creature back endlessly to the now empty clearing. Occasionally he
crashed his single-minded bulk against a shuddering tree, as we heard
him out in silence. Surely there could have been no frustration greater
than that of His Unholiness while waiting—as I've come to think that
he must have in fact been waiting—for me to shoot him.

"By the middle of the third day, which was only the day before
yesterday of course, we knew that there was no point in waiting any
longer and decided that we'd give Harrison one more night of sleep
and that on the morrow Rex would fly Harrison back to Juneau and
then, stopping only long enough to refuel and drink a cup of coffee,
return for Johnson and me and the others, who could not have been
more mortified at the way everything was working out. Actually, Fitzgibbon's problem was more than mortification since I had emptied his
entire remaining store of bottles. Emptied them all. He saw me doing
it and knew beyond a doubt that there was not a drop of whiskey to
be had in about sixty thousand square miles of wilderness.

"So it was shortly after noon on the third day, as soon as Harry
drifted off into his midday doze and as soon as we heard His Unholiness
banging about in the empty clearing, that we went back for the bear.
We told Fitzgibbon and his partner that they had to stay behind and
stand guard over the sleeping Harry, which they were loath to do, of
course, since they wanted to be in on the fun of the bear's death, and
pouted and scowled like a couple of boys and begged to be allowed to
join us. But I wouldn't have it. I simply wasn't going to let them taint
my shooting of that bear.

"So off we went, Rex and Johnson and I, with Johnson using the
branch I had chopped for him as a cane and the still as-yet-unfired Four-
Hundred-and-Five ready and perfectly balanced in my right hand. It
was drizzling, all around us were wisps and shreds and patches of fog
like lengths of hair, but for Johnson and Rex and me the midday sun
might have been beaming down in triumph, we were that elated at the
prospect of my first bear. We weren't smiling, no one made any unseemly remarks displaying pride or levity, but the three of us were
tingling, I can tell you, and had tacitly agreed that no one was worthier
than me of taking the life of His Unholiness.

"We approached in silence. At the edge of the clearing we paused in
silence. It was understood that Rex and Johnson would remain just

behind the screen of dripping boughs and up to their knees in skunk cabbage while I alone entered the clearing. They'd have a perfect view but the stage would be mine—as it had to be.

"I rubbed my beard—my beard had grown like a dead man's, Frank— and I knew that in their comradely silence Rex and Johnson were wishing me good luck. I wasn't fearless, I was far from putting on the cloak of overconfidence, despite our elation at setting off. There was too much danger for fearlessness, as I well knew, and in fact, now that I was on the verge of pushing aside the boughs and facing at last the bear Fitzgibbon had thought was his but which would soon be mine, suddenly my mouth became so dry that my tongue and teeth felt like someone else's, while my heart was racing and pounding as if I already had His Unholiness fixed in my sights.

"Then without a word to Rex or Johnson I stepped into the clearing.

"He was snarling and rubbing his great humped back against a tree. I was startled, Frank, and for a moment thought of giving up or of beckoning to Johnson, since Johnson was carrying his thirty-ought-six slung from his shoulder. Suddenly I thought of Johnson standing there beside me in case I missed, unlikely though that prospect was—because I had not until this moment seen the living beast that had given Fitz-gibbon his comeuppance and had nearly taken Harry's life. In the three full days since our arrival His Unholiness had become a legend: I'd heard him; I'd seen him in my sleep and in my mind's eye. But there he was, not ten yards away, and nothing of the three-day vigil or of what Johnson had told to Rex and me had prepared me in any way for the living beast. He was taller than myself even on all fours; the fur of his coat was longer and shaggier than Johnson had led me to believe, though bare patches of hide shone through where he had been clawed and bitten by others of his species not strong enough or vicious enough to prove his match. And the smell? Even from where I stood his smell was hotter, spicier, more foul than Johnson had thought it was, and the clearing was so filled with it that I knew I was smelling an actual history of regal savagery, the meat and teeth of his combats, the grass and ferns and baby deer he had devoured and then excreted in all the steaming piles I'd seen.

"Looking at him face-to-face I knew that I was witness to a lifetime of aimless prowling, marauding, plundering now brought to a halt in a clearing which he could hardly recognize, thanks to my thoroughness, but which he could no longer leave, at least for long, a tormented captive of instincts forever aroused, forever denied. As he rubbed himself sore against the tree trunk he'd worn smooth as skin and worked his jaws and twisted his head, still for some reason or other I thought of him as already dead for eons, as merely a collection of great bones like those of the mastodons they sometimes discover in that country above Icy Inlet.

"It was not a mere act of sport to shoot His Unholiness, and I knew it. But who was to say that I might not go the way of Harrison, despite all our differences of character, physique, upbringing, and fare worse than Harrison and in mere moments die in those furry arms that were like bands of steel?

"I thought of it, Frank, I can tell you. I could feel my skull cracking between the yellowed teeth as long as my thumb, could feel the claws that were sharper than Sitka Charley's blades. And I was not dauntless, Frank, not dauntless. What decent man wouldn't fear for his life in such circumstances?

"But do you know that the old fellow was eying me all this while? Swaying back and forth and snarling yet looking at me the whole time with those little pink pig eyes of his? Of course I knew that the eyesight of the bear is poor and that their tiny eyes are the only telltale attribute of their ignoble nature. But I knew that he was looking at me craftily, straight in the eye, and that he saw me as clearly as I saw him. And the eyes were worse than I had imagined—smaller, wetter, redder than I had thought they'd be, more appropriate to pig than bear, an evolutionary failure and surely the true indication of what was lurking inside his shaggy hulk.

"I grew tired of waiting finally and, feeling more composed, began to toss things at him—small rocks, chunks of wood. But he was not to be disturbed in his long and not unfriendly perusal of his nemesis, and I was perturbed a bit, I must confess it, to find my expected act of slaughter turning into an amusing game.

"And then just as I was stooping for another rock and was least expecting it, in a trice he was standing on his hind legs like a wrestler, as Johnson had said—you know how much I dislike wrestlers, Sissy, those dumb bunnies who want nothing more than to rub themselves against each other from head to foot, each of those disfigured and unnatural fellows smearing himself against the other—and holding out his forelegs like bowed and furry arms, and flexing his claws.

"And before I knew it he was upon me. I suppose at last I must have reminded him of Harrison, must have jogged his killer instincts into play, must have presented myself to him suddenly as something alive that needed hugging and breaking. The grace and speed of the otherwise ungainly bear are as well known as his impoverished eyesight, and yet I was not prepared for this terrible swiftness of his—how he had covered the distance between us I would never know; certainly I had not seen him even begin to move—and was prepared still less for his imposing height. Eight feet is tall, Sissy, a third again of the average height of the Deauvilles, and an animal that looks like a prehistoric man that tall and that close and that ferocious—it's enough to induce paralysis if you lose your wits, I can tell you. And he was so close that I could see that his fur was bristling and the mouth salivating. He seemed to know that I justified again his presence in the empty clearing; his ferocity was so complete, was such a handsome venting of his pent-up rage that I could not help but marvel at what was after all a perfect specimen of his species. He was noble. He was certainly noble. And yet even then I noticed that there were whole colonies of winged insects nesting in the poor creature's fur.

"Well, Johnson knew that he was speaking out of turn yet couldn't help himself as he told me later. 'Shoot!' I heard him say behind me through the dripping boughs, 'shoot!' But I smiled to myself and waited, convinced that Johnson would not lose his nerve on my behalf and fire at His Unholiness before I fired, since the prolongation of this moment, which could never be equaled by another, was worth the risk—even the risk of dying or of losing my first chance to shoot a bear.

"But Johnson bit his tongue and refrained from shooting. I stood my ground. I stood there in proper position with one foot before the other and torso leaning toward the target and the Four-Hundred-and-Five well seated against my shoulder. Dwarfed by His Unholiness, I waited.

"Now that I think of it, Frank, I believe that at the last moment I would have been happy to let him go. I believe I wanted as much to spare his life as I wanted to know the joy of destroying it. But the moment came, there was no more hair for quartering, to borrow Johnson's frontier figure of speech, and if I had not then squeezed the trigger—slowly, as if she wasn't loaded, or as if I did not expect her to go off then or ever—the great stinking creature would have had me, would have treated me to the bear hunter's waltz of death, Johnson or no Johnson. In that moment death or maiming were the only alternatives.

"But he was impressive, Frank, impressive! I wanted to laugh at my good fortune!

"But I was not paralyzed and I was not foolhardy. I noted in passing the black and dripping snout, the tiny eyes which at this range were only tiny in proportion to the great head itself, and even while his breath rumbled like water sloshing in the belly of one of my father's horses, I made my choice: not the heart, which was the safest but which would tear the pelt, but the head, since it was the most dangerous but least damaging to the trophy—as we all know, Frank, even we che-chaquas.

"He was lowering down at me, thank goodness, or else even the massive slug of the Four-Hundred-and-Five might have glanced off that long and sloping skull of his and left me wishing that I had let Johnson shoot him after all. But he gave me a good angle—on purpose, Frank?—and I was aiming directly at the fifty-cent piece between his eyes. It was a handy metaphor and later I was grateful to Johnson for giving it to me, without any condescension, of course, only minutes before we'd set off to rid the world of His Unholiness.

"She sounded, Frank! The old Four-Hundred-and-Five let go! She blazed fire from her muzzle, the shot went home. My shoulder is still black and blue, my ears still ring. But the day before yesterday I found only clarity in that concussion, felt as if I myself was the source of the detonation and not the gun. It was a beauteous blast, the clearing rocked from it. And yet I might have been sealed in some enormous bell jar with His Unholiness, since in that blast nothing else existed except the two of us. Though he was towering even taller while I was trembling, still we were locked together in what I can only call the purest sort of mutual concentration. I had thought that the Four-Hundred-and-Five would blow the top of his head right off. But it did not. I saw the round black hole between the eyes, the crown of smoke and the extrusion of little bits of brain, and saw the unwavering look in his eye that was locked on mine.

"I did not move. I was determined that I would not move. And as he toppled he reached for me with his teeth and claws, holding me steady in the eyes that never clouded, and had I been a lesser man or less lucky, he might have at least buried me under his dead weight. But he did not. When I recovered he was stretched out full length with his claws embedded in the forest floor and the head not a yard—not a yard, Frank!—from the tips of my boots. Eight feet long and as big around as a barrel and absolutely horizontal and stone dead. I heard Rex and Johnson yelling and calling out congratulations, but the only thought in my head, Frank, was that I might just as well have shot him in Guns & Locks & Clothes, it was that easy. But I was wet to my skin, I can tell you, and not from rain.

"Well, Rex shook my hand and Johnson went back for his camera which was loaded and waiting since he had expected to have to take Fitzgibbon's picture in the ordinary course of things but now was hopping about on both feet, despite that knee of his, at being able to take mine instead. I tried to compose myself, I was determined never again to look into those still-open eyes, though in fact I stole a final glance into what looked to me like living marbles of clear glass. I posed beside him with the Four-Hundred-and-Five athwart my chest, I knelt by his head with the rifle upright and my chin high, and every time I glanced down at him he was grinning.

"Johnson promised me a set of the pictures as soon as they're ready.

"Well, we skinned him out then and there and the next morning— yesterday morning, that is—I strapped Harrison into the basket stretcher and we got him safely aboard the plane. By late afternoon—yesterday afternoon, of course—Rex was back. And the next morning—this morning—the whole crowd of us took off in the Fairchild. And here we are, only five full days after our departure, Sissy.

"But what do you say—Frank? Sissy?—shall we take a look at His Unholiness? Well then, let's roll him out!"

But Uncle Jake had a flair for silence. He enjoyed his dramatic silences as much as his delaying tactics of his accordion narration, as he called it. And so in the chilly darkness he fell abruptly silent, except that after pausing for several minutes he commented to the room at large that my eyes looked like the eyes of a little fox in the night, and despite the promised displaying of his trophy, of the boon he'd brought back from his sojourn in the dark country above Icy Inlet, he made no move toward the massive, lopsided bundle that loomed at his side. He knew that Sissy and Frank Morley wanted to be left for a while just as they were: stunned by his story. He knew that it would be some minutes yet before they found their voices, as they continued listening to the sound of his in the cold silence, and that they could not move, though they were stiff enough from sitting. He knew that the power of the storyteller is greatest when the story's done, and no one enjoyed his own power more than Uncle Jake, or more enjoyed the pleasure of a speechless audience—even an audience as small as this one. So he waited, allowing time for the fading of both voice and visions, gauging the moment when Sissy and Frank Morley would themselves be ready to abandon Icy Inlet for the very different tangibilities of coldness and darkened room and of what he wanted to show them.

"Well, Frank," he said at last, in a voice that had clearly lost its gusto, "will you give me a hand?"

Sissy stirred herself then and turned on a light, which, dim as it was, nonetheless exposed to the three of them the starkness of the room and the dismal quality of the festive table set with tinware and paper napkins and bereft of its four bottles of ginger ale which Uncle Jake had drunk. Frank Morley and Uncle Jake cleared away Sissy's few sticks of furniture, as Uncle Jake was fond of calling the more important of Sissy's domestic purchases, moving table and rocking chair and the foldaway bed and the two wooden folding chairs against the walls. A bell buoy was ringing down in the channel, it was going to be another night of rising wind and heavy rain. There were no stories to give saving color to Sissy's home or to the strings of widely spaced electric lights going down our steep hill to the docks, no aura of expectation to make the black and rain-drenched mountains rising behind us any the less awful. There would never be a storyteller to make this bleakness tolerable to Sissy, though tolerate it she surely did. And she was terrified of the wind.

Frank Morley knew that Uncle Jake wanted no assistance untying his bundle and so stood by appreciatively with Sissy and me as Uncle Jake dragged the bundle to the center of the bare floor and began struggling with Johnson's knots. The ropes fell away; Uncle Jake looked up to measure the anticipation in our faces, and then proudly unfolded what was left of the bear.

There it lay, the furry hide flattened to the bare floor, with fat legs sticking out to the sides as if the creature were doing the dead man's float, and the great black head as still as a rock, eyes open and chin rigid against the wood. He was grinning, one of the dead ears was torn, the shaggy hide filled the room with its dusty blackness and livid stench.

"It smells pretty ripe," said Uncle Jake, with feet wide and hands on hips and chest inflated. "But I'm going to cure it. Actually we'll cure it together, won't we, Frank? Then Sissy will have a splendid rug for her living room. And didn't we do a good job? We scraped away most of the meat and cartilage, Johnson and I, though of course we didn't do anything to the head, so that you see his head just as I saw it in the clearing. But don't worry, Sissy, Frank and I will take care of that skull of his and the eyes.

"Well," he said then in a voice betraying hoarseness and fatigue,

"His Unholiness isn't going to persecute any more hunters, I can tell you that." And then after a pause that was not intended and that was not dramatic: "As for Robert Fitzgibbon," he said to himself thoughtfully and in a rare display of at least partial self-understanding, "that's what he gets for not saying good morning when we left the S.S. *Alaska*."

Sissy then asked Uncle Jake if he minded tying up his bear again until he and Frank were ready to do whatever they were going to do with it. And mightn't he keep it on the porch instead of inside the house? It was a beautiful bear, she said, but she honestly wouldn't want to see it spread out this way and grinning at her when she awoke.

That night the wind began whistling around the house, though it was May, and the rains came down on Juneau and on the empty clearing in the woods near the lake above Icy Inlet. Like Uncle Jake I loved the wind, and in the middle of that night I left my double bed and joined Uncle Jake and Sissy in the foldaway bed. Lying between them and pressing myself to Uncle Jake's smooth bare arm that was as large as another person's leg, as it seemed to me then—he always slept in his undershirt and drawers—thus I spent the long night of his return rocking side by side with Uncle Jake in the gale.

For the next few days Frank Morley and Uncle Jake worked on Sissy's rug, as Uncle Jake had started calling it. They removed the skull from the head and the brain from inside the skull, and scraped it clean inside and out and soaked it in Sissy's window-washing bucket with spoonfuls of the lye brought up to the house by Frank Morley. When the bear's skull had been restored to its essential bone, Uncle Jake shellacked the whole thing and, one afternoon, made a great show of presenting it to me. I kept it in my room, cradling it in my arms or removing the great lower jaw from the rest of that gleaming skull—Uncle Jake had decided against wiring the jaw in place. I fondled and tilted the bear's jaw this way and that, thinking that it was like a giant wishbone filled with teeth. But the hole between the eye sockets pleased me most and I used to study it and caress the smoothness of that black hole with careful fingers.

I still own the denuded skull of His Unholiness. The shellac has deepened to the color of burnt umber, the skull is smaller than it looked to me as a child. But there it sits beside Sitka Charley's knife on my imposing desk.

Why do I keep it? How can I stand to look at it? But then I'm nothing if not loyal to my Alaskan childhood and the sins of my father.

As for Sissy's rug, Frank Morley and Uncle Jake spent hours rubbing rock salt into the underside of the hide and talking about Uncle Jake's first bear and admiring the stiff black fur. Then they nailed it up to the side of the house to dry, where after a day or so of drizzle or heavy rain it began to rot. Never was Uncle Jake so dark of visage, so silent, never had his hopes been so unjustly dashed as on the day when he and Frank Morley took down again that bearskin, which was now crawling with maggots and smelling worse than ever, and when Frank Morley, to Sissy's great relief, disposed of it. At least Uncle Jake had the consolation of Johnson's photographs—those scratchy snapshots which I keep in the back of Sissy's journal.

It was not the anxiety induced by Uncle Jake's first Alaskan exploit that established the rhythm of Sissy's nightly crying. It took more than the dismaying town, the bad weather, the little house that shook in the wind, her four nights alone with me while Uncle Jake was off acquiring his mannish mannerisms, more than her fear of bears and her fear for Uncle Jake's safety—more than all this to induce her nightly crying. After all, she didn't begin her journal until three months after Uncle Jake, in the first of his angry depressions, tore down his handiwork from the side of our house, turned his back on the whole affair, and left it to Frank Morley to get rid of what Uncle Jake had planned as a mighty enhancement of the living room in Sissy's home.

By the time Sissy began her crying Uncle Jake's good humor had long returned with a vengeance.

But no matter the treachery of his innocence and misguided masculinity; no matter his Alaskan history of ever-increasing brutal flights of fancy that finally broke Sissy's spirit and caused her death; and no matter that his entire life was my seduction and betrayal—all this aside, Uncle Jake was a storyteller. He laughed and ranted and soared in his odd rhetorical fashion, extolling himself and maligning others, making jokes and moralizing and exaggerating all that was injurious. Generally he missed the point of his own stories, yet he held us in the thralldom of those endless stories until Sissy suddenly tired of them and died, and until he finally abandoned me to the bumbling care of Frank Morley. No wonder at my late age I've embarked on telling his story and mine. No wonder I know his story so well and have the words for it.

Give the devil his due.

20 —

Sworn to Fun, Loyal to None reads the bumper sticker on my customized ex-army jeep, which, my jeep, is like the conventional military machine except for the nine coats of olive-green lacquer that my friend Hank Laramie applied to the hood and lower body, and except for the gleaming black fiberglass cab that Hank affixed in place as a weatherproof substitute for the familiar gawky canvas top, and except for the six-foot aerial and shortwave radio and custom seat covers fashioned from the whitest fur of the mountain goat—all thanks to the taste and ingenuity of Hank Laramie, whom I met fifteen months ago—in mid-August of 1963, that is—and lost precisely nine months later.

As for the bumper sticker on the jeep, it doesn't exactly represent my private views, isn't exactly true to me in the way "Heed Hedonism" is. I'm *sworn to fun* as the bumper sticker says, but given my situation and my commitment to the Alaska-Yukon Gamelands, I've been remarkably loyal to the men in my life, among whom I number Jimmy though he was only a boy. I have not forsaken Sitka Charley since 1940 when, on my initiative, we lost our virginities to each other, he at the age of thirty-five and I at fifteen. And for nine months I was loyal to Hank Laramie and Jimmy until I lost them both. My work at Gamelands and the Willies I enjoyed occasionally at Gamelands didn't interfere with my loyalty to Hank and Jimmy and Sitka Charley.

Exactly as Spooky Ruth prophesied, this has been my time of change, my final days in Alaska, the high and narrow bridge to my premature change of life, which, according to Spooky Ruth, is looming on my horizon, tied tubes or no tied tubes and despite my relatively young age. I may be old for storytelling but I am young for the hormonal changes that please some, strike others down. At any rate in mid-August

of 1963 I first encountered Jimmy and Hank Laramie; three months
later Spooky Ruth read my palm, my heart, my mind, and told me,
in her own colorful way, that for me Alaska's a swamp that's drying
up, and that soon I'm going to a place where vines are tender. In mid-
May of 1964 Martha Washington, who insisted that her name was not
invented, came on the scene. It was then that I made my decision to
leave and then that Uncle Jake began to hold me back in dreams.

Can such a dry chronology be loaded like Gamelands itself with sex?
It can.

21 —

It was an unseasonably warm and dry and clear late afternoon in
mid-August. My cabin door was open; for one more time, and not the
last, I was sitting at my fancy desk and reading Sissy's journal. At that
hour and on that day Gamelands was floating in a sea of fireweed. In
all the fields surrounding our dark woodland, and on the low ground
rimming the lake, whole acres of fireweed were flowering, knee-high
and pink, and filling all the space I couldn't see with their pinkish light.
The fir and Sitka spruce, the birch and alder, the cranberries and the
salmonberries and the wolfberries, not to mention the rose berries big
enough to fill a teacup—all this profusion of natural growth was floating in the pink light of the fireweed. The birds were singing, the fish
were spawning. It was enough to make me admit to Alaska's grandeur,
despite poor Sissy's tearful journal or the old bear skull grinning at me
from its place on my desk.

Then came a sharp little rap, the girlish voice.

"Sunny," said Jenny, for it was she, standing barefooted on the split-
log flooring of my veranda, "hey, Sunny, we need you."

I turned and noted the naked feet, the tight jeans, the green hunting
shirt hastily donned and hanging open like two filmy petals around the
small torso that was otherwise as naked as her skinny feet. Despite my
refusal of the role of mother, I was partial to the "Little Whore from
Idaho," as she called herself, and still am. I liked the way she cut her
own hair—short and ragged, forgoing the stylist's shop in the Bar-

anof—and I liked the pack of cigarettes usually stuck in her shirt pocket, matches tucked into the cellophane. I approved of her refusal to use cosmetics, except for the bright red lipstick with which she turned her tiny mouth into a big cupid's bow.

"We have this Willie," she said, "and nothing works."

She was leaning heavily against the jamb; the lipstick, I saw, was smeared all over her upper lip and chin.

"I tried, Elaine tried, Joan tried, so did Liz. That leaves only Sue and Marie and Freckles, since we don't dare interrupt Spooky Ruth and Thelma. Sue's doing the best she can right now, but she's getting tired like the rest of us. And Freckles and Marie both say they hate his looks and won't have anything to do with him. His name's Jimmy," she said, yawning and drawing the shirt around her thin bare chest as if she were one of the women from the old Baranof and the shirt her kimono.

"And he's just a kid. I don't know what he's doing out here anyway."

By the time we found them in Susan's Mastodon mobile home, the most roguishly painted of all our mobile homes in pink and white, it was clear that Susan too had given up on poor Jimmy.

"Hello there," I said, "I'm Sunny."

"Boyoboy," said Susan and rolled her eyes.

The interior of her mobile home was a rounded blaze of aluminum suffused with the pink light of the fireweed outside; the plush carpeting was pink and purple; the white satin-covered divan, on which they sat like two suffering adolescents on a blind date, was low and soft and, strewn as it was with plump bolsters and perfumed cushions, could not have been more inviting. Through the open louvered door to the bedroom I could see the rumpled bed and one of Jimmy's thin black shoes sitting incongruously on a fat pillow: they had already tried the bedroom. Clearly they had tried the divan, since the bolsters were lying at odd angles or on the floor and the wide space between the two of them was filled with silky undergarments, as if Susan had donned and discarded her entire wardrobe of feminine frippery as a last resort. A half-empty bottle of almond-scented hand lotion was wedged between two pillows; clouds of Susan's body powder were slowly settling. By all the signs they should have been lolling together with fingers touching and bodies still faintly colored with the pink flush of satiety. Yet there they were, Jimmy bolt upright at his end of the divan, Susan cross-legged in boredom, Jimmy beginning to dress himself, the bony white-ness of his narrow torso rising from his as yet unzipped black trousers in a shame of nakedness; his face was a chalky wedge, thin and sharp, his lips were compressed, his close-set eyes were dark with pride and sullenness. From the way he held the second scuffed black shoe in both hands he looked as if he were unable to finish dressing. Susan was slowly drying herself with a lime-colored fluffy towel.

"Susan, Jenny," I said, sticking my hands in my tight hip pockets and leaning against an imitation French wall hanging depicting youths and roses, "I'd like to talk with Jim. OK?"

With knowing glances at each other and with evident relief, they took themselves off to the other end of the mobile home. At once there came the sound of the record player and behind it the sound of the shower gushing and steaming.

"Jim," I said then, stooping and retrieving his shirt and drawers and dirty socks, "I want to ask you a question."

He started, blanched though he was dead white already, and looked up at me, then quickly away. If he had been frightened by Jenny and Elaine and Joan and Liz and now Susan—and Susan was a young voluptuary if there ever was one—how much more incapacitating was the sight of me and my compact womanhood, how much more threatening than anything those girls had done to him. He trembled and caught the tip of his tongue between his thin lips and gray baby teeth.

"Jim," I said, after a long pause, "here's the question. Have you ever been up in a plane?"

Surprise. A breath of relief. The faintest dissipation of his distrust. He shook his head, frowned, stared down at his lap, which he noticed then and tried to hide with both hands.

"Well," I said, "would you like to go up? I'm a pilot."

Again his eyes met mine and he nodded; his eyes were as large and as near to brimming as a girl's. I turned my back while he dressed.

So down we went to the float, Jimmy and I, and from all around us came the voices and sounds of Gamelands—boisterous, simmering, muffled—in arousal, in climax, in the mumbled disarray of the aftermath; they were all kissing, fingering, laughing, drinking cold beer. And here were Jimmy and I walking swiftly down to the Cessna where it waited in the pink light safer and more inviting than any girl or woman to poor Jimmy. I let him climb on the wing and hold the nozzle while I worked the pump, a calculated ritual that made him look like a bird crouched up there on the Cessna's wing.

We climbed aboard. I offered to let him wear my leather jacket, which he declined; he sat beside me as bolt upright as on Susan's divan, but now he was clothed, attentive, suddenly attractive with his narrow shoulders squared and his poor hands tight on his knees. As soon as the engine turned over he looked at me, studied me a moment while I stared ahead through the propeller's slow circle of broken light as we taxied out onto the lake and headed into the gentle wind. I saw that he had dandruff and a hole in his shirt and a high forehead white and smooth despite his concentration. He was looking about him quickly at the instruments, the controls, the handle of the directional antenna thrusting down from the roof of the cabin. I dropped one hand into the tight lap of my jeans; he allowed himself one short surreptitious glance. Appreciatively he sniffed the smells of rubber, gasoline, musty fabric, craned happily to left and right—and what boudoir could possibly compete with Sunny's Cessna? Just before we left the surface of the water he reached for the ancient fur-rimmed goggles which were hanging down as always from the instrument panel—my good luck charm like Sissy's elephant or the green-eyed plastic skulls dangling in the fast cars of high school boys old enough to drive—and abruptly, without self-consciousness, he put them on. His face was narrow, but his cranium was as big around as a man's and the goggles fit. When he faced me he looked like a baby owl in Granny's goggles—for they were indeed the goggles of my long-dead oldest uncle—and I smiled, risked reaching over and giving his poor thin knee a squeeze.

Then we were climbing and banking and he was pressing his face to the plexiglass and looking down—lost to me yet mine, more mine at five hundred feet than if we were back in my log cabin.

We leveled off. I throttled back the engine, and flew low across the glacier and then circled Juneau and idled on down the channel, between the mountains on either side, dipping our wings at a seiner. I decided to show him the top of Mount Juneau. The color heightened in Jimmy's neck and cheeks as the sunlight faded from the patches of snow and slabs of bare rock below us.

"Jim," I said then, leaning toward him and raising my voice, "how old are you?"

"Fourteen," he said, still watching the peaks and ridges as we circled.

"When I was fourteen," I said, "I already knew how to fly. Do you want to take the controls?"

More unbelievable good fortune, more surprise, and now the rapt passenger gave way abruptly to the elated student of flight, and sitting forward, and staring through the blurry lenses of Granny's goggles, and with his poor thin rodent paws clamped to the wheel, for those few moments Jimmy flew us toward the thick orange mass of the sun that was already half sunk below the horizon. His thin lips were pursed, his smooth gray-white brow was furrowed, occasionally he turned his head sharply in my direction—the ancient fur-rimmed goggles made him look still more the rodent and aged him as well—and I nodded, drew his attention to the bank-and-turn indicator, our rate of speed.

"That's fine, Jim," I said, twisting so that my open-collared shirt stuck to me like wet cloth draped on a nude artist's model, "next time we'll try some takeoffs and landings."

Then I took over again, the light turned green and purple, the lake adjacent to the glacier became a black pearl. For a moment we skimmed across the water with the nose of the Cessna high and the tail low and spray shooting out behind us in a white fan, and then we lost most of our speed and headed in to the float as quietly and peacefully as an old dory powered by an outboard motor. Jim pushed the goggles up onto his forehead and sighed, reluctantly removed them altogether and hung them back where he'd found them. At my suggestion he climbed out first and made us fast; then I asked him to help me down and in the stillness of the now dead engine and massing mosquitoes I stood beside him on the narrow pontoon, one hand gripping a strut, the other warmly holding his.

"The teacher gets a kiss," I said and laughed, presented my soft cheek to his thin cold lips. "And now," I said, "after the first lesson there's always a banquet. So off we go to my private lodge, Jim, where I'm going to cook you a feast fit for a young god newly admitted to the pantheon."

I took him back to the cabin, where I asked him to build a fire while I cooked the meal, which revived his confidence somewhat and allowed me to hide my quickening desire in the demands of the stove.

"Steak and eggs, Jim, what do you say?" I called over my shoulder, and in response there came only silence and sudden billows of smoke from the fieldstone fireplace that was twice the size of my great aluminum and cast-iron stove. But could it be, I thought, a person of my age and experience all aquiver because of a thin young pasty-complexioned boy with guarded eyes, soiled underwear, and dirty socks? But no matter how improbable, I told myself, such was the case, and I attempted to restrain my exaggerated clattering of the pots and pans, my too hasty movements from stove to chopping block to steel sink, my all too eager handling of brown eggs, pound of butter, red meat. I felt like Jimmy in the Cessna; I tried to control my breathing, the warmth that was rising in my compact womanhood like osmotic heat in a flower. Careful, I told myself, or he'll go running off into the night with shirttails flapping.

I poured myself a full tumbler of the red wine and drank it down, then fixed the salad, fried the eggs, cooked the rare filets, all the while floundering through the rolling smoke of Jimmy's fire. Of course this was his first chance to build a fire in anything but a cranky little tin stove, I thought to myself, and smiled.

"OK, Jim," I called, "it's ready. Help me serve it up!"

"The fire's smoking," he said as he carried his plate to the table and returned for wine.

"That's all right," I said, "it smells good."

My china is heavy, white, thick-lipped, plain, the sort of china racked in the galleys of seagoing boats, while my silverware is sterling and my glassware is of the purest crystal, though I keep on hand a set of tumblers as modest and utilitarian as my china. I live for paradox, I've created my own brand of Alaskan elegance, striving all the time, no doubt, to simulate French rarities, French forms of indulgence. Now I was using the heavy tumblers for our wine and ordinary kitchen knives and forks instead of the sterling. Even so, Jimmy made no move to eat, to drink.

"Hungry?" I asked, swirling the wine inside my mouth from habit, and putting my arms on the table and sniffing my masculine cuisine like a connoisseur.

He shook his head, went back to his scowling.

"Well," I said, "there's nothing like fried eggs and steak after flying. And there's no steak like Sunny's."

So saying I rolled up my sleeves, brushed back my short-cropped hair, tore off a chunk of bread, looked down at my plate, then ground the bread slowly into the big yellow eye of my fried egg and let it soak, then stuffed it dripping into my mouth. Jim stared, his face relaxed, he glanced at his eggs and steak—I had given him four fried eggs to my one and a charred brick of steak larger than mine—and then, before he could move, I cut myself an enormous bite of the red meat and stuffed it into my mouth along with the egg-soaked bread. I winked and began laboriously to chew. I was hunched over, my face raised to Jim and my chin dripping with egg yolk and the pink juice of the steak, and my cheeks were bulging. I had broken out in a faint sweat, and my eyes, like his, were red with the smoke.

"Come on," I said then, "join me."

Through the mush of half-chewed meat, bread, eggs swelling my mouth, I could hardly talk, and it was this muffled invitation that caused us both to laugh, suddenly, just as I'd planned, and caused Jim to take up his knife and fork awkwardly, shyly, and begin to eat. He tucked his napkin into his shirtfront, he wiped the entire lower portion of his face at every mouthful. Obviously he enjoyed my performance, had never seen a woman pretending to eat like a ravenous truck driver, and yet the greater my self-indulgence the shyer and more reserved he became, though he did in fact eat his four eggs and all of his steak.

"Here's to the day you solo," I said and raised my glass. He resisted the wine, intuiting seduction in my vintage claret, but nonetheless he sipped it with increasing frequency throughout the meal. Across the table Jimmy looked like a little old man all but snared by a widow in her sultry lair. He even ran his fingers around the inside of his shirt collar as if to loosen it, though his collar was unbuttoned. Poor Jimmy.

We moved to the fire, which had stopped smoking. I made him sniff and sip my cognac and share a dish of refrigerated mint chocolates. Together we sat on our Barcelona chairs positioned side by side on my twelve-foot polar bear rug before the fire—Sissy never had her bear rug but I had mine—and I learned that Jimmy had been born in Anchorage and that he lived in Juneau with an uncle and that he earned his keep by working after school in the cannery. There he sat, leaning forward on the edge of the chair and clasping his hands between his legs and staring sadly into my romantic fire.

"How did you get out here, Jim?" I asked.

"Walked," he answered.

"No one stopped for you?"

He shook his head.

"Well," I said, "you wanted to come out to Gamelands pretty badly. What gave you the idea?"

"The poster," he said at once. "I saw it in a store window and made up my mind."

"Oh yes," I said softly, "the stockinged leg. But Jim, what did you expect to find out here?"

"Girls," he said quickly, "what else?"

"Well, Jim," I said in my lowest and softest register, "I'm a woman."

"I know that," he said simply.

So by the light of the fire I showed him the shapeliest silhouette he'd ever seen and then, without a word, I went into the bedroom and stripped off my boots, my shirt, my tight worn jeans, and, last of all, the pink triangular shield that cupped me as snugly as the palm of my hand. As quickly as I could I got myself up like a woman insisting on satisfaction in a silent film, donning nylon stockings and my sheer negligee—no garter belt or black net stockings, nothing to suggest the glitter of old-time artificiality, just the modest negligee and ordinary stockings, achieving thereby the image of a real woman in need of love. And in fact I was nothing if not a real woman, image or no image.

"Hello there," I said when I returned to the warm leather of my Barcelona chair. "I'm Sunny."

He did not laugh but neither did he frown or turn away, nor was he slumped in mere submissiveness. I was carefully veiled in the negligee and had arranged the lower folds so as to reveal only one leg as high as the top of the stocking. Yes, mine was the image of the oldest of male fantasies—and why not? I was not averse to feminine wiles, and Jimmy was not immune to my image. He may have been offended by Susan's image or Jenny's, but he was not by mine.

With its foot-thick logs for walls hung here and there with Chilkat blankets, and the raftered ceiling and the genuine kayak suspended horizontally above the mantel—the room was that wide—and the fur of the polar bear and the fire pulsing in a darkness like an Arctic night— what was my private cabin if not a citadel of sex, as if the queen of the Baranof women had set herself up in a museum? Alaskan lore and contemporary luxury—what a context for the oldest of male fantasies, I thought, what a world for a woman.

The empty wine bottle lay beside my chair, my breasts were full, Jimmy was taking longer and longer looks in my direction. Now, I thought to myself, now or never.

"Jim," I said, in a voice that I hardly recognized, "will you do something for me?"

He nodded.

"Well," I said, and there was an edge to my whisper, "I'd like you to come over here and roll down my stockings."

I held my hips in my hands. I was leaning back with one leg bent and one straight. I looked him full in the face so that he couldn't miss the fact that I too was vulnerable. I watched him. I heard a dry snuffling sound in his nose, his throat—Good Lord, I asked myself, is he going to cry?—and then at last he stood up and I could not forbear a glance at his crotch.

"Jim," I whispered, "roll down my stockings."

He knelt at my feet. I held my breath. And slowly, and unaware of the smells of the cannery in his clothes and the blatant smells of his boyish loneliness on his body, slowly he drew aside the lower folds of my negligee and sighed, sat back on his heels.

"Jim," I whispered, "do what you want."

My pelvic tilt was like a fracture in the earth's crust beneath the sea, like a tropical plateau tipped up to the sun. My legs were straight and quivering; I untied the negligee, watched as Jimmy who had never looked full upon a woman's breasts now paused with the second and last of my stockings gathered into his two hands, and stared up at mine. And the sight of my womanly breasts was lodged, as I could clearly see, in his virgin groin.

Late the next morning I fried him up four more eggs and led him back to Susan, who, surprised and flustered, discovered what it was like to have some fun with Jimmy. Within three days the showered and shiny Jimmy had become the favorite of them all. They bragged about him to their Willies, they preferred him to most Willies, they competed openly for his time. He accepted his role as sex-mascot of the Alaska-Yukon Gamelands.

But he remained my darling.

22

Hank Laramie. My friend Hank Laramie.

Hardly a week after Jimmy won the affection and admiration of everyone at Gamelands Hank suddenly appeared, from nowhere it seemed, and stunned them all with his prowess. He was my age to the day and winsome, open-hearted, sure of himself, a bronzed and limber man six feet tall. He had spent the last five years in Montana as the workingman consort, as he described himself, of an auburn-haired woman who, with her three young children, had been deserted by her burly, black-bearded husband for the sake of his full-time career in stock-car racing. The woman was as blond as she was auburn, with skin appropriately soft and milky, and she was small—slightly smaller than myself—with a body so perfectly curved in the right places, as

Hank said, that it made the hair stand up on the backs of his hands every time he saw her, whether she was fully clothed or naked. Her children were so beautiful, Hank said, that he never knew which was the boy and which the girls except when he got all three of them into the wooden tub for bathing. Hank himself was auburn-haired or blond, depending on the light, and he appeared the more likely father of the woman's children than the father himself, though he was not, in fact, but always wished he were.

The burly, black-bearded husband had left his family in a small frame house that stood in a condition of bleak disrepair on a plot of bare ground littered with automobile parts—old tires, fenders, head-lights, rusted chassis—which the squat and massive husband hoarded for his career in racing. With Sheetrock, plywood, and paint Hank restored the house for the woman and her children. He installed wood-burning stoves in most of the rooms, repaired the ceramic fireplace in the parlor, hung a swing for the children from the limb of a half-dead tree in the littered yard. He put stained glass in one of the windows in the main room, but left the wreckage in the bare yard to remind them all of how he had found them and also because he himself liked cars, even in pieces.

The family revolved around that golden woman. The children ran to and fro, unasked, to help their mother, and made the beds and stood around her chair when she rested, raced to bring her a fresh pack of cigarettes, a cup of tea. Hank generally maintained the house, fixing leaks, laying new floors, and did most of the cooking. Day and night he kept a ten-quart kettle of kidney beans bubbling and simmering on the stove, and read the children their fairy tales and brought the woman her glasses of white wine or sometimes vodka when she was in the mood. As for the woman, she gave them all her beauty, her plans for the day, her nervous love, and sustained herself in motherhood with pills—to lift her spirits or to slow them down depending on her wom-anly needs of the moment.

Having sex with that woman was, according to Hank, like eating a peach that had no pit or swimming in a lake of honey. It was always she who summoned him to sex when she was in the mood and never the other and more conventional way. But her needs were his and his were hers, he said, and whenever he felt the urge she summoned him, though he gave her no sign of his longing, and whenever she summoned him he felt the urge. Harmony, he said, could never exist except in a matriarchy, and with that woman he lived as husband and father both,

though in fact he was only her workingman consort, as he told me
more than once with a rueful laugh.

When the woman finally went off with her children to live in faculty
housing with an untenured professor of Asian studies at the nearby
state university, Hank Laramie went on a week-long drunk with the
stock-car racer and woke up clearheaded and ready to come to Alaska.

Jimmy was the harbinger of Hank Laramie, the boy-man calling into
being the boyish man. If Jimmy was my darling, Hank was my friend.

Hank Laramie. My friend Hank Laramie.

"Sunny," said Jenny, for it was she again, this time grinning in my
doorway and totally naked except for underpants and the wide open
shirt that exposed her little breasts to full view. "Hey, Sunny, come see
what we've got!"

For five days, or since young Jenny had last stood on my veranda,
we'd had nothing but fog, drizzle, rain, typical weather dragged in by
clouds of ravens and bad spirits. Now for the second time in less than
a week the heraldic sun was steaming through the surrounding pines,
warming clear skies overhead, drenching Gamelands in a warmth of
light. And here again, the same and not the same, was Jenny—worn
out, alert, covered with the sweat of a new Willie, as I saw at a glance,
and so sated that she made not the slightest effort to hide the signs of
what she had been doing—hair rumpled by the stranger's fingers,
underpants only partially hitched up on the shiny hips, thigh imprinted
with the red palm of a man's caressing hand—and so pleased with
herself that she could hardly wait to give me the news.

"We've got this Willie," she said, shaking her head and leaning stiffly
with an outstretched arm against the doorjamb, "who doesn't stop."

"Oh?" I said, swiveling around to her and smiling.

"The thing is," she said, showing me the brightness in her sleepy
eyes, wiping her nose, and shifting to the other arm and shaking her
head, "the thing is, he's been here all day and just keeps going from
one to the next, one to the next, then just starts over again. Three times
apiece so far. Like that. And we can't keep up with him. We've stopped
paying any attention to the rest of the Willies, and the place is full of
them. We can't tear ourselves away from Hank—that's his name—but
we're finished. He's used us up. All nine of us. But the main thing,"

she said, "is that he's wonderful! Hank's just wonderful, Sunny. Come see!"

I followed her readily enough to the sky-blue Mastodon where Joan, who was nineteen years old and from Illinois, enjoyed her privacy or entertained her share of Willies, and where, at the moment, all of them—Elaine, Susan, Spooky Ruth, and the rest—were congregated. Never had I seen the womanhood of Gamelands so gathered. Never had I seen them so spent or so adoring. They were in the nude, the entire lot of them, except for Marie, who had pulled on the stranger's boots. Beyond the wide-open louvered bedroom door, four of them sprawled together on Joan's bed; two were draped on either side of the stranger on the divan, leaning their heads on him, holding him loosely in their tangled arms; and two, Liz and Susan, sat propped against the divan at his feet, leaning their cheeks against his knees, tracing imaginary languid lines up and down his calves. They were all inert, softly laughing, uncharacteristically embarrassed.

"So you're Sunny," said this paragon of Willies, raising his face and smiling up at me from where he lay with his arms around Susan and Elaine on the divan, and I could not suppress an unaccustomed tingle of girlish pride that they, the girls and women of Gamelands, seduced as one, had been boasting the day long about their Sunny.

"I'm Hank," he said in his nice ordinary voice. "Hank Laramie."

He was attractive, as I saw at once, and not in the least what I'd expected. Bulk, muscles, a rowdy laugh—not with these had Hank Laramie stormed our Gamelands. He was as thin proportionately as Jimmy, and he was relaxed, good-humored, ordinary. His boyish manhood, that was his charm. He was wearing an old tan felt hat with a feather in the band, and except for the hat and a blue shirt unbuttoned but nonetheless concealing casually his loins, he was as naked as Liz, Joan, Elaine, and the rest of them. Even supine he was tall enough to be willowy, thin enough to be lean; he had an easygoing face that was strong enough to inspire confidence and boyish enough to arouse compassion and angular enough to suggest an endearing shade of male beauty. He wore a wedding band which I later learned he had bought on the verge of leaving Montana because he had lost his woman but had not been married to her.

"Oh, I'm not married," he said when he saw me glancing at the ring. "I'm just wedded to all these women here."

"Girls," I said then, "do you mind if I borrow Hank Laramie for a moment?"

They shifted, raised their heads, mumbled in mock dismay their obvious approval. So I reached for his waiting hand and pulled him up, kept the lean hand in mine as we stood face to face and as I surveyed him frankly, frankly admired the slender suntanned body, the clear eyes.

"Sunny," he said, "I knew they'd go get you if I waited long enough."

His posture was straight yet slouching, he appeared to be unaware of his naked loins framed in the open shirt.

"Well, how do you like that!" said Spooky Ruth from the bedroom. "All nine of us just to prime the pump for Sunny!"

"Now ladies, the day's not yet done," he said and retrieved his boots from Marie and followed me out across the gravel toward my handsome lodge.

"Bring him back!" called Liz.

"Bring him back, Sunny!" cried Elaine.

We laughed and held hands, and his body looked like sunlit rivers. Never had I seen such male nakedness, thanks to the open shirt, the old hat tilted downwards over the youthful face, the white high-heeled boots with their bright red decorative designs. Never had I seen a man strolling more than naked in plain sight of anyone who might come along, and I told him how much I liked the sight of him.

When we got to the door, which I'd left open, I dropped his hand, caught hold of the bottom of his shirt, and pulled him after me straight to the bedroom that was filled with the smells of wood, rawhide, wool, my Cachet Noir. Mine was the only bed of its kind in Alaska, and had a six-by-eight-foot frame built of varnished logs six inches in diameter, and tight white sheets and red blankets bordered in great checks of black and white. The two white pillows were propped up on two more pillows in red cases. Hank made no comment on my lavish furnishings—the bed, the Chilkat rugs, the deer skull hanging above the bed, the stainless steel lamp on its black pedestal—and I left him standing there while I went back to lock the door and get what we needed from the kitchen.

I put the glasses and bottle on a small black tray as shiny as coal and waited, ran my hand through my hair. I couldn't remember the last time I had felt such aching—not even with Jimmy had it been this strong.

"What have you got there," he asked, "Alaskan hooch?"

"Hudson Bay rum," I said, and placed the tray on the bedside table of split logs and sea-green glass. I had wondered what he would do in my absence and now I knew. He was waiting for me stretched out full-length on my bed, and it was as if he were the courtesan and I the stately old visitor in black tie and tails. He had left his boots on the floor beside the bed but still wore his shirt and hat. He had clasped his hands behind his head. I filled the glasses with the black rum, left his within easy reach and took mine over to the rawhide chair and sat down.

"When did you get up here?" I asked him.

"Just off the boat."

"And you came right out to Gamelands."

He nodded.

"You came all the way to Alaska looking for women."

He nodded again.

"Well," I said, "Jenny and Liz and the rest can't all be wrong."

"They're not wrong," he said in his honest lighthearted voice.

"What's your secret?"

It was then that he told me the story of his five years in Montana. I listened, drank the rum, and thought about touching his pectoral muscles, his thin flanks, his kneecap, the side of his face, and wished that I had been the woman with the three children.

"I miss her," he said. "But I'm not trying to make up for losing her."

"Still," I said, "she's the one who made you so good with women?"

He waited. Without a word he bunched my fresh pillows so as to raise his head more sharply forward and reached out and took a slow drink of the rum.

"Maybe they've worn you out after all," I said. "Have they?"

But Hank Laramie and I knew better. No woman ever made to cry; no woman who wasn't grateful for having seen Hank Laramie and chased him and become his friend. His pectoral muscles were shifting on his breast like leaves.

"I'm not like your Montana lady," I said. "I'll never marry."

"Me neither," he said at once.

"Sworn to fun is my motto," I said. "Loyal to none."

"That's good," he said. "I like that. Sworn to fun..."

I stood up then and went over to the window and watched an anxious-looking figure come out of the evergreens and stand gawking at the entrance to Gamelands. With my back to Hank I watched the man while I pulled off my shirt, stripped down my pants.

"Yet the thing about you," he said behind my back, "is that you're nubile. No matter what you say about not marrying. All women approach the ideal of course. But I've never met a woman who's all woman, knowing what every woman knows, and who is still nubile, which is the way you are. They told me about your flying and the way you run this business. They called you the toughest and sexiest woman in Alaska. And it shows. But I'd never expect to see your kind of body except on a young girl on a basketball court. And yet there isn't a young girl of marrying age whose nudity could ever be a match for yours.

"A professional," he said in his low good-humored voice, "and yet nubile. That's what you are.

"Listen," he said then while I smiled and watched our new Willie hurrying up to the reception lodge, "I'll grow marijuana for you. I'll cook for you. And I'm good at cars. I'm good at doing customizing jobs on cars."

I turned around. I studied him. His gray-blue eyes were looking at me, and made me think of the eyes in the head of a sad old dog.

"Well," I said, "you can do a customizing job on me, and then we'll talk about the car."

I lay down beside him.

"Hot lava," he said, "hot lava..."

And for the rest of that afternoon we engaged in what would have been deemed unlawful cohabitation back in Uncle Jake's day in Juneau. It was the longest Klondike dogsled ride I'd ever taken. Inside me there was nothing but exfoliation, and the bed, my big Alaskan bed, was filled with Mexican saddles and little golden babes crawling all over us. But I was not the woman in Montana. I was Sunny.

At twilight we strolled outside, walked across the gravel into the approaching night. On impulse I led him down to the entrance to Gamelands, slowed before the Gamelands totem pole. It was new but was already the best-known landmark in southeastern Alaska, if not in the entire state. We craned up at my ceremonial totem pole that had been carved to my design but under the supervision of Sitka Charley, and though the sun was gone, small tongues of light still flickered up and down the freshly painted height of my wooden monument. It rose a full thirty feet into the air, and except for the traditional winged creatures of Indian lore which divided it into quarters, and except for the greater-than-life-sized figure surmounting it, the entire totem pole was entwined with the bodies of nude women. Around and around my totem pole they went, snaking their way upwards, climbing on each other's shoulders, hanging on to the wings of the sacramental birds, hugging the cruel beaks.

"Well," he said, putting his arm around my shoulder, "that's some totem pole. But who's the gent on top?"

I waited, watching the women spiraling upwards like stripes on a barber's pole, reaching and clamoring up my wooden rainbow toward the noble bareheaded man who soared above us in the darkening night. He wore his wooden parka, held aloft his wooden gun. He was pointing north to adventure.

"My father," I said at last. "He was afraid of women."

23 —

Seven months of dreams. Seven whole months. And my dreams lie on the shores of my sleeping self like washes of dead fish. Or my dreams are like geese drifting across leaden skies, disappearing, returning to view, sinking below the treetops, falling off the horizon of white ice. And I have no one to tell them to, I can't bear to tell them even to Spooky Ruth.

I am not my own woman.

I do not want to wake into still another dream, do not want to see my father in this dream or the one to follow. Why does he fill my sleep with dreams? Why does he sail through my dreams like a gray bird in a cold time between seasons? Why must I suffer him each night and then every morning try to cast him out? But so I must.

I am not my own woman.

Sunny, he cries. Look, Sunny. Baby seals!

I refuse to look. I bury my face in my arms. I close my heart, stop my ears. I deny the wedge of light that has forced its way into my deepest sleep.

Uncle Jake is closer now, insistent, demanding my attention as if to do so is the most natural thing in the world. Sunny, he says, and I feel

the hair rising on the back of my neck. Take a look at them. Good
Lord, have you ever seen so many baby seals?

I roll over, torn from my cocoon of fur, bundled and swathed in my
fur wrappings, I too might be a baby seal—except for my age, my one
hundred and twenty-eight pounds, the size and shape of my womanhood. I am on my belly, my arms are like flippers, and even with my
eyes squeezed shut I know that I am lying on the edge of a flat world
of the brightest light. Yes, I awake to the certainty of his voice, now
clear and optimistic, now wheedling, and to the certainty that I am
dressed in furs: without cracking my eyelids I see myself clothed in fur,
in mukluks and clumsy mittens, pants with the fur turned inwards, the
hood of my parka blanketing my head, the fur around my face long,
silky, all but hiding my pink face with my eyelashes and wisps of hair
frosty, frozen. An Eskimo papoose. A big baby seal.

Hear them, Sunny? he says. Thousands of them. Hear them crying?
Don't they sound just like babies?

I raise myself on my forearms and finally open my eyes and perceive
rather than see the white horizon, the white sky, the whiteness of the
ice floes sculpted from the nothingness of light. Behind me is black
water, a kayak that has been hauled out onto the ice and Uncle Jake,
who is turned half to the north, half turned to me, and is looking down
at me and filling the Arctic air with the innocent breath of his narcissism.
He is hatless, the hood of his parka is thrown back, his face is strong.
There is not a trace of frost in the now unruly hair as black as the wing
of a crow. Beyond him are the herds of seals painfully collected and
heaped together on a beach of ice—and they are moving, slowly moving. I hear them, the crying of the baby seals. They sound human, they
fill the cold regions with their little cries massed in the music of hunger,
confusion, fear, thousands of them sweet and pathetic, clamorous, making sounds that might as well be words. The nursery of the far north,
I think, and climb to my hands and knees and see them—the bulls, the
females, the pups squirming, flopping about on the ice.

Uncle Jake is carrying a heavy club.

Think of it, Sunny, he says, gesturing with his free hand toward the
prostrate seals while looking down at me and giving me the gift of his
smile, the pale blue of his eyes, just think, he says, the babies are crying
for their mothers. It's one thing to kill seals on terra firma. That's the
way it's done. Killing seals on terra firma is fair play as long as it's done
with clubs. But there are those rascals who do their seal hunting out
in the open waters, rascals who gun down swimming seals with shot-

guns. And it's mostly mother seals who are swimming around out there in the black waters. The mother seals go out there looking for food and get themselves shot by the rascals. But here's the thing: a female seal will not give suck to a pup who's not her own. Think of it! To each her own is the law of the mother seal! Nature has been strict with the female seals; no mothering of orphaned pups! So they're hungry, all those baby seals. That's what's the matter with them, Sunny. Victims of nature's cruelty. It goes against the human spirit, especially when they've got the voices of baby seals. But there it is.

He is close to me, and now he reaches down with his free hand as if to help me to my feet. The club swings from his other hand and I stare at it, watch it swinging, wonder where he could have found such a weapon. It's heavy. And there's something about the leather thong that's tied through a hole in the smaller end, which is the end he holds, and is tightly looped around his wrist, that I don't like.

Come on, Sunny, he says at last, we have to go!

Without another glance at me he strides off, swings his club like a policeman. I follow, and I am clumsy, afraid, too furry and dazzled to keep up with him.

Then I see the men, a band of squat men. The clubbers. They have come in umiaks that they have abandoned on the edge of the floe. It is the emptiness of those boats that makes me afraid of the squat men and their clubs.

Sealers! calls Uncle Jake over his shoulder. Sealers up from the Pribilof Islands, Sunny. Professionals. Not just a bunch of thieving rascals. These fellows know how to get furs, you'll see. In only weeks the fur they take today will be in the hands of C.E. Lampson & Sons, of London! Alaska to London, Sunny, that's how they work!

He strides ahead of me; I flounder behind. He waves to the sealers, who do not wave back. And now we are pushing our way among the shy seals, and the little pups are flopping along and crying and brushing against me, and I who have no use for motherhood, no use for babies, shove them off, shove them aside. To me their fat and formless little flippers are mere deformities; their heads are all mouth. And they are wet, slimy, wild-eyed. With my foot I give one a shove that's vehement and away he slides foolishly across the ice. And I am dragging through this Arctic nursery of barking and weeping baby seals, Sunny who is no better than a fat seal herself and joining the savages.

Hello there! calls Uncle Jake. I'll give you men a hand!

He waves in his friendly fashion, taking for granted that he belongs with the sealers and that they will welcome him into their party with slaps on the back, shouts of surprise. Again he waves, again he calls, but the men of the Pribilof Islands make not the slightest sign of recognition. For a moment, only for a moment, he is crestfallen. Suddenly he stoops, singles out one of the baby seals and, as if to teach me not to kick them, or simply in one of his typical gestures of endearment, he catches the wriggling creature by one of his flippers and picks him up. He cradles the baby seal, allowing the stout club to hang by its thong, and smiles wanly at the twitching whisker, the eyes like raisins. Oh Sunny, he says, the sealers are going to do their job. They are. And they'll leave behind not one survivor. Not one. Not even this little tyke. But, he says as he squats and releases the baby seal, the riches of the land must be harvested! C.E. Lampson & Sons can't be denied! He laughs, stands tall, takes a good grip on the handle of his club. Again he outdistances me. Again I follow.

In that ruthless light I see that the sealers have brought ashore their gear and have made numerous orderly stacks of knives, axes, coiled ropes. They are sailors, these fur hunters, and the parkas and bright yellow oiled skins they wear are bejeweled with the frozen salt of the sea; together they move across the ice with the same precision with which they paddle their umiaks. They are moving in unison and with purpose; I see their black clubs. The silence in which they work is worse than the emptiness that fills their waiting umiaks. Methodically they catch the stragglers; methodically they divide the herd and bunch the baby seals—hordes of them—into smaller groups that are more manageable, more easily dispatched. I hear the silence as distinctly as I hear the crying of the gathered seals.

Wait! cries Uncle Jake. Wait! And on he hurries, club aloft, destined, or so he hopes, to join the kill, though in his excitement and as an afterthought it occurs to him to shout back in my direction: Clubbing is painless, Sunny! Painless! Remember that!

The sealers begin to use their clubs. In unison and slow motion the black clubs rise and fall, swing up and down silently, as if the sealers are chopping wood or beating paths through high grass, and as the sealers make their way through the herd, the crying of the baby seals diminishes. The silence expands, the crying dies away voice by voice, note by note. Even Uncle Jake is shocked. And would it be better if we could hear the blows? Hear the shouts of the men? Yes, I tell myself, let me hear the shouts and blows, let them give vulgar sound to this vulgar event. But they do not, and now the number of clubs in motion lessens, only a few baby seals are still crying, and the ice is running red with crimson rivulets that cross and recross the ice as far as I can see. Ice, dead seals, seals attempting to escape, the sealers themselves—everything is turning that color of red that is like no other, the wet red color of blood when it is first exposed to the air, the shining red color of blood before it blackens.

My own blood is draining.

Slowly he turns back to me and there is blood on his club, and his every feature is forced to the self-consciousness of the heroic male. Sunny! he calls, it's the slaughter of the innocents, that's what it is!

The hair rises on the back of my neck, my eyes are burning, and I see his startled smile and hear his brave voice. I want to shout an answer to him. But nothing happens. I cannot move my lips. I make no sound. Behind him a bloody fan spreads open across the horizon and there is only silence and the smell of what the departed sealers have left in their wake.

Oh Sunny, he calls, and he is looking to me for help. Oh Sunny, it's the slaughter of the innocents. That's what it is.

When I awake from this dream, as from my others, I know that I have been crying in my sleep. Sunny crying. Sunny no better off than Sissy. But who or what have I been crying for? Baby seals? Missing father? Myself? How can I know?

24 —

No Jimmy. No Hank Laramie. Sitka Charley morose in his loft above what used to be Guns & Locks & Clothes. I have made the right decision, despite the dreams: France and a French boyfriend. Six years older than Jimmy, nineteen younger than Hank Laramie, as fresh to sex as Jimmy was and as gently strong as Hank used to be—there he is, my French boyfriend, the best of both. He'll be taller than Jimmy, a shade shorter than Hank, another winsome fellow with black hair uncombed and tending to curls around the ears and collar. His voice will make me think of Paris, little bars, sex cinemas, roses going to seed behind iron railings. I see him already, know him already, my twenty-year-old French friend.

Sex is the syrup in his veins, but horsemanship will be his art. He is a reader of books, the much loved son of an old gallant, still living, and a lavender-scented mother, long dead. Poetry, quick-tempered girls in eyeglasses, pinball machines in underground arcades—he's a young roué, my sweet dilettante, and old for his age.

But he's not in Paris. He's given up his intellectual young women, his old father, the sound of cathedral bells over the city, has gone to the south of France and become monastic, except for the occasional young widow or village daughter, and has decided at last to lead a lonely life devoted to his love of horses. He's a mere groom, a mere stableboy, a mere hireling on a vast estate. But never has there been such a cosmopolitan young man engaged in such lowly work. And though he conceals well his aristocratic heritage and his overly sophisticated erotic past, still the charm of what he hides is evident enough to elicit agreeable puzzlement from the owner of the vast estate and to make him—my boyfriend—a favorite of everyone on the estate and in the nearby village. He has refused so far the advances of the lady of the estate, and decorously, without arousing her anger, so that she continues to seek him out at the stables or on horseback in the dawn hours.

His name is Pascal.

He is not some French-Canadian Pascal mushing a team of famished dogs across the Nizina Glacier, or lying down on a bed of scurvy in a log cabin sheeted over with a film of ice. He is not an Alaskan Pascal, a Yukon Pascal, a sly Pascal with a stubble of beard and yellow teeth, familiar up and down the Tanana for his Canadian French and broken English.

My Pascal is Parisian, even in a village in the south of France.

I'll meet him among the plane trees on a dusty road leading into the village of rouge-colored stone houses, or at the cafe in the village square. He'll speak English to me of course, perfect English filled with the slangy, cultivated tones of his Parisian French. A pigeon will be sitting on the stone soldier in the all-but-empty square; nearby a fat man in an apron will be chopping meat. I shall be the only foreigner in the village, the only Alaskan woman ever to join Pascal at an outdoor cafe table in the orange light of a summer's dusk. We'll hear the ringing of a distant bell, the pigeon will take to the air, the wine will smell of casks and vineyards, a girl will laugh her tremulous French laugh.

And Pascal will lean toward me then.

"Let me put my little saint in your chapel," he'll say, my twenty-year-old Parisian with a Provençal turn of mind.

And that's how I'll learn my French, on Pascal's pillow.

In the little rouge-colored village I shall not suffer as a result of French elegance as did my father in Chantilly. And I shall not find my father's France but mine. And that's who I'll be at last: Jacqueline Flowers in the south of France, and in six months or a year or two there will be hardly a trace of Alaska in me, and not a single trace of Deauville. Father forgiven, Alaska purged, Sissy's family name become my own.

I'm on my way.

25 —

It was only days after Frank Morley had gotten rid of the rotten bearskin that Uncle Jake's good humor came back, to Sissy's great relief, and allowed Uncle Jake to devise his plan, to see the shape of the summer that was to be our first in Juneau. He could do nothing without a general plan, and it came to him: he needed more money, he needed a boat. General planning wasn't much to Uncle Jake's liking and fortunately for him there came along one more rescue mission, one more adventure in an airplane, that made him able to put up with the duller work of that summer.

Uncle Jake found it difficult to think about money. He had found it more difficult to ask his father, whom he did not respect, for money, and still more difficult to admit that the money he had accepted from his father, who thought little of the Alaskan scheme, was not enough. And it was not, though Uncle Jake's worry about the scarcity of funds, as he called them, had nothing to do with Sissy and the meager needs of our family. Uncle Jake did not once worry that Sissy suffered because of the lack of money, or that there wasn't enough money for our needs. Uncle Jake was never interested in replenishing the funds except to fuel his vision. He knew that airplanes were limited in purpose and effectiveness, as much as he enjoyed sailing off in them; he knew that he would get nowhere without a boat. He did not have enough money and needed more.

But if Uncle Jake had a compunction about taking money from his father, even an inadequate amount of money, he had no compunction about taking money from Frank Morley. It was ever my father's way: to worry about his standing with people for whom he had no use, as he put it, while remaining shamelessly indifferent to the welfare of those he loved. Such was the sum of his honor, and he was proud that his concept of honor was opposite from the general view. He was proud that personal concerns, as he called them, had no place in his thinking. Furthermore, what he had already shared with Frank Morley made Frank Morley worthy of being more than a friend of our family. In an instant, while standing on our porch and staring down the length of Gastineau Channel on a day when the sun shone periodically through the drizzle, it came to Uncle Jake to his immense relief: Frank Morley was worthy of being not just his closest friend but his *partner*.

Partners saved each other's lives, cooked for each other, defended each other against bears, wolves, claim jumpers.

The ties between partners were closer than the ties of marriage. There was no loyalty like the loyalty of one partner for another. Marriage was sanctified, but unlike people who merely married, men became lifelong partners in order to face the turbulent mysteries of the wilderness, to stake their claims, to overcome the universal fears. In coldness, darkness, driven mad by mosquitoes—Uncle Jake had heard about the mosquitoes from Frank Morley—partners carried each other bodily if they had to, helped each other along desolate trails, doctored each other's wounds. Partners shared all they had. And that was the crux of it: partners shared all they had.

So Uncle Jake solemnly invited Frank Morley to become his partner. Frank Morley accepted. They went immediately to Doug's and celebrated what they had pledged together over mugs of coffee. They talked about their joint bank account, which came into being within hours, and within hours contained half of Frank Morley's savings and the scant remnants of the money which Uncle Jake, who at the time was going strong, as he said, into his fifty-first year, had borrowed from his old and scoffing father. And it was during that same conversation, spoken in low and confidential voices in a booth at Doug's, that Uncle Jake brought up the subject of the boat. Frank Morley did not hesitate: Doc Haines, the only dentist in Juneau and a young fellow temporarily down on his luck for having lived too many months beyond his means, had a boat to sell. Frank Morley wisely omitted any reference to the women in the Baranof Hotel who had caused Doc Haines to live beyond his means. Uncle Jake wanted to know the length of Doc Haines's boat. Oh it was long, Frank Morley said, blowing on his second cup of coffee, long and with an unusually wide beam. Uncle Jake nodded. The only trouble with that boat, Frank Morley said, was that Doc Haines, who knew nothing at all about seagoing vessels, had torn out half the bottom on a rock that had been clearly marked by a buoy. She was tied up down at the wharf with an old pump going night and day. Uncle Jake frowned. He looked out the plate-glass window and saw Patsy Ann hightailing it toward the harbor: ship coming in. He frowned more deeply and took an envelope from the inside pocket of his suit coat and began to jot down figures, though Frank Morley had made no mention of the price of the boat. He shook his head. Then, by what stroke of good fortune he would never know, suddenly and casually he thought to ask the name of Doc Haines's boat. *The Prince of Wales,* Frank Morley said, and Uncle Jake smiled, put away his envelope, and told Frank Morley that of course they would buy the boat.

"The Prince of Wales," said Sissy when they climbed our hill to tell her the news. "Oh Jake, what a wonderful name for a boat!"

"She's ours," said Uncle Jake, and Frank Morley nodded. "And Doc Haines came down in the price. You bet he did. We skinned him, didn't we Frank?" Again the expression on Frank Morley's face, an expression that lit up the sagging jowls and sallow complexion and the eyes like the brown and slightly bloodshot eyes of a bloodhound with a pride that was akin to love, confirmed the reasonableness of Uncle Jake's newfound happiness. "And Sissy," Uncle Jake added, "Frank and I are partners."

"Partners?" said Sissy, and smiled her sweet and somewhat baffled smile.

"That's right," said Uncle Jake. "Partners. We're in this thing to-gether, aren't we, Frank?"

The two men, who had already shaken hands in Doug's, looked long and gently at each other and Sissy shivered, a ship's whistle blew, and the bells of the old Russian church began to ring, which allowed the three of them to laugh self-consciously at the ways of fate.

That afternoon we all went down for a first look at *The Prince of Wales.* It was drizzling; there were pale streaks of sun on the water.

Sissy wore her Scotch hat and a coat thrown over her shoulders. At an otherwise empty wharf that we reached only by skirting the disreputable docks where the Indians tied up their boats—the eyesore of Juneau as Uncle Jake was already fond of saying—we found the lonely berth of *The Prince of Wales*. The tide was low and the old boat, her belly awash and keel resting on the muddy bottom, despite the faint thumping of the pump, was not merely tied in ordinary fashion to the pilings: she was lashed to the rotten wharf by numerous ropes that were stretched taut from bow, stern, even the top of her mast to ring-bolts, cleats, a telephone pole on the street side of the wharf, to anything that might hold the old boat fast. They had gone so far as to wrap a weary hawser around her pilothouse and to tie the other end of it to a rusty wreck of a truck that had been abandoned at the edge of the sagging wharf.

"Sunny," said Uncle Jake in his proudest voice, though he was in fact speaking for Sissy's benefit, "Doc Haines is not as dumb as I thought. You see," he said, appraising the unlikely sight of *The Prince of Wales* bound grotesquely in her web of ropes, "if he hadn't been smart enough to tie her up this way, she would have tipped over. Tipped right over! Her superstructure's high, you see, and her bottom's sprung and full of water. So at low tide she sits on the mud instead of floating, so if they hadn't put up all that rigging to hold her, why she would have just rolled over. Right over! What a mess!" he said happily, and raised his chin, stared proudly at the old boat in all the glory of her averted catastrophe. "But Doc Haines knew what he was doing, and they've done a good job. A good job, all right. I'll have her seaworthy in about ten days."

Sissy listened, nodding soberly and looking up askance at the high and rusty smokestack, the pilothouse with newspaper stuffed into a broken window, the seagull droppings that crusted the rails, the wooden plank that was affixed to the top of the pilothouse and into which had been cut and painted her proud name: *The Prince of Wales*. The old boat had been painted in two stark colors, black and white, which in itself stirred poor Sissy's superstitious nature, and now the paint was flaking fore and aft, from stem to stern and top to bottom, peeling away from the deadness of the old ungainly boat in little chips and curls, and Sissy shuddered.

"But Jake," she said as cheerfully as she could, "is it safe?"

He laughed, he thrust his hands into the pockets of his camel's hair coat and cast an approving eye at the rusty iron rudder towering up from the black waters. *"The Prince of Wales?* Why, with a name like that I'd sail her anywhere in the world. Anywhere. And we'll make a sailor of you yet, Sissy. You'll see!"

It took him two months to repair the damage done to the old boat and to set her to rights and to take her off in August for the month-long accumulation of mishaps and accidents that was her maiden voyage. He did not know what Doc Haines had already discovered for himself: namely that the boat was dangerously flawed in her design and could not be trusted to weather rough seas or a gale. But Uncle Jake had his boat and his partner and in the two months that it took him, he did most of the restorative work himself, laughing and wallowing knee-deep in the mud at low tide. Despite the disasters that were to come, the old boat outlasted him, no matter her treacherous nature, and did not finally sink beneath the waves as Doc Haines thought that one day it surely would. As for Sissy, she came quickly enough to rue the day, as Uncle Jake would have put it, when the four of us stood in the drizzling rain, and in the stench of low tide, and admired the shabby and sinister grandeur of *The Prince of Wales*.

26 —

Uncle Jake was summoned to his second mission of mercy much as he had been to his first. Again the call came to Frank Morley by radio; again Uncle Jake's spirits soared as he prepared once more to test his powers of self-sacrifice; again the rescue required the use of an airplane, and thanks to Rex Ainsworth Uncle Jake now considered himself an old hand at flying. But Uncle Jake's trip to Icy Inlet was nothing compared to his visit to Disillusionment Bay, which was where his second mission took him. He may have been a misguided moralist and a good shot in Icy Inlet and may have enjoyed himself at Robert Fitz-gibbon's expense, but he wreaked havoc in Disillusionment Bay and suffered for it. At the outset even he had an inkling that the prospects

of his second mission were very different from those of the first, and
his misgivings showed. Nonetheless he cranked up his enthusiasm and
couldn't wait to be off.

"Again? Oh not again," Sissy said when the two partners appeared on
our porch that early morning and entered in silence and by their silence
conveyed to Sissy that the worst was once more to come. Sissy had
had her morning cigarette behind the house, and again had tied up her
hair in one of Uncle Jake's bandannas and was humming. The windows
were open, as they rarely were, to a few hours of warm sunlight and
to the heavy scent of the evergreens surrounding us. Sissy had just
made up the foldaway bed and my double bed, using the hospital
corners that she had learned from her newfound friend, the government
nurse, and drawing tight the covers. I was seated on the floor and lacing
my boots. In they came, Frank Morley and Uncle Jake, and never had
they looked so grave and at the same time so sheepish—which was
another favorite word in Uncle Jake's colorful and inexhaustible lexi-
con—as well they might have.

"Again?" said Sissy and sank down onto one of the folding chairs.

Uncle Jake nodded, pulled at his chin, indicated the rocker to Frank
Morley, who hesitated, then took his place in it, though throughout
this short encounter he kept his feet flat on the floor, his forearms on
his knees, and the rocker absolutely still.

"Another hunting expedition?" asked Sissy.

Uncle Jake frowned and cleared his throat. Frank Morley shook his
head, stared down at the narrow tips of his high-topped shoes, then
raised his eyes to Sissy's.

"No," said Uncle Jake at last. "No hunting."

"The thing is," Frank Morley said, "the call just came. From Olaf
Olafson down in Disillusionment Bay."

"He's a fox farmer," added Uncle Jake.

"That's right," said Frank Morley. "He's the only white man down
there and he's got the only shortwave radio in the entire region. It
wouldn't be safe for a fox farmer without a radio."

Sissy frowned.

"Well," Frank Morley said, trying to warm to his story, "one of them
rowed over this morning—"

"Rowed over?" asked Sissy, looking from one partner to the other
in alarm and incomprehension. "What do you mean?"

"Olaf Olafson lives and runs his fox farm on an island," said Uncle Jake hastily. "He's only about fifteen minutes by skiff from White Eye, the Indian village that's on the beach right across from him. On the mainland."

"Skoots," said Frank Morley. "The Indians in White Eye are Skoots." Sissy frowned.

"So it was just this morning," said Frank Morley, "that one of the Skoots, a fellow named Too-Much Jackson, rowed over to ask Olafson to radio for help."

"Sissy," said Uncle Jake suddenly, standing beside her and looking down at her firmly, "you don't understand. This thing's serious. A man has gone crazy and may be dangerous—"

"From the mosquitoes," said Frank Morley.

"Just a minute, Frank," said Uncle Jake, "she doesn't understand. Sissy," he said as calmly as he could, "what Frank says about the mosquitoes is true. Up here men who spend their lives alone in the bush, carrying their packs and picks and shovels, panning for gold on the muddy banks of creeks where no man has ever been, get eaten alive by mosquitoes. Eaten live. In Alaska the mosquito is a menace. A genuine menace. As bad as the wolverine, the copperhead. Why, the mosquito is worse: he infests the wilderness with pure torment. So prospectors in the wilderness protect themselves as best they can, and ingeniously too. But every year two or three prospectors can't stand it—the incessant whining sound, the dark clouds of them, the pain, the itching, the impossibility of escape. Every year at least one prospector can't stand the mosquitoes and goes mad. Then his partner has to tie him up and bring him out of the bush. They stumble along for days, for miles, the mad partner raving and weeping by turns, the other one doing all he can to keep his wits about him, to outlast the hordes of mosquitoes, to persevere until he drags his partner safely back to civilization. Do you understand?"

Uncle Jake's voice had risen despite himself, and there were tremors along his clean-shaven jaw; his smile, usually kind and boyish, was as close to hardness as it would ever be, fixed as it was on the derangement he had been describing. His eyes might have been following the cruel flights of invisible birds of prey. Poor Sissy listened obediently, fearful not for herself, not because of Uncle Jake's harsh animation and what he was saying, which could not help but stun her inmost sensibilities, but fearful for Uncle Jake's own sake, for what he himself seemed to be suffering. She smiled weakly. From where I sat on the floor with my forgotten leather laces dangling, I watched as Sissy tried to rally herself and placate Uncle Jake, saw the flickerings of alarm on Frank Morley's face, but most of all looked up with unnoticed devotion at my father, who was beginning to blush. Never had I seen him so grandly vehement.

"Do you understand?" he said again, more gently, and put his hand on her shoulder. "Do you, Sissy?"

She nodded and smiled without conviction.

"What Olaf Olafson told me," said Frank Morley, struggling on despite the sudden frowns of both Sissy and Uncle Jake, "was that last night two prospectors turned up in White Eye. Their names are Jones and Brewster, and Brewster is the one who's mad. Now the Skoots have got him tied up in a smokehouse and we need to bring him back to Juneau."

Nothing that either of them had said had made any sense to Sissy, and she knew that by all rights she should blame Frank Morley for what was happening. But she could not, and while the incongruous sounds of early summer filled the house—the cawing of a crow in the tall fir beside the porch, the cascading of freshly melted snow down a ravine on the steep side of the mountain behind us, the honking of a 1928 Chevrolet roadster in the streets far below us—Sissy gave Frank Morley one of her gentlest smiles of forgiveness but at the same time could not resist voicing, in a final try, her objections to Olaf Olafson, Too-Much Jackson, Brewster, the mosquitoes, the whole oppressive, frightening, nonsensical affair, even if in only a sentence or two and whether or not Frank Morley and Uncle Jake would choose to listen.

"Well," she said brightly, "I suppose there's no point in arguing. You two are incapable of hearing what I have to say, or of giving in."

They demurred immediately, they launched into a tangle of disclaimers, without intending to they made her laugh.

"You see," she said, "you won't let me say a word. Not one word."

"Of course we will," said Uncle Jake.

"Well," said Sissy, "you want to bring that poor tied-up man back to Juneau."

Uncle Jake nodded.

"But why?"

"Good Lord, Sissy," said Uncle Jake. "We can't just leave him captive in an Indian smokehouse. Now that his partner went to all the trouble to save his life we need to restore his senses. It's only humanitarian, Sissy. It has to be done."

"And he may be dangerous," said Frank Morley. "We'll probably have to send him back to the States."

"Well, I won't even ask why you instead of Hilda," said Sissy, referring to her newfound friend the government nurse.

They waited.

"But why," said Sissy, and flashed her eyes, "why doesn't Rex Ainsworth just go alone?"

There was silence. Uncle Jake and Frank Morley looked at each other, and Uncle Jake frowned and carefully removed his camel's hair coat and draped it over his arm while Frank Morley, still hunched forward in the rocker, absently raised his right hand and between yellowed thumb and forefinger began to fondle the elk's tooth dangling from the watch chain that spanned the sagging front of his black vest. Then Frank Morley drew out his watch—it was a large railroad watch, a Hamilton in a gold case, that he had inherited from his father in 1910—and studied it, closed the cover, returned the watch to its warm pocket in his vest.

"Sissy," he said and stared at her with what Uncle Jake would have called his most doleful expression, "a bush pilot wouldn't dare fly alone with one of those fellows driven crazy by the mosquitoes. The fellow might get loose. It's been known to happen. Right now I can think of about three bush pilots who thought they were good enough to go after a crazy prospector alone. And in each case the fellow who had lost his mind got free. And then there was a terrible tussle, and then they crashed."

Slowly, but still smiling, Sissy looked up at Uncle Jake. "So," she said, "you'll be the one to hold this Brewster? Up in an airplane and trying to prevent a madman from killing all three of you?"

"But Sissy!" exclaimed Uncle Jake. "I can do it!"

"Oh I suppose you can," she said and reached for his hand.

"He shot the bear," said Frank Morley in a happier voice.

"Well," said Sissy, shaking her head and laughing, "at least I can trust Rex Ainsworth."

Silence. Covert communion between the partners. Darker looks than ever.

"Well," said Frank Morley at last, "that's the thing—"

"Sissy," said Uncle Jake, drawing himself up before her as he might have stood before some naval tribunal in the Great War if dishonor could ever have befallen someone like Uncle Jake, "Rex's engine is in pieces."

"That's right," said Frank Morley in the same breath, "Rex is down at the docks right now working on his engine."

"In fact," said Uncle Jake, "he's still taking it apart. He hasn't begun to put it back together."

"That's right," said Frank Morley, shaking his head and gloomily fondling the big crooked elk's tooth between his fingers. "The Fairchild won't be ready to fly for days."

Sissy stood up. And from where I sat on the floor between the three of them, I saw how prettily Sissy stood in her trim blue slacks and old green sweater and with Uncle Jake's bandanna tied around her curly hair. Suddenly I had eyes only for Sissy, who was young and slight and, standing there beside Uncle Jake, was actually not much taller than I was and might have been my sister. But was she angry, overcome with fear, ready to admit defeat? Could even Sissy's loyalty be destroyed? Or was she still herself, still resilient, trusting, girlish, no matter what Uncle Jake and Frank Morley were trying to do to her? For a moment I was afraid that she was going to walk out of the house. What if she went outside and lit up one of her cigarettes and puffed on it until Uncle Jake smelled the smoke coming in through the open window? I had spied on her trying to light the wooden matches and coughing and then smoking the cigarette until it burned her fingers, a habit Uncle Jake deplored in male smokers, and I knew that her smoking was a private pleasure. I did not want Uncle Jake to find her out and spoil the enjoyment she gave herself in secret. But she did nothing of the sort and merely stood looking now up at Uncle Jake, now down at Frank Morley. I could smell the perfume she had taken to daubing behind her ears.

"Do you mean," she said, "do you mean that Rex Ainsworth is not going to be your pilot?"

They nodded.

"But if not Rex," she said, "then who?"

"Sissy," said Uncle Jake, "it can't be helped."

"It's only a short trip," said Frank Morley, "and the weather's good."

"Chippy's not a bad soul," said Uncle Jake. "I don't believe half the stories they tell about him."

"That's right," said Frank Morley to his own confusion, "he's quite a character."

They waited.

"Chippy Smith," she said.

They watched her.

"Do you mean to say," she said, "that you're going up in an airplane with Chippy Smith? Oh Jake, how can you do it? Chippy Smith, of all people. You know that man's reputation. You've told me yourself that he's reckless and unreliable. You've told me yourself that he's lost his license more than once and that Rex Ainsworth considers him to be the poorest pilot ever to fly in Alaska. Oh Jake, you know that if you had your way Chippy Smith would be grounded. That's what you told me. How can you do it? As if riding in an airplane with a man who has gone berserk isn't bad enough."

She paused. She caught her breath. Not one of them, including Sissy herself, could believe that from her sweetness had come passion as well as reason, and while the two men looked at her in shocked surprise Sissy clutched her elbows, frowned, then suddenly thought of herself as Cassandra—in all her future days Sissy took comfort in likening herself to Cassandra—and set her heart-shaped face as if she might never speak again. She had not meant to tell Uncle Jake the truth but she was pleased to be right.

"Sissy," murmured Frank Morley.

"Sissy," said Uncle Jake.

"Oh it's all right," said Sissy.

"Jake," said Frank Morley, "you can't go."

"Of course I can't," said Uncle Jake. "Sissy," he said, "it's not like you to flare up this way. Forgive me."

"Oh Jake," she said, "don't apologize. It's just that Chippy Smith ... that you've never had a good word to say for him, Jake ... it's just that you gave me such a bad impression of him that I never thought ... But of course it's all right. You know that. You know you mustn't talk about not going."

"Actually," said Frank Morley, "Chippy's Curtis is a better plane than Rex's Fairchild."

"That's right," said Uncle Jake. "It's a flying boat."

"Flying boat?" said Sissy, pretending interest while seeing disaster after disaster in her far-off gaze.

"It doesn't have pontoons like the Fairchild," said Uncle Jake quickly and once more put his hand on Sissy's shoulder. "It has a hull like a boat with the wing on top and the engine facing backwards on top of the wing. You'll see."

He paused. The driver of the Chevrolet called out to a friend far below us. Frank Morley coughed.

"Jake," said Sissy, "this time I won't see you off if you don't mind."

He nodded and smiled in a distracted way. "You know, Frank," he said, "I've always wanted to go up in a flying boat."

Frank Morley nodded.

"Well," said Uncle Jake, "I better get dressed. But I guess I don't need to bring along the old Four-Hundred-and-Five, eh Frank?"

Uncle Jake's checked woolen shirt was still torn and still smelled of smoke, his britches were faintly stained with the blood of His Unholiness, and his leather boots, laced high to his knees and bulging about his heavy calves, still bore the scuffs of his sojourn in Icy Inlet. Happily he strode ahead of Frank Morley and me, swinging his knapsack and turning his face so that it caught the sun—though for the first time the set of his jaw betrayed what he had done to Sissy. If he had had another chance he would not have denied her. As for Frank Morley and me, my father's partner was, in his pleasure, wheezing—his mild asthma generally became more pronounced at the onset of seriously masculine pursuits—while I was clutching Frank Morley's hand, which was as soft and warm as a woman's despite its size, and could not contain my eagerness to see the flying boat.

"Jake," called Frank Morley, "let's stop by for Charley. Shouldn't we bring Charley along with us down to the docks?"

Uncle Jake agreed at once, shifted his knapsack to his shoulder, and led us across the street from the two totem poles that guarded the portals of the old Baranof Hotel to the shadow of the great key suspended above the door of Guns & Locks & Clothes. A woman with her hair in curlers was leaning against one of the totem poles and smiled at us and said good morning to Uncle Jake, who stood taller in passing and handsomely returned her greeting.

"That woman's name is Nancy," said Uncle Jake to Frank Morley. "She's a nice person."

But little did the partners know what the lounging Nancy portended at the start of Uncle Jake's second rescue mission; little did they know that in her womanly attributes and proximity to the totem pole set up for tourists was a message, if they had had the wit to read it. Who could have seen Nancy lounging outside the old Baranof on a Tuesday morning and not looked to his future? Not Uncle Jake. There had been a day when Uncle Jake had unintentionally slighted the gently emboldened Nancy, as he had slighted most of the women in the Baranof, and now he again failed to hear the tones of her voice or to understand the way she looked at him. Frank Morley was even blinder to Nancy than Uncle Jake, though at least he did not think of her as nice.

Sitka Charley, on the other hand, was careful not to look across the street when Frank Morley called him out from the darkness of Guns & Locks & Clothes. Deliberately he averted his gaze from Nancy as if he had known beforehand that she was there, and joined the partners without a greeting or any indication that he was pleased to be included in our group on this occasion. And though Sitka Charley did not acknowledge my presence, as he usually did, still I was happy that I was wearing my knife on my new belt that was decorated with all the talismans—bear, bird, tree—of Sitka Charley's art.

"In a bad mood, Charley?" asked Frank Morley with sudden concern in his voice.

"I'm OK," said Sitka Charley.

"Of course he is," said Uncle Jake over his shoulder. "But Charley, do you know any of the Indians down in Disillusionment Bay?"

"I know them," said Sitka Charley.

"That's good," said Uncle Jake. "I don't want to go in there a complete stranger."

"They know who you are," said Sitka Charley. "Don't worry."

The two airplane floats belonging to Rex Ainsworth and Chippy Smith lay side by side in the cold waters, and there was Rex Ainsworth, just as Frank Morley had said he would be, wearing white coveralls over his suit and tie, and across from him, on the other float, sat Chippy Smith smoking a cigarette and sitting on an empty oil drum. He was small, unshaven, and wore tight denim pants like Sitka Charley's and an old leather flying jacket with a fur collar and, on his otherwise bare feet, a pair of floppy moccasins that had been chewed by a dog.

No two bush pilots could have been more different than Rex Ainsworth and Chippy Smith, and the two airplanes were as different as the men who flew them. The yellow Fairchild was conventional, trustworthy, and stood tall from the water on its pontoons, while the flying boat—could any anomaly have more pleased a child?—was smaller than the Fairchild and sat low in the water like a feeding bird. Its small hull was a skin of wood and was a light brown in color and highly polished; two miniature pontoons hung down from the tips of its wings on struts; the engine, of shiny metal blackened by exhaust, sat high above the wing like a small windmill. And to the nose of the hull in brass letters Chippy Smith had affixed the name of his flying boat:

Mabel. The Fairchild had no name; the Fairchild, in which I had first longed to soar, was no match for the flying boat in shocking my expectations. Except that today the Fairchild had no engine. Rex Ainsworth had removed the engine and there it hung, a great metal heart suspended inside a steel tripod from chains and pulleys. And the partially dismembered engine and the gaping front of the Fairchild, with its disconnected pipes and tubes and wires, made the Fairchild as much a marvel as the flying boat. I clung to Frank Morley's hand in my excitement.

"Rex," said Uncle Jake as we trooped along behind him down the sloping gangway to where Rex Ainsworth's wrenches gleamed in the bright air, "you picked a fine time to work on her!"

Rex Ainsworth gave Uncle Jake a level glance and nodded, pulled loose a rubber tube and caught its sudden gush of oil in a tin can.

"I wish it were you," said Uncle Jake in a low voice, "instead of Smith. I'll be lucky if that fellow doesn't crack us up."

"That's unlikely," said Rex Ainsworth, wiping his fingers on a rag.

"Nonetheless," said Uncle Jake, "I'd rather be in your hands than his."

Rex Ainsworth leaned forward into his engine and slowly, carefully, applied his ratchet wrench to a bolt that was like a nugget of silver.

"Well," continued Uncle Jake into the silence broken only by the faint slurping of the Fairchild's pontoons and the pinging of Rex Ainsworth's tools, "it's a pretty kettle of fish, but I guess I've got to go."

They shook hands.

Then Uncle Jake sighed and led the way across the two planks that bridged the floats, and Chippy Smith stood up to greet us.

"Thought you'd never get here!" he said and laughed and pinched the little hot stub of his cigarette between his thumb and forefinger and put it to his lips and inhaled. Uncle Jake frowned at the yellowed fingers, the pale lips, the glowing coal.

"Isn't it dangerous to smoke around airplanes?" asked Uncle Jake.

"Don't worry," said Chippy Smith. "There's an extinguisher inside the ship."

"Well," said Uncle Jake, "this is my partner, Frank Morley, and this is Sitka Charley. And this," he said, looking sideways at the flying boat and tousling my hair, "this is Sunny."

"Hello, Sunny," said Chippy Smith and winked.

Sitka Charley made a move behind me and Frank Morley cleared his throat. But Chippy Smith was already squatting and holding me around the waist with both hands—a gold identification bracelet hung from one of his thin wrists—and he smelled of toothpaste, gasoline, cigarettes, and beer, and in the breast pocket of his flying jacket he had hooked a pair of amber-tinted glasses that caught the sun. The leather of his jacket was cracked and flaking; his fur collar was musty, mildewed; under the open jacket he wore only a tee shirt and a tin religious medal on a chain. On one of his sunken cheeks a white worm of a scar showed through his two-day growth of beard. He was young and lively and was squeezing me playfully around the waist.

"So," said Uncle Jake quickly and in a jocular voice while drawing me to him by the shoulder, "so this thing really flies?"

"Mabel?" said Chippy Smith, who sprang to his feet and flung away his cigarette. "You bet she does. She was just a heap of wood and wire when I bought her down in Seattle. Three people were killed in her in that crash. But flying boats are rare, and even wrecked and dangling from the crane they'd hauled her up with she was pretty. I could see that much. So I bought her with a little money I got from my mother and rebuilt her myself. Ainsworth can have that old Fairchild of his. I'll stick to Mabel."

"Rebuilt her yourself," repeated Uncle Jake, his brows working and one palm resting against the wing.

"Sure did," said Chippy Smith.

"And then you flew her up here to Juneau? Well," said Uncle Jake, "I know something about boats. I like boats. And I can see that this hull has good lines. She's sleek, she's trim. Why, she looks like a winged fish. I think everything's going to be all right. Anyhow, Chippy, I'm ready whenever you are. Shall we go?"

Uncle Jake embraced Frank Morley, shook Sitka Charley's hand, gave me one of his bear hugs, as he called them, and then handed his knapsack to Chippy Smith as if he were a porter instead of the owner and pilot of the flying boat. It was then that Sitka Charley stepped forward and spoke a few low words to Uncle Jake. He told Uncle Jake to watch out for Too-Much Jackson. He said that Too-Much Jackson was a dangerous man even if he was a Skoot. Uncle Jake listened, frowned, thanked Sitka Charley for his warning, and then after smiling broadly at Frank Morley, he allowed Chippy Smith to settle him comfortably inside the flying boat.

"See you tomorrow, Sunny," called Chippy Smith, who donned his tinted glasses and started up the engine that was louder than the Fairchild's and shot thick tongues of flame from its ports.

Slowly they taxied out into the harbor, vibrating and pounding to the waves below them and to the angry top-heavy engine above them. The little plane turned bronze in the morning light, wallowed in a trough, skirted a mass of pilings, fought its way out of a sudden patch of crosscurrents, nearly sank from sight in the wake of a seiner that passed close enough to run them down. And then the flying boat was roaring before its pearly plume and skimming the surface, rising. Not a hundred feet in the air it banked, raced back and forth across the choppy waters, barely missing the corrugated iron roof of the Alaska Steamship Company's loading shed. Then it dropped down and shot viciously across the bow of the offending seiner, to a frantic blast of the seiner's whistle. Lower it fell, faster it came toward the three of us standing on the now empty float, and then passed just above our heads with wings wagging and Uncle Jake's terrified white face pressed behind one of the little cabin windows still awash with salty spray and flecks of foam. And then in a blast of wind and fire they were gone. Frank Morley was shaking his head and wheezing. Sitka Charley said something in a tongue I did not understand. Slowly we crossed over to Rex Ainsworth's float.

"That man is the worst pilot in Alaska," said Rex Ainsworth to Frank Morley as we paused before starting back to await Uncle Jake's return. "And when he crashes, it's going to be the worst crash in the history of aviation in Alaska."

That night I heard Sissy pacing in the darkness between the living room, where lay the foldaway bed which she had turned down but could not bear to sleep in, and the empty kitchen. Back and forth she paced, testing the front door, testing the back door, testing the windows in both rooms. I heard the little rattling sounds she made to convince herself that she and I were safe and that she had not forgotten to lock the back door, the front door, one of the windows. She did not pause to prepare herself a cup of warm milk in the kitchen; she did not lie down on the foldaway bed between her rounds. I heard her wispy anxious movements as she tried not to interrupt my sleep in her determination to protect us both from intruders. I heard her stop to listen for unfamiliar sounds; I knew she was searching for movement in the shadows.

Then abruptly she gave up her vigil. I heard her standing outside my door, heard the door opening, and in that instant she forgot about her need for caution, forgot her fears, came into my room and sat beside me on the bed as if she had not been walking about all this while in her green robe and furry slippers, attempting to guard us, and as if she suddenly had no further need to conceal from herself as well as from me what she had in fact known all the while, namely that I too was awake in the darkness.

She did not touch me. She did not hang her head or sigh. From the way she sat I knew that her eyes were clear and that she was alert, composed. From the cheerful sound of her voice when she finally spoke it might have been midafternoon instead of 4 A.M. I could not see her little elephant but I knew it was there, tied to her wrist.

"Well, darling," she said at last, peering into the night beyond my window, "at least I have you for my partner!"

But Uncle Jake did not come back as promised. The trip to Disillusionment Bay took him not a mere twenty-four hours, as he had expected, but three days. Yet when Frank Morley arrived on our porch that first morning, just as Sissy and I were finishing breakfast, Sissy knew at once that Uncle Jake had been delayed, which was exactly what, she told Frank Morley, she had expected. Frank Morley sat down at our kitchen table, still wearing his hat, and complained of always bringing her bad news, but Sissy only patted his hand and told him that she was getting used to bad news. While he rolled and smoked one of his wet cigarettes, Sissy put the skillet back on the stove and fixed Frank Morley three fried eggs and a thick portion of corned beef hash from a can. According to Olaf Olafson, Frank Morley said, the problem was engine trouble and nothing serious. Sissy replied that she had surmised as much and went on to say that she knew that Uncle Jake was not in danger. She would be the first to admit, she said, while pouring Frank Morley a second mug of coffee, that Uncle Jake was not at all in danger of dying in a plane crash, no matter what she had said the day before about Chippy Smith. And surely, she said, there couldn't be anything else she had to worry about.

The engine trouble continued. The sun continued to burn away the fog and the threat of rain. Frank Morley brought his binoculars with him when he visited, and Sissy was amused at the sight of two bear cubs playing on the slopes above us but refused to test the power of Frank Morley's binoculars by peering through them down the length of Gastineau Channel. Sissy and Hilda Laubenstein, the nurse who had spent nearly ten years working for the Bureau of Indian Affairs in Alaska, sat together over games of double solitaire while Frank Morley hunched beside them and looked on. On the second afternoon Sissy decided that she wanted to see the Russian church and persuaded Hilda Laubenstein to join her for a few moments in the heavily scented darkness just inside the massive doors. Sissy was afraid of Orthodox religious services, as she told Frank Morley, and was not a person to intrude where she did not belong. Frank Morley declined to accompany her inside the church but agreed to walk down with her and wait outside if she needed him to. It was understood that Uncle Jake wouldn't go anywhere near the Russian church, or any other church for that matter, even for Sissy.

We waited.

27 —

"Jake!" called Sissy. "Welcome back!"

From our porch she had suddenly spied Uncle Jake and Frank Morley climbing the wooden steps and wooden sidewalks that rose to our high ridge—all over Juneau the sidewalks were like narrow rickety bridges of bare weathered planking propped up on two-by-fours to avoid the mud—and together Sissy and I stood waving down at them.

"Sissy," said Uncle Jake, "I'm home!"

"Oh Jake," said Sissy, tucking in her blouse, "and nothing's wrong? You're not hurt?"

"Fit as a fiddle!" said Uncle Jake and kissed the top of her head and swooped me up into the crook of his arm. Frank Morley had insisted on carrying Uncle Jake's knapsack and still held it by the straps, relief and loyalty as thick as dust in every crease of his stooped figure, though he managed to keep a straight face, in Uncle Jake's vernacular, despite his intense desire to smile. It was an early afternoon, the sun was warm, some gulls were circling the half-bare fir that rose up beside the porch.

"And Brewster?" asked Sissy. "Is he all right?"

"Brewster?" said Uncle Jake, suddenly remote in the magnificence of his return. "Oh, Brewster. Yes, we've got him well in hand. Your friend Hilda Laubenstein was waiting for us and gave him a shot." And then, turning to Frank Morley: "Just put the knapsack anywhere, Frank," he said. "And why don't we bring some chairs out here? We might as well have the story on the porch."

Sissy and Frank Morley arranged the rocker and folding chairs and Sissy produced the ginger ale and the glasses. She was quick, she was pleased to be busy, she gave Uncle Jake one of her swift loving glances and caught hold of Frank Morley's arm. I thought that Uncle Jake was taller than ever, with his handsome head held high and his eyes strong and distant, brilliant and rock-hard with all that he had seen and would soon recount. He smelled the way he did whenever I slept between them—of soap, of manly talc—and his face was freshly shaven and freshly sunburned, his black hair was parted perfectly in the middle and stiffly, formally lacquered with the tonic he had carried along with him in his knapsack. Below us lay the roofs of Juneau—glinting or green with fungus, silent.

"You look wonderful, Jake," said Sissy. "And you had a good trip!"

He waited. We heard the faint sharp whistle that meant that they were changing shifts at the Alaska-Juneau Gold Mine. Frank Morley rolled a cigarette and with his yellowed thumbnail struck a flame from the sulphurous head of a wooden match. We heard a rumbling sound from the mine. Uncle Jake leaned back in his rocker, crossed a booted ankle over a heavy thigh, and squeezed me secretly. He knew that Sissy and Frank Morley saw in his flaring nostrils, his agitated brow, his steady jaw, his eyes that were becoming wilder as he prepared to speak, all the sure signs that something extraordinary had happened to him, and he laughed.

"We were worried," Uncle Jake declared in abrupt and unexpected soberness. "We were all worried. Weren't we, Sissy? Weren't we, Frank? The whole thing seemed ill-omened from the start. I thought that I had made a mistake, I can tell you. I've never known much apprehension in my life, but I knew it down there on the docks with Chippy Smith. At the last minute I was ready to give it all up. You know I was."

"Oh Jake," said Sissy, smiling in her consternation, "it's over now."

"Yes," said Uncle Jake, "it's over. And I can tell you, Sissy, that trip was a success! That trip was the most successful one I've ever made! And to think I might have lost it. . . . But I didn't. And we needn't have worried. I did the right thing, I can tell you, despite our worries."

"Of course you did," said Sissy.

"I don't mean it was easy," said Uncle Jake quickly. "God knows it wasn't easy. But I never thought I'd accomplish what I accomplished out there in Disillusionment Bay. I found myself in a pretty ticklish situation, Sissy, but it turned out all right. I managed. I did better than that if the truth be known."

"Oh Jake," said Sissy, "we're proud of you ... and even the engine trouble wasn't serious?"

"No," said Uncle Jake, "it wasn't. But that Chippy Smith is a rare bird. We weren't in the air two minutes," said Uncle Jake, launching into his story, "when I shouted to him to behave himself and stop showing off. He had me holding on for dear life and I knew I was as white as a sheet—you saw the way he came at you, Frank, at you and Sunny and Sitka Charley—so I shouted at him and told him that he had better respect my life if not his own. But he wouldn't have it. Not a bit of it. He just reached between his legs—you saw those moccasins of his, Frank—good Lord!—and brought up a bottle of cold beer. 'Want one?' he shouted back and popped the cap off with an opener that hung down from the instrument panel on a piece of string. 'You're not going to drink up here!' I shouted, but he only took a long swig and shook his head. And that flying boat of his—why, I never felt anything shake and shimmy and rattle as much as that thing did. I think you may be wrong, Frank, about its being a better plane than the Fairchild. Why, everything was loose—the seats, the rudder pedals, the little half-wheel—and I thought it was going to shake the teeth right out of my head. I could tell that the bursts of flame coming out of the engine above our heads were as long as my arm. I could smell the smoke—thick black rancid smoke—and thought that we'd catch fire any minute. I looked around for the extinguisher, but Chippy Smith is a liar, Frank, an outright liar, and it wasn't there. Along with the smoke and gasoline—the smell of the gasoline was terrible—there were the smells of salt and kelp and sea water, which was only natural since she was a boat as well as a plane. But good Lord, she smelled as if she'd been sunk for a week instead of just tied up down there at Chippy's float. Later I learned that he had about five ten-gallon tins of fuel stored behind us under a canvas flap, so it would have been an explosion, Frank, and not a fire.

"Then he started telling me stories. I won't repeat them, Sissy, but they were all about a woman called Nancy, and I never heard such filth in my life. Of course I tried to stop him, but on he went, giving the ship her head or so it seemed to me, and telling me the most atrocious things about this Nancy. You wouldn't believe that any man could use such words or that any woman would allow what this woman allowed. It was vile. I noted the coincidence of the names, Frank, but of course I knew that that nice woman couldn't possibly be the person Chippy Smith was carrying on about in his smutty way."

"Jake," said Sissy gently. "What woman?"

"Woman?" said Uncle Jake, still aloft and red-faced with Chippy Smith. "Oh she's just some nice person who used to say hello to us in the Baranof. Don't you remember? Her name is Nancy. Anyhow, Frank," said Uncle Jake, laughing and scowling at the same time, "just when I'd had enough of Chippy Smith we heard a tremendous sputtering and the engine went dead. That stopped him. He forgot all about his Nancy, I can tell you.

"Well, it was nothing, thank goodness. But he took forever to switch over to the auxiliary tank—that's all he had to do—and there we were in the grip of the wind like a pigeon in the talons of a falcon, and I couldn't do anything except stare at him in stupefaction, absolute stupefaction, while he chuckled to himself and felt around for the gadget that switched us from the empty tank to the full—at least I hoped that he had remembered to fill the auxiliary tank, and he had. We lost around three thousand feet in that little maneuver, but then the engine started up again with a bang, and naturally I thought he'd shoot us back up to a safe altitude, as any sane man would. But not him. Not Chippy Smith. In fact he did the opposite and shoved the controls forward and took us down, straight down, or so it seemed to me, until our shadow on the water was nearly as big as the plane that was casting it.

"The curious thing is that though I didn't trust him—how could anyone trust Chippy Smith?—nonetheless I was beginning to share his devil-may-care attitude. Forgive me, Sissy. There was something about him that I couldn't help admire, though everything about him was repugnant. The reason he had dropped us down so low—we couldn't have been more than fifty feet above the water—was that we had come to the Candle Creek Islands—you know them, don't you, Frank?—which fill those black and treacherous waters for miles. The Candle Creek Islands are small, uncountable, uninhabited, and wild, absolutely wild, just little ragged gems of wilderness scattered cheek by jowl across those inland waters. And Chippy Smith wanted me to see them, that's all, and I couldn't exactly hold the risk against him. Our air speed was

one hundred and forty knots, or thereabouts, and Chippy banked and
turned and skittered and flew us through that labyrinth of islands as if
he could have done it blindfolded. I couldn't help admire the man, I
can tell you. The light was changing, coming down at a fierce angle,
and each one of those islands was turning into its own dark night. We
were going so fast that we shot between three or four islands with
every breath, and yet I could see distinctly the rocks heaped up like
skulls on their steep shores and the masses of black and shattered trees
that rose above us. Well, zigzagging through the Candle Creek Islands
in the failing light, I decided that there was something of the artist in
Chippy Smith, and considering how he behaved later for most of our
stay with Olaf Olafson, that's the only thing that saves him in my eyes,
Frank. That's the reason I don't just flatly condemn the man, as Rex
Ainsworth does. You can't just totally condemn any man who's got a
touch of the artist in him, that's my firm belief.

"I had to give him credit for his sense of timing. He extricated us
from the Candle Creek Islands and headed us into Disillusionment Bay
at sunset, precisely at the stroke of sunset when the waters of the entire
bay were ablaze with reds and greens and purples and the black night
was descending. It was a spectacular approach and I had to admit it.
Chippy climbed, made a large circle, straightened, leveled out, and
before I knew it we were across the bay and there below us was the
dark coast of the mainland, the little cluster of shacks where the Skoots
were keeping an eye on Brewster, and, just offshore, Olaf Olafson's
island—it's a big island, Frank—looking like an open hand in the water.

"'There he is!'" Chippy shouted. "'The Swede himself. And wait
until you see his wife!'

"Well, I didn't like the sound of that business about Olafson's wife,
but I let it go. Chippy was back to his old tricks of low-level flying,
and when he dipped our right wing and made a tight circle, I looked
down to where he pointed and was impressed by what I saw: a man
about twice my size, Sissy, standing on the end of a log jetty and slowly
waving. He was a brute, I can tell you, and he was flanked by two of
the fiercest dogs I've ever seen. I recognized them for what they were
at a glance: malamutes. They had a lot of wolf in them, Frank, and
they were big fellows. Olafson's boat was tied up alongside the jetty
and it looked like a diesel and looked as sound as the man himself. But
I was wrong, Frank. I couldn't have been more wrong, as I was soon
to see.

"Then Chippy, who was clearly trying to put on a good show for Olafson, smacked us down so hard that I thought we'd crack right open, and gunned the engine as hard as he could as if we were having a race with some invisible high-speed boat, and then just as suddenly throttled it back down from a whine to a grumbling whisper. I couldn't see for the spray. But we slowed and the dripping windows began to clear. Chippy opened the hatch and climbed out onto our bow; Olafson tossed him a rope and made us fast.

"'Good work, Chippy,'" I said as he gave me a hand and I stood up and stretched and jumped down onto Olafson's jetty.

"Face-to-face, Olafson wasn't impressive. Not at all. He was just big. We shook hands, and as soon as he gave me his big paw I could feel his reluctance, his unfriendly manner, and disliked him instantly. I had thought he was a man of stature, one of those blond fellows from Sweden with clear features and honest strength. He was blond all right, and Swedish, but that's as far as it went. He was just big. He was at least a head taller than I am, Sissy, and had shoulders on him like an ox. You'd think we would have hit it off, but we didn't. He was so big that his character had to be weak, and it was, and when I introduced myself he only grunted and took back his paw as soon as he could. He wasn't my sort at all. But he grinned at Chippy and the two of them shouted greetings at each other at the tops of their voices, and before I knew it Chippy had ducked back down into the plane and was handing up to Olafson a couple of large wooden boxes that were heaped high, as I should have known, with bottles of beer. So I saw how things were going to go, and then in the bright colors of the failing light I glanced over at Olafson's boat. You wouldn't believe it, Frank, but that boat had been burned in a fire, badly burned, and half of her was just a char. Olafson didn't even care enough for his boat to make even the simplest repairs—he was that kind of man. And that's how wrong I had been about both the boat and the man. They just weren't sound, Frank. Not at all. But Olafson's dogs were fierce all right. At least I could respect his dogs.

"'Tell us about Brewster,' I said as we started up to Olafson's cabin. 'Is he all right?'

"'Sure,' said the Swede, hugging his case of beer to his chest. 'Sure. He's all right.'

"'Well,' I said, 'what are we going to do? Bring him over here?'

"'Hell no,' said the Swede, and you know how much I dislike profanity, Frank. 'Hell no. He doesn't set foot on my place. He's crazy.'

"'Olafson,' I said, 'do you mean we're not going to see Brewster until tomorrow?'

"'That's right,' he said. 'Tomorrow.'

"'But he's already spent one night over in that native village,' I said. 'This will be his second night with the Skoots. Who knows what shape he's in, Olafson? Now that Chippy and I are here we ought to do what we can to make him comfortable until we can fly him out of here in the morning.'

"'Comfortable hell,' said the Swede. 'It's not my business. It's too dark to do anything.'

"That's how impertinent the man was, Frank. Impertinent, lazy, no good. And of course he was afraid of Brewster, that much was clear.

"Olafson kicked open the door and in we went, and Sissy, you wouldn't believe the smell. The cabin was a large one-room affair built crudely of logs, with wooden bunks along two walls and a potbellied stove in the middle. The logs were unpeeled and whoever built it had used moss, not mortar, to chink up the spaces between the logs. In the shadows at the far end of the room was a cooking range being tended by Olafson's wife, and from the rafters in the roof hung kerosene lanterns flickering and smoking to beat the band. And the smell? It was partly the kerosene, partly the smoke from the range and stove, partly the filthy blankets heaped up in the bunks, partly the fish Olafson's wife was cooking, partly the dogs. But it was more than all this. It was a slippery smell, a hot smell, an aroma that rose to high heaven, I can tell you. And of course it was nothing other than the smell of Olafson and Olafson's wife themselves, and I could hardly choke down each foul breath I had to take in that cabin.

"'Come on,' said Chippy, nudging the Swede, 'make her come out here where we can see her. Jake wants to take a look at her, don't you, Jake?'

"Of course I wanted to do no such thing and by now was thinking of very little except that the four of us and the two dogs—two big malamutes—were going to spend the night together in one room and without the slightest chance for privacy. Sticking out from under one of the bunks was a fat old-fashioned chamber pot that belonged in an antique shop, I thought, rather than in a fox farmer's cabin, and the sight of that chamber pot was making me ill, I can tell you, along with everything else. But the Swede made a grunting sound and the woman stopped what she was doing at the stove and joined us in the middle of the room.

"'Just look at her!' said Chippy Smith and nudged the Swede. 'What a woman!'

"'Mrs. Olafson,' I managed to say and tried to smile.

"'You don't have to call her that,' said the Swede. 'She's a Skoot.'

"And that's why I faltered, Frank. Olafson's wife was an Indian. A full-blooded Indian. And that's not what I had expected. Not at all. And wasn't it just my infernal luck to be piloted by a man I couldn't trust? And to be greeted by a man I didn't like? And then to find out that the fellow's wife was an Indian? There it was, the first Alaskan Indian woman I'd ever seen—except for that woman in Taku Bay, Sissy, and she doesn't count—and all three of us were going to have to spend the night in the same room with her. I faltered, all right. Who wouldn't? Every woman should have her privacy, including Olafson's wife.

"'Come on!' said Chippy, forcing the poor creature to accept one of his bottles of beer. 'Join the party, Passuk!'

"'Do what he says,' muttered the Swede.

"I was aware of her discomfort, Sissy, and wondered if she was aware of my indignation, which I tried not to show. If she was she gave no sign of it and instead, and while we watched, she merely raised the bottle to her lips and drank, and then wiped her mouth on her sleeve like a man. You know how flat their faces are, Frank, and Passuk's was no exception. Round as a pie tin, flat as the back of your hand, shiny as a greasy skillet. It was the face you might find on a walrus, Frank, and yet she was young and with those cheeks and those dark eyes of hers I thought she was probably one of the belles of White Eye across the way from us—or had been. But it was her size, I knew at once, her considerable size that had made her such a curiosity for Chippy Smith and such a catch for Olafson. Her face was nearly level with mine and she wore one of the Swede's shirts and one of his pairs of pants with ease. The shirt was loose here and there and the pants were a little long, so that she wore them rolled up at the bottoms. But those pants were tight on her, Frank. They were actually a bit too small for her, which shows you how large that woman was! On her feet she was wearing nothing but a pair of Olafson's thick woolen socks, she was that disheveled. Clearly she was a good worker, a girl as large as she was, and Lord knows what Olafson had traded to win her hand in marriage. Not much, I thought to myself. Some pittance or other. It was then that I began to take a liking to Passuk despite myself and to think that it was she and not Olafson who had been demeaned by the marriage.

"At first the evening made me only mildly uncomfortable, though it was obvious that they were taking advantage of Passuk every step of the way. She went back and forth between the range and table waiting on us; she served up the fish and some sort of cornmeal fritters; every once in a while they made her sit down and drink another bottle of beer. I asked Olafson about his fox farming and got another one of his rude replies. Chippy started to tell Olafson about that woman Nancy, which is when I went outside and stood under the clear heavens and listened to the foxes barking. There were no lights in the village across the way; for a moment I considered trying to sleep in the flying boat but decided against that idea. I took a few steps into Olafson's woods and stopped and listened. He and Passuk had harvested their pelts the previous December, shortly after the new cubs were born—that's how they do it, Sissy—and now the young foxes were barking right along with the breeders. They don't really sound like dogs, Sissy, and yet barking is the only word for the wonderful shrill sounds they make. I listened and I knew that their eyes were gleaming all over the island.

"There was no stopping the way things were going to go, and by the time I forced myself to return to the cabin they were well under way. Chippy and Olafson and even Passuk—I was surprised to hear her laughter sandwiched between the drunken voices of the two men—caroused all night at the far end of the cabin. I cleared the bedding out of one of the bunks and made the best of it.

"'Hey,' Olafson called to me at the height of their revels and in tones that were none too pleasant, 'hey, she wants you to come drink a beer.'

"I did not answer him of course but noted that Passuk's invitation confirmed that she was aware of my concern for her situation, as I had suspected she might be. For a while I thought that they were going to bring the cabin crashing down around our ears with their drunken carousing, but then they quieted down and I got some sleep.

"You can imagine the shape that pair was in the next morning. When the first crack of light came through the parchment windows I found myself wide awake and oddly refreshed and listening to Passuk, who was already outside and chopping wood. I knew it was she because only men could snore as loudly as that pair was snoring at the other end of the cabin. I decided to wait for them down at the jetty, where

I found Olafson's boat looking like a derelict and Chippy's plane covered with dew and looking as if it would never fly again. The sun rolled up over the iron-colored water and a hawk sailed across from White Eye, where I could see the first trickles of wood smoke starting to rise. Passuk brought me a cup of java, as Johnson called it back in Icy Inlet— and that's how I spent my time, sipping my coffee and staring out across the water, until that pair finally joined me at the jetty, grumbling and as red-eyed as I thought poor Brewster probably was over there in his smokehouse. Even Chippy Smith had lost some of his perkiness, and the Swede, as I could see, had been sick and was so sullen that I began to feel sorry for him despite the way he had treated Passuk.

"They bailed out Olafson's dinghy and fumbled with an old outboard motor until they got it going. Off we started at last, and the only thing I could think of, Sissy, was getting home to you and Sunny. Oh I was pleased that we were only minutes away from Brewster, poor devil, and that now we could do our job and be done with it. But do you know, Sissy, that sitting in the bow of Olafson's dinghy and feeling the sun on my shoulders and hearing the sound of our outboard motor putting and fading away in the distance—why, suddenly it came to me that we were leaving the plane behind and that perhaps I would never find my way back to you and Sunny."

Uncle Jake paused then, as he knew he must, and shifted me on his lap and waited for Sissy to leave her place in the darkness, which had descended while Uncle Jake had been talking, and to lean down and put her cheek to his, which she did.

"Oh Jake," she whispered, "what a terrible feeling it must have been."

Uncle Jake nodded and Frank Morley struck another kitchen match on his thumbnail. We waited.

"It was irrational," said Uncle Jake as Sissy quietly returned to her chair and the stars came out over Gastineau Channel. "I had never felt such a feeling before and don't expect to soon again. But when I looked back and saw the plane, and then turned around and in the morning light saw the approaching shacks of that native village, suddenly I knew how far I had come from you and Sunny and Frank, no matter that we were only a few hours apart as the crow flies and that you could practically shout from Olafson's place to the village. It was grief that I felt, Sissy, pure grief for you and Frank and Sunny. But it was irrational, as I say, and before I could moon a moment longer I received a jolt that took me out of myself, I can tell you.

"'Mister,' came the sound of the Swede's voice behind my back. 'Mister, I got news for you.'

"Was he threatening me? Was he attempting to be agreeable? His more formal mode of address was insulting, and his friendliness, if that's what it was, was even more insulting. Rarely in my life have I ever cringed, Frank, but when I heard his Swedish accent, which I detested anyway, and heard it slow and stupid with his night's carousing, I tell you I cringed and went rigid with suspicion.

"'Mister,' he said, when he understood that I was not going to answer him, 'there's a young squaw over there who wants to divorce her husband. She wants you to give her the divorce.'"

"Why Jake," said Sissy, unable to control herself, "whatever did he mean? How strange..."

"Yes," said Uncle Jake, "it was strange. It was like being struck dumb, I can tell you. At first I waited for Chippy Smith to laugh or for the Swede himself to laugh. But they didn't, and I knew that I had to be careful and also that I loathed Olaf Olafson more than ever for his mockery or impertinence, whichever it was.

"'Olafson,' I said at last, without turning to look at him. 'I don't know what you're talking about. But I don't like it.'

"'No,' he said. 'What's the matter?'

"'What do you mean by saying such a thing to me?' I said. 'Are you joking?'

"'No,' he said. 'I'm not joking. Why should I joke?'

"'Lord only knows,' I said. 'You're a funny bird.'

"'Listen,' he said. 'You're new up here. You're a chechaqua. You don't know what we do up here.'

"'I know enough not to trifle with divorce,' I said. 'It's preposterous.'

"'Well then,' he said, and I heard plainly enough the shade of triumph in his voice, 'who gives her the divorce?'

"'Lord knows,' I said. 'But not me.'

"'You!' he said. 'You!'

"'There are laws, Olafson,' I said. 'There are laws even in Alaska.'

"'Hell no,' he said and laughed. 'Not out here. Nobody ever comes to Olaf Olafson's island or to White Eye. Nobody. So what's the difference?'

"'Well,' I said, 'you can grant this woman a divorce if you want to, Olafson. But not me.'

"'Oh,' he said, 'I'm married to one of them. They don't think I'm a white man anymore. Besides, there's a burial ground full of dead

Skoots on my island. They don't want me fox farming on that island. They hate my guts.'

"'Olafson,' I said as patiently as I could. 'How did you marry Passuk?'

"'Took her to Juneau,' he said. 'How do you think?'

"'Well, then,' I said. 'Let this woman go to Juneau.'

"'Jesus,' he said. 'She's got no boat!'"

"Oh Jake," said Sissy, interrupting him again, "is that what you did? Did you separate that woman from her husband?"

"I don't like it," said Frank Morley, speaking up suddenly and leaning forward in the darkness. "There could be trouble, Jake."

"Well," said Uncle Jake, "I was flabbergasted and anyway I didn't have time to make a decision there in Olafson's dinghy because just then we nosed onto a shelf of soft mud—the tide was out—and came ashore. As luck would have it, there was Too-Much Jackson himself standing in the muck to meet us. Olafson had barely had time to tell me that this fellow Too-Much Jackson was the husband that the young squaw wanted to get rid of, and that the husband had a mean temper, just as Sitka Charley had said, and didn't know anything about his woman's plans. Then it turned out that Brewster wasn't in the smoke-house as we had thought, Frank, but was in the shack belonging to Too-Much Jackson, which was why the Indian had come down to meet us. We had hardly climbed up the bank into clouds of freshly risen mosquitoes—there's irony for you, Frank—when it came over me that the dead Skoots on Olafson's island were beginning to revenge themselves—and not on Olafson but on me.

"Too-Much Jackson's shack was the most run-down shack in White Eye, and that village wasn't a prosperous place, I can tell you. There was grass growing a foot high on the roof and gunny sacking nailed over the windows. A pile of muskrat traps was rusting away near the door that was covered by a tattered blanket, and sitting on a barrel near the traps was poor Jones, who didn't seem to mind the mosquitoes and who jumped up to greet me like a long-lost brother. And thin? Why, I've never seen a man as thin as Jones, excluding Brewster, of course, and for the life of me I didn't know how Jones had survived such emaciation as long as he had. But he was a lively little fellow and hurried us right in to take a look at Brewster, which was when I got my second shock of the day. Some sacks of meal, a tin stove, a woman sitting on a broken chair in a corner—I saw the glance she gave me, Frank, don't think I didn't—and an old brass bedstead without a mattress which was where Brewster was lying, trussed up hand and foot—

that's all there was inside Too-Much Jackson's cabin. The place was like a sieve despite the grass on the roof, and it was cruel the way the sunlight came through the chinks and cracks and lit up the misery of that hovel and lay warmly and brightly on Brewster as if he wasn't the picture of despair. But it was not the trussing or the clothes—or what was left of them—or Brewster's emaciation that shocked me. It was his face. His face was nothing but a gray mask, a thick gray mask cracked and featureless except for two mad eyes staring out at me and a couple of holes for the nostrils.

"'Good Lord,' I said, averting my gaze, 'what's wrong with his face?'

"I couldn't help myself, Frank. I couldn't hold back that exclamation. After all, I hadn't expected that Brewster would not look human. Deranged, yes. But human. Well, all this will be nothing new to you, Frank. But the thing is, Sissy, and as Jones explained to me right away, when men in the bush get driven far enough and are at their wits' end with the predicament of the mosquitoes, they give up everything and search until they find a creek, and then they squat and scoop up great handfuls of wet clay—imagine their relief, Sissy!—and pack it onto their faces as a last resort. Then off they go again, searching for another creek. Gold is no match for mosquitoes, I can tell you. Jones had scrubbed the clay from his own face as soon as they stumbled out from the tangle of dead trees and into White Eye, but Brewster had screamed whenever his partner had made a move to clean him up, which was why Brewster's face was still a disfigured mask of dried clay. It was an awful sight, Sissy. Just awful.

"The pathetic part of the story, as Jones explained it, was that they had started off wearing old felt hats with netting tied around the brims and covering their faces, and though their headgear wasn't foolproof, still it did a pretty good job, as Jones said. But when Brewster lost control of himself—it was high noon in the worst mosquito country Jones had ever seen—he stopped suddenly and before poor Jones's very eyes removed his hat and quick as a flash tore and ripped his mosquito netting to shreds with just the fingers of his two hands. Then he snatched off Jones's hat and did the same thing to it. Can you beat that, Frank? I suppose the poor devil thought that total affliction was what he deserved after what he had suffered already and that his only recourse was to spite himself once and for all and drag poor Jones along with him. So there they were without even the meager protection that they had started with, which is when Brewster somehow understood what he had done and began to howl, and Jones somehow got a rope around him and hauled him off in search of their first creek.

"Jones had plenty of courage, I can tell you. He was a devoted partner.

"It was then, just as Jones was finishing his story, that I realized that Chippy Smith was missing."

"Oh no!" whispered Sissy in the darkness.

"Yes, Sissy," said Uncle Jake. "Just when I needed him most he was gone. I had been preoccupied with Jones's story and with my first sight of Brewster and with the young Indian woman who never took her eyes off me from start to finish, so that I hadn't noticed that Chippy Smith had slipped away. But he had.

"He had gone off with Too-Much Jackson. And do you know why?"

"Yes," said Frank Morley, bestirring himself in the darkness, "I have an idea."

"Oh Jake," said Sissy. "What was it?"

"Drink," said Frank Morley and shuffled his feet.

"Exactly!" exclaimed Uncle Jake. "You've got it, Frank! Hoochinoo! You don't know about hoochinoo, Sissy, but it's terrible stuff. Bad whiskey. The Indians make it by putting a fermented mash of molasses, flour, sugar, and Lord knows what else into a kerosene can—isn't that the way it goes, Frank? Then they use a long piece of kelp for piping and run the kelp from the kerosene can through another barrel filled with freezing sea water. They build a fire under the kerosene can, steam rises, and hoochinoo drips out of the other end of the length of kelp. One drink of the stuff can make a man steal the thongs from his own snowshoes, as Olafson had the nerve to tell me when we finally found Chippy stretched out flat on his back with Too-Much Jackson swaying over him, bottle in hand. It was the only time Olafson used a colorful expression, but I didn't appreciate it at the time. Not only had Chippy incapacitated himself with Too-Much Jackson's help, but Olafson had noticed the two of them slipping away and knew full well what they were up to. He didn't make a move to stop them, and he deceived me in the bargain. And did he care? Not on your life he didn't. I could only think that I had had a picnic with Fitzgibbon and his crowd and that no Swede had ever stooped so low as Olafson."

"Well, the problem was that Chippy didn't wake up."

"So that was the engine trouble," said Sissy timidly. "The hoochinoo."

"Exactly," said Uncle Jake. "That's what it was. I couldn't bear to talk to Frank myself, but I made sure that the Swede gave Frank that lame excuse so you wouldn't worry.

"Well, it took us about twenty-six hours to bring Chippy back to his senses as a matter of fact, and I don't believe I've ever worried as much about any man as I did about Chippy Smith. Why, he had drunk enough squirrel whiskey, which is another name for hoochinoo, Sissy, to kill him, and for all I knew he wasn't going to regain consciousness but just die in his coma. Anyhow, we had no sooner come upon Chippy out cold and Too-Much Jackson swaying above his prostrate form than Too-Much Jackson passed out on his feet and sank down, while we stood there helplessly, until he too was flat on the ground and dead to the world like Chippy. The way he went slithering down might have been comical if I hadn't already taken such a strong dislike to Too-Much Jackson. The Skoots are a bad lot, Sissy. In the old days they used to amuse themselves by putting one of their slaves into a leather sack and then jumping on the sack—the whole tribe of them taking turns—until they had broken every bone in the body of the wretched creature still alive in the sack. I didn't need Olafson to tell me that Too-Much Jackson was the same sort. You could see it in the fellow's eyes.

"So we took Chippy back to Olafson's cabin—he was like a corpse in the bottom of the dinghy, I can tell you—and wrapped him in blankets and left Passuk watching him until I could return and take up the vigil myself. Then Olafson ferried me back over to White Eye, where I told Jones what had happened and insisted that we take the ropes off Brewster. I had noticed an old sheepskin coat hanging from a peg near the tin stove and told Jones and Olafson that we could use the coat instead of the ropes. As soon as we loosened them, Brewster began to fight with fury—and silently, Frank, without making a peep— but we held him down and managed to bundle him into the coat backwards with his arms down at his sides instead of in the sleeves. The old sheepskin coat made a pretty good straitjacket, you see, and we tied the empty sleeves to the bed frame with a length of line. That way Brewster was more comfortable.

"It was then that Olafson persuaded me to let Sipsu say her piece, as he put it—Sipsu was the poor young woman's name, Sissy—which reluctantly I agreed to do. We were right there after all and I had seen the way she'd been watching me and had not the heart to deny her. Olafson took Jones outside. Brewster lay still. Sipsu rose to her feet— she's a small person, Sissy—and looked up at me and with a simplicity and dignity I had not anticipated, and with Brewster watching and listening, though it made no difference of course, she told me why she no longer wished to be the wife of Too-Much Jackson. I was formal with her, Frank, don't think I wasn't, and I was touched by Sipsu's manner and angered by what she had had to endure. Passuk never spoke a word of English in my hearing, but I could tell that Sipsu's English was superior to Passuk's. And Sipsu was a nice person, which I knew as soon as she began to talk, and was in an entirely different class from Passuk.

"Sipsu was alone, Sissy, except for that infernal husband of hers, with no one to grant her justice and no way to escape the desolation that was her lot. She only asked to be freed from Too-Much Jackson and to move out of his cabin, and she had plenty of cause for wanting the divorce. Then she said that no white man would ever come again to White Eye except for Olafson, who was not empowered to do what I could do. She said that I had greater powers than the missionary who had married her to Too-Much Jackson. She said that I should do what she asked.

"I told her that I would weigh what she had said and then I left her.

"Well, one minute I wanted nothing more than to wash my hands of the whole affair and the next minute I was ready to slam down my gavel, so to speak, and to give poor Sipsu her divorce. I don't know how I got through the twenty-six hours. At least that night there was no carousing, since the beer was gone and Chippy was still in his coma and Olafson had the sense to stay away from squirrel whiskey. Once— it must have been toward dawn—I heard Brewster howling over in White Eye unless I was dreaming.

"Toward midmorning of the next day Chippy began to come around, and that's when Passuk and I went to work on him. We forced scalding java down him; every hour we dragged him stark naked to Olafson's rain barrel and doused him good; we walked him up and down, still naked, all morning long. He shivered, he sagged between us, and slowly he came around. I didn't have to worry about Chippy's modesty, since it made not the slightest difference to either one of us that Passuk was helping me to parade him up and down in front of Olafson's cabin in the raw. If she had been a white woman it would have been something else again of course.

"Berate him? Oh I berated him, Frank. Shoveling hot food into his mouth, propping him up outside, dousing him in the rainwater—all those hours I told him what I thought of him and that I had not expected him to go this far. To jeopardize the whole trip and the lives of the men in his care was an outrage and I told him so. He only laughed and said that chain lightning, as he called it, was the best stuff in the world.

But I've never seen a man so pale, Frank, and I thought that he had learned a lesson.

"We spent the rest of the day reviving him and letting him rest. At one point Olafson's dogs suddenly decided to fight, and Olafson beat them apart with a two-by-four. Late in the day I heard Brewster howling again across the water. That evening I listened to the foxes barking. It was another quiet night.

"The next morning Chippy was still groggy but he thought he was well enough to fly. Of course by then it was drizzling and had turned cold. Olafson kept shouting at his dogs. But finally we took the dinghy over to White Eye and picked up Brewster. I didn't see anything of Too-Much Jackson—for all I know he's still lying out there in the grass in White Eye—but while Jones and Olafson were settling Brewster into the dinghy, I went back and without any fanfare told Sipsu that she could consider herself divorced."

"Oh Jake," came Sissy's voice through the darkness, "you didn't!"

"Yes," said Uncle Jake, "I did. It was one of the hardest things I've done in my life, but I had made up my mind. I'll never forget the way she looked when I told her.

"Well, we went straight to Olafson's jetty and helped Brewster aboard the flying boat. We put him into the seat I'd occupied on the trip down— the one next to Chippy's seat, that is—and I sat directly behind him, so that I could hold him if the need arose. Chippy had already filled both tanks from the tins of fuel he'd brought along, and the engine was finally turning over. At the last minute, just as Chippy was about to close the hatch, Olafson leaned down and shouted that Passuk wanted me to come back to see her. I was fed up with that Swede, I can tell you, and I almost shouted back that it was Passuk and not Sipsu who needed the divorce and that I was ready to give her one too. But I kept my temper and said nothing and Olafson cast us off.

"Brewster howled only once on the flight home. This time Chippy was minding his P's and Q's, I can tell you, and we were flying at ten thousand feet through broken clouds. I had my hands resting on either side of the back of Brewster's seat, ready to hold him, when suddenly I heard Chippy's laugh—it was a pretty awful laugh, Frank—and saw him pointing dead ahead. Before I knew what was happening, I heard him shouting—'Goose!' just that one word, 'Goose!'—and there it was, a great fat gray goose hurtling head on toward us with its wings wide, its feet tucked up, its head probing forward on its long neck. Brewster howled, Chippy laughed, and we crashed right into that poor goose.

I felt the impact and grabbed Brewster's shoulders and thought sure that the goose had smashed a hole in the wing or hull and that we'd go down. Actually it struck higher up on the engine nacelle and didn't do any damage to speak of except to itself. As for Brewster he howled when he saw the goose approaching us but didn't move. He just sat there as quiet as a church mouse and perfectly content in his sheepskin coat, with no need for me to hold him.

"Then we were down and taxiing and tying up. And your friend Hilda Laubenstein was waiting to give Brewster his sedating shot. There it was, Sissy. I had done what I had set out to do and more and had found my way back to you and Sunny after all. That's what I call a successful trip. Don't you think so, Frank?"

Uncle Jake stopped and leaned his head back in pride and exhaustion and asked Sissy to bring something to put over me. Later, after Frank Morley had said good night to Sissy and started down the hill toward Guns & Locks & Clothes, the three of us sat silently in the darkness until we heard the whistle announcing the next shift at the mine. Then we watched the long single file of miners winding down the mountain trail, or rather watched the bright flickerings of the carbide lamps they wore on their hats. Sissy said that they looked like fireflies. Then, softly, she said that Uncle Jake was a noble man.

28 —

I awoke in the late night to the sound of their voices. Uncle Jake had been home three days from Disillusionment Bay and had already gone back to work on *The Prince of Wales*. Now it was the smallest hour of the night, and their voices—on edge, consoling, now loud, now soft, broken—were rising and falling beyond my door, shifting octaves like night breezes, and the very sound of their voices was filled with the dire consequences of what had happened in Disillusionment Bay. I sat up wide-awake and listened.

"... failure," Uncle Jake was saying. "Two months in Alaska and a failure. An abject failure."

"Oh Jake," said Sissy. "It's not so."

"Of course it is," said Uncle Jake.

"You did the best you could," said Sissy.

"It's my fault," said Uncle Jake. "It's all my fault. To think that I meddled in that poor woman's life and Too-Much Jackson killed her."

"It was bound to happen," came Frank Morley's voice, sad, dispirited, thick with his sleeplessness.

"No," said Uncle Jake. "I'm to blame. I can't kid myself any longer."

"Oh Jake," said Sissy, "please..."

"And you say that Rex is going down there tomorrow morning? With the Marshal?"

"That's the plan," said Frank Morley.

"And they didn't want me to go along."

"The Marshal's got his deputy, Jake," said Frank Morley. "Young Cuthbert."

"But they could have used another man," said Uncle Jake.

"I don't think so," said Frank Morley.

"All right," said Uncle Jake. "There's the Four-Hundred-and-Five. I'll go get the Four-Hundred-and-Five."

"Oh that's silly, Jake," said Sissy. "You know it is."

"I'll just take the Four-Hundred-and-Five!" came Uncle Jake's voice in a burst of rage, "and...use it! I'll just settle the whole thing! It's what I deserve."

"No," said Frank Morley. "You won't do that."

"Don't you see, Jake? You're hurting us," said Sissy. "You're just hurting us all."

"Good Lord, Sissy," said Uncle Jake. "I'm low. I'm as low as a man can get."

"Partner," said Frank Morley, and there was a long pause, "you've got to listen to old Frank Morley."

"But the poor woman," said Uncle Jake. "That poor woman."

"Jake," said Sissy, "you're an honorable man. You know you are."

"There was just no way to stop the thing," said Frank Morley. "It had to happen."

"I went down there," said Uncle Jake, "and failed."

"That's not the way to think of it," said Sissy.

"What about the Marshal? What's the Marshal going to say? Why, I'm probably an accessory to the crime!"

"No," said Frank Morley. "That fellow's got a reputation. I knew it was going to happen sooner or later."

"Good Lord," said Uncle Jake. "Jake Deauville involved in the scandal of a couple of Indians. Why, Sitka Charley warned me. Why didn't I listen? Sitka Charley told me to watch my step."

"No, Jake," said Frank Morley. "Charley just wanted you to be careful. For your own sake. He didn't want you to get stabbed in the back. That's what he meant. Charley's a Siwash, Jake. The Skoots don't mean a thing to him, dead or alive."

"It's a tragedy," said Uncle Jake, "that's what it is. A tragedy."

"Jake," said Sissy. "Please... We should send Frank home and try to get some sleep."

"I'm not going to sleep," said Uncle Jake. "Sleep is out of the question. At least for me."

"Don't worry," said Frank Morley. "We'll stay up with you. We'll work this thing out."

Silence. The sound of them moving about in our darkened living room. The smell of coffee. I sank back down on my bed, drifted off, came suddenly awake.

"... all right!" Uncle Jake was saying. "All right! We'll make amends!"

"Exactly," said Frank Morley.

"Here's what we'll do. We'll get that fellow acquitted."

"But he's guilty, Jake."

"If I'm going to make amends, then that fellow's got to be acquitted. Then we'll buy out Olafson and drive him and that wife of his right off that island and give the island back to the Skoots. They've got to have their burial ground, Frank. That's all there is to it. And the last thing we'll do is this: we'll make Sitka Charley our partner! We'll take Sitka Charley in with us, and make him our third partner! That ought to do it!"

There was a long pause. "He'll be pleased, Jake," said Frank Morley. "There's no one more loyal than Charley."

"And Jake!" exclaimed Sissy. "I'll help you work on *The Prince of Wales!* I'll become a sailor!"

"Sissy," said Uncle Jake, "you can be the skipper."

In the morning I found Uncle Jake and Frank Morley red-eyed at the kitchen table, and Sissy as bright as ever at the stove and heaping high the plates of her two men, as she now thought of them. Uncle Jake and Frank Morley were unshaven, careworn, relieved, and looked as if they had slept in their clothes. Sissy's face was pale and faintly puffy, but still she was a quick and vigorous cook in her clean kitchen though she burned the toast as she often did. A large blue platter, chipped and cracked, was already warming on the stove with fried eggs, bacon, sausage, corned beef hash, and fried potatoes enough for second and third helpings for her hungry men.

"Darling!" she exclaimed when I entered the kitchen, "good morning! Would you like some hot cakes this morning?"

"That's what she wants," said Frank Morley, using his knife to pile a mouthful of hash on the back of his fork, "a good mess of your hotcakes, Sissy, with Log Cabin syrup."

"Sunny," said Uncle Jake, "kiss the beard!... And Frank, as soon as you finish up we can go give Charley the news."

29 —

The murder that occurred in June of 1930 in White Eye, the Skoot village until then unknown even to most of the residents of Juneau, survived as a newsworthy event for several weeks, or until after the hanging of the culprit. For that short time it served to remind the residents of Juneau that theirs was still a frontier town. Townspeople and a few tourists who could not believe their luck packed Doug's and the Red Dog Saloon and the lobby of the Baranof Hotel and other public places, and raised their glasses and their voices and elaborated on the story, dressed it up, in Uncle Jake's vernacular, and argued about how exactly the lurid deed had been done and what sort of punishment would best fit the crime though they all knew that they were going to have their hanging. There were those who hazarded the opinion that the gossip would have been more worth their time had the murderer been the white fox farmer who lived down there, as the local newspaper and local radio station said, and had the victim been the native woman who was his wife. A murder committed by a drunken Indian was not so out of the way, whether or not they had ever heard of White Eye. Nonetheless a murder, any sort of murder, was not to be scorned, especially when everyone knew that Alaskan justice demanded two eyes for an eye, two teeth for a tooth. Juneau's nine hundred Indians kept off the streets.

Uncle Jake said that the whole thing was an outrage and went to bat, as he put it, for the accused. He stalked out of Doug's when he

saw three men sitting with their heads together and heard them ex-
claiming loudly in tones inappropriate to the gravity of the affair about
the doings in White Eye. He insisted that if there was nothing to be
done about the victim—and of course there was no helping that poor
woman—then it was all the more important to save the life of the
accused. He insisted that there had been extenuating circumstances and
even a provocation of sorts; he contended that the very fact that the
murderer was an Alaskan native was cause enough for the crime in the
first place and should be considered a strong factor in his defense. Day
after day Uncle Jake argued the case with Sissy and Frank Morley, who
were on his side and needed no persuading of the merits of what he
said, though they knew he was wrong. He had his tan suit pressed by
the only Asian tailor in Juneau, known to Uncle Jake as the Chink, and
in his most formal and handsome attire spent thirty minutes with the
Governor of the Territory of Alaska, who declined to act on the precepts
Uncle Jake brought forth. Uncle Jake then cabled his friend in Washington, requesting that the friend carry the case to the proper quarter
and intercede on the murderer's behalf. But his campaign was of no
avail. The date for the execution was set and Uncle Jake's determination
wavered in the face of his returning depression.

At last he admitted to Sissy and Frank Morley that he had lost the
battle; he had done all he could to force the powers that be, which is
what he called them, to spare the life of the White Eye Skoot. And the
terrible thing, he said, was that he had been in error and that it was
not the Skoots who had been so cruel and barbarous in the early days
of Alaska's history, but the Metlakatlas. The Skoots had always been
a kindly people. So this, said Uncle Jake, was one more failure to add
to the fiasco of his trip to White Eye. But Uncle Jake had a last card
up his sleeve and he would play this trump and would not be denied.
There was nothing left for him to do but to attend the execution. If he
could not be instrumental in mitigating the poor devil's sentence, at
least he, Uncle Jake, could be present to dignify the poor devil's death
and, in a sense, to share it. Uncle Jake made this announcement proudly;
Sissy and Frank Morley heard it in horror. Sissy and Frank Morley
reasoned and remonstrated and pleaded with Uncle Jake, but he held
firm. And Uncle Jake was true to his resolve. Thanks to a second cable
to his friend in Washington, he was told that he would be admitted to
the execution if he wished to attend it. Sissy and Frank Morley became
as dispirited as Uncle Jake.

The execution was to occur outdoors and adjacent to the Federal

Building, which contained a few offices, a small courtroom, and, in its basement, three cells, one of which was occupied by the condemned. Shortly before the day appointed for the execution, heavy tarpaulins were erected and arranged so as to form three high canvas walls behind which, and clumsily concealed from public view, the hanging could take place.

The designated dawn arrived. A crowd gathered outside the canvas walls. Uncle Jake performed his duty, as he saw it, and assumed his place among the handful of witnesses huddled inside the canvas walls. The crowd outside could see nothing, but they could hear, and they listened attentively, thus experiencing the execution aurally, from the last rites to the final thump of the sprung trap and fallen body. The rain had ceased moments before the hanging occurred and resumed even as the workmen were dismantling the scaffold and taking down the tarpaulins.

Uncle Jake was unable to sleep or eat or speak for three days following this primitive event, but finally allowed himself to be nursed back to confidence by Sissy and Frank Morley. He told them that he had been a stalwart witness, and had withstood the draining of the blood from his head, as others in the same predicament had not, and had not succumbed to vomiting as had the rest. He said that it had been the blackest day in his life and that he would not forget it for however few or many years he had remaining.

White Knight. White god with the soul of a Sundown warrior. Meddler.

30 —

No matter his claims to the contrary, Uncle Jake was proud of the havoc he had wreaked in White Eye, and of the way he had punished himself and made amends. Not many of his kind would act on principle as he had done; not many of his kind would welcome a Siwash Indian for a partner and, without any obligation whatsoever, or any function to perform, attend the hanging of a Skoot. Catastrophe and triumph were twins in the house of Fate, as he often said, and it took as much courage to cause the one as to earn the other. And *The Prince of Wales* was waiting.

As for Sissy, she was as true to her word as was Uncle Jake to his. She who had never touched a tool or been anywhere near the sea, except for her journey on the S.S. *Alaska,* rolled up her sleeves and learned to use hammer, saw, paintbrush, pliers. She swept the trash from the pilothouse of *The Prince of Wales,* hosed down its decks, set the galley to rights and hourly encouraged Uncle Jake to make his repairs. It was she who laughed and turned the hose on his hip boots whenever he climbed the rotted ladder covered with mud. It was she who made pitchers of lemonade for Uncle Jake, which he savored nearly as much as his ginger ale, and she who, with the help of Frank Morley, provisioned *The Prince of Wales* for her maiden voyage. Together they bought and stowed away six pounds of coffee, ten pounds of sugar, two dozen tins of Carnation milk, twenty-five pounds of flour, six pounds of butter, six dozen eggs, twenty-five pounds of potatoes, twelve loaves of bread, five T-bone steaks and four bars of yellow Lenox soap, which was not at all sufficient for the voyage, as Uncle Jake soon ruefully found out. And when Uncle Jake hired his crew— a wiry consumptive named French Pete as mate and a small fat filthy cook whom Uncle Jake nicknamed the Belly Burglar on the spot—it was Sissy who received those two into her house on the ridge above Juneau and charmed them in her living room and fed them in her kitchen until *The Prince of Wales* finally departed—though, as she confessed to Frank Morley, she was afraid of the consumptive and repelled by the cook. And it was she who saw them all off without crying.

"Do you know," said Frank Morley, as Uncle Jake headed the old black and white boat out into the channel and gave two toots on the whistle, "I believe that she's still listing."

31 —

Uncle Jake was reported missing. *The Prince of Wales* was assumed to have gone down. Uncle Jake had planned the maiden voyage to last eight days. On the twenty-ninth day since she had left port Frank Morley came up to High Ridge Street bearing a copy of the local newspaper that had appeared that morning. In Sissy's presence Frank Morley chided himself again for always bringing her bad news. But he knew that she preferred knowing the worst to having her feelings spared, and so he showed her the brief story in the local paper. "Fear for Safety of Juneau Men Long Overdue," the headline in small type on the back page read. There followed a short account, which Sissy read aloud though Frank Morley was already familiar enough with its contents, of how Jake Deauville, formerly of Sound Beach, Connecticut, along with Peter Barnou and Wesley Pitts, was long overdue at the Killisnoo Coal Mine. In a report to U.S. Commissioner J. F. Mullen from Purser David Ramsey of the *Estebeth,* the article went on to say, Ramsey said that Postmaster Frank Brandes at Angoon had been informed that the three men had left Juneau some time ago en route to the Killisnoo mine and were reported long overdue there. The watchman at Killisnoo reported no trace of the men, who were to have gone by way of William Henry Bay. Mrs. Deauville, the article concluded, is said to be living in Juneau.

"But of course I'm living in Juneau," said Sissy. "Don't they even know I'm living here? Why didn't they ask me?"

Frank Morley had no answer to her question.

"But what are we going to do, Frank? Is he lost?"

"He'll be all right," said Frank Morley. "That watchman at Killisnoo doesn't know what he's talking about. They weren't headed for Killisnoo, Sissy. You know that."

"But where are they, Frank?"

"Don't worry. They'll be all right."

"Oh Frank, I don't think those men he's got with him are any good. Will they come back?"

"Of course they will," said Frank Morley. "Don't worry."

It was at this time that Sissy began inviting her friend Hilda Laubenstein up to High Ridge Street for watery highballs, as Sissy called them, thus acquiring her second vice as she confided to Hilda. If Uncle Jake had known of Sissy's journal he would have found its pages studded with cheery references to highballs and cigarettes, except that Uncle Jake would not have read Sissy's journal even had he stumbled across its hiding place, which he never did. Long before her death Sissy jokingly confessed her vices to Frank Morley, who, much to his credit, did not betray her confidence to Uncle Jake.

32 —

"Get your hat!" called Frank Morley, who had just arrived unannounced on our veranda. "We're going down to the docks!"

"Oh Frank," said Sissy, hurrying to meet him, "he's back!"

"Well, no," said Frank Morley, "he's not back. But we're going down to the docks anyway. Where's Sunny?"

"Why, Frank," said Sissy, once again concealing her disappointment, "what is it?"

"You'll see," said Frank Morley, and stood by shyly watching as she hurriedly draped her coat across her shoulders.

"Sunny," called Sissy, "Frank's got a surprise!"

But I had been watching and listening from my bedroom and was catching hold of Frank Morley's hand before the words were out of Sissy's mouth.

Four days had passed since Frank Morley had come bearing the folded newspaper under his arm, and the weather had partially cleared. Now he was chuckling to himself over what he had in store for Sissy. He looked more than ever like a long-retired Colorado sheriff, with his old hat, collarless shirt, black vest and stooping back, and he kept eying

Sissy for signs that she knew that he was brightening her day.

There were six hundred wooden steps from the top of our ridge to the sloping streets of downtown Juneau, and we descended them as quickly as we could, making allowance for Frank Morley's arthritic joints.

"Oh look!" said Sissy. "The ship's in."

"She just docked," said Frank Morley.

"What do you think of that," said Sissy. "I didn't hear the whistle."

"Well, there she is," said Frank Morley. "The S.S. *Alaska.*"

"It seems so long ago, Frank," she said, and he understood what she meant.

The dock was empty when we arrived except for Patsy Ann lying in the sunlight wet and shivering, and a few aged stevedores beside a pile of skids and a little tractor.

"You know, Frank," said Sissy, "I don't like it down here. I don't like standing so close to a ship—isn't it an awful sight?—and to tell you the truth I don't like that poor dog. Oh Frank, there's nothing lonelier than a big ship in port."

"Cheer up," said Frank Morley. "They're getting ready to unload."

Winches began to turn and whine high above us on the deck of the *Alaska.* Booms swung into place and the nets of cargo rose into view, looking as if they would surely drop suddenly and shatter the very planks where we stood, and then slowly descended to the waiting skids. The dock shook, steam from the donkey engines hissed in the air, machinery clattered.

"Ah," said Frank Morley, "there it is."

Up from the dark hold of the ship came Sissy's prize, a single wooden crate shaped like a coffin and large enough to hold a horse, as Frank Morley said, and trapped up there and swaying in a cargo net suspended by an iron hook from the end of the rusty cable.

"Frank," said Sissy nervously, "what is it?"

"It's a present," said Frank Morley. "For you."

"For me?"

"Yes," said Frank Morley. "All the way from Seattle."

A lone voice called down from the deck of the ship; the indifferent stevedores steadied the all-but-lowered crate until it settled gently onto the dock. Patsy Ann turned her head toward the looming crate and began to whine. Frank Morley glanced at Sissy, who for her part was responding to the mystery as he had hoped she might—nervously and by standing close to him and putting her arm through his. Then to her further surprise there came the sound of an engine and the sight of a familiar pickup truck backing toward the two old men who were now leaning casually against the crate. The driver of the truck, the same fat early-morning beer drinker whom Sissy had enlisted to bring us fresh tanks of propane when we had first arrived in Juneau, climbed down and joined the stevedores and, under Frank Morley's direction, helped the men load Sissy's present into the bed of his truck.

"Frank," said Sissy, "you're the one who made all these arrangements. Aren't you?"

"Come on," said Frank Morley, "let's pile in with Karl and go up to the house for the unveiling."

Sissy expressed her concern that the pickup truck would not be able to manage the steep grade to High Ridge Street; she worried that the beer drinker and Sitka Charley, who was awaiting us when we arrived, would not be able to unload the crate; she laughed in fright when Sitka Charley applied his crowbar to the crate which filled the narrow space of our veranda.

"Charley," said Frank Morley. "Be careful."

"All the way from Seattle, Frank," said Sissy. "Think of that!"

Frank Morley nodded happily and told Sitka Charley to watch what he was doing.

"But it's awfully large, Frank," said Sissy. "Whatever it is."

Sitka Charley pried off another plank and the nails screeched, the plank groaned, Sissy shivered and drew her coat closer around her shoulders.

"Easy," said Frank Morley.

The sunlight flickered, the smell of impending rain was heavy on the summer air. We heard the distant roaring of waste rock from the Alaska-Juneau Mine being dumped into Gastineau Channel. Sitka Charley flung aside another plank and Sissy told me not to get in Sitka Charley's way. And Sissy, who did not like surprises and did not like change and who had already furnished our three rooms exactly as she wished them to be furnished, now stood girding herself to face the unavoidable fact that this crated object had lurched into her life from nowhere, Seattle or no Seattle, and in mere moments, her own wishes or interests notwithstanding, was to be lodged somehow inside her house. She had not been consulted. She could not think how to accommodate the bulky thing that was invading her home. Even I could see the look of alarm on Sissy's face.

Sitka Charley stepped back and wiped his cheek on his sleeve. Discarded planks and splintered boards lay everywhere, bent and pointed nails gleaming. Before us stood Sissy's gift strapped and swaddled in protective quilting. Frank Morley was perspiring as freely as was Sitka Charley.

"You didn't forget the wire cutters, did you, Charley?" asked Frank Morley.

"Poor Charley," said Sissy, "what a lot of work."

"Easy there," said Frank Morley. "Let me do it, Charley."

There was silence. The sun bathed us all in a burnt orange light.

"Oh Frank," said Sissy.

We waited.

"Oh Frank," said Sissy. "A piano..."

He nodded.

"A Steinway piano. Oh Frank."

Half-dead fir tree. The smell of rain. The orange light. And there, crowding our veranda, was Sissy's new piano, an upright model that was golden mahogany in color and highly polished. Silent in the wreckage of its crate, as pristine and massive as it had been on the showcase floor, there was Sissy's new piano awaiting the first quick touch of her fingers, her first crashing chord—this musical instrument that dwarfed our house in size and richness and had no place in Alaska.

"Do you like it?" asked Frank Morley.

She nodded. She clasped her hands.

"Jake said you needed a piano up here," said Frank Morley at last. "Of course Jake expected to be back by the time it arrived. He'll be disappointed that he wasn't. But he made sure that Charley and I could install the piano for you if he wasn't here."

He paused. He smiled at Sissy. The sun lit up the elk's tooth on its gold chain across his vest.

"So Jake wanted me to have a piano," said Sissy.

"Yes," said Frank Morley, "that's what he wanted."

"A Steinway," said Sissy.

"Yes," said Frank Morley. "He wrote down to Seattle for it. Weeks ago."

"And Frank," said Sissy, "it's not too large. It will go nicely in the corner beside the bookcase."

"The only one in Juneau," said Frank Morley. "Except for that old thing in the Presbyterian church and the one in the school."

"And do you know, Frank, I had an upright Steinway when I was a girl."

"I told him you'd be happy. Now you can play the piano as you did back east."

"Oh Frank," said Sissy, "thank you."

"No thanks to me," said Frank Morley. "But will you play for us?"

"Now? Today? Oh I can't do that, Frank," said Sissy. "It needs to be tuned, I'm out of practice, I didn't bring my music..."

"When you're ready," said Frank Morley. "Come on, Charley, let's move Sissy's piano indoors where it belongs."

Sissy cried herself to sleep that night, and the next morning awoke with wet eyes, red nostrils, sore lips, and in the certainty that now she was going to cry at night forever. She had cried, she knew, because Uncle Jake had given her a piano, and not because Uncle Jake was reported missing in the area of the Killisnoo Coal Mine, or because of anything else that had happened or was sure to happen. Frank Morley and Sitka Charley had left us with the piano. Darkness had finally come. Sissy was finally able to go to bed. But she could not sleep. She thought of Uncle Jake. She knew that she would not be able to bring herself to touch the piano for weeks to come. But lying in the darkness she heard herself playing silent music for the rest of her days in Alaska, and knew that that was all she had—the piano—and that she was doomed to solitary enjoyment of the music she had once loved, and would die alone in the midst of some sonata she had learned as a girl.

By the time Uncle Jake returned, a week later, Sissy had grown cheerfully accustomed to her grief and adept at concealing it.

33 —

"Juneau, Alaska. August 17, 1930. Last night cried myself to sleep as usual. Awakened 10 P.M. by Frank Morley. Jake down at the docks! Safe and sound! Bundled Sunny into her clothes and off for the rendezvous at Doug's. Jake ravenous. The other two drinking at Red Dog Saloon. Sunny sleeping on my lap in the booth. Salisbury steak for the three of us. My second dinner! Jake scoffed at story of 'Men Long Overdue.' Said David Ramsey and Frank Brandes were fools. Tied up whole time at mouth of Beardslee River. Engine trouble. No danger but harrowing nonetheless. Peter Barnou refused to follow orders. Wesley Pitts filthy the whole time. Cooked up everything in sight in first ten days. Fatter than ever. Whining. Jake showed them how to fish. Shot a deer. Constant trouble with Peter Barnou. *Estebeth* finally returned with much needed part for engine. David Ramsey failed to inform U.S. Commissioner of facts. No one with any brains but Jake.

"More coffee. More pie for Jake. Jake says he's fed up with Barnou. Get rid of him, says Frank. The Belly Burglar too, says Jake. I thank Jake for the Steinway. To bed at 2 A.M. Talk until dawn."

Sissy's journal, which she kept in her telegraphic style for five years, makes no further mention of the piano. But play it she did, in time to come, first from memory and then using sheet music she ordered from Seattle. She bought herself a chair and cushion and every afternoon she sat before the glossy keys and played. When Sissy took her place at the piano, she pushed up her sleeves and assumed the posture of the concert pianist, with spine straight and shoulders squared, as in a packed hall. Small and light though she was, nonetheless she most enjoyed striking sharp and shocking chords that made her chin and elbows quiver. She played the piano as she played tennis, like a man. Down would come both hands, driving, determined, and in the instant we would have the triumph of the shuddering chord and then the self-chiding little grimace for the one faulty note. There were days when she stopped at each mistake, days when she rushed over them. She was proud of how the thumb and little finger of both of her hands were jointed so that she could stretch them to encompass an entire octave in one easy blow, no matter that her hands were as thin and fragile as a child's. She was proud of her natural talent as a pianist. She was proud of the strength of her fingers and the way that she could turn the tips of them into little mallets, as she liked to say. So Sissy played the piano, full of chagrin that she had not fully appreciated its arrival, surprised that she had ever thought of herself as doomed to music, though she knew she was.

When the rains fell and the Taku Wind came up the channel at eighty miles an hour—Sissy's special fear was the Taku Wind—and when Uncle Jake was off on *The Prince of Wales* or allowing himself to be carried far and wide as an honored guest aboard the Coast Guard cutter *Haida,* as he sometimes did, Sissy fought back strenuously at the keys. She played on command for Frank Morley, hardly at all for Uncle Jake. Hilda Laubenstein, highball in hand, was her most appreciative audience.

Sissy did not die in the midst of a sonata with her little elephant whirling from its ribbon on her wrist. And she did not die alone. But the piano represented all that killed her.

34 —

"Good Lord," said Uncle Jake, frowning and returning the letter to the inside pocket of his suit coat, where he carried his papers, "Mother says that Robert McGinnis is having trouble and wants to come to Alaska. She says that it's up to me to help him."

"Who is Robert McGinnis?" asked Sissy.

"Oh he was some sort of buddy of poor Barney Lewis, that inventor friend of mine who took his own life. I never met the man."

"Well," said Sissy, "you mustn't disappoint your mother."

"But is this Robert McGinnis fit to live in Alaska? Not all men are, you know."

"Let's hope he is," said Sissy.

"Mother calls him Bobby. I'll never be able to call a grown man by such a name. I'll call him Robert. His wife's name is Annie."

"Oh," said Sissy, "he has a wife."

"So Mother says."

"Well," said Sissy, "it will be nice to have some new friends."

"I'm not so sure," said Uncle Jake.

But encouraged by Sissy, and pleased that his mother had sought his help, and fully aware that no favorite son ever denied his mother, Uncle Jake engaged in a lengthy correspondence with Robert McGinnis, and throughout the fall became increasingly interested in assuming responsibility for Robert McGinnis and his wife. The wet fog came down on Juneau, never to lift again as Sissy thought. One late September night the Taku Wind first blew, and no sooner had it struck with a sound of hammers crashing on our thin roof than Sissy cried out for Uncle Jake, who obligingly awoke and told her not to worry. The Taku Wind, he said, was the strongest wind in the world and colder than the glacier of the same name. But the Taku Wind, said Uncle Jake, wouldn't pull the house from its moorings, though it felt that way.

By October Sissy and Hilda Laubenstein had tired of double solitaire and had persuaded Frank Morley and Uncle Jake to join them in bi-weekly games of hearts, a card game that Uncle Jake played only with the greatest reluctance. Each month Uncle Jake waited until the S.S. *Alaska* had been in port long enough for the mail to have reached the post office, and then hurried down to his box to pick up the latest, as he put it, from Robert McGinnis, which Uncle Jake read to himself at once in the post office, and then aloud to Sissy, and then again aloud at the next game of hearts, the amusement he experienced in the post office mounting to the final moment when Sissy and Frank and Hilda put down their cards and listened. Uncle Jake said that McGinnis wrote a good letter but was the most finicky fellow he'd ever come upon. McGinnis, said Uncle Jake, wanted to know everything from the size of the Alaska-Juneau Mine to the price of eggs. And the worst thing was that the fellow couldn't make up his mind to come north even after all the time Uncle Jake had spent on his questions.

"We could tell him a thing or two about the weather," said Uncle Jake, laughing and ridding his hand of another heart. And three weeks later: "Listen to this!" cried Uncle Jake. "He wants to know about getting orthopedic shoes up here! Says he's got bad feet! That's a good one, eh Frank?"

"The poor man," said Sissy. "You mustn't make fun of him, Jake."

"Good Lord," said Uncle Jake, "he won't last a day up here, will he, Frank. If he ever condescends to join us."

"Does he say anything about his wife?" asked Sissy.

"No, he doesn't," said Uncle Jake, "but I don't know how she stands him."

Hilda Laubenstein told Sissy that she wished that they could drink their highballs in the presence of the men, which Sissy said was out of the question, and complained that Uncle Jake always won at hearts when he didn't even like the game. Sissy said that Uncle Jake was restless waiting for Robert McGinnis to make his appearance in Juneau, which was why he bragged so much about beating them all at hearts. Hilda, a tall and bony woman with outspoken legs and a head of hair the color of faded strawberries, said that she could not understand why Uncle Jake bombarded them all the time with Robert McGinnis. Sissy said that that was just his way.

"Well," Uncle Jake announced in the middle of their last Saturday night game in November, "he's booked his passage."

"Good for him," said Hilda.

"He's really coming?" asked Sissy, passing a saucer of cashew nuts to Frank Morley. "That's good news, Jake. You must be relieved."

"The *Alaska* gets in on the twenty-first of December," said Uncle Jake.

"In time for Christmas!" exclaimed Sissy.

"Frank," said Uncle Jake, as Hilda pushed back her chair and left the room, "this is what we'll do. We'll buy out Olafson, but instead of giving his island back to the Skoots we'll keep it and send McGinnis and his wife down there. We'll turn the McGinnises into fox farmers. How's that for an idea?"

"Oh Jake," said Sissy. "Do you think you should?"

"Fox farming isn't so difficult," said Frank Morley.

"A fox farmer," said Uncle Jake as Hilda returned, tugging at her skirt. "That'll fix him!"

•   •   •

Late on the afternoon of the twenty-first of December, a pitch-dark hour violent with wind and wet snow, Uncle Jake and Frank Morley met the *Alaska* and escorted Robert and Annie McGinnis to the Baranof Hotel. Uncle Jake was not back by the time Sissy had finished preparing her Spanish rice, the staple dish of my childhood, and when he did at last return he was alone.

"Why Jake," said Sissy, "what's the matter?"

He stood tall and dripping and white-faced in the center of our living room, where Sissy had set the table for seven instead of our usual three. He had long recovered from the aftermath of the White Eye incident but was now once again silent and staring. I wondered if he was going to threaten us again with the Four-Hundred-and-Five but he did not.

"Here," said Sissy, "let me have your things."

The house was shaking so badly that his empty rocking chair was rocking slightly and erratically of its own accord.

"Where are they?" asked Sissy.

"The Baranof," he said at last.

"They're not coming to dinner?"

"No," he said, and raised a hand to his face. "I didn't invite them."

"And Frank and Hilda are not coming?"

"No, they're not."

"But Jake," said Sissy, "what's the matter?"

Outside, there was nothing but darkness and a thin wet silt of snow. Inside, Sissy's empty table waited. I knew that her fear of the wind had fled before the shocking sight of Uncle Jake.

"Jake," she said. "Sit down. Won't you?"

He shook his head.

"What is it?"

He waited. He looked as if he might demolish the house, the three of us, the night itself if he so much as opened his mouth to speak. But then he spoke.

"They're deaf."

"What?"

"Stone deaf. The two of them."

"Oh Jake..."

"Orthopedic shoes," he said, black smoke curling around his slow enunciation of the word. "The fellow writes to me about orthopedic shoes when he's deaf. Stone deaf! I don't know what sort of fool he takes me for."

"And his wife too, Jake?"

"Both of them. Congenitally deaf since birth. And they can't talk either. At least not as an ordinary person talks."

"Can't talk?"

"Cleft palates. They were born with them. It relates to the deafness."

"How strange."

"Strange," Uncle Jake repeated bitterly. "I can't understand a word that woman says, that's how strange it is. He's a little better."

"But what are we going to do?"

"They read lips," said Uncle Jake, his anger visibly collapsing. "But I'd like to see anybody read lips on a shortwave radio. And can you imagine poor Frank trying to understand someone with a cleft palate on a radio? With all that static? Good Lord."

"But am I not to meet them, Jake? We mustn't be rude."

"Oh you'll meet them all right. On Christmas eve."

"With Frank and Hilda? That's lovely."

"A fine Christmas eve," said Uncle Jake. "And a pretty kettle of fish, I can tell you."

The wind did not abate. The snow fell and melted, fell and melted and froze. Christmas lights were strung around the totem poles in front of the Baranof. The stove in Guns & Locks & Clothes was fat and fiery. Not fifty paces from where Sissy smoked her cigarettes even when the weather was at its worst, Uncle Jake chopped down the largest spruce that he and I could find—Sissy was afraid of fire and wanted a little tree that she could stand on a table—and gathered armloads of thick green boughs which we tacked up everywhere inside the house. The day before Christmas eve Uncle Jake returned from downtown with two brown paper bags and grandly displayed their contents on the kitchen table.

"Liquor?" said Sissy, smiling and raising her eyebrows in mock alarm. "It's not like you, Jake."

"I'm going to make a punch," said Uncle Jake. "You and I won't drink it, needless to say. And I don't think Frank will either. But it might help."

"Just a sip?" asked Sissy. "It's Christmas."

Uncle Jake smiled and said that maybe she could have a drink of his Chain-Lightning Punch, as he had decided to call it, just to fortify herself against Robert McGinnis and that little wife of his.

.   .   .

The Taku Glacier. The Taku Wind. Frank Morley, whose soft arms
and sunken chest had become nearly as familiar to me as Uncle Jake's
embrace. Hilda Laubenstein with her Red Cross pin and cherry lipstick
and her legs of a Juno, as Uncle Jake had described them more than
once for the sake of the pun. (I liked nothing better than sitting backwards on Hilda's lap during their games of hearts and leaning forward
and bracing my hands on her stockinged knees, all the while feeling
her warm flesh shifting beneath me as she concentrated on her cards.)
And Sitka Charley, who told me legends of the Siwash tribe. And the
knife he had given me. And my boots and belt. What were they? What
were they all compared with a man who could read lips and could not
talk?

By Christmas eve of 1930 I thought of nothing but Robert McGinnis.
I longed only to see Robert McGinnis. The more Uncle Jake had read
aloud from his letters and had worried about him and had scoffed at
him in the presence of Frank Morley and Hilda Laubenstein, the more
devoted I had become to the man who was surely like no other. Now
for three days and nights Uncle Jake had denounced the deafness of
Robert McGinnis, and now I wanted to see Robert McGinnis's shoes
but more to watch his eyes while he read my lips. I was convinced that
he would be powerful, round-shouldered, bearlike, this man who was
worthy of the tirades of Uncle Jake. I was convinced that I would
recognize on his face the marvels of his infirmities. Uncle Jake had said
that Robert McGinnis talked like an animal caught in a trap, and I
wanted most of all to hear those sounds, to see the great head turning,
to touch the hair on his hands. Sitka Charley had declined Sissy's invitation to dinner on Christmas eve. But the deaf man would be our
guest that night. What more could I ask?

Sissy wore her apron and her dark green dress and the string of pearls
that Uncle Jake had given her shortly before their marriage. Hilda, who
had just arrived with Frank Morley, wore a dark blue velvet dress that
set off her red hair and showed her knees. Frank Morley had had a
haircut and was wearing black trousers, a leather vest, a new green
shirt and a western-style tie consisting of a rawhide lanyard looped
through a disk of hammered silver. Uncle Jake, who had already gone
down to get the McGinnises, had donned his navy blue suit and white

shirt and blue polka-dotted tie for the occasion. As for me—the important one, as Uncle Jake had begun to call me—I was wearing a red dress, black shoes, a red hair ribbon, and smelled of Sissy's perfume which she had daubed behind my ears. Thus our finery for the festive season and for our special guests, and now the Taku Wind was performing at its best, as Uncle Jake had said before setting off for the Baranof, and we were more than ever safe from the winds of night with our red-hot kitchen stove and kerosene heater and our spruce boughs and the spicy scent of the two tinned hams and rice casserole that Sissy was baking in the faulty oven.

"Well," said Hilda, standing with her back to the heater and hiking up her skirt, "where's the Oaf?"

"Jake's getting them now. But Hilda," said Sissy, and laughed in spite of herself, "you mustn't call that poor man an oaf. What a terrible thing!"

"Jake calls him the Oaf. So I call him the Oaf," said Hilda.

"But Jake's terrible," said Sissy. "It isn't nice."

"McGinnis was in the store today," said Frank Morley. "Nearly bought me out. On Jake's credit."

"Oh dear," said Sissy.

"He's not a bad sort," said Frank Morley. "I catch every tenth word or so."

"Flatfooted," said Hilda. "And deaf and dumb, for God's sake. I can't wait to see him."

"We don't know a thing about him," said Sissy. "Be kind, Hilda."

"He's unusual," said Frank Morley. "I'll say that much."

"Frank," said Sissy. "You got a haircut!"

"Clippers," said Hilda, and put her hand on Frank Morley's arm.

"Frank looks beautiful," said Sissy. "You do, Frank."

They laughed, all three of them. But I was the important one who waited, content to admire the heady smell of the barber's lotion on Frank Morley's skin, and to admire the sight of Sissy's pearls, and to admire Hilda's red hair, which she was wearing loosely up like one of the Baranof women, and content to wait in the luxury of Sissy and Hilda and Frank Morley for Robert McGinnis. The Oaf, the Oaf, the Oaf, I said to myself and smiled at my reflection in the rattling and banging window.

"Oh," said Sissy, "they're here!"

The wind at the door. Three wet figures out of the night. Confusion. Introductions. Robert McGinnis blinking vacantly behind his fogged-

up eyeglasses and sniffing the aroma of the brown sugar melting on
the baking ham.

"Come in, come in," repeated Uncle Jake. "Nearly couldn't make
it up the hill, Sissy. That old Taku Wind."

Sissy and Hilda took their coats. Frank Morley blocked my view.

"Sunny," said Uncle Jake, and I went to him. "This is Sunny. She's
the important one around here."

"Say hello to Mr. McGinnis," said Sissy.

And there he was and there I was at last. And though Uncle Jake
was saying something to Sissy, and though off to my left there were
muffled nasal sounds as of someone trying to speak while being
gagged—it was Annie McGinnis asking Hilda Laubenstein a question—and though I was aware of Sissy rushing off to tend her stove,
and vaguely saw that Frank Morley had taken out his tobacco sack
and orange packet of cigarette papers, nonetheless I was suddenly
alone, completely alone with the man who was like no other. I looked
up at him. I opened my mouth. I thought of my lips. I could not
speak. And to my overwhelming joy I found that I could not hear
either. Deaf! I said to myself, as deaf as a stone like Robert McGinnis!
In the silence only we two could know, I stared at him, and Robert
McGinnis was all I had hoped he would be and more. He was short,
compared with Uncle Jake, with a chest as big around as a barrel,
and with shoulders fatter and broader than Uncle Jake's, and with
legs that were thick and twisted, as if he had never quite learned
how to stand on them. His head was round, he had no neck that I
could see, his hair was short-cropped and bristling—like the hair of
a German uncle, Jake said when the night was over—and his round
face was so pushed in that I longed to run my fingers over all the
wonder of his great sunken face. He had visited Guns & Locks &
Clothes as Frank Morley had said, and had especially dressed himself
tonight in his bright new woolen shirt and tight new pants and
gleaming boots laced to his heavy knees.

"Good Lord," I heard Uncle Jake say distantly, as my hearing returned like the clap of a hand, "what a get-up. Where does he think
he is? In a logging camp?"

"Hush, Jake," came Sissy's voice, "they'll hear you."

"Nonsense," said Uncle Jake. "I'm not looking at them."

But I had seen Uncle Jake when he himself had first worn such
clothes, and now I knew what Robert McGinnis looked like: a bulging
Uncle Jake, an enigmatic Uncle Jake, an Uncle Jake even readier to

show off his new hunting clothes than Uncle Jake had ever been. I could smell the camphor in Robert McGinnis's new clothes; I saw the tiny eyes behind the little round misted lenses; I saw the battered ears that could not hear. I watched as the bulldog face inclined toward mine, watched as the crushed mouth began to move, listened as the face worked and the guttural high-pitched sputtering commenced.

"Important," was the word embedded in the veils of his strange speech. "Important... one!" And Robert McGinnis was laughing down at me, laughing rather than speaking, and I too was laughing.

"All right, everyone!" exclaimed Uncle Jake in a voice unnecessarily loud, "now I'm going to make Jake Deauville's Chain-Lightning Punch! Gather round!"

Sissy, Hilda, Frank Morley, and Annie McGinnis formed a little circle at the table where Uncle Jake stood before his array of bottles and a bowl he had borrowed from the desk clerk at the Baranof Hotel. Majestically he unstoppered the bottles, seized a small tumbler, and with a flourish prepared to concoct for the first time his famous celebrative drink. Then he paused, tumbler and one of the bottles raised, and glanced significantly at Sissy.

"Punch," she said, hurrying over to Robert McGinnis, who was still standing with his hands behind his back and laughing down at me. "Punch," she repeated, anxiously enunciating the word as clearly as she could though in a whisper. He stared at her, agreeably baffled, and then allowed himself to be led to the table.

"Chain-Lightning Punch," said Uncle Jake, "requires one pint of brandy, one pint of Hudson Bay rum, one pint of blended rye whiskey, and six quarts of ginger ale. How does that sound, Frank? And then you give it a shot of Tabasco and a shot of gin and two cups of sugar and a packet of dried mint leaves for good measure. And let me tell you," he said, speaking suddenly to Robert McGinnis, who grunted eagerly, "this punch can't be made anywhere except in Alaska!"

So Uncle Jake poured and stirred and laughed while the bowl filled and his little party crowded around him and urged him on. Respectfully they accepted their sparkling tumblers, carefully they drank.

"Everything but the kitchen sink!" cried Uncle Jake, looking directly at Robert McGinnis, who was smiling at the golden chain sagging across Frank Morley's vest. "What's that he says?" asked Uncle Jake, turning to Sissy. "I can't make him out. Not a word, Sissy!"

"Elks," whispered Sissy. "He says that he belongs to the Elks like Frank."

"Well, ask him what he thinks of the punch. He may be good at reading lips, but he can't read mine. And remember, Sissy, just a sip of this stuff. It's strong enough to knock down a moose."

"Jake," said Hilda, putting her arm around his waist, "I like your punch. You ought to make it more often."

"Once a year," said Uncle Jake stiffly, "is enough."

"Back home in Colorado," said Frank Morley, "my father used to make what he called his Black Tar Punch for Christmas. It was good, but not as good as your punch, Jake."

"Go easy on it, Frank. It's bad medicine."

Just then we who were capable of hearing heard a crash from the kitchen. The wind stopped, the talking stopped, we heard the unmistakable sharp crack of breaking china and a faint cry. Then Uncle Jake led Hilda and Frank Morley off on another medley of conversation, as if there hadn't been two small alien sounds to disrupt the rhythms of his Christmas eve. I alone acknowledged the interruption and in the kitchen I found Sissy on her hands and knees beside the smashed and still steaming casserole. Shards. Rice. Lopsided rings of pineapple.

"Darling," she said, looking up at me, "I dropped the casserole. Do you want to help?"

I squatted, she wiped her forehead with her arm.

"The important thing," she said, "is to be sure we get out all the pieces."

But newspaper? A sheet of newspaper? Yes, there it was, the sheet of newspaper which she had seen and had impulsively spread flat on the floor where she was kneeling—in her effort to remain calm, in her effort to salvage the casserole, in her effort to get the meal on the table, a phrase that was never far from Sissy's mind. And now with her bare hands she was busy sorting out the wreckage—rice and pineapple on the newspaper, bits of china in a separate pile on the floor.

"Just scoop up the rice," she said, "and pick out the broken pieces. And let's hurry, darling. We don't want them to catch us like this, do we?"

By the time we had emptied the contents of the newspaper into another dish and had put one of the baked hams on a platter and had carried everything to the living room, Frank Morley was looking helplessly at Uncle Jake and holding a half-filled glass, and Uncle Jake was freshening the punch with another pint of Hudson Bay rum.

"Oh no," said Sissy to Annie McGinnis as if she could perfectly understand the small woman's new burst of nasal agitation, "there's nothing you can do to help. There isn't, really."

Somehow Sissy got us into our places while Uncle Jake stood at the head of the table and with his thumb tested the blade of first one knife and then the other.

"Sissy," he said, "these knives..."

"I've done my best, Jake. They'll have to do."

Elaborately Uncle Jake began to sharpen the knives against each other like crossing swords. Robert McGinnis watched attentively, the sweat standing out on his brow, as if he could hear the singing of the flashing blades as well as I could.

The table was small, the glazed ham had shrunk, the seven of us were crowded together thighs and elbows and shoulders. And the ham, half hidden behind the punch bowl which no one had bothered to remove, was all but lost in a forest of dark and deadly tumblers and Sissy's candles on chipped saucers. Uncle Jake could not have known what had happened in the kitchen. And yet he was no more immune in his way than Sissy was in hers from the infectious spirit of unease that the McGinnises, in all their innocence, had brought to this Christmas eve. Now Uncle Jake leveled a long knife between the tumblers, the candles, the fat-lipped china mugs. A sudden pinging of steel on glass. A falling tumbler. Uncle Jake stabbed at the ham with his bone-handled fork and away skittered the ham off its platter and across the table as if determined to land in Hilda's lap.

"Jake," said Sissy, "are you all right?"

"A drop too much," said Hilda. "Here, let me help."

"You know I'm a teetotaler, Hilda," said Uncle Jake. "But these knives are dull, Sissy. Dull!"

Frank Morley served himself more punch. Annie McGinnis, whose face was as narrow and wrinkled as a baked potato, was shaking her head and going on at a great rate with her watery incomprehensible advice. Sissy was fanning herself with a paper napkin. And Robert McGinnis was nodding encouragement to Uncle Jake while at the same time furtively conversing in the language of the manual alphabet with his little wife. How swiftly and mysteriously their fingers moved! How eloquent the speech no one else could hear or read!

"Oh dear," said Sissy, "I wonder what they're saying."

Then Uncle Jake put down his fork, surveyed the table—with disdain? chagrin? bemusement? anger?—and slowly reached out his hand and, looking not at his hand but at Robert McGinnis, seized the unruly ham in a firm grip. Frank Morley groaned. Faster went Robert

McGinnis's fingers, voluble became his grunting. Sissy gasped and Hilda, our brazen judgmental Hilda, leaned slowly and sedately forward toward the captive ham. And slowly, all eyes on hand and ham, Uncle Jake tightened his grip, the juices of the red meat and the crusty glaze of the brown sugar oozing up between his fingers and around his rings—his wedding band, his Deauville signet ring—and in long deft revengeful strokes began to carve. And carve he did, never relinquishing his hold on the now hapless ham, and suddenly, squirming as I was beside Uncle Jake, hardly able to contain my child's pleasure at this new sign of the unexpected, suddenly I wanted Uncle Jake to lick his fingers and to allow me to put my own small hand where his had been. I wriggled, I laughed, I watched as Uncle Jake held Hilda hypnotized while he stared straight at Robert McGinnis as if there were no other way in the world to carve a ham. Uncle Jake could do whatever he wanted to do—so said the dripping knife, the ruthless greasy hand which he himself ignored.

They passed the plates. Sissy trembled as she served the rice. Frank Morley talked about shooting wild turkeys in Colorado. Hilda looked long and quizzically at Uncle Jake as she ate, chewing each bite of the red ham slowly and licking her lips.

"Robert!" Uncle Jake exclaimed halfway through the meal, turning sideways and crossing his knees, a habit that Sissy particularly disliked, "the main thing about Alaska is its bigness. Isn't that right, Frank? Big glaciers. Big mountains. Big men. Alaska's no place for the puny nursling! Why, weaklings go mad up here or die. Alaska's blizzard freezes a fellow's heart, her long cold nights chill the brain. You fellows from back east don't know what you're in for, Robert. Only the biggest, strongest, bravest, smartest men survive up here.

"Up here the call of the moose at twilight rings in your ears. You smell the dark undergrowth of ancient forests. You meet a snarling grizzly on an empty trail in the silent north. But the main mood up here, Robert, is desolation and death, I can tell you—"

"Jake," said Sissy, gently interrupting him, "I think Hilda needs more ham."

"Desolation and death," continued Uncle Jake undaunted. "Why, the very names of our grand mountains tell the story. Starvation Peak. Death's Head Rock. Poverty Point. Mount Weariness. Mount Disappointment. Mount Despair. Not to mention our bays, our lakes, our inlets—hopeless bodies of water, all of them."

"Jake," said Sissy, more anxiously, "he can't hear you."

"Death," said Uncle Jake, as Hilda slowly looked at Sissy, and Robert McGinnis wagged his head, "up here death isn't the way it is back east. Up here we don't have some alcoholic weakling like your friend Barney Lewis drowning himself off the prow of a pretty twelve-foot sailboat in a quiet little cove in Connecticut. I'm not talking about the death of weaklings. I'm talking about Alaskan death, Robert, death as big and important as this Territory itself. Why, up here a fellow's winding sheet is a whole winter of icy snow. The howl of the wolf dog is the howl of death. Hardship. Privation. Misfortune. Up here a fellow dies in a gulch filled with skunk cabbage or on some bare and lonely mountain. Up here, Robert, we respect the death that awaits us on the heart-breaking way to failure or in a nameless grave. Up here a man embraces death. He walks along, he mushes along, he crawls along until he stops. Then someone else, years later, gaunt and near death himself, finds the first man's note tacked to a tree: 'Hell can't be any worse than this trail,' says the dead man's note. 'I'll try it.'

"In Alaska, even the man whose courage finally dies," said Uncle Jake, staring at Robert McGinnis, "and has no other recourse but to take his own life—why, even this man knows what he's doing. He doesn't just drink half a quart of whiskey and then, with a silly grin on his face, drown himself while his unsuspecting wife and little son lie sleeping in the dawning light of what that new day holds in store for them. The Barney Lewises of this world are not welcome in Alaska, I can tell you that. Up here we don't tolerate weakness, Robert, of any kind. . . ."

Sissy stood up abruptly as Frank Morley steadied her vacated chair and Hilda pushed herself back from the table. Both McGinnises were staring at Uncle Jake. Gone was Annie's incomprehensible monologue; in turn she looked from host to husband and back to her speech-making host, crushed by the dark passion of her handsome host and frightened by the wrinkles of delight that were disfiguring still further her husband's round and oddly unformed face. In this moment of silence, and in his excitement, Robert McGinnis shoved aside his plate and, with a sound as of bubbles hotly bursting, eagerly agreed, it seemed, with all that Uncle Jake was saying, which Uncle Jake had certainly not expected. As for Frank Morley, never had he been so excluded from Uncle Jake's attention, never had his eyes been so dim with sad love for his partner.

"Hilda," said Sissy quickly, "I think we had better clear off the things."

"Jake," said Frank Morley, "have you heard what's going on over at Rangoon?"

But Uncle Jake was not to be deterred.

"Now let me ask you a question," he said, ignoring Frank Morley and Sissy and the little deaf woman and Hilda Laubenstein, who was gently leaning down to extricate the platter of now cold and half-carved ham from where it sat like a sullen island in the litter of the meal, "just let me ask you this question. Do you know anything about foxes?"

Sissy and Hilda fled to the kitchen, Frank Morley tried again to intervene, and the house shook and the green boughs crowded in upon us and the immense spruce tree, its ornaments and strings of popcorn all atremble, swelled and glittered and filled the room as if ready at any moment to burst into flame.

"Two hundred foxes," declared Uncle Jake, "are a lot of foxes. You've got to grow potatoes—lots of potatoes—to supplement their diet of birds' eggs and the mice that overrun your island. You've got to keep your foxes from being frightened. The least thing and they go out of their heads with fright and kill each other—and for each dead fox we lose about eight hundred dollars. And then you've got to keep those foxes from eating their young, which means you've got to keep a few good cats around and give the young foxes to the cats to rear. The cats won't eat the baby foxes. Then there are the poachers. The Skoots down there are not beyond rowing over in the dark and stealing a couple of foxes—sixteen hundred dollars!—and there are Swedes who'll come two hundred miles to raid your place. Some night you'll hear them—in your case feel them in your bones, I guess—and you'll know that they've come ashore and are creeping up on your foxes. Then you've got to trust your dogs and the Winchester you'll just have to learn to shoot. Oh, every six months we'll be down there with your provisions. And once a year you'll do your trapping and your killing and your skinning and we'll be there to bring back the pelts. That's when you'll see your fellow man—two times a year—since you better keep away from those Skoots in White Eye, I can tell you that. But at least you'll have Annie down there. And your dogs and cats. And the foxes. Why, the foxes get so tame you'll end up keeping three or four of them right there in the cabin with you, along with the cats, though even the tamest fox can give a fellow a pretty nasty bite. But the thing about those foxes of yours—ours, really—is that they're blue. Blue foxes. Not red as you probably thought all this time but blue. It's the blue color—the pale and silky blue of one of our Alaskan lakes in summer—that brings those handsome prices.

"Mother might not have mentioned fox farming," said Uncle Jake, raising his chin and showing his teeth, "but you'll make a go of it. Anyhow, she sent us the fare for your return passage just in case."

Then suddenly Robert McGinnis began to move. While Sissy and Hilda hovered in the kitchen doorway—Sissy smaller than ever in her green dress and the apron she had forgotten to remove, Hilda hot and heavy in her blue velvet gown and smiling crookedly—and while Frank Morley blinked and Annie McGinnis squeezed shut her eyes and Uncle Jake stopped talking, clearly taken aback, slowly Robert McGinnis pushed himself up from the table. Awkwardly he bulged in his red shirt, perspiring and shrouded in the fumes of the Chain-Lightning Punch. Heavily he stood peering down at Uncle Jake. Clumsily he worked his shoulders, his fat hands, his tiny eyes, looking for all the world, as Uncle Jake said later, when we three were at last alone, like the ghost of His Unholiness come back to haunt the man who had shot him. Robert McGinnis was struggling with himself to refrain from touching Uncle Jake or to summon the courage to embrace him. He struggled, he beamed, his mouth disappeared beneath its sputtering.

"Oh," said Sissy weakly, "he can't get the words out, Jake. He's going to do something."

It was embrace, the tenderest embrace that Robert McGinnis had in mind because helpless in the very tangle of himself, and too overwhelmed, too overwrought, too frustrated to pursue any longer his attempts to express himself directly to his rigid host, now Robert McGinnis turned away from host and table and lumbered in a few steps to Sissy's piano. And still swaying and lumbering, Robert McGinnis sat down at Sissy's piano, exposed the keys, and grandly, liltingly, lovingly played the golden Steinway for Uncle Jake. Stars in motion, dominoes falling, pebbles shifting beneath a clear stream—on he went, and on, up and down the icy scales with stubby fingers as light and nimble as Sissy's fingers, and in all the continuum of his chords and trills not one mistake, not one wrong note, only the misshapen paws tumbling about the keyboard, the clear notes sounding. At the end of every measure he glanced furtively and happily over his shoulder at his coldly smiling host. And played on.

"Schumann," whispered Sissy, leaning toward Uncle Jake, "deaf and playing Schumann! I do believe he's serenading you! How lovely!"

"Well," said Uncle Jake, indifferent to Sissy's closeness and oblivious to Hilda Laubenstein's warm hand stroking his cheek, "I wish he'd stop!"

35 —

Early the next morning, Christmas morning, the left side of Sissy's heart-shaped face was as swollen as the rounded flesh of a hard-boiled egg fresh from its shell.

"Toothache," she said apologetically as I cupped my hand to her swollen cheek and Uncle Jake struggled into his trousers.

"The luck that that fellow has brought us," said Uncle Jake.

"It's not his fault," said Sissy.

"That man," said Uncle Jake, buttoning his crumpled white shirt of the night before and hurriedly adjusting his blue suit coat but forgetting his tie, "that man is the reincarnation of His Unholiness."

"Oh Jake, he's not," said Sissy.

"The reincarnation of His Unholiness. Come back to haunt me."

"You'll soon be rid of him," said Sissy. "But could we hurry, Jake? It hurts."

"Don't worry," said Uncle Jake, unshaven and white-faced in the darkness, "we'll rouse out Doc Haines and have you fixed up in no time at all."

"I hope he doesn't have to pull the tooth," said Sissy in a voice as muffled as Annie McGinnis's and holding her hand to her mouth.

"He'll do nothing of the sort," said Uncle Jake. "We just want it filled."

"Let's hurry, Jake."

"Good Lord," said Uncle Jake, reaching for his camel's hair coat but forgetting his hat, "I haven't even wished this child a merry Christmas!"

He hugged me then but his skin was cold, his movements brusque, his breath filled with agitation. Uncle Jake prided himself on his ability to bear pain. He was generally untouched by the suffering of others and openly contemptuous of his own personal injuries no matter how severe, and in Alaska some of his injuries were, as he called them, beauts. He liked nothing better than peril and pain; he thrived on mayhem; rattling sabers and bloody decks were just the thing for him since his days in the Great War. He was good at extricating the near-dead from their wreckage; there was no analgesic strong enough, he bragged, to subdue his senses, so acute they were, and hence to afford him the slightest relief from pain. But he did not want relief from pain. He did not want to be spared the pain of others. He thought that pain's position in the general order of things was privileged, and he welcomed it at every turn, on every hand. Except in the case of Sissy. Sissy's smallest hurt meant chaos of the most appalling sort to Uncle Jake, meant sweat and flaring nostrils and wild eyes. Uncle Jake was infatuated with his own ills and the ills of mankind, yet had no tolerance at all for even minor discomfiture in Sissy. He did not wish to know about her ailments, he could not bear to listen to her complaints. He spoke readily of this odd failing of his and was quick enough to declaim to friends, acquaintances, and sometimes to strangers as well that his wife's pain was the only pain in the world that he could not stand, except for his daughter's.

So now Uncle Jake led us off into the darkness and wet snow—the wind had died in the night—more bent on relieving his own anxiety than Sissy's pain, driven more by his own dramatic urgency than by Sissy's muffled request for haste, which he had by now forgotten. Down we went into the dark pit that was the sleeping town, and through the narrow streets until at last Uncle Jake stopped us before a three-story wooden building on a back alley behind the Baranof Hotel and declared that here the dentist lived and conducted his practice, unless the wretched building had a creaky twin in another back alley more sinister than the one in which we were now standing.

"Here?" asked Sissy through the scarf she had wrapped around her face.

"Yes," said Uncle Jake. "On the second floor if it's the right place."

Uncle Jake had already climbed the slippery outside stairway to the middle porch and, as we hurried after him, was pounding on the darkened door and stamping his feet. We waited. A light went on.

"Doc," said Uncle Jake when the door finally opened, "we've got an emergency here. Can you help us out?"

"What's the trouble?" asked young Doc Haines.

"My wife," said Uncle Jake. "She's in agony."

"So I see," said Doc Haines as Sissy lowered her scarf and gazed forlornly at the dentist, who, without bothering to dress—he was wrapped in a crimson robe and had a face like a penny though he was not yet fully awake—took Sissy by the arm and escorted her through the empty waiting room and directly into his office. For a moment we saw poor Sissy seated in the electric chair, as Uncle Jake scornfully called it, before Doc Haines closed the door.

"Good Lord," exclaimed Uncle Jake, "I wish he'd turn on the heat."

Bare plaster, an overhead bulb, a large dead kerosene heater white with frost—such was the room where I sat and listened to the youthful voice beyond the closed door and Uncle Jake paced up and down composing himself for the ordeal.

"...Cecily," we heard the dentist say, and Uncle Jake stopped, frowned, turned up his collar and thrust his hands into the pockets of his camel's hair coat.

"Why, he's using her first name," said Uncle Jake. "Her first name just because I bought his boat? There's nerve for you, Sunny. And that fellow's the only dentist in all of Juneau. They say he's good but I have my doubts."

We waited, we watched our breaths, the first gray light of morning appeared in the window.

"...afraid?" came the young dentist's voice, and then, "I'm going to use laughing gas, Cecily, and we'll take our time."

"If he hurts her..." threatened Uncle Jake vaguely, facing the window. "And I tell you, Sunny, I don't like the sound of that laughing gas. What's the fellow up to anyway?"

It was then that a woman wearing only a nightgown, fluffy slippers, and a crimson robe to match Doc Haines's robe entered the waiting room from the hall, smiled at Uncle Jake, wished me a merry Christmas, and, producing a box of matches from her bathrobe pocket, stooped down and lit the kerosene heater.

"Smokes at first," she said, indicating the heater, "but it'll be hot as Hades in here soon enough."

Uncle Jake inclined his head at the smiling woman. A machine began to whine in the other room.

"Is the little girl's mother in there with Doc?" asked the woman, soothing her crimson flanks and listening to the little angry sound of the machine.

"That's right," said Uncle Jake. "My wife."

"I hope it's not too bad," said the woman.

"Oh," said Uncle Jake, watching the woman's hands and forcing a smile, "I don't think it's going to be too bad."

". . . wider, Cecily, wider," came the nice young voice beyond the door.

"Well," said the woman, "we know each other from the Baranof. Don't you remember?"

"Why, of course," said Uncle Jake with a sudden laugh. "You're Nancy!"

"Yes," said the woman, "I'm Nancy. The last time I saw you and your little girl I was wearing curlers. Now I'm not even dressed."

"But it's hardly morning," said Uncle Jake. "I guess I woke you up with my pounding."

"Just so you don't think that I look too indecent," said the woman, stooping again to the heater, adjusting a knob, brushing at the sooty smoke with a fluttering hand. Now the kerosene heater appeared to demand her full attention; from the waist she bent down to it and waited, tightly sheathed in her crimson robe. And now the intensifying heat and brightening glow of the burning kerosene appeared to issue not from the old and dripping heater but from the broad red haunches of the stooping woman herself. Uncle Jake stared uncomprehendingly and then looked away.

". . . good girl!" came the voice of young Doc Haines as the minuscule ripsaw sound of a second machine joined the whine of the first, "you're doing fine."

"I tell you," said Uncle Jake abruptly, "I just can't stand her pain!"

"It's harder on you than it is on her," said Nancy, who had given up stooping at the heater and now stood facing Uncle Jake like a great and glorious tulip in waxy bloom. With both hands she was drawing closed her robe and all at once concealing from chin to toe the florid filigrees of lace which Uncle Jake had already seen with only a minimum of discomfort.

A smell of disinfectant seeped around the edges of the closed door. We heard a faint cry.

"Good Lord," said Uncle Jake, scowling and bracing himself as between invisible pillars, "what's going on in there? What's he doing?"

"Listen," said Nancy, "maybe your little girl would like a cup of hot milk."

"Perhaps," said Uncle Jake slowly, "perhaps it would be better if you just stayed with us until we've seen this thing through."

"Gladly," said Nancy and smiled, tucked herself still more securely inside her robe.

A sound as of a pedaling bicycle shook the closed door. Then stopped. And again we heard the faint cry and then a rapid clicking of switches, a sudden upward surging of the cruel duet of the other two machines.

"He must be ripping out every tooth in her poor head!" cried Uncle Jake.

"Now, now," said Nancy.

"Well," said Uncle Jake, "have you ever seen a grown man faint? Have you?"

"You ought to keep moving," said Nancy, putting her arm through Uncle Jake's. "Let's walk awhile."

"Wait!" cried Uncle Jake in a sudden new spasm of alarm. "What's that?"

Silence as of a fallen blade. Silence awaiting only the victim's cry. Uncle Jake took a step toward the closed door, Nancy hung back on his arm. We listened. At last there came the ring of a spidery steel instrument against a porcelain tray. Then the gentlest undertones of the young dentist's most soothing words. And then faintly, unmistakably, the prolonged and silvery quavering of Sissy's voice.

"She's laughing!" exclaimed Uncle Jake, shaking off Nancy's hand and facing the door. "My wife's in there and laughing!"

"You see," said Nancy, "Doc Haines wouldn't hurt a hair on her head."

"Nonsense," said Uncle Jake. "It's just that infernal laughing gas. She's in pain, I tell you!"

"Well, it doesn't sound that way to me," said Nancy.

"Listen to her," said Uncle Jake. "Why, that fellow has made some sort of mistake. He's pierced the gum! He's shot right through to the root! My wife wouldn't be laughing in that crazy way if she weren't suffering. Don't you hear it?"

Suddenly, as if Doc Haines had replaced a fuse, which indeed he had as Sissy told us later, the now three machines began to pulse and probe while Sissy's laughter rose to gay heights, subsided to low and throaty depths, changed to a sweet patter of giggling, and then soared on uncontrollably. Beneath the audible medley of Sissy's ninety minutes in Doc Haines's care, there lay the inevitable intimate conversational sounds of his consoling voice.

"Honestly," said Nancy, once again seizing Uncle Jake's right arm and allowing her cheek to graze the shoulder of his camel's hair coat, "I don't think she's feeling a thing. Honestly."

"Laughing," said Uncle Jake. "Helpless in that infernal electric chair and laughing."

"You poor man," said Nancy.

"I think I'd better sit down," said Uncle Jake, and dragged a chair to mine and sat close beside me and crossed his knees.

"Well, Sunny," he said, "we'll have to take good care of her when she gets out of there."

"She won't be long," said Nancy, standing beside Uncle Jake and resting one hand on his shoulder and holding her robe with the other.

But I did not want the closed door to open. I did not want Sissy to stop laughing. I did not want the low persuasive tones of the other voice to cease. I had caught a glimpse of the forbidding chair and had seen Sissy swinging up her pretty legs and reclining weak and trusting under Doc Haines's guiding hand. I had seen his small quick face and square-cut coppery beard; I had seen the wires and metal arms surrounding Sissy's heavy chair, and had seen the way Doc Haines had nudged shut the door with his elbow. I knew that he should be wearing a white coat but was instead leaning over Sissy in a crimson bathrobe. And out here in the waiting room the kerosene heater was now white hot, and the woman Nancy—a much sought after billiard player as I well knew—was as large as Hilda Laubenstein and smelled as only a large and friendly woman can smell in the early morning. And now Uncle Jake was more upset than he had been the night before and his breath was cold, his eyes a paler blue than ever, his massiveness all the more majestic for the weakness running through it like a thin vein of gold through a cliff of quartz. Last night there had been the Oaf, the Oaf, the Oaf. Now there was Doc Haines, Doc Haines, Doc Haines. The next best thing to lying in the great oak and steel and horsehair-cushioned chair myself, and to being the one Doc Haines was crooning over instead of Sissy, was sitting just as I was in the warmth of a wintry wooden tenement and listening to the two of them in there.

"...ouch!" said Sissy, choking on her interrupted laughter and then finding her breath and sailing off again into the lively sounds of a young woman being pushed high in a swing in summer or rippling with unexpected pleasure behind a tree. Doc Haines said something, dropped something, spoke again, and for the first time joined in Sissy's merriment.

"Listen to that," said Uncle Jake, wincing and sitting tall on the edge of his chair, "he's laughing too!"

"Why don't you take off your overcoat?" asked Nancy. "It's hot in here. I'm getting pretty warm myself."

"I'm all right," said Uncle Jake. "But I had a cousin who died in a dentist's chair. The scoundrel jammed a gleaming blade into my poor cousin's rotten tooth and that was the end of him. It was a single jab but it sizzled right up the nerve to the brain and killed him. I don't trust dentists, I can tell you. Especially your Doc Haines."

"But everybody loves Doc Haines," said Nancy.

"Well, I don't," said Uncle Jake.

The machine that whined sank to an ugly dispirited tone, the buzzing of the second machine grew momentarily as loud as any sound we had heard so far, the pedaling sound of the third machine climbed to a clatter. Then silence. Then running water. Then a tapping we had not heard before, sharp tapping noises that came in measured sets of three. Sissy moaned and then began laughing at herself for moaning. Then she sighed.

"Good Lord!" cried Uncle Jake, bolting once more to his feet, "he's using a hammer!"

"Honey," said Nancy, "you can't go in there!"

She had been watching him with her quick dark eyes, seeing how far she could go with her warm and hesitant hand (on his tight shoulder, on the tight muscles in his handsome neck), anticipating his every move. She was ready for him. And now the crimson-clad Nancy blocked the closed door and held firm before Uncle Jake, who in his momentum had stopped just short of her. They were together, touching and not touching, the towering man elegant, disheveled, dressed for the street in his beige and crisply tailored overcoat, the robed and slippered woman dressed for warm darkness and quilts and pillows. She took the half-step necessary to push herself against him. She seized his soft lapels. She made certain that the tall man was breathing in the very breath that she exhaled.

"... breathe deeply," came the young and confident voice beyond the door, "a few more deep breaths, Cecily."

The tapping hammer. A crunching sound. A splintering sound. A sound of steel thread unwinding from a silver spool and stretching, tightening, wrapping around and around the head and jaws of our invisible Sissy with one long high-pitched whistle of expiration that had no start, no finish, no crescendo, no diminution. Then Sissy groaned, cried out, and once more began to laugh. But now she laughed as if into Doc Haines's shoulder or against his chest, and now she was laughing in submission, exhaustion, gratitude, certainty—Sissy's own certainty that never again would she laugh so happily, so freely, or in such delicious pain.

"It's nothing," said Nancy quickly, struggling to comfort Uncle Jake, struggling to hold and support him though he had not moved, was no longer moving, this easterner who was now staring over Nancy's head, aghast at the sounds he heard, confounded by the drama in which he had no part, more distraught than he would ever be again because of Sissy. "It's nothing," repeated Nancy. "This isn't anything compared to what happened to Chippy."

Was he not listening to her? Did he not understand what she was saying? Did he neither see nor feel the slackening of the robe, the sudden appearance of one naked leg? I watched as for one long moment Uncle Jake stood wonderfully immune to Nancy and set his hard aristocratic face.

"Wait!" said Nancy, offering herself as a loving and fleshy bulwark against his pained despair. "Listen! You should have heard the way poor Chippy hollered! Chippy couldn't see straight for a week, that molar of his hurt so much, and when he said he was going to kill himself if it didn't stop, despite the state of drunkenness I kept him in—it was all I could do—well, he finally let Doc Haines take the pliers to that screaming tooth of his, and you've never heard anyone yell and holler the way poor Chippy did right in that same chair where your wife is now. He kicked, poor Chippy did, and shouted to beat the band, despite the whiskey and the laughing gas, and the whole thing was so terrible I had to help hold him down."

Silence. Silence fit for secret whispering. A protracted low chortling from Sissy. More silence. And slowly Uncle Jake disengaged himself from Nancy, drew Nancy's hands away from his lapels, calmly stepped to one side of her and buttoned up his coat, hot as it now was in the waiting room.

"What's the matter?" asked Nancy quickly, and in one swift gesture banishing the bare unruly leg back to its proper place inside the robe.

"I suppose you mean Chippy Smith," said Uncle Jake coldly. "The airplane pilot."

"Oh it was terrible," said Nancy, relieved and determined not to understand Uncle Jake's knit brows, flaring nostrils, restrained severity. "Chippy tried to change his mind at the last minute. As soon as he saw

Doc's white coat he turned cold sober and headed out the door. But I had a good grip on his arm and that abscessed molar was kicking up a storm. So poor Chippy let us lead him to the chair and let Doc tie on the sheet. Doc was patient and used about half a tank of gas, joking with Chippy all the while, just to get things started. The gas seeped into the room and even I began to giggle. (Everything's quiet in there now, do you hear?) But Chippy told Doc that the gas wasn't doing a thing and that he'd come back some other time. Well, Doc knew that that was the foulest molar he'd ever seen and went after it. And the blood? And the kicking? And the howling? I've known some pretty unhappy men in my time, but the day poor Chippy had his molar out took the cake. . . . Is something wrong?"

It was then that Uncle Jake became the master of his distress. Reluctantly, politely, with a minimum of irony he took his leave once more of the best female billiard player in the Baranof Hotel, though he had not the slightest recollection of having once declined to join her in a game.

"Come along, Sunny," he said, "we're going."

"But what's wrong?" asked Nancy.

"It appears," said Uncle Jake, "that this town is populated by women with the name of Nancy."

"Not that I know of," said Nancy.

The door. The closed door opening, swinging wide. And there before us at last stood Doc Haines and Sissy side by side as in some typically Alaskan portrait. Doc Haines was perspiring; in his exertions the top of his crimson robe had fallen open displaying the hairy medallion of his boyish chest. He was drying his hands on a paper towel; he was still laughing and looking not at us but at Sissy—Sissy who, with her damp hair, her green dress awry, her poor cheek more swollen than when she had first entered Doc Haines's office, nonetheless was smiling half a smile and tilting her head and shyly showing Uncle Jake the unexpected serenity in her soft eyes. The chair, the machines, the spattered sheet, the bowls, the tufts of cotton, the lurid lamp beneath which she had trusted herself to the skills and kindness of Doc Haines—gone was it all, floating off on the wistful aftermath of Sissy's ninety minutes under gas.

"Jake," she said thickly in the doorway.

"There you are," said Doc Haines. "Good as new."

"Jake," said Sissy.

"That tooth was so far gone and so impacted," said Doc Haines, "that we practically had to blast it out. Isn't that right, Cecily?"

"So you pulled her tooth," said Uncle Jake, helping Sissy into her coat.

"Pulled it? I'll say I pulled it," said Doc Haines. "But I saved three others. And Cecily enjoyed the laughing gas, that's for sure."

"Jake," whispered Sissy, "it's over."

"Now," said Uncle Jake, putting his arm around Sissy and taking hold of my hand, "now if you'll just send your bill I'll pay it by return mail."

"There's no rush," said Doc Haines.

"Just send it," said Uncle Jake.

"Jake," said Sissy, after we had propped her up in the foldaway bed and wrapped her warmly, "what's the matter?"

"Matter?" asked Uncle Jake.

"You're not yourself," said Sissy in her thick dreamy voice. "He's a wonderful dentist, Jake. I may look terrible but I hardly felt a thing."

"I can't help it, Sissy. It will take me a while to calm down."

"Poor Jake."

"I'm beside myself, Sissy. That's all I was the whole time."

"You shouldn't care for me so much," said Sissy, happily laughing as she had behind Doc Haines's door.

"That fellow really didn't hurt you?"

"Of course not. I don't think I ever laughed so much in my life."

"Well," said Uncle Jake, "I suppose we had better call off the dinner."

"Oh no," said Sissy, "don't call it off for me. I'll be fine."

"If you think so," said Uncle Jake.

At 11:45 A.M. the Deauville party assembled according to plan in the dining room of the Baranof Hotel for the Christmas day dinner intended to spare Sissy having to cook twice in a row for that famished bunch, as Uncle Jake had said, and to exemplify Uncle Jake's largesse. (He paid the check and then reimbursed himself from the funds of the Deauville-Morley partnership, which was entirely agreeable to Frank Morley.)

Red and green streamers from the light fixture overhead. Commiseration for Sissy. Toasts to Uncle Jake. Jokes about Frank Morley and Hilda Laubenstein and the aftereffects of the Chain-Lightning Punch, the wallop of which, said Hilda, was well worth a little stumbling and a puffy face. The McGinnises in their best clothes and looking like the guests of honor, as Uncle Jake at once proclaimed them, relenting from his attitude of the night before.

Grapefruit juice tasting of the tin. Filet of Brown Bear Steak. Fool Hen Fricassee. Caribou en Croute. Vanilla Ice Cream with Strawberry Jam. Dawson City Java.

Sissy cleverly concealing her inability to eat. Uncle Jake's long story about the Christmas dinners they used to have at Deauville Farms.

Then back at High Ridge Street the yield of our giant spruce: hand-kerchiefs for the men; Glacier Vanity cosmetics for Hilda Laubenstein and Annie McGinnis; the specially cut-down .22-caliber Remington rifle for me; and for Sissy *"Old Yukon,"* which she was never able to bring herself to read.

That night Uncle Jake declared that once he got the McGinnises out of the Baranof Hotel he would never set foot in the place again. Sissy expressed surprise. Hadn't Uncle Jake enjoyed the dinner? The hotel was nice enough as she remembered it. Why, she asked, was Uncle Jake suddenly so unhappy with the Baranof Hotel? What could possibly have made him so angry? But for the only time in his life Uncle Jake stopped short, thought better of what he was about to say, understood that for once he had best not burden Sissy with the shocking ways of the world and his injured pride, and so kept to himself and for the rest of his days his undeniable and guilty encounter of that morning. He mumbled evasively; he did not mention Nancy's name; Sissy did not press the matter. Then Uncle Jake began to snore and Sissy, as usual, to cry. In the night the swelling in the side of her heart-shaped face went down.

36 —

It took Uncle Jake two months to negotiate the purchase of Olaf Olafson's island and to arrange the McGinnises' new life. Olaf Olafson did not want to sell. On the occasion of Uncle Jake's first return to the environs of White Eye, and in the presence of Rex Ainsworth, Olaf Olafson called Uncle Jake a fool, a meddler, a no-good crooked businessman from the outside. He said that Uncle Jake was a stuck-up easterner who thought so much of himself that he couldn't even be civil to a fellow's wife. He said that no one, especially not Uncle Jake, was going to destroy his livelihood, his good name, his peace of mind. No one, he said, was going to kick him off his own island. No one was going to take him away from his foxes which were the best blue foxes in Alaska. What kind of a thing was this? asked Olafson, to come pussyfooting back where he wasn't wanted with a pilot dressed in city clothes and to try to trick a poor Swede into ruin? No sir, said Olafson, they weren't going to get rid of Olaf Olafson without a fight. Uncle Jake told Olafson that they would be back. Olafson told Uncle Jake not to bother.

Three weeks later Rex Ainsworth made another perfect landing and tied the Fairchild to Olafson's float. Uncle Jake watched calmly as the Swede came swearing out of his cabin rifle in hand and shouted to Uncle Jake that he and his stuck-up pilot better get out and get out fast. Uncle Jake, who was not about to lose his temper to such scum as the Swede, as he put it, merely ignored the rifle, the snarling dogs, the vile cursing, the face of the frightened Indian woman peering around the corner of the cabin, and then in silence presented Olafson with a shiny new leather satchel which, as Olafson knew at once from Uncle Jake's expression and by the rich and formal appearance of the satchel itself, contained more cold cash than Olafson had ever held in his hands or would again. Olafson clutched his rifle in one hand and the unopened satchel in the other. He began again to swear—in English, in Swedish, in the language of the Skoots. Uncle Jake calmly bore what he called the Swede's abuse until at last the fox farmer had no more to say. Then

Uncle Jake ordered him off the island and back to Juneau within a week. And within a week Olafson's charred boat was tied up at one of the Indian docks in Juneau and the duly signed and sealed deed to the island lay safely in the little iron strongbox in Guns & Locks & Clothes.

Sissy and Frank Morley along with Robert McGinnis, no matter that he had begun complaining about his feet, provisioned *The Prince of Wales* with an arsenal of new tools, a six-month supply of food and home remedies for the McGinnises and, in the final hour, with a thousand pounds of fish heads for the foxes. It had come to Uncle Jake in the night that the Juneau-Douglas Cannery was dumping tons of useless fish heads into the channel every day, and that he, Uncle Jake, could buy for a song, as he said, enough fish heads to make the McGinnises' foxes—our foxes, really—lick their chops in ecstasy for half a year. The weather was cold enough to preserve the cargo from the cannery in the hold of *The Prince of Wales* until he and French Pete and McGinnis and Frank Morley, who had suggested that he might come along this time, could build a log ice house on the island. They picked their day of departure.

Sissy told Uncle Jake that she hated to see Annie McGinnis leave and that she, Sissy, could not have stood being left behind without Frank Morley had she not had me to love and Hilda to entertain. As it was, she said, she was already beginning to feel what she called her palpitations. But Uncle Jake said that Hilda was a fine girl and that everything would be all right.

Against his better judgment, Uncle Jake had not gotten rid of French Pete (Peter Barnou) or the Belly Burglar (Wesley Pitts) and had ordered them aboard *The Prince of Wales* by noon of the day before the scheduled 3 A.M. departure. Frank Morley and the McGinnises and Uncle Jake were to spend the night on board with the two-man crew in order to facilitate the early sailing. Sissy, with the help of Hilda Laubenstein, hosted a final supper on High Ridge Street for her brave travelers, as she called them, all of whom were eager to be off.

"Frank and I will be back in about two weeks," said Uncle Jake.

Sissy nodded.

"We have our double solitaire," said Hilda.

"Take care of Annie," said Sissy.

Uncle Jake said that it was time to leave and that there was no point in saying our good-bys down at the dock in the darkness. They all kissed Sissy and me, including Robert McGinnis, and shook Hilda's hand.

"Come on," said Hilda to Uncle Jake, "I get a hug too!"

Everyone laughed and Sissy concealed her depression. Then they were gone. Sissy and Hilda allowed themselves two highballs each. Then Hilda was gone. I joined Sissy in the foldaway bed.

But in the middle of those dark hours Uncle Jake came back. We awoke together, Sissy and I, and heard his long strides in the night, heard his boots on our wooden steps, were fully awake and out of bed when he flung wide the door.

"Sissy!" he cried, "I think that darn Belly Burglar is dying!"

"Dying?" asked Sissy while Uncle Jake turned on all the lights and picked me up in his arms. "Do you mean it, Jake?"

"Well," said Uncle Jake, "he woke me out of a sound sleep practically in tears and holding that little round belly of his for all he was worth. He said that the pain was bad enough to give a dead man babies, and was obviously so miserable that I overlooked his language—he knows how I dislike that kind of language—and helped him over to Hilda's as fast as I could make him go. He was bent double, I can tell you. And moaning."

"Oh Jake," said Sissy, "will he be all right?"

"I think he'll have to go under the knife. Hilda's got him in one of the beds down there in that Indian infirmary of hers and Doc Robinson is already sharpening his scalpel."

"They're going to operate on Wesley Pitts?"

"Looks like it," said Uncle Jake. "They'd better wash him first."

"Oh dear," said Sissy.

"I guess he poisoned himself on his own cooking," said Uncle Jake.

"What are you going to do?" asked Sissy. "Postpone the trip?"

"Well, no," said Uncle Jake, squeezing me in his arms and giving Sissy one of his boyish looks. "That's the thing. Frank and I have talked the whole matter over. We want you to come along."

"Me?" asked Sissy after a pause and shivering in her nightgown and smiling her most worried smile. "Me?"

"That's right," said Uncle Jake in his grandest voice. "We want you to come along as cook."

"Jake," said Sissy, "you can't be serious!"

"Of course I'm serious," said Uncle Jake. "Frank and I have made our decision. We can't get along without you, Sissy."

"But there's Sunny, Jake. What are we going to do with Sunny?"

"We'll bring her along!"

"Oh Jake, are you sure we're doing the right thing?"

"You bet we are," said Uncle Jake. "Aren't we, Sunny?"

"But I'm not ready," said Sissy in a little wail. "I don't even know what to bring!"

"Just get your hat," said Uncle Jake, "we'll be out of here in fifteen minutes!"

So Sissy and I were in the darkened pilothouse with Frank Morley and Uncle Jake, who was at the wheel, when *The Prince of Wales* pulled away at 3 A.M. on schedule. The McGinnises were happily asleep below; French Pete, who had cast us off, and was the thinnest man I had ever seen, with sideburns down to his jaw and a fish-bait knife on his hip, was in the galley stoking up the stove for coffee. Uncle Jake stood with his legs apart, sailor fashion, and one hand on a spoke of the tall wooden wheel. In the faint glow of a green light he glanced at the compass, stared out through the broad wet windows into the blackness of the harbor, gave the great wheel a judicious quarter turn. He was serious. He was wide-awake. He was in command. He knew that we were watching him by the glow of the green light.

"Well, Frank," he said at last, allowing himself to relax a moment into a smile and a low laugh, "we shanghaied them! No better cook, no better cabin boy even if she is a girl! Quite a crew, eh Frank?"

"Oh Jake," said Sissy.

"And we're going to have a couple of happy McGinnises in the morning," said Uncle Jake, "I can tell you that."

37 —

I awoke on that first morning, as I did on each succeeding morning until we finally dropped anchor in the narrow stretch of waters between White Eye and the Olafson island, into that condition rarest and most enjoyable of all to the expectant child: disorientation. I slept as in a nest or den, warm, peaceful, secure, dreaming of hordes of fat blue foxes crowding an empty shore. I awoke to disorientation, to the suspense of total uncertainty, to that blank consciousness from which the genie of unexpected life leaps forth. I awoke in a narrow bunk built against a curving wooden hull, awoke to liquid motion and to the smells of diesel oil, a mildewed mattress, paint like curdled cream, seasons of brine and rust and corroded copper. What boat was this? Where was it going? Who was I and what had happened to me, what lay ahead? I prolonged my disorientation as long as I could, savoring the concreteness of a self and setting that meant nothing, that called to mind no names, no time. When I could hold it off no longer, recognition would suddenly be mine; when I could keep it closed no longer, my little shutter would flick open on the world that was mine. *The Prince of Wales,* I would say aloud; Sunny, I would say aloud, and know that only steps away were Sissy's boys, as she called them, and Sissy herself. The shivers of emptiness gave way to everything that was familiar; everything that was familiar led onward to the unknown.

"Well," said Uncle Jake each morning, "here we are in all our glory!" And so we were.

In the fifteen minutes that had been allowed her, Sissy had had no choice but to dress herself in slacks and blouse and to cram the merest essentials into the little canvas bag that Uncle Jake had held open for her while laughing and extolling the pleasures of the trip that would now be hers. Uncle Jake repeated that he and Frank Morley could not do without her, which was all that Sissy had ever wished to hear from him, and rushed me into my boots and shirt and britches, crying, "Off we go, Sunny, off we go!" Sissy and I had come aboard *The Prince of Wales* with only the clothes on our backs, as Uncle Jake pointed out to

Frank Morley once we were safely under way, and with little more. We were cold, Sissy and I, we were not outfitted for the rigors of the journey. So they dressed us, Frank Morley and Uncle Jake, not below in one of the small cabins but right there in the pilothouse where then and always Uncle Jake was at the helm. Uncle Jake told Frank Morley to bring up a pair of his, Uncle Jake's, canvas duck-hunting pants and an armful of his stiff woolen shirts. Uncle Jake told Sissy to pull on the canvas pants over her slacks and said that she would have to wear one of his checked and baggy shirts on top of her blouse. Sissy demurred, laughingly, and said that she didn't want to dress like a man or spend her days on *The Prince of Wales* swimming in clothes that were Uncle Jake's, even though he was her husband. But Frank Morley steadied her, and Sissy struggled into the shirt and pants, and Frank Morley then rolled high the flapping sleeves and bulky bottoms. As for me, Uncle Jake said that one of his shirts would make a splendid pair of pants and that I had only to wear the shirt upside down with my already booted and trousered legs through the enormous sleeves. Now Sissy joined Frank Morley, and they held me up and tugged and fastened the wadded shirttails around my waist with a length of brand-new rope as thick as my little finger. Sissy said that she could hardly move and that she and I were the funniest-looking pair she had ever seen. But I felt more exalted than I had when I had first been transformed in Guns & Locks & Clothes, while Sissy too was plainly proud of what Uncle Jake called her Alaskan getup.

Uncle Jake's domain was the pilothouse, Sissy's the galley. Uncle Jake kept a canvas army cot in the rear of the pilothouse so that occasionally he could catch a snooze, as he said, while entrusting the wheel to French Pete. Sissy was afraid that she and I were especially vulnerable to French Pete's consumption, but nonetheless she learned from him how to fuel and control the heat of the iron coal-burning stove in the galley. Uncle Jake had his compass, his charts, his sextant, his newly purchased shortwave radio, his place of prominence on *The Prince of Wales*. Each morning he and Frank Morley shaved in the pilothouse from a porcelain bowl that Frank Morley readied with hot water; each morning Uncle Jake carefully plastered down his black hair.

Hour after hour, day after day, Uncle Jake surveyed and directed our northward passage toward the Candle Creek Islands and the safe anchorage that lay sixty miles beyond them. Sissy mastered the iron stove and stoked it, nursed it, perspiring and always chipper, as Uncle Jake was proud to say, even when we rolled and pitched and Sissy had no recourse but to brace herself by hip and elbow not an arm's length from the fiery stove, avoiding burns as best she could and braving the pots, the crashing lids, the flying gouts of the baked beans she prepared according to Uncle Jake's recipe and that was his favorite dish at sea. Boiling water spilled and sizzled; her place in the galley was a place of grease and heat, confinement, where she wielded knives that were razor-sharp and heavy, and where the iron coffeepot slid back and forth across the deadly surface of the stove like a scalded goose. Day after day I watched her until she sent me up to the pilothouse, where, she said, I would be safer. Day after day French Pete stood leaning into the narrow doorway of Sissy's galley, coughing, until she ordered him to report to Uncle Jake, which he never did, and to leave her alone. Once when she was pumping sea water into the galley sink she told me that if Wesley Pitts survived his operation, as she was sure he must, she was going to do everything she could to befriend him, although, she said, she would never be able to appreciate the virtues of French Pete, if he had any.

Whenever I had the chance, and when I was not perched on my high stool which Uncle Jake had assigned to me in his pilothouse, or was not watching Sissy at her cooking, or not studying the features of Robert McGinnis, who spent most of the trip playing cribbage with Annie in the forecastle, I followed French Pete about the slippery decks or into the engine room, only to be sought and found by Frank Morley and taken by the hand from the consumptive mate. The curls in French Pete's hair and sideburns were like tight masses of small black fishhooks which I longed to touch. He was young; he smoked a pipe despite his cough; he spoke to me in his French-Canadian patois when I asked him to. Not being able to understand French Pete was as great a delight as not being able to understand Robert McGinnis. The thrill of spending a few minutes with French Pete was equaled only by the thrill of being retrieved by Frank Morley.

Sissy served Uncle Jake his beans in the pilothouse and fed the rest of us in the forecastle. Annie McGinnis did not lift a finger, in Sissy's words. French Pete helped himself from Sissy's pots whenever he felt like it and ate alone.

The Prince of Wales was still listing, still temperamental, an aged eighty-foot boat that rose high from the water and lurched from wave to wave with all the elegance her name implied, like an aged European proceeding loftily across a wintry garden. Uncle Jake did not speak of the contradiction between her name and gender, conveyed to Frank

Morley that they were to speak no more of her last owner, and was never more in his glory, as he said, than when assuming his rightful place in her pilothouse and assuming responsibility for boat and loved ones both. Whenever he could, French Pete told Sissy that *The Prince of Wales* was an old tub that would drown us all sooner or later, an opinion Sissy chose not to pass on to Uncle Jake.

There were squalls, onslaughts of hail, sudden calms, high seas. The exterior of *The Prince of Wales* was a skin of ice. In the worst weather the McGinnises rushed up the forecastle companionway to the nearest rail, suffered seasickness holding hands and taking their chances on the wind's direction, and then returned white-faced and exhausted to the ivory cribbage board that had been their only purchase in the Curio Shoppe in Juneau. Uncle Jake paid sober attention to his nautical devices, spoke reassuringly to Sissy when the elements, as he called them, threatened *The Prince of Wales* with the first hints of violence, and confessed to Frank Morley his regret that this trip was such that he was obligated to restrain on all counts his natural longing for a good blow. But the weather was unpredictable enough to suit Uncle Jake— snow and icy fog were the challenges he most appreciated—and yet not so continuously bad as to destroy Sissy's resolve to justify her newly discovered worth in the eyes of the two partners.

Northward we went up Lynn Canal through darkness or a sludge of yellow light, through choppy waters blanketed in ice. The perils, as Uncle Jake told Frank Morley in a quiet voice, included drifting logs concealed just beneath the surface of the ice-strewn seas, or some Indian fishing boat running without lights, or even a chance rock not shown on the charts. Frank Morley nodded gravely.

"Pete," Uncle Jake would say, his ordinarily garrulous speech giving way to the terse economy essential, as he thought, to his authority, "the pumps." Or, "Pete," he would say, "another sounding," which meant that French Pete would go grudgingly to the bows and measure the depth of the water with a lead weight affixed to the end of a knee-high coil of rope. The pilothouse, always warm and orderly, smelled of brilliantine and Union Leader.

Toward dusk of the fourth day out Uncle Jake suddenly exclaimed, "Red sun at night, sailor's delight, Sunny!" At that moment the heavens cleared, the patchy black and white seas glittered, and a benign and spectral sun sank across our bows as far as we could see and guaranteed bright and spectacular days to come.

"Frank," said Uncle Jake in his mildest manner, "let's get them all out on deck tomorrow morning to see the islands."

Thus on the fifth morning, by the light of a climbing sun that more than lived up to the old adage, Sissy and the McGinnises and French Pete lined the port rail as *The Prince of Wales* began to wend her way through the small black frozen gems of the Candle Creek Islands. The wind had dropped, nothing stirred the dark seas but the dory that bobbed along in our wake at the end of a long rope fastened to a cleat at the stern. The snow on the slowly passing rocky shores or towering trees spoke not of harrowing blizzards but of the tranquillity of winter's mysteries. Frank Morley had lowered the port window in the pilothouse and was leaning out head and shoulders and sniffing the sun, admiring the scenery, sharing the voluble pleasure of those at the rail. Sissy and I had discarded for the day our outlandish garb. Uncle Jake was at the helm in his shirtsleeves; I was perched beside him on my stool. A crow as big as a kite flew gently from the island on our port side to join a colony of silent crows filling the treetops of the smaller island to our starboard. Heads turned. Even the old diesel engine, running steadily and softly at its slowest speed, sounded as if it would never break down again.

Then it came.

Suddenly Uncle Jake's strong face was stricken. An awful readiness was in his eyes, though he was still smiling. My tall stool began to tip, to tilt, to sway slowly on two legs toward the starboard side of the boat. A strong hand stopped my fall. *The Prince of Wales* rolled, lifted, hoisted itself bodily from port to starboard, slowly. Higher the port side climbed. Higher it rose. High above our heads on the port side Sissy and the McGinnises clung to the rail; the angle of the floor of the pilothouse became precarious, the starboard rail dipped low, shipped brackish water.

"She's going over," said Frank Morley.

"I don't think so," said Uncle Jake.

Then as *The Prince of Wales* continued on her unchecked course toward capsizing, her bow began to rise out of the placid sea so that the old boat turned and twisted in the serpentine motion of an immense oceangoing monster doomed in the next instant to sink, to disappear in all her dignity, to make her stately way to the dark caves of the deep.

"Jake!" cried Sissy.

"What the hell!" said French Pete, loosening his hold at the rail and sliding feet first through the open door of the pilothouse, where he landed heavily against the starboard wall.

"Pete," said Uncle Jake, "the dory." French Pete got to his knees, crawled out of the pilothouse, and struggled for once to obey orders.

"What is it?" asked Frank Morley.

"A partially sunken wreck," said Uncle Jake, lashing about with his icy eyes and gripping the wheel. "Or a rock."

"Jake!" cried Sissy.

"Well," said Frank Morley, "she's going over."

"Not yet," said Uncle Jake.

French Pete was calling in his French-Canadian patois for help. High above us Sissy and the McGinnises were stretched out flat on the nearly perpendicular deck and clinging not to the rail but to its stanchions. Warm sunlight was pouring through the open door and window of the pilothouse. Uncle Jake had braced himself with his legs apart and was still clutching the wheel with one hand and me with the other.

"Shouldn't we swim for it?" asked Frank Morley.

"Too cold," said Uncle Jake and threw the switch that stilled as if forever the valiant engine.

Then it stopped.

Our bow and port side hung high above the horizon. The starboard rail was all but submerged in the icy surface. We were not moving. In the silence we heard the colony of crows.

"Jake!" cried Sissy.

"Just stay where you are, Sissy," called Uncle Jake. "It's going to be all right."

"Well," said Frank Morley, exhaling a long and wheezy breath, "it looks as if you've gotten us out of this one, Jake."

"We'll see," said Uncle Jake.

"Do you want me to give Pete a hand with the dory?" asked Frank Morley.

Uncle Jake nodded and Frank Morley, devoted as he was to the only partner he had ever had in his nearly fifty-nine years, made his way aft on hands and knees, brittle bones and arthritic joints notwithstanding, in search of the terrified French Pete and the dory.

We waited, Uncle Jake still holding the now lifeless wheel, I still perched on my tilted stool and safe in the grip of Uncle Jake's massive hand. He listened, knowing, as he finally confessed at the end of his ordeal, that the slightest shift in weight might well dislodge *The Prince of Wales* and send her straight to the bottom.

"Jake!" cried Sissy, "what is it?"

"We're hung up on a rock," called Uncle Jake. "Just stay where you are. Frank's coming around with the dory."

We heard Annie McGinnis. We heard Sissy trying to comfort her. We heard the sound of oarlocks, the splash of oars. The invisible Frank Morley said he was ready. At last, and after only the briefest hesitation, Uncle Jake relinquished his post at the wheel and, with me at his side and my hand in his, proceeded as light as a cat up the sharp incline of the deck on hands and knees until we reached the McGinnises and Sissy.

"Now, Sunny," said Uncle Jake, "we're going to abandon ship!"

We were straddling the topmost edge of *The Prince of Wales* and, once again, could see: the two islands, the black water in which the old boat was marooned, the half-exposed rounded hull, and, knocking gently against it, the dory manned by Frank Morley and French Pete. Uncle Jake told Robert McGinnis that he would have to help and Robert McGinnis, showing no sign of comprehension and making no attempt at speech, nonetheless did as he was told.

Uncle Jake and Robert McGinnis formed a two-man chain with Robert McGinnis anchoring himself to a stanchion and Uncle Jake firmly holding his free hand; with his other hand Uncle Jake held tight to me, to Annie, to Sissy, in that order, passing us down the wet and barnacle-covered slope of the hull to Frank Morley, laughing and saying that we would only have to stay on the island a few hours.

"Aren't you and Bobby coming?" asked Sissy, hugging me in the prow of the dory and peering up at Uncle Jake, who was standing as tall as a statue on the upturned gunnel of *The Prince of Wales*.

"Not now," said Uncle Jake, calmly enjoying the sun and smiling down at her, "just go with Frank."

Frank Morley did the rowing as French Pete bailed out the dory with Frank Morley's hat while Annie, no longer weeping and once more opening the floodgates of her little torrential mind, screwed up her tiny spluttering face to questions, advice, and a variety of accounts of what had happened, though only Sissy was able to interpret what she was saying.

Frank Morley put us ashore with French Pete and without a pause rowed back to *The Prince of Wales*. We watched him pull away, Annie and Sissy and I, and, huddling together amidst icy boulders and pulsing beds of kelp, watched and waited until he returned with Robert McGinnis and a wet pile of blankets and tins of beans and tins of peaches, which was the best that Uncle Jake could do for us at the moment.

"Frank," said Sissy, helping to unload the dory, "what about Jake?"

"Well," said Frank Morley, "Jake says the old *Prince of Wales* is high and dry on a reef and he wants to try to pull her off."

"You mean he's going to stay out there?"

"Pete and I are going back with the dory to try to pull her off. Jake's gassing up the outboard motor now."

"I don't like him out there alone," said Sissy.

"He knows what's best," said Frank Morley.

"Well," said Sissy, "Bobby's going to take care of us. Aren't you, Bobby?"

A short distance above the narrow stretch of rocky beach where we had landed, and with a good view of *The Prince of Wales,* was a small open patch of humus, fungus, ancient earth surrounded on three sides by underbrush and deadfalls and tall trees, and there Robert McGinnis pitched our camp, raising the aged canvas tent that Uncle Jake had kept aboard *The Prince of Wales* in the unlikely event, as he said, of some emergency, and stacking the tin cans neatly and cutting boughs for the floor of the tent and chopping wood, as surprised as Sissy and Annie that a person like himself, who had never even mowed his own lawn back in Connecticut, could do such work.

The sun rose higher. The humus, the fungus, the underbrush, the trees—everything began to steam, though splinters of ice still gleamed at the edges of our narrow beach. All day we stood or sat before the tent and listened to the sounds of the outboard motor and watched the dory straining backwards this way and that at the end of its tether. Uncle Jake was the little figure standing in the stern of *The Prince of Wales* and shouting directions; Frank Morley and French Pete were the little figures riding the dory as it bucked and sagged, lurched and slacked off from its hopeless task. The three tiny figures removed their shirts, the distant outboard motor screamed and died. *The Prince of Wales* looked like a ghostly and dangerous mirage canted upwards crookedly for no reason anyone could see in the calm waters. The unseasonable sun burned down on the white boat and the buzzing energetic salvage efforts that lasted throughout the day.

The hot sun began to sink. All around us the black and wintry woods were on fire. Robert McGinnis shook his head. Through pools of purple and orange light the defeated dory started back to us.

"Frank," called Sissy, trembling at the edge of the black tide as the dory nosed ashore, "where's Jake?"

"Well," said Frank Morley, as he and French Pete disembarked and dragged the dory as far as they could above the high water mark, "he's going to spend the night on *The Prince of Wales*."

"No!" said Sissy. "I won't have it!"

"Jake told me to tell you that the wind might come up. A squall might come up. Wind or shifting seas might free *The Prince of Wales* and Jake has to be on board to save her if that happens."

"It might tip over," said Sissy. "He might drown."

"There's nothing we can do," said Frank Morley.

"Must he remain out there alone? Couldn't you stay with him?"

"He wants me here with you," said Frank Morley, shaking his head.

"French Pete," said Sissy sternly, indifferent to the young and sullen mate who was lighting his pipe.

Frank Morley looked at Sissy and said nothing.

Despite the ice that glazed the beach and trees and darkness in which we were camped, the tent, when Sissy and Annie and I crawled into it, was hot. Frank Morley had shown Robert McGinnis how to build a fire and how to open the tins of beans with the ax. Frank Morley and French Pete had smoked in silence. Then the men had wrapped themselves in blankets, and Sissy and Annie and I had retired to the heat of our tent. I would have preferred to sleep in a blanket between Frank Morley and Robert McGinnis, but the hot tent smelled like the clothes of men, like the unwashed bodies of long-departed hunters, and was compensation enough for having to sleep with those among us who were considered timid. Even in the tent I had my Frank Morley and my Robert McGinnis—they were that close by—and when I awoke periodically throughout the night and saw the small dark shape of Sissy sitting in the mouth of the tent with her knees to her chest, keeping her vigil over Uncle Jake, it was Uncle Jake himself who, as I fell back to sleep, smelled of Union Leader and brilliantine and swept me off alone with him on *The Prince of Wales*. Intermittently Annie McGinnis snored, and snored as strangely as she talked. I heard Frank Morley reaching reassuringly for Robert McGinnis's as-yet-untried .30-30. There was a moon. I put my head in Sissy's lap and she stroked my hair. I lay back in the hot tent, smelling the heavy scent of the boughs we lay on, Annie and I, and heard Uncle Jake calling me down to him where he stood in a phosphorescent blaze in the waiting dory.

"I don't understand it," said Frank Morley the next morning, as the sun rose and we ate our cold peaches and hot beans. "I've lived up here for forty years and I've never known such weather—not even in summer."

"Well," said Sissy, who had seen Uncle Jake waving to her with both hands at the break of day, and who had waved back until he had disappeared, "it's exactly what Jake needs, isn't it?"

Frank Morley nodded.

"Crazy," said French Pete. "Crazy stinking hot."

All that day the island wilderness kept melting. All that day the dory tugged hopelessly at *The Prince of Wales*. Robert McGinnis removed his shirt. The colony of crows in the treetops of the island facing ours was silent. Robert McGinnis found a trickle of fresh water a few feet from our camp and we slaked our thirst. Those of us confined to shore, the three men struggling on the water, the spectacle of the immobile boat— all were held in clear oppressive shimmering balance under the low sun. Precarious balance.

"We're giving up," said Frank Morley at the end of that day.

"But what are we going to do?" asked Sissy.

"Wait," said Frank Morley.

For five days nothing happened. The light of the sun was like the new light of spring, the heat of the sun was like the heat in a latitude far south of ours. Still we watched, still Uncle Jake was faithful to his duty out on the old boat that waited proudly, forlornly, helplessly in the hot sun. Sissy maintained her nightly vigils.

"Has he radioed for help?" asked Sissy.

"Yes," said Frank Morley. "The *Haida* is going to start our way when she can. It may be a while."

"If we can only last," said Sissy.

But a wolverine had discovered our presence—Frank Morley showed me its tracks—and now the smell of wood smoke was in my clothes and there were pine needles in my hair and we were shipwrecked— shipwrecked in the Candle Creek Islands—and two unimaginable pleasures, the greatest of all so far, were mine: the fear known only to the castaway, the hope of rescue. And all, I thought, because of Uncle Jake, who several times a day stood upon the highest point of *The Prince of Wales* so that we should see him and know that he was still in charge. He never waved except in the early dawn, when there was only Sissy to wave back.

"Look what he's got us into," said French Pete.

"I wish you would be quiet," said Sissy.

Then at dawn of the sixth day, when the air was still and the barely risen sun hotter than ever, we heard the sound of a motor. We leapt to our feet; we gathered before the tent; Uncle Jake, we saw, was already poised atop the dangerously tilted pilothouse, where he was the most visible and could not be refused.

"Indian fishing boat," said Frank Morley, and there it came around the tip of the far island, a small disreputable boat weighted down with dried nets and empty oil drums. It veered toward *The Prince of Wales*.

"They see him!" said Frank Morley. "They're going to help!"

"Oh darling," said Sissy, kneeling down and hugging me, "it looks just like the little boat we saw in Taku Bay. How wonderful!"

There were in fact two Indians, a man and a woman, standing in the cockpit of the small boat now cautiously approaching *The Prince of Wales*. We yelled, we clapped, we hopped about—Sissy and Annie and Robert McGinnis and I—as Frank Morley and French Pete hurried down to the dory. Uncle Jake cupped his hands and shouted. The Indian reduced his speed. The dory kicked up a lively spray.

Uncle Jake threw the Indian a line, threw Frank Morley a line, and while we watched and waited the Indian and Frank Morley conferred with Uncle Jake out on the water that was like a sheet of white tin beneath the sun.

They were ready. We could see they were ready. The lines were attached. Uncle Jake looked shoreward for a moment and then disappeared—forever, for all he knew, as he said later—and then the fishing boat and dory began backing off from *The Prince of Wales*, tightening the ropes between them. The Indian put on full power, spumes of bright spray rose from behind his boat and the dory, and then Uncle Jake undertook what he later called the risk of his life. He started up his engine. We heard it throb, we saw the water churning around the partially sunken stern of *The Prince of Wales*. Uncle Jake's raised arm emerged from the pilothouse window. The Indian and Frank Morley understood its signal. The engines roared. And *The Prince of Wales* did not capsize, did not remain impervious against the forces exerted upon it by the fishing boat and the dory and Uncle Jake, but like an island of ice, or like a stranded whale, began to slip, to move, to yield to the determination of easterner, westerner, and the Indian to save her, keep her afloat.

She righted suddenly and without a splash moved slowly sternward, gave up her place on the underwater ledge, and there before our eyes sat gently rocking as if nothing at all had happened, as if she had not spent nearly a full eight days on the verge of doom.

Confusion. Celebration. Flying ropes. Uncle Jake blew three times on his whistle, the Indian answered with three toots and then pulled

away and turned and disappeared back around the island from which
he had come and over which the colony of crows was now loudly
circling.

"Darling," whispered Sissy, "we're saved. You have the most wonderful father in the world."

By the time Frank Morley had returned to us and had helped us to
break camp and had ferried us back out to *The Prince of Wales,* Uncle
Jake had already determined that *The Prince of Wales* was still as sound
as a dollar, as he said, and had already radioed the Coast Guard cutter
Haida that her assistance was no longer needed. Back on course, the
dory once again riding along behind us, everyone except French Pete
congregated in the pilothouse with Uncle Jake. Those of us who had
stayed on shore looked the survivors that we were—Frank Morley and
Robert McGinnis with their scratchy beards, Annie and Sissy uncomfortable in the clothes they had not changed, I with the pine needles in
my hair—and were all the more admiring of Uncle Jake, who had
shaved each morning despite the tension of his death watch as he called
it, and were all the more relieved to be reunited with him on *The Prince
of Wales.* Sissy went below and returned with coffee, saying that we
would soon be eating the fanciest feast that she could cook; I was
perched again on my stool; Uncle Jake was once more at the wheel—
alert, good-humored, farsighted. Shoulder to shoulder the McGinnises
were exhausting the manual alphabet and at the same time happily
haranguing the rest of us with the audible speech that they thought we
could understand. Sissy stood close to Uncle Jake with no need to talk.
To a rapt audience Uncle Jake discussed the risks, the chances, the
nautical technicalities as he had known or soon discovered them from
that first moment when disaster struck.

Uncle Jake said that in about eight hours we would be dropping
anchor just off Olafson's pier. Between here and there, he said with a
laugh, there were no more reefs.

It was then that Sissy asked about the smell.

Frank Morley looked at Uncle Jake. Uncle Jake looked at Frank
Morley.

"The cargo," said Frank Morley, frowning.

Uncle Jake nodded.

"Those stinking fish heads!" cried French Pete, lunging into the
pilothouse with his fist to his face, "those damn stinking fish heads are
rotting!"

Uncle Jake said nothing.

"Chuck them overboard!" cried French Pete.

"That's not so easy to do," said Uncle Jake.

"Besides," said Frank Morley, "by nightfall it may drop back down to freezing. There may well be ice on Olafson's island. We needn't lose the entire cargo, Jake."

"Stinking fish heads," grumbled French Pete and held his nose.

Sissy said that she regretted bringing up the subject and that after what had happened it would take more than a smell of dead fish to dampen her spirits, and everyone except French Pete agreed. We were safe, we were exuberant, we were only hours from our anchorage, and, as consensus had it, the day's clear sailing was more important than its heat. Valiantly Sissy prepared and served her meal; handsomely Uncle Jake held us on course. Even *The Prince of Wales* no longer listed as far to starboard as when she had set off from Juneau. And yet by early afternoon there were frowns, long periods of silence, dismal glances furtively exchanged. In the pilothouse the doors and windows were tightly shut; we perspired. The McGinnises fled the forecastle, returned to it in desperation, fled again to the airless deck that brought no relief.

"Well, Jake," said Frank Morley as the day began to wane, "I have to admit it's pretty bad."

The smell of fish. The sickening overpowering smell of rotting fish. Ten miles from White Eye the fact could no longer be overlooked, the smell no longer denied. Ten miles from White Eye *The Prince of Wales* was an embarrassment to everyone aboard. She was immodest, unclean, pestilential, a floating grave filled with the gases of decomposition. In her hold was packed a thousand pounds of fish heads, large and small, gone bad, reduced to pulp, and though the hatches were tightly battened down, the hold as tightly sealed as any hold could be, nonetheless the pressure of those gases was increasing, the hold was readying to burst, the smell was crying out for escape. And escape it did. There were cracks, there were crevices, *The Prince of Wales* might have been riddled with secret pipes and jets that forced the smell unmercifully to every part of the boat. Up it came through fissures in the deck; the pumps that pumped sea water now gushed only with the smell of rotting fish. Even the smoke from our diesel engine smelled of dead fish. We were sailing northward in white and shimmering clouds of our own stench.

"You've got to do something," said Frank Morley at last. "We can't hold out much longer, Jake."

"All right," said Uncle Jake. "All right. We'll jettison the whole darn cargo."

"The idea was a good one," said Frank Morley. "But you can't fight the weather, Jake."

"We'll just waste half a ton of perfectly good food for the foxes," said Uncle Jake. "We'll just chuck it overboard as that darn French Pete said."

"Poor Jake," said Sissy through the handkerchief she was holding to her face, "don't be angry."

But he only laughed grimly and set his jaw. He was angry—I had never seen him become so angry. He had a cast-iron stomach, as he always said, and there was nothing in the world to make him queasy except any form of fish or meat or fowl that was undercooked. He could not bear the sight of even so much as a trace of blood in his food and sent many a plate back to Sissy's stove. And he could not bear even the faintest of bad smells. Otherwise no man had a stronger constitution, as he always said, or a greater appetite.

"Pete!" called Uncle Jake through the speaking tube, "the anchor."

We were drifting forward, ceasing to move, coming to rest at last in the clear hot light of the day's end. We had arrived. Fifty yards to our port side were the cabin, sheds, and jetty that had once belonged to Olaf Olafson but now were ours; two hundred yards to our starboard lay the village of White Eye as if abandoned. Again we were all collected in the pilothouse, except for French Pete. The McGinnises were struggling not to breathe or to breathe as little as they could and Sissy and Frank Morley were glancing uneasily and sadly at Uncle Jake.

"Pete!" shouted Uncle Jake through the window he had just opened a crack, "the hold!"

"No, sir!" shouted French Pete. "No, sir! That's one rotten job you can do yourself!"

"All right," called Uncle Jake in his grimmest voice, "I will."

"McGinnis and I will help," said Frank Morley.

"Look at him," said Uncle Jake. "He's green in the face."

"I'll help," said Frank Morley.

"You can work the boom," said Uncle Jake after a pause. "I'll work in the hold."

In the clear hot twilight *The Prince of Wales* sat like a boat in quarantine between the silent island and the village deserted as under its shaman's curse. And there was no colony of crows, no distant sound of a gasoline engine. We were alone, as far as we knew, alone in the lingering anger of both Skoots and Swede, and ripe—good and ripe—as Uncle Jake said with an angry laugh, leading Frank Morley forward to the hatches.

Frank Morley tied a bandanna around his lower face. He and Uncle Jake removed their shirts. Frank Morley removed his ankle-high black shoes and Uncle Jake his boots. Together they unlashed the boom and rigged the block and tackle by which they would haul topside the overflowing drums. Then they approached the hatches. They stooped, pulled aside the tarpaulins, unfastened the hatch covers, and heaved them off. Even the loyal Frank Morley leapt away from that now open pit of stench and the silent, all-but-invisible detonation that belched upwards from its dark and slimy depths as if, as Uncle Jake said later, some great cavern of sewer gas had just let go. Uncle Jake stood his ground, Frank Morley disappeared from view—even the loyal Frank Morley—and then returned weaker, paler, but determined to do his part of the job. While Frank Morley held fast to the rope that traveled the length of the boom and from its tip descended into the still-fuming hold, Uncle Jake stepped forward and climbed down the iron ladder to his appointed task.

"Look," said Sissy through the handkerchief bunched against her face, "there are people over there in that little town!"

Robert McGinnis erupted into excited noise and pointed, shook Annie's arm, and where before there had been no one, now, as Sissy had been the first to see, the entire population of White Eye—thirty or forty Indians wearing black hats and blue denim shirts and pants— stood massed on the shore. Profoundly they watched us, profoundly they stared at *The Prince of Wales,* profoundly they bore witness as Uncle Jake and Frank Morley began dumping rotten fish heads into waters belonging to the Skoots.

The rope descending into the hold grew taut; Uncle Jake had made it fast to the drum. Frank Morley waited; Uncle Jake climbed back up from the hold, wiping his chest and restraining his anger. Side by side and hand over hand Frank Morley and Uncle Jake pulled until the first drum rose into view, sloshing and dripping, and then in unison they pulled it almost high enough to clear the starboard rail. They waited, Uncle Jake rippling and rigid, Frank Morley faint, and then the partners pushed the boom so that the bottom edge of the swinging drum rested against the rail. We watched, Sissy and the McGinnises and I, for the moment oblivious to the attentive Indians, watched for the instant when Uncle Jake would embrace the bottom of the drum, holding it in place against the rail, and when Frank Morley would slowly slack off on the rope and the drum would lean, lean further, and slowly pour its contents safely over the side. But it was not to be.

"Oh!" gasped Sissy, and the rope slipped, the first drum slipped, and Uncle Jake threw himself against the suddenly careening drum and hugged its steel girth with both arms, despite the bodily harm he risked, and wrestled with the dreadful weight—but to no avail. Down crashed the drum, spewing its sloppy contents not into the sea as planned but across the deck. Frank Morley yelled, Uncle Jake leapt away in time to avoid the full flood of fish heads that fell and splashed or lay half floating in their rancid milky liquid everywhere between the partners.

"Jake!" cried Sissy, no matter that we were sealed inside the pilot-house, "are you all right?"

The bandanna slipped from Frank Morley's face. With his bare hands Uncle Jake wiped his chest, his arms, his face. Everywhere were fish heads as white and soft as bars of soap—dead-eyed, mouths stretched as if to dislodge the hook. They flopped and lay against Uncle Jake's bare feet; they settled into their pools of putrefaction. Uncle Jake said something consoling to Frank Morley. Then Uncle Jake strode stiffly to the hold and once again disappeared into its noxious depths. Slowly Frank Morley replaced his bandanna.

"Oh dear," said Sissy, "what a mess."

There were nine more such steel drums in the hold and nine times, without further mishap, Uncle Jake and Frank Morley treated the attentive Indians to the sight of rotten fish heads cascading down into the still waters. Without a hitch, they rid *The Prince of Wales* of its precious cargo that had spoiled right under Uncle Jake's own nose, as he said later, laughing and dispelling the last of his anger. All along our starboard side floated white triangular fish heads in search of bodies. The water along our starboard side grew white. When it was plain that the last drum had been emptied and that this irrational ritual of defilement was at an end, the Indians turned away as one and were gone.

In growing darkness Uncle Jake and Frank Morley hosed out the drums, hosed down the deck and, giving Sissy and Annie fair warning to protect their modesty, hosed down each other. That night doors, windows, portholes, the offending hold were all left open to the clear air and a sudden chill. By dawn the smell had all but evaporated and the deck was icy. In the dawn light I was the first on deck, alone and shivering, and suddenly near the bow I found one last fugitive fish head lodged in a scupper. I squatted, studied my find, picked it up, this flattened head with its spiny teeth and eyes like white rubbery raisins. Then slowly I dropped it over the side and listened until, with childish satisfaction, I heard the splash.

38 —

"Look what he's done!" cried Uncle Jake, fully recovered from having been the dupe of nature, and leading us energetically up from Olaf Olafson's jetty. "Why, that miserable Swede has destroyed the place, Frank! He's left us nothing but a ruin!"

Uncle Jake and Frank Morley and Sissy exclaimed together and made dark faces over what the villainous Swede had done, whereas Robert McGinnis and even Annie were as pleased as I was to find ourselves not on some ordinary fox farmer's tidy place but in the midst of a ruin. We three trailed along behind Sissy and Frank Morley and Uncle Jake, surprised and elated at every turn by the parchment shredded in the windows of the log cabin, by the door torn from its leather hinges and flung to earth, by the moose antlers ripped from above the door and smashed to pieces, by the black remains of one of the sheds that Olaf Olafson had deliberately burned down, by the interior of the log cabin, where we found the iron stove on its side and the bunks and crude furniture lying in splinters thanks to Olafson's ax and the tearing and clawing of his dogs. One corner of the cabin was heaped with evidence of drink.

"How terrible," said Sissy, once more bunching her handkerchief to her nose and mouth.

"It's an outrage, Frank," said Uncle Jake. "I've never seen such an outrage."

"I guess he didn't like selling out," said Frank Morley.

"Why, that man," said Uncle Jake, "is a reptile. That's what he is."

"But where are the foxes?" asked Sissy in a small and worried voice, which is when Uncle Jake and Frank Morley discovered, by obvious signs within the windowless log hut used for trapping and slaughtering the foxes, that Olaf Olafson had already gone ahead with the slaughtering, as Uncle Jake had warned him not to, and had already made off with this year's pelts that were ours.

"He's a crook," said Uncle Jake, emerging from the bloody darkness. "He's a no-good pussyfooting crook, Frank, and he's robbed us blind."

Frank Morley nodded.

"Well, I won't have it," said Uncle Jake. "I'm not going to be robbed blind by a no-good Swede who couldn't even find a white woman for a wife. We'll go after him, Frank. That's what we'll do. We'll go after the reptile."

Sissy shivered, Frank Morley turned up the collar of his duck-hunting coat. Robert and Annie McGinnis and I peered into the log hut where Olaf Olafson had killed our foxes.

"Jake," said Frank Morley slowly, "we better leave well enough alone. If the McGinnises had been here when all this damage was done, it would have been worse."

"Do you mean he might come back?" asked Sissy.

Frank Morley nodded.

"I'd like to see the fellow behind bars," said Uncle Jake.

"No," said Frank Morley. "We better leave well enough alone."

"All right," said Uncle Jake at last, "if you say so, Frank."

No one commented on the icicles that began to form from the branches, from the eaves of the log cabin, or in the rigging of *The Prince of Wales*. No one commented on the snow that fell intermittently for the next three weeks. There was no further mention of Olaf Olafson. Uncle Jake refused to allow French Pete ashore, though Frank Morley murmured that there was lots to be done and that they could certainly use an extra hand. But Uncle Jake was adamant. After he and Frank Morley and Robert McGinnis had set up the tent and cleared out the cabin, and had transferred all the provisions and new tools and equipment to the two sheds that Olaf Olafson had left unharmed, he, Uncle Jake, moved the rest of us ashore, leaving French Pete alone on *The Prince of Wales* with only the meagerest supply of food and water, which was the fate that Uncle Jake thought fitting for French Pete. But as Uncle Jake himself discovered one afternoon toward the end of our three weeks devoted to relocating the McGinnises and refurbishing our fox farm, French Pete was happy enough to remain idly aboard *The Prince of Wales,* where he spent most of his time catching halibut off the stern and sleeping day and night on Uncle Jake's army cot in the warmth of the pilothouse.

Uncle Jake was nearly as much in his glory on Olafson's island, that now was ours, as he was when in command of *The Prince of Wales*. He and Frank Morley set up the portable gasoline ripsaw and taught Robert McGinnis how to operate it in order to produce rough boards. They rebuilt the shed that Olafson had burned down. They installed new walls and floors inside the log cabin, righted the stove, constructed new bunks and chairs and a table. They put up ample shelving for Annie McGinnis's foodstuffs, and filled the air inside and out with wood chips and the sound of hammering. Uncle Jake gave careful thought to selecting the best trees for felling, and then he and Frank Morley and Robert McGinnis built in less than a week the log ice house which Uncle Jake said that Robert McGinnis could fill with ice well in advance of the time when *The Prince of Wales* would return with a fresh cargo of fish heads for the foxes. Uncle Jake and Frank Morley taught Robert McGinnis how to shoot his .30-30. They built what Uncle Jake called the most luxurious outhouse in Alaska—an airy structure with its own wood stove and a fluted kerosene lamp instead of candles. Olaf Olafson had tried to smash the generator in his final act of vandalism, but Uncle Jake repaired it. The shortwave radio was missing and reluctantly Uncle Jake transferred the radio from *The Prince of Wales* to the totally restored log cabin.

The woods rang, the chips flew, the circular ripsaw sang its brutal tune, and Uncle Jake and Frank Morley called to each other through the now wintry air and gave Robert McGinnis the privilege of sitting with them on the jetty, which they had also repaired, when they gave themselves a few manly minutes of respite from their labors. Robert McGinnis chopped and stacked five cords of wood; Sissy and I were once more dressed in what Uncle Jake called our outlandish garb; Sissy did all the cooking but Annie, she said, was learning. All day wood smoke of the purest blue rose from the new tin chimney so firmly fastened to the four corners of the roof by sturdy rustproof wires that even the Taku Wind couldn't blow it down.

The cribbage game sat ready and waiting on the new table. The McGinnises' new clothing hung the length of one entire wall from horizontal young saplings stripped of bark. Uncle Jake told Robert

McGinnis that he, McGinnis, could probably build a fieldstone fireplace and chimney when the next summer rolled around. Finally Uncle Jake estimated that there was only a week of work remaining and suggested that he and Frank Morley and Robert McGinnis move out of the tent and into the cabin with the ladies, as he said, for that last week. At night they divided the cabin in half with a thick gray Hudson Bay blanket and thus preserved the necessary division between the sexes, though Uncle Jake did not use the word and refused even to consider the conventions of marriage.

"Well, Frank," said Uncle Jake, hands on hips and laughing ruefully, "the only thing we need now is a bearskin hanging on the wall."

"And a pair of antlers," added Frank Morley, "above the door."

"If McGinnis doesn't lose a hand on that saw—it's a pretty wicked contraption, Frank—and if he and Annie aren't at each other's throats by the end of the first month, I guess they'll survive."

"They'll survive," said Frank Morley.

"Mother will be pleased when she hears what we've done," said Uncle Jake.

A cold dawn, a clear dawn, and Robert McGinnis was trespassing beyond the men's side of the blanket. I awoke with a happy start and found his great face close to mine and a thick finger signaling for silence.

"Important one," he said in a whisper I understood, "important one," and I knew that he wanted me to dress and follow him stealthily out of the cabin for some reason that only he and I would share.

Robert McGinnis had found a path, a faint and secret path which even Uncle Jake had not yet discovered, or so I thought, and I followed Robert McGinnis further and further from the still-sleeping cabin. The skunk cabbages, the devil's clubs, the ferns and windfalls were silent, ice-covered, spotted brilliantly, transparently with the first cold light of day. On went my waddling guide, impulsively looking back with every other step and nodding, smiling, encouraging me to follow. Would he show me a den of blue foxes? A dead wolf in a trap? A she-bear and her cubs? What could he possibly have found to lure the two of us so far from the cabin? What that would please me so much as obviously he knew it would?

The frozen undergrowth was suddenly higher than I was tall. Robert McGinnis cleared the way, forced our passage, held aside the grasses and nettles and branches so that I could pass by. His face was splotchy and disfigured with eagerness. He was trembling.

He stopped, listened, once again put his finger to his lips. High in the trees the sun flashed. All around us the icy darkness was turning blue. Robert McGinnis cocked his head. I nodded and smiled at him. As if surrendering suddenly to the happiness that would be mine he turned and, haunches high, crawled through an opening in the underbrush with me at his heels until abruptly we entered a small clearing, or what was left of a clearing, and regained our feet and side by side stood looking around at Robert McGinnis's marvel.

He tried to speak. He peered down at my face. Slowly and carefully he began to form on the fingers of one hand letters from the manual alphabet which he knew full well that I could not understand, despite his recent and secret tutoring.

There before us in the overgrown clearing in the sun-spotted gloom stood six small weathered wooden houses on spindly and crooked stilts. They were large enough to hold a person, those small houses, but no person, I understood—manual alphabet or no manual alphabet—had ever lived in them. They had steep wooden roofs, no windows, and large dark open cracks between the withered strips of wood that formed their sides. There were patches of glistening green moss on their roofs. And best of all, as I began to see, these strange gray silent houses had once been brightly painted, were streaked and tinted with the faintest shades of what had once been bold reds, bold blues, bold greens.

Quickly Robert McGinnis cautioned me not to laugh in my excitement, not to speak, not to move. Looking around him as if we were being spied upon by foxes, wolves, malamutes, an entire forest of unfriendly eyes, slowly he approached the nearest house, as obviously he had done before, and peered at the silent house on its stilts. From the front of the house he removed the papery square of wood that had once been a door and extended both arms, reached as far as he could inside the opening, and carefully withdrew and held out to me this prize—a skull, a small human skull that had no lower jaw.

He thrust it toward me, he who knew well the workings of a child's mind and had only a child's mind himself, gifted though he was at the piano. "Dead... Dead..." he was saying, "oots... oots..."

So Robert McGinnis had prowled Olaf Olafson's island, had stumbled upon the sacred burial ground of the Skoots, and had thought of me. He thought that the secret of the little houses was our own and except for me intended to keep the secret to himself. Here he would come to be alone, here he would sort the bones and stir the ashes and look at the darkened skulls of the long-departed Skoots inhabiting this overgrown miniature village of the dead. He would restore the clearing. He would be the sole proprietor of six dead Alaskan Indians and their relics.

He thrust the skull into my hands.

I accepted it. I held it as I might have held a brimming bowl of water that must not be spilled. And if I prized the skull of His Unholiness, which was only the skull of a bear, how much more I prized this small and smoky skull that chilled my palms. Its eye sockets were filled with soot and appeared intended for eyes as large as eggs, despite the skull's small size; on top of the fissured cranium there remained a few fluttering strands of hair, though this Skoot like the five others had been cremated, as we later learned from Uncle Jake, before being laid away where Robert McGinnis had found him. And which was better, I asked myself, the empty eye sockets or the tiny teeth? There was not one tooth missing from the curve of bone where they belonged, and those teeth were smaller than my own and of a bluish-purplish-greenish black—black from the decay that had attacked them long before this young Skoot had died. They looked like hardened kernels of corn.

An icy snow had begun to fall despite the cold sun spotting the sacred ground where we stood. Robert McGinnis's head was close to mine. Then I did what only a child would do and what even Robert McGinnis would not have thought of doing, as close as we were, as childlike and magical as he was to me. Suddenly I ran the middle three fingers of my left hand lightly around the surface of one of the skull's eye sockets and, raising my eyes to Robert McGinnis's, stuffed my fingers into my mouth and licked them clean of the soot which was all that remained of the smoke that once had been the dead man's flesh.

Robert McGinnis slapped his thighs, nodding and laughing, peering at me with admiration that was little short of awe. I tasted the ancient smoke in my mouth. He took back the skull and replaced it. He put his fingers to his lips. We returned to the path and to the still-sleeping cabin where no one was the wiser for what we had done.

And what kind of child receives the skull of a bear from her father and the skull of an Indian from her father's friend? An important child as I had been told. A child loved unusually and at an early age by men. A child deprived at that early age of a fear of death.

· · ·

"Frank," said Uncle Jake early in the afternoon of that same day, standing bareheaded in the snow with ax in hand, "we've got a visitor."

We had heard no sound of oarlocks, no slapping of a skiff's bottom on water. Yet there at the end of our jetty stood a person who was unmistakably one of the Skoots from White Eye. He too was bareheaded, motionless with his arms at his sides, an apparition that might have come up out of the sea or out of the snow, waiting patiently to be seen.

Robert McGinnis seized my upper arm in his hand and jerked suddenly in the direction of the jetty, though he could not have heard what Uncle Jake had said, and for one terrible instant Robert McGinnis and I both thought that we had been found out. But we had not. Uncle Jake strolled down to speak with the Indian. He listened, nodded, and walked back to us, leaving the Indian on the end of the jetty, still motionless.

"He says they've got a problem over there," said Uncle Jake.

"What is it?" asked Frank Morley.

"I don't know," said Uncle Jake. "But he says they need my help. He wants me to go with him."

"Don't do it," said Frank Morley.

"Oh," said Uncle Jake, "I don't think we need to worry."

Frank Morley shook his head. Robert McGinnis tried to interfere.

"I won't be long," said Uncle Jake.

Sissy opened the cabin door.

"Jake?" she said.

"I'm just going over to White Eye for a little while," said Uncle Jake.

"You know what happened there," said Sissy.

"This is different," said Uncle Jake.

"I don't see how," said Sissy. "It's dangerous."

"Sissy's right," said Frank Morley. "You'd better listen to what she says."

"Frank," said Uncle Jake, "this is a chance to make amends. I can't turn it down. Besides, that fellow down on the jetty says he's got something for us in his skiff. Let's see what he's brought us."

The village offering proved to be a freshly shot young deer, which Uncle Jake and Frank Morley carried up from the jetty and hung head down from an icy tree limb near the cabin. No one among us had ever seen a dead deer until now, except Frank Morley and Uncle Jake, but only Robert McGinnis and I were drawn to the still-warm creature with its white and fluffy scut, its slender legs, its silken coat, its coronet of antlers barely formed, its large and quiet eyes, its grace and stiffness, all of which Robert McGinnis and I inspected carefully, though Robert McGinnis was still afraid, I knew, of the Indian.

"There you are, Sissy," said Uncle Jake. "Frank will skin him out and you can roast the haunches and cook up the steaks. There's nothing sweeter in this world than venison."

So Uncle Jake, not knowing what to expect, as he said, assembled an assortment of small tools and medical supplies, though the problem, he said, might well prove to be one of morals or the human spirit as it had been before, a declaration Sissy and Frank Morley received in silence. Then Uncle Jake kissed Sissy, shouldered his pack, and rejoined the waiting Indian on the jetty. The snow had become so heavy that we on shore could see nothing of their progress across the water.

We heard two distant foxes barking. In the driving snow *The Prince of Wales* was as invisible as it would have been had French Pete hauled up the anchor and sailed the old boat back to Juneau alone.

"Sissy," said Frank Morley, "I'm just going to skin out that buck right now. You and Annie better wait inside."

And now there was only the silent snowbound cabin, the hanging deer, the day that was already dying, the gloomy unspoken knowledge that Uncle Jake was gone. Frank Morley, stooped and slow and methodical though he usually was, worked with swiftness and concentration against the fading light, against the threatening emptiness around us. Robert McGinnis and I, his silent acolytes, stood watching the progress of Frank Morley's blade. The blade slid down, sliced across, guided by the old arthritic hand, and as closely as I watched the spilling of the entrails and the slowly emerging mysteries of the dead deer, nonetheless I too suddenly wished only for the end of Frank Morley's work and for the warmth and safety of the cabin.

Off came the creature's head, antlers and all, and lay in the snow like the head of the deer that was mounted in the window of Guns & Locks & Clothes. The hide lay crumpled in the snow like an old cast-off coat. Then Frank Morley halved the carcass—hurrying as we could see—and trimmed and chopped and, followed by Robert McGinnis and me, stored the butchered meat in one of the sheds, carried away the head and hide, swept the snow as clear as possible of the signs of his butchering. It was dark by the time Frank Morley presented Sissy with a round dozen venison steaks that were each as large as Robert McGinnis's hand.

Outside the wind was howling through the snow and pounding against the cabin doors that Frank Morley had barred. The stately kerosene lamps were lit, the wood stove was throwing off a steady heat, Sissy was frying potatoes on the iron range. Robert and Annie McGinnis sat across the table from each other unable to touch the cribbage game between them. We were warm, we were secure, we smelled the potatoes and the sweet clean smell of unseasoned wood. But we were beleaguered.

"He's not coming back tonight," said Sissy.

Frank Morley shook his head.

"I've given up worrying about him," said Sissy.

"I wish you had," said Frank Morley.

"I guess I better cook the steaks," said Sissy, smiling the smile she reserved only for such occasions and only for Frank Morley.

Sissy burned herself, laughed at her carelessness, served up the meal. No one talked except Frank Morley, who with an effort told us about his days in Dawson and the time that another fellow and he rescued a St. Bernard from being torn to pieces and eaten alive by two Siberian huskies. He and the other fellow, Frank Morley said at our silent table, effected the rescue of the St. Bernard with axes. There wasn't much left of the huskies, he said, but at least the St. Bernard, the only one that was ever seen in those parts, got off practically unharmed.

"Oh Frank," said Sissy, laughing and nursing her hand, "I never knew that you had done such things!"

Frank Morley nodded shyly and said that he had. And things much worse or better, depending on how you looked at it, if the truth be known. The wind howled. Silence fell again at our table. Frank Morley and Sissy once more looked dejected.

The storm continued for two more days, whirling occasional birds of prey through sudden clear pockets in the snow, and obliterating the shapes of trees, the sheds, the jetty, the most luxurious outhouse in Alaska. We stayed as much as possible inside the cabin. We waited. Sissy prepared a large pot of blackly crusted baked beans for Uncle Jake's return.

"Cheer up, Bobby," she said, and then sadly told Frank Morley that she did not know what was wrong with our new fox farmer but that she thought that he was no longer even bothering to read her lips.

"He'll be all right," said Frank Morley, "when he's on his own."

Before dawn on the third day since Uncle Jake's departure, Sissy and I were up and dressed and Sissy was warming the baked beans and preparing the batter for the flapjacks she intended to serve for breakfast when Frank Morley and the McGinnises awoke. She was bustling as quietly as she could in her slender athletic way and smiling, every now and then opening the door and listening, peering out into the silence and the dawn light on the snow. Today was the day, she said, that Uncle Jake was coming back—and in time, she said she knew in her bones, for breakfast. She was going to give him venison steaks with his beans, and told me to set his place at the table along with ours. She made two pots of coffee, flinging in the egg shells to settle the grounds, and laughed at the sight, which was ordinarily denied us, of the two boys, as she called them, snoring away in their long johns.

And then we heard him calling—Uncle Jake calling out to us from the jetty—and Frank Morley and Robert McGinnis were hurrying into their trousers while Annie McGinnis, working her little face and swinging her hips that were as wide as an ax handle, as French Pete had said, was making her usual enthusiastic noises and taking down the blanket.

"Jake!" said Sissy, dropping a chunk of lard into the skillet and turning to the open door, "you're just in time!"

"I could smell the beans all the way down on the jetty," laughed Uncle Jake, and there he was—rumpled, unshaven, smelling of smoked fish, thinner than when he had left us, as Sissy thought, but nonetheless tall and strong, unharmed, bluer-eyed than ever, and ready and waiting for the commotion his return now caused.

"To the table, everyone!" cried Sissy.

"Welcome back, partner," said Frank Morley.

"Sunny," said Uncle Jake, "come kiss the beard!"

"Don't start the story," said Sissy, heaping the one plate with steaks and beans and the others with six flapjacks each, and pouring the coffee, "until I can sit down and listen, Jake."

"Oh," said Uncle Jake, winking at Frank Morley and sitting sideways and crossing his knees, "it's not much of a story."

"But there's no trouble over there?" said Frank Morley, looking significantly at Uncle Jake.

"No trouble," said Uncle Jake.

"The Skoots aren't riled up?" said Frank Morley, as Robert McGinnis watched Uncle Jake's face for the answer and Sissy finally took her place not opposite from Uncle Jake, which traditionally was where

Frank Morley sat, but beside Annie McGinnis where she could be close to the stove.

"There was nothing wrong with the Skoots," said Uncle Jake, as Robert McGinnis nodded vigorously at Uncle Jake and me, his round face creased and squeezed in his relief and pleasure, and suddenly began to eat.

"Thank goodness," said Sissy.

"Well," said Frank Morley, "what was it?"

"Teeth!" said Uncle Jake, and took a hot mouthful of his black and caramelized baked beans and savored the sounds and expressions of surprise around the table.

"Teeth?" said Sissy.

"That's right," said Uncle Jake, laughing and sipping his coffee and winking again at Frank Morley. "Teeth."

"Well, partner," said Frank Morley, smiling and shaking his head, "I guess I'm just dense today. What do you mean?"

"Frank," said Uncle Jake, slicing into one of his steaks and laughing, "it was the darnedest thing. I couldn't refuse to go with Nam-Bok— that's the fellow they sent to get me—but I didn't know what to expect, I can tell you. It might have had something to do with that unpleasant business, as you and Sissy were afraid it might. Or it might have been their burial ground."

"Burial ground?" said Sissy as Robert McGinnis shuddered and dropped his fork.

"Yes," said Uncle Jake. "You remember what the reptile said—that the Skoots didn't want him fox farming on this island because some of their dead are buried over here. So naturally I thought that that might have been the problem. An Indian burial ground can cause a lot of trouble, as you well know, Frank. Or maybe it was something easier— the fish heads," said Uncle Jake, coloring beneath his three-day growth of beard, "or something they wanted to trade for food, or an engine they wanted me to fix. At least I wasn't going to build them another still for their hoochinoo," said Uncle Jake with a boyish laugh, "that's for sure. Anyhow off I went with Nam-Bok through the snow. He was rowing Indian fashion, standing up in the stern of the skiff and facing forward, while I was seated in the bow with my back to the driving snow and facing Nam-Bok, who obviously didn't want to talk.

"It gave me a pretty peculiar feeling to be back in White Eye, I can tell you, especially with the snow and no sign of life except for a few welcome traces of wood smoke on the air. And it was worse when I realized that Nam-Bok, who was leading the way, was taking me to the same cabin—the very same cabin, Frank—where I had found poor Brewster tied to the bed and tried to help that unfortunate woman."

"Oh Jake," said Sissy, interrupting from where she was standing at the stove, "how strange."

"It was strange all right," said Uncle Jake. "Enough to give a fellow the willies, to use your expression, Frank. Well, Nam-Bok pushed open the door—there was a dead deer just like ours hanging from the eaves beside the door—and I went in. And ventilation? Why, there was so much snow piled up around the log walls outside and so many deerskins hung on the walls inside and such a wicked fire burning in the potbellied stove that there wasn't a breath to be had inside that cabin. Not a breath. And the smell? Why, the smell in that cabin was worse than the reptile's winter underwear, I can tell you. The thing that made me uneasy, Frank, was the number of people in that hot and foul-smelling little room. There were three old squaws, four younger men, besides myself and Nam-Bok, and seated cross-legged on the famous bed a Skoot so old and shrunken that he was about the size of Sunny. They didn't welcome me, they didn't say a word. It was ominous, Frank. Pretty ominous. Then the ancient Skoot on the bed made a sudden sound and grimace of pain, and I thought that he was giving voice to the wounded spirit of the village and that I had been summoned to White Eye to atone for it. The heat was terrible and those Skoots weren't looking at me kindly, I can tell you.

"But I was wrong. In the next minute the old fellow said something, one of the squaws spoke up, and Nam-Bok finally found his tongue. Well, what I thought was ominous was merely pathetic, Frank. The old fellow's name was Olo—it means the person who's always hungry, Sissy—and the squaws and younger Skoots as well as Nam-Bok were the last of his family, as Nam-Bok explained. Naturally I was curious about why they were all crowded into this particular cabin, and it was with Nam-Bok's answer that the whole thing turned pathetic. In the first place Olo was chief of the Skoots in White Eye—he looked like a chief, Frank, despite his faded blue denim clothes and the shabby blanket over his shoulders—but more important, as I should have guessed, Olo was the father of that unfortunate young woman. When his daughter died the old fellow, in his grief, moved into her cabin, bringing along his squaws and sons, who of course included Nam-Bok. That way, as Nam-Bok said, Olo could spend his last days where the spirit of his dead daughter still lived on. According to Nam-Bok, the old fellow found his daughter in everything he touched and saw in that miserable cabin. I had never heard of such a thing, have you, Frank? As soon as I understood the situation, and understood how devoted to that poor unfortunate young woman old Olo was, I knew that he didn't bear me any grudge for what had happened. I told Nam-Bok to tell the old fellow that I regretted his loss, which Nam-Bok did. Olo's reply was to the effect that his daughter had sought and received my wisdom and who could quarrel with that? So I asked Nam-Bok what his father wanted, just as the old fellow made another grimace of pain and, as if he had understood my question, launched into a lengthy speech to his most trusted son, who was not a person I would have trusted, I can tell you.

"Well, you can see what's coming, Frank, but there in that poor young woman's cabin with the heat and the smoke and the old chief sitting cross-legged on Brewster's bed in his grief, I didn't, and was not at all prepared for what was coming.

"'Teeth,' said Nam-Bok when the old fellow finally stopped talking.

"'Teeth?' I said, just as surprised as you were, Sissy, a few minutes ago. Here I had thought I had come on some sort of serious mission, even a mission of dire consequence, and now this sullen young Skoot was talking about his father's teeth. I was relieved, naturally, and even a bit amused. But of course I didn't see how I could possibly have anything to do with Olo's teeth.

"'My father is old,' said Nam-Bok in that sullen voice of his. 'All his life he has lived in hunger. Eating is what my father does. He chews the meat of the bear, the elk, the moose, the deer, the caribou. Olo is famous for his hunger and the strong way he eats. No one eats as proudly and fiercely as Olo, though he is very old.'

"'So now,' I said, 'there is something wrong with his teeth?'

"The old fellow spoke again to Nam-Bok and the squaws nodded up at me agreeably, I saw, despite the fact that my eyes were smarting and the smell kept reminding me of those darn fish heads, Frank.

"'Olo,' said Nam-Bok as the old fellow suddenly clapped his smoky wizened hands to his mouth, 'has good teeth and bad teeth. His top teeth have never hurt or broken and have stayed in his head for all the years of his life. But the bottom teeth were traitors. All of his bottom teeth have fallen out, except for two. And now these last two bottom teeth are on fire. You see how old Olo suffers.'

"Well," said Uncle Jake, pausing to compliment Sissy on the steaks and to request another helping of her baked beans, "by now what I was beginning to understand of the old fellow's plight was making me uneasy. I didn't like the implications of what Nam-Bok was saying. I didn't come to Alaska to be a dentist, Frank, even if the patient was only an old and superstitious Skoot. To go anywhere near a person's mouth when you're not trained is a risky business, we both know that. Ordinary physical injuries are one thing. Teeth are another.

"'Nam-Bok,' I said at last, as cautiously as I could, 'I am sorry that Olo is in pain. But why did he give me the gift of the deer? Why did he summon me to White Eye? What does he want me to do?'

"'Take them out,' said Nam-Bok promptly. 'Take them out now.'

"'Do you mean that Olo wants me to extract two of his teeth?' I said.

"Nam-Bok nodded.

"'But Nam-Bok,' I said, 'I don't know anything about extracting teeth.'

"'You know,' he said.

"'The Skoots have their own way of dealing with such things,' I said. 'I don't want to tamper with tribal customs.'

"'You,' said Nam-Bok. 'He wants you.'

"'Good Lord,' I said, thinking of my poor cousin, Sissy, 'Olo might die if I attempt to extract his teeth. Don't you understand?'

"'He hurts,' said Nam-Bok. 'He doesn't care about dying. He won't die.'

"'Well,' I said, 'I suppose I could at least take a look inside his mouth. But I don't like it, Nam-Bok. I don't like it a bit.'

"Nam-Bok nodded and as the squaws stirred about where they were squatting and the fire crackled, he concentrated on the ground he had won from me so far. But suddenly I knew that there was more to all this than met the eye. I looked hard at Nam-Bok and then at old Olo, who suddenly grinned and with one shriveled finger made stabbing motions toward his jaw.

"'Take them out,' said Nam-Bok, sounding more and more like some shyster lawyer, Frank, 'and then give Olo white man's teeth. That's what Olo wants. White man's teeth.'

"'What!' I cried, 'dentures? That old fellow expects me to provide him with a lower plate?'

"'New teeth,' said Nam-Bok. 'On the bottom.'

"I was stunned, Frank, and not a little angry. I stared at Nam-Bok, disregarding the squaws and the four young men who were all gesticulating now and smiling at me as if the deed were done.

"'Nam-Bok,' I said, finally getting control of myself, 'I can't. I might be able to pull the two bad teeth, but I can't possibly make Olo some sort of makeshift lower plate. It can't be done.'

"'Pull the teeth,' said Nam-Bok just as the old fellow, who was clearly stoical as well as brave, grunted, grimaced, and then seized the two offending teeth as if to wrench them out with his own fingers.

"Well," said Uncle Jake, holding his third cup of coffee in midair and recrossing his knees, "what could I do?"

There was a pause as Frank Morley ruminated on the question. Annie was holding her hand to the side of her face and staring at Uncle Jake in horror. Sissy lingered by the stove, bravely awaiting the rest of the story. Seated now on Uncle Jake's lap, though he was still eating, I waited impatiently for the outcome. Only Robert McGinnis had given up listening to Uncle Jake's adventure to bury his happy face in his flapjacks.

"Well," said Frank Morley at last, "I've heard some Alaskan whoppers in my time, Jake. But nothing like this."

"It's not a whopper," said Uncle Jake. "It's true."

"I know it is," said Frank Morley.

"I'm not upsetting you, Sissy, am I?" asked Uncle Jake.

"Oh no," said Sissy. "But what did you do to that poor old man?"

"Well," said Uncle Jake, "I didn't give him laughing gas, that's for sure!"

Sissy and Frank Morley reacted appropriately to Uncle Jake's well-intended joke, and then Uncle Jake pushed away his plate—another habit that Sissy had always found annoying—and resumed his story.

"Nam-Bok knew he had me," said Uncle Jake, using his razor-sharp pocketknife to fashion a toothpick from one of Sissy's wooden matches, which he had begun to do at the end of every meal in imitation of Frank Morley, "and actually I was becoming interested in trying to relieve old Olo's pain though for the life of me I still didn't know what I could do about coming up with a homemade lower plate for the old fellow. Well, the wind was howling, we were snowed in, there was nothing I could do but give it a try. So I told Nam-Bok that I needed leverage and that Olo would have to get off the bed and sit on a chair—there was one chair in the cabin, a spindly thing constructed of rawhide and hand-hewn slats, presently occupied by one of the four young men. The squaws and Nam-Bok's other three brothers were naturally seated on the floor around the stove. As soon as I spoke the young man sitting in the chair vacated it, and the old fellow, who was not much bigger

than Sunny here, as I've said, began trying to move in little fits and
starts—he was eager to help me, Frank, I knew that from the beginning—while the three squaws got to their feet and went immediately
to the old fellow's assistance. I had never seen an Indian so small and
old, and standing weakly upright between the bustling squaws he looked
even more the mummy—with his brown skin shrunken tight to the
tendons and his oily black hair that might have been growing for a
hundred years. The only sign of Olo's rank as chief was a necklace of
bears' claws around his skinny neck, meaning that he had once killed
a bear in single-handed combat with only a knife. Anyhow I told Nam-
Bok that I had to have some water and that I would need him to hold
the flashlight which fortunately I had brought along.

"Well, they sat Olo in the chair. It was easy to see that the old fellow
was weak from hunger—wasn't that a sad irony considering his name?—
and they crowded around to watch. I told Nam-Bok that I had to have
some elbow room but the old squaws and the young men wouldn't
give an inch, so there I was with the jostling, the crowding, and of
course the smell. I had removed the flashlight, the iodine, the rolls of
gauze and the pliers from my pack, and Nam-Bok had handed one
of the squaws a pail of water. I told Nam-Bok to ask his father if the
old fellow didn't want a last minute stiff drink of hoochinoo, but Nam-
Bok said that they had already drunk up all the hoochinoo they had.

"'Nam-Bok,' I said, 'tell Olo that it's going to hurt.'

"'He knows,' said Nam-Bok. 'He doesn't care.'

"'Tell him he'll have to hold still,' I said.

"'We'll hold him,' said Nam-Bok.

"For a moment Olo and I looked at each other, he with his little
bony head tilted back, I from my vantage point of what to all the
Skoots was my unusual physique, and do you know, Sissy, that old
fellow had the most beautiful eyes I'd ever seen—present company
excluded. I saw that his eyes were golden, Sissy, just like the eyes of
one of Mother's cocker spaniels back home, and the beauty of old Olo's
eyes was a shock, I can tell you. Then while we were looking at each
other in this steady gaze of mutual companionship, suddenly, and before
I had a chance to speak, the old fellow snapped his mouth wide open,
inviting me beyond a doubt to get to work, and laughing at me with
those golden eyes of his.

"'Nam-Bok,' I said, 'the light.'

"And there it was—the mouth filled with the beam of light, the
upper teeth that were just as good as Nam-Bok had said they were,

and in the middle of the lower jaw the two scraggly traitors standing side by side, ready, as I saw it, to resist me to the very end. They were long and crooked and mean-looking, Frank, the color of a thumbnail struck a hard blow by a hammer. I knew at once that it wasn't going to be easy.

"It would have been less difficult if the two rotten teeth had been growing down from the upper jaw instead of poking up from the rubbery and otherwise empty gum of the lower. It meant that I had to put one arm around the old fellow's head and to grip his jaw from underneath and try to hold it down while pulling up with all my strength on the pliers. It was an awkward business but I had to go through with it.

"'All right, Nam-Bok,' I said, 'here we go.'

"I felt Olo's fragile jaw between my arm and chest. I seized his lower jaw. I held the pliers in my right hand and tried to get a grip on one of the teeth. I could hardly see what I was doing for the heads of the three old squaws and their frowning sons. The pliers slipped off immediately, as I should have known, and I lost my hold.

"'Nam-Bok,' I said, 'tell them to give me a little room. I can't work this way.'

"But they didn't budge.

"Then I tried again and felt the pliers catch and I squeezed my hand and had that scraggly devil right where I wanted him, I can tell you. But what now? A steady upward motion? A little twisting to help it along? Or should I put all my strength—and you know that I'm no weakling, Frank—into one swift and single effort, not to just yank out the tooth of course but to pull it out quickly and evenly, once and for all, without coaxing? I didn't want to break it off in the old fellow's jaw, but nonetheless I decided on a bold attempt without the coaxing.

"I braced myself. I exhaled. And then I tightened my fist and at the same time that I drew in my breath I pulled up on the pliers like someone determined to pull a young tree out of the earth by its roots. Well, I had feared the worst, but I needn't have. Can you believe that, Frank? Here I was, a novice, standing in as awkward a position as I'd ever been in and with good reason to fear the worst. But I must have found the proper angle, must have exerted exactly the right pressure, because contrary to what I had expected, my arm, hand, and the pliers all flowed upwards together—for the longest time, Frank—until to my surprise I was holding up the tooth protruding from the bite of the pliers for everyone to see. I hadn't felt a thing, Frank. I hadn't known the tooth was out. Pulling that tooth was like drawing a long and slippery and utterly compliant cork from a bottle. I couldn't believe my luck and didn't even mind the old squaws pushing and crowding around me in their pleasure. I had expected blood, but there was no blood. Not a drop. I gave the extracted tooth to Olo, who accepted it, looked at it, poked one finger into the spot where the tooth had been. And then shaking with tiny spasms of laughter he made another speech that Nam-Bok saw no need to translate. I was pretty pleased, I can tell you.

"But that's the very moment when I had my premonition, Frank," said Uncle Jake, and paused.

"The second tooth," said Frank Morley.

"Exactly," said Uncle Jake.

"Your luck couldn't hold," said Frank Morley.

"That second tooth," said Uncle Jake, "fought back. That second tooth was as malignant as the first tooth was benign. I might have known it and in a way I did."

"Jake," said Sissy, interrupting again and glancing worriedly at the McGinnises and Frank Morley, "we understand."

"I know you do," said Uncle Jake, "and it was even worse than that. The pliers slipped off about five times. Olo's tongue got in the way. And what happened when I finally managed to clamp the pliers to that tooth and for the second time to coordinate my long slow inhalation with the steady motion of my hand and arm? Why, nothing of course. Nothing at all. I exhaled, I waited, I tried again. The old squaws looked at me in alarm. Olo's courage deserted him. Nam-Bok spoke to me in his own tongue, as if I could understand a word of it, and I told him that his job was to hold the flashlight and that he better stop talking and pay attention to what he was supposed to be doing.

"Did I twist that tooth? Did I try to rock it back and forth? Did I yank on it while the old fellow howled? Did I pit my will against the will of an eighty-year-old incisor that was harder to even wiggle than a spike of iron? You bet I did."

"Jake," said Frank Morley quickly and leaning forward, "look at her. She's faint."

"I'm all right," said Sissy.

"Of course she's all right," said Uncle Jake. "Anyhow the docility of the first tooth was matched, as I say, by the stubbornness of the second. I forgot all about trying to coordinate my breath and hand, forgot my audience, lost my patience, staked everything on overcoming the last of the traitors with brute force. Olo was yowling and slithering about in his chair despite the headlock in which I held him, and the last of the incisors was still there and as solid as a rock no matter how violently I tried to wrench it loose. Well, I won of course. And do you know how? I just unscrewed that tooth! That's right, Frank. I just unscrewed it! Suddenly I realized that if the first tooth had been like a slippery compliant cork in the old fellow's jaw, the second was like a corkscrew that had been ground to the limit into the bone. So I waited and then I gave it a quick twist, just a quick sharp little twist, and sure enough it moved. Not much, Frank, just a crack that I could hardly feel—but it was all I needed. I composed myself and gave it a few more slow and steady turns. I listened to the faint screeching and splintering with satisfaction, I can tell you. When I had it good and loose I threw caution to the winds and in one great victorious tug just tore that spent devil from its socket. Olo screamed, I smelled the squaws, I released my hold on the old fellow's jaw and head. That's when I needed the rolls of gauze, Frank, and the iodine and the bucket of water. But when I finally staunched the flow, and when old Olo recovered himself and understood what I had done—by this time the squaws had carried him back to his mildewed mattress and his furs and blankets—he was as happy as a clam, I can tell you. As for the tooth, its root was about an inch long and exactly the spiral shape of a corkscrew, as I had guessed. No wonder it gave me such a tussle. If I could have brought it back to Sunny I would have."

"Jake!" said Sissy, "you're being awful!"

"Oh well," said Uncle Jake with a laugh, "I needed those two teeth as you'll soon see."

"For the lower plate," said Frank Morley.

"Exactly," said Uncle Jake.

"Tell us," said Sissy in her once more sweet and mollifying voice.

"First of all," said Uncle Jake, "they made me eat a whole smoked salmon. I sat on the floor with the squaws and Nam-Bok and his brothers, who shared one salmon comfortably—it was that big—while I had to eat one long fat fellow alone while they watched me, which wasn't easy. You know what the wind and snow were like—you were all just as trapped as I was in that storm—and the smoke was worse than ever as was the smell. That night and the next two nights we all slept together wrapped up in furs on the floor like dogs, except for Olo, of course, who had Brewster's bed. That first night I slept lightly, listening to Olo dream—about having his teeth pulled out I thought—but sleeping with Olo and his family was a lark compared with my nights in the reptile's cabin.

"Well, the next morning Olo was in fine shape and I decided to face the problem of the lower plate. I was stormbound, I had nothing better to do, I began to think that perhaps I could give Olo his white man's teeth after all. And the funny thing, Frank, is that there was nothing to it. As soon as I got my idea the job I had thought impossible was as good as done. First I asked Nam-Bok to bring me the head of the deer hanging out there in the ice and snow. My audience sat around laughing and nudging each other, and I understood their amusement and joined in. No doubt they had never seen anyone, white man or Indian, pulling the teeth out of the frozen head of a deer. I hadn't, that's for sure. Then I spent most of those two days snapping off the roots and filing smooth the crowns—fortunately for me I had brought along the file—and carving from an old piece of soft pine an inverse version of Olo's lower jaw. It was something like a little wooden horseshoe hollowed out so as to fit down over old Olo's gums, and it was a snug fit all things considered. Then thanks to my sewing awl and pocketknife and pliers and the spool of fine steel wire, soon I had all the holes I needed in the wooden plate and in the crowns to be affixed to it, and soon had all those crowns securely wired to the wooden plate. That's the way it was done, Frank, and when it was finished everyone kept passing around my handiwork, trying to fit it into their own mouths.

"Well, the head squaw cooked up half the venison and Olo had his first good meal in years. Of course he couldn't wear his white man's teeth except when actually eating, but that was enough. The beauty of the thing," said Uncle Jake with a proud laugh, "was that I fastened what was left of Olo's own two front teeth right where they belonged in the center of the wooden plate. How's that for artistic achievement, eh Frank?"

"Oh Jake," said Sissy, "you're wonderful!"

"Anyhow," said Uncle Jake, "I guess I showed that Doc Haines a thing or two!"

"I guess you did," said Frank Morley, slapping his knee.

"And now," said Uncle Jake, swinging me down and pushing back his chair and standing up and stretching, "now the only thing we have to do is to move the burial ground."

"What's that?" said Frank Morley as Robert McGinnis choked and sputtered.

"Why, just move their burial ground," said Uncle Jake. "I want to put it on that little island behind this one."

"Jake," said Frank Morley, shaking his head. "I don't know about that. Tampering with their dead is the one thing that could cause real trouble between ourselves and the Skoots."

"They won't know about it," said Uncle Jake.

"The reptile," said Frank Morley. "You remember what the reptile told you."

"That's just it," said Uncle Jake. "The reptile was wrong. I talked enough with Olo and Nam-Bok to know that that burial ground is as old as the hills and that there's not a Skoot in White Eye who remembers it or knows it's here."

"Why move it?" asked Frank Morley.

"Because I respect them, Frank," said Uncle Jake. "I respect their spirits. It's the spirits that could cause the trouble. Right now we're contaminating the spirits of all Skoots dead or living, and sooner or later we'll suffer for it—or the McGinnises will. It doesn't matter that the Skoots in White Eye don't know about this thing."

"I still don't like it," said Frank Morley.

"Well," said Uncle Jake, "I just want to do it for old Olo, Frank. I think we'd better."

With a sweep of the hand before the face, Uncle Jake took the burial ground away from Robert McGinnis, though Uncle Jake could not have known about Robert McGinnis's secret discovery, just as Robert McGinnis did not know that Uncle Jake had already studied the six small wooden houses before Robert McGinnis had found them, as became obvious enough when, that afternoon, Uncle Jake took Frank Morley to view the burial ground and to consider the work that they still had to do. But with his usual unerring aim, and without even knowing that he was doing so, Uncle Jake deprived Robert McGinnis of his childish dream. In a mere two days the village of the dead ceased to exist on our island. Gone were the houses, the smoky skull; gone, for Robert McGinnis, was his wondrous selfishness that only the child-ish mind can know. Now there was nothing left for him but the blue foxes that he had yet to see.

Glumly Robert McGinnis and I accompanied Uncle Jake and Frank Morley to the small forbidding tree- and snow-covered island that Uncle Jake had selected as the new resting place for the sacred bones

and ashes. Glumly we stood by watching as Uncle Jake and Frank
Morley decided on the clearing that best duplicated the overgrown
clearing on our own island. Glumly we watched as Uncle Jake and
Frank Morley cut down slender saplings and hammered them horizontally to the trunks of close-standing trees from which they had
stripped the lower branches. Moodily we too rode along in the dory
as Uncle Jake and Frank Morley ferried our six ancient houses, without
mishap, to the new isle of the dead, as Uncle Jake called it, and hoisted
them to their safe platforms in the trees. We heard the skulls—one of
which was Robert McGinnis's gift to me—rolling about in the houses.
We saw the six ghostly houses perched in the trees. Back on our own
island we watched in mute despair as Uncle Jake and Frank Morley
chopped the remaining spindly stilts from the frozen ground and halved
and quartered them and burned them like brittle bones in the iron stove.

"Well," said Uncle Jake as we sniffed the fading acrid smell of the
smoke, "we've done all we could, eh Frank? No more reptile. No more
dead Skoots. Now it's up to Robert McGinnis to make a go of this
place."

The McGinnises came out to see us off. The dawn was cold, the sun
sharp as a blade, the dory loaded with our scant gear and waiting at
the jetty. We were milling for a last time in front of the cabin.

"Robert," said Uncle Jake, "I've come to the conclusion that this
island of ours has got to have a name. I propose we name it Olo Island.
That's the last thing I can do," said Uncle Jake, turning to Frank Morley,
"to atone."

Frank Morley nodded in silence.

"Robert," said Uncle Jake again, "I believe that we can get this thing
done officially. As soon as I reach Juneau I'll go down to the Bureau
of Geodetic Survey and persuade the powers that be to put this island
on the map. Literally. Which means that you and Annie will be the
first people ever to live on Olo Island. Well," he said, looking from
face to face and then upwards toward the smoke rising from the new
tin chimney, "I guess we better say our good-bys."

"Just one more thing," said Frank Morley.

Then Frank Morley, slow and careful and stoop-shouldered as always, stepped behind the cabin and returned with a flimsy ladder which
he propped against the cabin door. Despite his heavy breathing and

painful joints, he climbed the ladder and nailed above the door the small bright coronet of antlers that he had secretly removed from the skull of our first deer two weeks ago with this very purpose in mind.

The McGinnises stared up at the antlers mutely, neither pleased nor puzzled, but Uncle Jake and Sissy complimented Frank Morley on his thoughtfulness. Frank Morley put away the ladder.

I clung to my bounteous magical Robert McGinnis. Sissy clung to Annie.

The McGinnises followed us to the jetty, still in silence. Uncle Jake told the McGinnises that they would spend the following Christmas up on High Ridge Street in Juneau. That was his promise.

We cast off the dory.

Robert and Annie McGinnis, hand in hand and standing as close as they could to the edge of the jetty, then threw off their silence, screwed their faces into the agony that passed for their smiles, and suddenly and simultaneously launched into unending rivers of outpourings of the eager speech that we could neither understand nor answer.

We waved.

Uncle Jake thought better of sounding our whistle when at last we pulled away from Olo Island.

39 —

Seven hours out of Juneau, in the midst of high seas and blackened skies and fading light like congealed grease, and as *The Prince of Wales* rolled heavily from side to side, more seriously in danger of capsizing than she had been even in the Candle Creek Islands, and as Uncle Jake stood at the wheel with no thought in mind but to save himself and wife and child and partner if he could—French Pete could have drowned ten times over for all he cared, as he laughingly said at Doug's seven hours later—the old diesel engine, throbbing in the belly of *The Prince of Wales,* suddenly went dead. After all that Uncle Jake had already suffered because of this engine, and after all his efforts to repair it, and after all the old engine's recent steady service which had earned it the confidence of all concerned, here it was again—a faithless stone-dead silent worthless piece of machinery as Uncle Jake said later over his Salisbury steak at Doug's.

Sissy stumbled up from the galley. French Pete, crashing through the pilothouse door, began to curse. Frank Morley caught me and held me to him. Uncle Jake's army cot slid across the pilothouse floor and landed on its side against the wall.

"What's wrong?" asked Sissy, catching hold of the binnacle just in time.

"Engine's quit," said Uncle Jake.

"Now?" cried Sissy. "When we're so close to home? Can you fix it?"

Uncle Jake, frantic in his way and stumped, as he said later, gripped the now useless wheel and said nothing. Slowly we rolled from port to starboard and back again. The windows of the pilothouse were drenched in spray. We were helpless, wallowing, the boat itself as dead as its engine, and the long fatty line of orange light along the horizon heralded the utter darkness of a desperate night.

"Wait a minute, Jake," said Frank Morley. "Do you see it?"

"I see it," said Uncle Jake.

"What?" asked Sissy.

"A seiner," said Uncle Jake at the same moment that French Pete shouted that we had lost the dory. "Over there."

"She's close enough," said Frank Morley.

"And just in time," said Uncle Jake, who with his free hand reached up and seized the whistle lanyard and began filling the pilothouse and the surrounding dusk with the sharp vibrating signals of our distress. "Pete," called Uncle Jake between blasts of the whistle, "the bow!" Without one foul word, without one sign of recalcitrance, more swiftly than he had ever moved to obey one of Uncle Jake's commands, French Pete flung down the wrench he was carrying to the engine room and started forward to ready himself to catch and make fast the towline that one of the men aboard the seiner would heave our way.

"Jake!" cried Sissy, as Uncle Jake let go of the lanyard, "they're not stopping!"

"She's right," said Frank Morley.

"They're loaded to the hilt with a full catch," said Uncle Jake, "and are trying to get to Juneau as fast as they can. They're not going to heed our signal."

"They see us too," said Frank Morley. "Look at them."

The seiner, its long black iron hull low in the water, was within moments of cutting diagonally across the port bow of *The Prince of Wales* and leaving us astern forever. Uncle Jake had hooked back the pilothouse door, and framed in it was the seiner; in its iron midship stood two men smoking cigarettes and watching us. The seiner under full steam was steady, unmerciful, indifferent; without power *The Prince of Wales* was rolling at a near standstill in the heavy swells.

"To abandon a ship in distress," said Uncle Jake, "is the worst crime there is on the high seas."

"I guess they just don't care," said Frank Morley as the deep oily sound of the engine came to us and the two cigarettes winked on and off in the approaching night.

"We'll make them care," said Uncle Jake.

So saying, and with his mouth set half in a grimace, half in a smile, and with his eyes suddenly wild and with clear purpose, Uncle Jake left his post at the wheel, strode to the rear of the pilothouse, took down the Four-Hundred-and-Five from its rack on the wall among the rolls of charts, and pushed past Frank Morley and onto the deck. Frank Morley relinquished me to Sissy and joined Uncle Jake; Sissy clutched me and, hardly able to maintain her footing, nonetheless managed to drag me to the open door, where, with the wind and increasing darkness in our faces, we could watch the now desperate scene.

Closer came the brutal seiner on her diagonal course. In another moment it would be too dark to see.

Uncle Jake braced himself at our rail. Up to his shoulder went the Four-Hundred-and-Five. He fired. And the rifle that was meant for stopping bears in their tracks sent forth its flame, kicked mightily, shoving Uncle Jake off balance, and made a sudden deep report that knocked the wind out of poor Sissy, as Uncle Jake later said at Doug's, and caused even Frank Morley to shut his eyes and stagger.

"It's not working, Jake," said Frank Morley, recovering and watching the seiner continue on its way, "it's just not working." The smell of cordite drifted into the salty night.

"That first shot," said Uncle Jake grimly, as he levered another shell into the chamber of the Four-Hundred-and-Five, "went across their bows. This next one will pass within a foot of their pilothouse. The third will go right through their pilothouse window and take the head off that fellow at the wheel."

Up went the Four-Hundred-and-Five. Uncle Jake inhaled slowly, held his breath, leaned into his aim, and fired. The two men at the rail

of the seiner pitched high their cigarettes and fell to their knees and
scampered for cover while the seiner, without hesitation, sounded her
steely whistle in a few frantic blasts of capitulation and abruptly slowed
and circled around to pick us up. They came within yelling distance,
then close enough to take us in tow. One of the cigarette smokers threw
French Pete the towline, and swiftly he made it fast.

"That did it," said Frank Morley, gently clapping Uncle Jake on the
shoulder.

"I'll lash the wheel," said Uncle Jake, laughing and returning the
Four-Hundred-and-Five to its rack, "and we'll just sit back and enjoy
our free ride to Juneau!"

The Prince of Wales submitted to the full force of the seiner and, once
under way, ceased her rolling, her listing, and the rest of her usual
eccentricities at sea. Uncle Jake righted his army cot; Sissy served the
four of us a hot meal of tinned bully beef, as Uncle Jake called it, and
canned corn. Wrapped in blankets I lay at last on the army cot, waiting
drowsily for the dreams of Uncle Jake that were sure to come and
listening to the soft voices rising and falling in the green light.

"Partner," I heard Frank Morley saying, "I'm glad you didn't have
to fire that third shot."

40 —

Seven hours later I awoke on Sissy's lap in a booth at Doug's. There
were voices, electric lights, cakes on pedestals along the counter, and
heat, smoke, the smells of Doug's home cooking. Our oilcloth-covered
table was crowded with heavy white plates of Salisbury steak and ice
cream scoops of mashed potatoes changing color under Doug's gravy
that was as thick and shiny as hot chocolate sauce. Across from Sissy
and me sat Uncle Jake and Frank Morley, both famished.

"Awake, darling?" Sissy whispered to me, as she watched Frank
Morley upending the ketchup bottle and Uncle Jake smothering his
meal in salt and pepper. "Are you hungry?"

"She's starved," said Frank Morley, pausing to light one of his half-
smoked cigarettes and then returning to his food.

"Doug!" called Uncle Jake, "another Salisbury steak!"

Boots and hats and raucous voices. Men eating apple pie. Then Doug himself brought over my steaming plate and Uncle Jake detained him.

"Doug," said Uncle Jake, "I did the darnedest thing down there in White Eye. Pull up a chair."

And as the young blond and aproned Doug sat down to listen, Uncle Jake pushed away his plate and began to talk.

"Jake," said Sissy midway through Uncle Jake's story and in a sad sweet voice that only I could hear, "whatever are you going to do without me?"

The next morning we learned from Hilda Laubenstein that Wesley Pitts had died as soon as Doc Robinson had made his first incision.

"I'm going to miss the Belly Burglar," said Uncle Jake, "but at least I fired that darn French Pete."

Sissy unobtrusively left the room.

41 —

Uncle Jake had instructed Robert McGinnis how to use the shortwave radio and had given him to understand that he was not to touch the radio except in the worst of emergencies. Uncle Jake and Frank Morley did not cease to expect some desperate message from Robert McGinnis, though none came. Sissy regretted that she could not write to Annie. Uncle Jake turned his attention to three abandoned coal mines—blind alleys all, as he said—and, in the vicinity of a remote and distant place called Windy Arm, wasted eighteen weeks searching for outcroppings of molybdenite—a word he relished and a substance he enjoyed explaining as the source of molybdenum, which, he said, was of considerable value to the manufacturers of steel—which he never found. He took Frank Morley hunting for mountain goats and on regular fishing trips to Mud Lake. They became Rex Ainsworth's most frequent passengers. Now and then, seated beside the wood stove in Guns & Locks & Clothes, they remembered Olo Island and took a moment from their talk to joke about Robert McGinnis and his foxes.

In December of 1931, Uncle Jake first honored his promise to bring
the McGinnises back to Juneau for the holidays. *The Prince of Wales*
returned from Olo Island bearing not only the jubilant McGinnises but
the pelts of twenty-one blue foxes as well. Uncle Jake and Frank Morley
and Sitka Charley soberly removed the three bundles valued at just
under seventeen thousand dollars, as Uncle Jake remarked, to Guns &
Locks & Clothes until the pelts could be sold to the furrier's agent and
shipped to Seattle. In silence Frank Morley and Uncle Jake untied one
of the bundles and inspected what Frank Morley called the largest,
softest, bluest furs he had ever seen. In silence Uncle Jake allowed me
to comb the silky fur with my fingers, to hide my face in the smell
and color of the furs, to stroke the hides that had the texture of parchment and the suppleness of living skin.

"Seventeen thousand dollars," said Uncle Jake. "I guess he's making
a go of it down there, Frank."

Robert McGinnis might not have been the author of these riches for
all the interest he showed in the furs, and during this holiday season
and those that followed he was content to leave the yearly harvest in
the hands of Uncle Jake and Frank Morley, and to devote himself to
Sissy's Steinway, Uncle Jake's Chain-Lightning Punch, the ritual dinner
at the Baranof. The piano, the punch, and the dinner were all he needed
or expected in return for his exile, as Uncle Jake insisted it was, on
Olo Island—along, that is, with Sissy's affection and the chance to take
me walking on the Silver Bow Basin Road, a narrow track that made
its precipitous way two miles out of Juneau to a dead end where some
of the Alaska-Juneau miners had their bunkhouse.

Moodily Uncle Jake and Frank Morley acknowledged their good
fortune and Robert McGinnis's mysterious skills as a fox farmer; un-
wittingly they continued their pursuit of fish and game, freedom and
risk, and ever more astounding enterprises. On three more occasions
The Prince of Wales was reported long overdue. In Glacier Bay Uncle
Jake cracked four ribs and was nursed back to health by Hilda Laubenstein, who strapped the ribs and confined her patient to the same
bed once occupied by Wesley Pitts. Hilda allowed Sissy and me to pay
our daily visits to Uncle Jake, who, despite his pain and coughing, lay
propped on pillows, his thin and naked torso bound in Hilda's broad
white bands of adhesive tape, and told us day after day of how he had
sustained his injury—thanks to a tree, a narrow trail, and a blind moose.
Frank Morley started losing weight, mere pounds a year but steadily.

Uncle Jake failed in his attempt to construct a machine for sucking gold nuggets from pebbled beaches. Sitka Charley taught me to shoot a small nickel-plated onyx-handled .32-caliber revolver that had been concealed, he said, up many a mustachioed gambler's sleeve.

"July 10. Juneau. Palpitations. Tipsy with Hilda. Frank looks the other way."

"July 19. Juneau. Where's Jake?"

So they played their games of hearts while the ghosts of blue foxes barked on Olo Island.

42 —

The day came. Inevitably the day came. It was Thursday, the third of October, 1935.

"Darling," said Sissy, "will you take my place?"

"Are you winning?" I asked.

"Your poor mother is losing this game," said Uncle Jake. "Badly."

"And your father," said Hilda Laubenstein, who was suffering that day from a bad head cold, "is winning."

"Sunny's going to reverse my luck," said Sissy.

"Sissy," said Frank Morley, "finish the game."

"It's my back, Frank," said Sissy. "Sunny will take over for me."

"When Jake finally destroys us all," said Hilda, "Sissy and I have some business at my place."

"You girls are always up to something," said Uncle Jake.

"May I come?" I asked.

"Of course you may," said Hilda, dipping into her box of tissues and licking her reddened upper lip.

"You should have stayed in bed with that cold," said Uncle Jake.

"Don't worry," said Hilda, "I wouldn't give you my cold for the world."

"Look at her, Frank," said Uncle Jake. "Talk about wet eyes and a plugged-up nose. Why, that's the deadliest cold I've ever seen."

"Darling," said Sissy, "take over my hand."

"Four o'clock," said Frank Morley, peering at his Hamilton and then returning the gold watch to his vest pocket, "it's getting on, Jake."

"Stick around, Frank," said Uncle Jake. "I'll just finish off this hand and then we'll let the girls go down to Hilda's for their little tête-à-tête. You and I can stay here and talk."

"It won't be a tête-à-tête," said Hilda. "We're taking Sunny with us."

"What are you going to do down there?" asked Uncle Jake, expecting and receiving no reply.

I sat at Sissy's place, picked up her cards, and felt Hilda nudging me under the table. Sissy had somehow been dealt six hearts and the queen of spades. The windows were open, the rain had stopped, Uncle Jake's rocker began to creak slowly to Sissy's rhythm.

"Frank," said Uncle Jake, glancing at Hilda and putting his hand to his tie, "don't you think she has a fever?"

"Looks that way to me," said Frank Morley.

"A nurse," said Uncle Jake, "and she doesn't even know how to take care of herself."

"That's right," said Frank Morley.

"Sissy," said Uncle Jake, glancing again at Hilda, "where's your thermometer?"

"You two," said Sissy. "Stop joshing Hilda."

"Look at that flushed face," said Uncle Jake.

"Belongs in bed," said Frank Morley.

"I could say something," said Hilda, "but I won't."

Uncle Jake raised his eyebrows quickly several times and cleared his throat and studied his cards. I felt Hilda's warm and silky foot against my leg. In my turn I passed Uncle Jake two hearts and the queen of spades. Uncle Jake picked up his ginger ale glass and found it empty. Frank Morley's breathing was dry and leathery. He held his cards in a tight fan close to his chest like a poker player.

"They're laying off at the mine," he said.

"How are you feeling, Hilda?" asked Uncle Jake. "Shall we call it quits?"

"She's looking worse," said Frank Morley.

"Hilda," said Uncle Jake, "just doesn't know how to be hygienic, nurse or no nurse."

"In your books," said Hilda, "what woman does?"

"She doesn't even put her wet tissues in the wastebasket," said Uncle Jake, preparing to lead.

Hilda snorted, nudged me, and laughed when Uncle Jake, from lofty heights, led a diamond and took the trick, which is what he did not wish to do. The cards he picked up included one of Sissy's hearts. The set of his jaw remained the same but his eyebrows betrayed his displeasure. Without a moment's hesitation, Hilda readied her discard, holding it in two fingers by the corner, a practice of which Uncle Jake strongly disapproved, and sat gloating over the outcome of Uncle Jake's next play. He took his time, trying to outsmart Hilda and me, though he was still the possessor of the queen of spades, as we all knew. Finally, and with a handsome show of confidence, he led a club. I put down another of Sissy's hearts, again Uncle Jake was forced to take the trick, again he reached for his empty glass.

"What's going on here?" he said.

Twice more he led, twice more I glutted his tricks with Sissy's hearts. Hilda laughed, I laughed, Frank Morley said that he thought that the jig was up for his partner. Hilda crumpled a tissue and smeared her cherry lipstick, wiped her eyes, dabbled at her rabbity pink nose, and gave me two swift kicks under the table. Through the open windows came the oily fishy smell of Juneau.

"Not again!" cried Uncle Jake, staring at the little pile of cards and at Sissy's fat red nine of hearts that I had dropped on the pile and that was now indubitably his own. "Sissy!" he cried, "will you come over here and take away this daughter of yours? She's ruining my game!"

"Sissy," said Frank Morley, "you better do what Jake says."

"Don't listen to them," said Hilda. "They're bad sports. Both of them."

But Uncle Jake did not pick up the cards, though he reached for them. He frowned, arm still outstretched. Hilda's face grew hard. Frank Morley frowned. Hilda looked at Uncle Jake. Uncle Jake looked at Frank Morley.

"Sissy?" said Uncle Jake.

Hilda and Frank Morley stared at Uncle Jake. There was not a sound in the room.

"Sissy?" said Uncle Jake again. "Why, whatever is the matter with her, Frank? Falling asleep in the middle of the afternoon. Look at her head."

There was a prohibition upon us—not to move, not to speak, to deny by the very questions we did not ask this day's event. We listened, we turned our heads and looked at Sissy. Was the prohibition hers? Was it she who now in silence was telling us not to speak, not to move, not to look, but simply to allow what was now happening to pass?

She sat in the rocker with her hands in her lap and her chin on her chest. Her lowered head was tilted to one side. The rocker was not moving.

"She's just sleeping," said Uncle Jake.

There was a long pause.

"No, she's not," said Hilda in a low cold frightened voice.

"Sissy!" cried Uncle Jake to the still figure. "Sissy!"

Then we threw off the fragile prohibition and Frank Morley stumbled to his feet, Uncle Jake was at Sissy's side in a bound, Hilda lunged away from the table, I turned and watched the three of them rushing to my mother, hovering about my mother, frantically attempting to stop her flight.

"Sissy?" said Uncle Jake.

"Don't touch her," said Frank Morley.

"Put her on the floor," said Hilda.

"What have I done?" cried Uncle Jake, reaching for her shoulders, drawing back, suddenly lifting her out of the chair and turning, taking a step, staring at me with my mother still in his arms. "What have I done, Sunny?"

"For God's sake put her on the floor," said Hilda, flapping and spreading the gray blanket she had pulled from my bed. I sat and watched, my back to the table, my left hand slowly stirring the dog-eared cards which we had already given up for good. Hilda told Frank Morley to go after Doc Robinson, and poor Frank Morley went out the door, striking his old thin shoulder against the jamb and leaving the door wide open as he started downtown on foot.

Uncle Jake knelt with his burden. He held her head and shoulders in his arms. He kissed her forehead. A little totem pole toppled from the end table.

"Let me have her," said Hilda; she knelt, rolled Sissy onto her stomach, and gave her friend long minutes of artificial respiration, knowing all the while, as she told Frank Morley at the funeral and in my presence, that Sissy's heart had stopped the moment the rocking chair had ceased to move, a good fifteen minutes before any of us had heard the silence.

"She's gone," said Uncle Jake, sitting back on his heels and helplessly watching Hilda going through the motions of resuscitation. "She's gone, Sunny."

Doc Robinson arrived and down on his knees listened to the silence of the lost voice through a dusty stethoscope. Still sitting in her chair at the table, I watched as Doc Robinson and Frank Morley exited awkwardly but as unobtrusively as they could, bearing between them the slender blanketed figure. There was the sound of a car engine. Frank Morley returned. Then Uncle Jake, whom Hilda had pulled to his feet when Doc Robinson had first arrived, and who had been standing in the middle of our living room throughout the entire episode of the jostling, the embarrassed consultations, the head shakings, the awkward exit, suddenly became aware of the empty space on the floor and, blind witness that he had been, clutched Hilda's arm and stared about the room as if the impossible had just occurred and he had missed the most important event in his life.

"Frank," he said, "where is she? On Sunny's bed?"

Frank Morley waited and then told Uncle Jake that she was already gone.

"But where?" cried Uncle Jake. "Where have they taken her?"

"Down to Franklin's Funeral Parlor," said Frank Morley, barely able to get out the words. "You'll see her tomorrow."

Confusion. A glass crashing in the kitchen sink. Uncle Jake wearing his tie and fawn-colored suit and a white handkerchief in the breast pocket and refusing to calm down, refusing to stay put, as Frank Morley said at the funeral, refusing to stop searching in the kitchen, in my bedroom, in the room where she had died, for the object—the slender gently loyal object—of his grief.

"Coffee," said Frank Morley, tears in his eyes.

"Whiskey," said Hilda.

Another glass broke in the kitchen. The coffee boiled over. It was growing dark. Uncle Jake refused the whiskey.

"Calm down, Jake," said Frank Morley.

"Look at this," said Uncle Jake. "Just look at this."

He was holding her purse in his hands.

"Sunny," he said, suddenly looking in my direction and holding up the purse for me to see, "she's gone."

"Jake," said Hilda, "you're going to sit down."

She and Frank Morley forced him into the rocking chair and wrapped his knees in a second blanket that Hilda had stripped from my bed. Suddenly he made an effort, crossed his knees under the blanket, and set the rocking chair in motion, still holding the purse.

"Sunny," he said, "come here."

"Jake," said Hilda, "you've got to eat. Sunny and Frank are here. I'm just in the kitchen."

He nodded.

The smell of scrambled eggs and bacon. The smell of whiskey. Ordinary night descending. Frank Morley closing the windows. I left the card table and sat beside Uncle Jake. He was rocking, I was sitting motionless on my metal chair. He was staring toward one of the darkened windows. I was staring at his profile. His eyes were dry but his face looked as if it were covered with a thin coating of glycerin. My own eyes were dry but my face ached. The bones beneath my face were aching. I watched him.

Hilda brought the plate of eggs and bacon which he held in his hands while keeping the purse in his lap. Hilda gave Frank Morley a tumbler half filled with whiskey and poured one for herself. They drew their chairs close to Uncle Jake and me and watched him eat.

"Poor Sunny," he said.

I thought I heard something in the kitchen.

"Frank," said Uncle Jake, still rocking and eating.

"It was the best way," said Frank Morley.

I put my hand on the arm of the rocker and felt the motion. The card player had become an invalid in his suit and blanket. Hilda and Frank Morley leaned as close to him as they could.

"Frank," said Uncle Jake again.

"We wouldn't have wanted it any other way," said Frank Morley.

"It's my fault," said Uncle Jake.

"There was no pain," said Frank Morley. "That's the important thing, Jake. No pain. She never knew what happened."

"Hilda," said Uncle Jake, "I've changed my mind about the whiskey."

"Good for you," said Hilda, taking his plate and giving him her glass.

"I'll catch your cold," he said, resting one hand on the purse and with the other raising the glass to his mouth. Around the rim of the glass was a thin cherry-colored smear. The aching in my face was worse.

"Sunny," he said abruptly, "it's my fault."

"It's not your fault," I said.

"I shouldn't have brought her to Alaska. Why did I come up here anyway?"

"Jake," said Frank Morley. "She's been taken from us. You're not to blame."

"She just closed her eyes," said Hilda, reaching for Frank Morley's glass. "We were all together."

"Her father was a wonderful man," said Uncle Jake. "She and I were in the house when he died."

"She adored you," said Frank Morley. "She adored you, Jake."

"You have to control yourself," said Hilda. "For Sunny."

He smiled, he took a tighter grip on the purse, he continued rocking as if he were going to rock all night. Once Frank Morley rose slowly from his flimsy chair and left the room, carefully skirting the still-empty spot where she had lain, and went through the kitchen and stepped outside. I wondered whether he and Hilda had deliberately positioned their chairs so as to leave bare the empty place on the floor, but I understood that Frank Morley wanted to stand a moment where she had done her smoking. Then Frank Morley returned and Hilda finally began to cry. Her knees were showing.

Suddenly, Uncle Jake stopped rocking. He recrossed his knees, rested his head against the back of the chair, smiled up at the ceiling as he might have glanced skyward on a summer day. His face was dry and his eyes were clear. Absently he stroked the purse and mused. Suddenly this was no fifty-five-year-old grief-stricken widower of five hours but the Uncle Jake we all knew. Hilda and Frank Morley had promised not to leave him. They wanted nothing more than to spend the entire night allaying his bereavement as well as their own. What merciful relief was this now shining forth from Uncle Jake? Hilda and Frank Morley's glances at each other said that they had not known that they could comfort him so well.

"Frank," said Uncle Jake, smiling at whatever it was he saw on the ceiling, "did I ever tell you about the time my father took us all to France?"

There was a pause. A long pause. Hilda sniffled. Slowly Frank Morley raised his head. He and Hilda looked at each other.

"What's that, Jake?" said Frank Morley.

"France," said Uncle Jake. "My first time in France. Haven't I told you about it?"

Poor Frank Morley wheezed and frowned and looked at Hilda, who had stopped crying but was balling up a handful of wet tissues.

"Well, Frank," said Uncle Jake, as I clung to the arm of his chair and listened, "I was just a boy. It was in 1892—a long time ago—and

I was not much older than Sunny is right now. Well, my father decided he wanted to take us all back to France, which was his native country, and that's what he did."

"Jake," interrupted Frank Morley, "you're tired."

"Oh no," said Uncle Jake, "I'm not tired, Frank. Anyway my father packed us all off to France. Mother, my three brothers—Billy Boy was just a baby—our maids—we had a lot of pretty young maids in those days—the entire lot of us. He wanted to have a reunion with his eight brothers and the Old Gentleman, which is what they called my grandfather. Well, you can't imagine it, Frank—the chateau, the horses, the banquets, the pretty young maids..."

"Look," said Hilda, stiffening and glancing sharply at Frank Morley, "I'll put on another pot of coffee."

"That's all right, Hilda," said Uncle Jake, "I'm wide awake. I can't tell you how clearly I see it—the Old Gentleman in his red coat and white britches and riding out ahead of his nine sons. He was so old they had to lift him up onto his horse. Well, he gave us a grand time and even Mother, who is about as far from being a frivolous woman as any woman you could hope to find, began to enjoy herself. My grandfather had mutton chop whiskers and knew how to entertain his guests, I can tell you. Each week it was something different—concerts, visits around the countryside, exhibitions of dressage—which is a special way they have of riding..."

"Jake," said Frank Morley helplessly.

"This is a good story, Frank," said Uncle Jake. "Hear me out. You see, it's the grape harvest that I remember best. It was a wonderful affair. The Old Gentleman packed us all off in carriages to a great barn filled with what they call treading troughs—they were low stone tubs, large enough to hold about six people each. Well, my grandfather sat us all in red plush chairs on a stage he had had specially built for the occasion—think of it! red plush chairs in a barn!—and ordered all his old tenants to fill the treading troughs with the new grapes. I was seated in the front row between my father and my grandfather, and no twelve-year-old boy was ever happier than I was then. But the Old Gentleman had a surprise in store for us, I can tell you. He made a long speech about the ancient mysteries of the grape—he loved wine and had a splendid cellar, as my father used to say—and told us that no one was ever allowed to tread the grapes on his estate except the virgin girls he summoned out from the nearby village every year. Village virgins, he said, were essential to the quality of his wine. His servants passed around trays of last year's vintage and he proposed a toast to Mother, right there in the barn. Then he clapped his hands and all the girls who had been huddling in the shadows and who were clothed in nothing but blue smocks, came rushing forward to the treading troughs. They leapt into them like a flash, six or so girls to a trough. Well, I never saw anything like it. Those village virgins whipped off their smocks—what do you think of that, Frank?—and began dancing and hopping up and down squashing the grapes and spattering themselves so that they looked like a bunch of blue savages—except that they were pure young French girls in the pink. I sat there between my father and grandfather, who were both laughing, and watched those young girls for all I was worth. Well, Mother was furious. After the whole thing was over she stormed up to my grandfather and in front of everyone told the poor old man that he had destroyed my innocence.

"Can you imagine? Poor Mother worrying about my innocence? Why, I didn't lose my innocence until I married Sissy. . . ."

He faltered. He stopped. Abruptly he looked at Hilda and Frank Morley. His face collapsed. Then it filled with rage. Then it collapsed again.

"Sissy," he said weakly, coming back to himself. "Good Lord, Frank, what have I done?"

"It's all right," said Frank Morley.

"She's gone," said Uncle Jake. "Sissy's gone. And here I am telling crazy stories! I can't stand it, Frank. What's the matter with me?"

"It's all right," said Frank Morley. "You're not yourself."

Hilda left the room, carrying off what was left of the whiskey. Then Uncle Jake turned to me and looked down at me calmly and gently, as if Sissy had just spoken to him instead of Frank Morley. He took my hand. He looked at me. Then he spoke.

"Now you're not just the important one, Sunny," he said. "You're the only one."

It was then that I cried out and the terrible aching in my face was swept away by grief.

We were her faithful followers as Uncle Jake said when we assembled at 11 A.M. on Friday, the fourth of October, in Franklin's Funeral Parlor. There were only five of us but five faithful followers were enough. Bob Franklin himself officiated at the service. The casket was open, Bob Franklin's sister played "The Darkness Deepens, Lord with Me

Abide" on a small black upright piano. Frank Morley had helped Uncle Jake get dressed in the navy blue suit, the tie, the black socks and shoes. Uncle Jake had not forgotten the crisp white handkerchief in the breast pocket of his suit coat and he looked stunning, as Hilda murmured to Frank Morley, with his strained face and black hair parted in the middle. Uncle Jake—stricken and distracted—tried to comfort me when we stood in front of the casket, he and I, and I saw for the last time the green ribbon and the ivory elephant.

When the service was over and Sitka Charley had returned to Guns & Locks & Clothes, Hilda said that she wanted to pay a brief visit to the Russian Orthodox church and wanted Frank Morley to go along with her. She said that Uncle Jake and I should start on up to the house without them, and that they wouldn't be long. Uncle Jake nodded, there at the edge of the cemetery behind the Indian school, and put on his hat and took hold of my hand. A seagull flew overhead. Uncle Jake waited until Hilda and Frank Morley were out of hearing. Then he spoke.

"Sunny," he said, peering into the drizzle, "when I go—when it's my turn to go—you're the only person I want at my funeral. Not even Frank, Sunny. Just you."

That night, after Hilda and Frank Morley had left us and when the house was dark and Uncle Jake and I were preparing to face our first night alone, he emerged from the bathroom in his robe and pajamas and slippers and paused, looked around the room, and then carefully hung the purse from the knob of my bedroom door so that it would always be there, he said, for him to see. Then he said that he didn't think that he could bear to touch the contraption, as he always called it, and asked me to open it out for him and to turn down the covers, which I did.

"Well," he said, looking at the empty foldaway bed, "now I can send Robert McGinnis back to Connecticut where he belongs."

In the morning, before it was light, I heard him calling. "Rise and shine, Sunny, rise and shine!" I ran to him, hair and nightgown flying, and flung myself upon him where he sat on the edge of the foldaway bed. He was large and shivering and dismal, despite the way he had called me. We wept together as, still in our nightclothes, we made sandwiches for breakfast. We wept together as we sat at the kitchen table and tried to eat. We wept until at last he smiled, wiped his face, and suddenly inspired, began to tell me that once there had been palm trees that flourished up here in Alaska.

43 —

Sunny, he calls, look at this. A kangaroo court!

Again it is happening, again and as usual I know that I am dreaming and can feel, as if in total wakefulness, the cold slime on my skin, the terrible electric tingling in my cold feet, the pain in my chest. I know the word for what I'm feeling—anxiety. I have a waking consciousness of the anxiety that I experience only in sleep—because of Uncle Jake and the treachery of his Alaskan lore—but I am asleep. The anxiety is wrapping me in long fine strands of hair, in silken threads. Yet in the dream I am walking on a hot dry path, pack on my back and rifle in hand. There are clouds of mosquitoes, crackling underbrush, the smells of summer in the northland. The dream, as always, is the cause of the anxiety or anger that comes to me each night in sleep. Yet in this particular dream I am also at peace, despite the sudden sound of his voice. I am dressed like a man, a prospector, and am wearing an old crushed fedora. The netting that hangs around my face is black with mosquitoes. I am walking with a lively step, rifle in hand.

Sunny, he calls again. Look what's happening to me. A kangaroo court!

I hear him, I cannot breathe. Somewhere ahead of me they have captured Uncle Jake. I edge forward along the trail, convinced that I shall witness at last what has happened to Uncle Jake.

Sunny, he calls, they're going to string me up!

I come to a clearing where there are a small and windowless log cabin, forty or fifty square-bearded men and, beside a giant spruce, Uncle Jake standing on a barrel. The men have tossed a rope over a high limb and have settled the noose tightly around his neck. Nonetheless he still wears his hat which, I notice, is old and crumpled, like mine.

What's the charge? shouts one of the square-bearded men.

Unlawful cohabitation, comes the answer.

That's serious, says the first man. That's the most serious charge there is!

You're darn right it is, says the other.

I arrive at the edge of the crowd. They make way for me, and I smell them—their flesh, their matted hair, their teeth, their narrowed eyes, their clothes. I love their dry and sour smell, I who am disguised as one of them in my shirt and pants and my hat and mosquito netting. They make way for me and I move to the front. They seem to want me to have an unobstructed view of the proceedings, which is what I want to have. Uncle Jake is standing as proud as a peacock on top of his barrel—all the prouder for the noose around his neck and the trouble they have taken to bind his hands behind him. He is the only man in the crowd who is clean-shaven. His shirt and trousers are covered with dried mud. Fishing flies are stuck around the band of the old hat cocked on his head.

Sunny, he says, looking straight down at me from his barrel, they're going to lynch me. What do you think of that?

We're not going to lynch him, says a man beside me, we're going to hang him. This is a court of law.

I smile though I say nothing to the man beside me and give no sign of recognition to Uncle Jake. There is an impatient rumbling from the crowd of men, then silence. They have come long distances, I see by the packs and guns and tools they carry, and I wonder how they knew to find Uncle Jake in the desolate log cabin in this empty clearing. I do not know where I am, yet all these men know where they are. Even Uncle Jake appears at home on his barrel.

In my sleep I am wet and cold. In my dream I am for once a spectator among forty or fifty lonely men congregated in a clearing. I look at Uncle Jake, who seems to find his plight more entertaining than do his accusers. All around us the scrub trees are covered with dried and flaking lichen, the air smells of the dust and heat of a dead country.

Unlawful cohabitation! shouts the self-appointed chief magistrate of this kangaroo court. Who with?

Three Way Mary! comes an angry answer.

No! shouts the chief magistrate in disbelief.

Moose Neck Betty! cries another.

Skagway Lil! cries still another.

The Chinless Filly! shouts a man so close behind me that his expelled breath stirs the mosquito netting hiding the back of my womanly head of hair.

No! shouts the chief magistrate again. The Chinless Filly? Up at Thirty Mile? Wife of old Jack Hampton?

That's the one, shouts the man behind me.

Good Lord, says the chief magistrate.

And what about Sweet Pea Kate? shouts someone on the other side of the crowd.

And Finn Dora, shouts someone far to my right.

And don't forget poor Fighting Belle, comes another voice. He got her too!

Stop! shouts the chief magistrate. The man's a fiend!

Even Short Gertie who makes the best flapjacks on the trail! shouts another square-bearded man who steps from the crowd, shakes his fist, and then lets his arm fall to his side.

Enough! shouts the chief magistrate. I've heard enough!

Not a woman left unspoiled, comes a bitter voice. He's had them all.

The worst was little Utah Rose, shouts another man who steps out and faces the crowd. Caught red-handed by her brother, old Calamity Jim. That's a fact.

All right! shouts the chief magistrate. Are you ready to pronounce the verdict?

You bet we are! cry the forty or fifty old-timers down to a man.

But they fall silent. They make no move to seize the free end of the rope. They shuffle, they slap the air, they wait. The rope rises straight from Uncle Jake's neck to the limb of the tree, and there he stands patiently, expectantly, his tall body wrapped in the thick smoke of the mosquitoes and all but invisible—except for the head, the eyes, the long pink face, the rakishly tilted hat.

Guilty or innocent, shouts the chief magistrate, what'll it be?

They wait, they grumble, they menace Uncle Jake on his barrel. But they do not speak. In my dream my impatience and anticipation grow. I feel someone's hot belly in the small of my back. I smell the armpits of the old-timers. Then Uncle Jake speaks up.

Condemn me, Sunny! he says. Be my witness!

Boys, shouts the chief magistrate, just say the word!

They shuffle, they rumble, their bellies sound filled with water. But they do not give the chief magistrate his word.

I drop my pack, my rifle, and step forward and turn to face the mob of old square-bearded vigilantes. With both hands I lift my mosquito netting and prepare to address the crowd. My mouth is dry, I feel the tips of needles beneath my skin, never have I felt so bold. I work my jaws, I concentrate on making my voice as low and leathery as a man's.

Well, shouts the chief magistrate, what's it to be?

I take a breath. I know that my voice will sound like the voice of an old prospector when I hear it. I raise my right arm and point up at Uncle Jake, who is nodding and smiling down at me.

Hang him! I cry. He's innocent!

Damnation! says the chief magistrate. Who's this?

Now the men rub their beards—there are a few grays sprinkled among the blacks—and they jostle each other and shake their heads. Someone claims to have seen me at Easter Creek. Another says that I might be the fellow who finally served the warrant on Jim Glass, that native on the Yukekaket River who was always beating up his mother. Someone in the back of the crowd disagrees. They wrangle and shove each other and again fall silent.

You'll have to hang me yourself, Sunny, says Uncle Jake. It's the only way!

I spit into my hands and grip the rope, pull on it hand over hand, lean back. I feel his weight. Nothing happens.

Harder, Sunny, he says. Harder!

My feet slip in the dust and pine needles. My palms burn. His heels haven't even begun to rise from the lid of the barrel. A dead weight. An improbably dead weight.

Come on boys, shouts the chief magistrate. Lend a hand!

And suddenly they are climbing all over each other to reach the rope, and down I go, smothered beneath the clamorous old-timers, slipping this way and that to avoid their knees, their elbows, their yelling and their jets of chewed tobacco.

I crawl out from under them at last, my hat and mosquito netting still in place.

Look at me, says Uncle Jake, whom they have hoisted six inches into the air. They've hung me, Sunny! Now they'll have to dig my grave!

"Charley," I said thickly, frantically, and rolled against him, clung to him, "another crazy dream. Help me!"

He grunted. I hung on to him and in long spasms breathed in the wonderful familiar smell of his skin and the air from his mouth and lungs. He smelled like jerked beef. I kissed his shoulder. He told me to go back to sleep.

"I'll have another dream," I said.

"Go back to sleep."

I did what he said. I let go. I kept my nakedness to myself and slept and, just as I knew I would, I dreamed. By the time I escaped from my second dream of the night—last night—it was morning and I was alone in Sitka Charley's bed.

I can't move, Sunny, he calls in a voice I can hardly hear. Help me!

The saloon is in a large and crudely built log cabin. At one of the tables I am sitting on the lap of someone bundled up in furs. He is burly inside his parka, his sealskin pants, his mukluks, his fur mittens, a fat and massive musher with his whip on the table and his great face hidden within the fur that rims the hood of his parka. I know he is bearded though I cannot see his face. I too am swathed from head to foot in fur. I too wear fur mittens and my parka. There is no one else in the saloon, not even a bartender, and everything in that long and empty room is filmed in ice. The tops of the tables, the spittoons, the kerosene lanterns, the candles on cracked saucers, the mirror and pyramid of brightly colored bottles behind the bar— all are glittering in a skin of ice. Here I am sitting on the musher's lap with one of my furry arms around his padded shoulder and one of his mittened hands on my thigh. His long black whip lies in a coil on the table like a frozen snake.

Come on, French Camille, says the musher, give us a kiss!

But I am not French Camille and the musher won't show his face.

Sunny, he calls again, I'm frozen stiff!

There is a shout of laughter from outside, where the snow is packed into a semblance of a narrow street between the tents, a shout of men without women, of men who help each other and on the trail eat their own dogs when they are forced to. Again comes the shout of laughter, and a shard of ice drops from the ceiling and shatters on the barroom floor.

All right, French Camille, says the burly musher, trying to shove me off his lap, let's take a look.

We are as big as bears, the musher and I, and we move like bears prodded out of hibernation. Slowly we extricate ourselves, one mass of clumsiness coming unstuck from the other. I tug on the bottom of my parka, and the musher picks up his whip. We leave the saloon door wide open.

We join the little band of fur-hatted laughing men who make way for us, nudge each other, shake their heads, and point toward the object of their amusement. On either side of the snow-packed semblance of a street the tents, constructed of sagging tarpaulins on log frames, are empty and banked high with snow. There are no fires, no smells of cooking. The sky is clear, the light is as painful to the eyes as is the air to the lungs.

New man in town, says one of the laughing onlookers, pointing into the street.

Darn fool, says another.

He's been like that all day, says a third.

Came into town this morning, says the first, and won't even get off his sled.

Just sitting there like that the whole time, says a fourth. The darn fool.

And there he sits, Uncle Jake bolt upright in the rear of the cargo sled. He wears his wolf-fur hat, his fur mittens, and has wrapped himself in bearskin robes. His dogs sit forlornly in their traces, and their eyes are oddly servile. They are gaunt, despite their brute size, and suddenly I understand their patience and odd servility. The dogs are afraid.

Sunny, he says, without looking at me or opening his mouth or moving his lips, I'm cold!

Except for Uncle Jake the sled is empty. It stands where it has stopped, frozen into its tracks. The dogs are watching us with narrowed eyes.

He's a sight, says the musher, and begins to laugh.

He's crazy, says the first onlooker. Forty below and just sitting there like that.

What's he waiting for? asks another. A brass band?

Maybe he's waiting for French Camille here, says the musher.

They laugh.

He'll have a long wait if he doesn't watch himself, says a short onlooker who laughs and rocks against me like a ball of fur.

Well, boys, says the musher, let's not be stand-offish. Let's march right over to him and say hello!

The musher pushes me ahead of him and in a moment we are crowding around the silent visitor and the musher is introducing himself and the other men are laughing. The musher leans down, I hang back.

Hold on, says the musher.

Too late, says the first onlooker.

Frozen solid, says the second.

Dead the whole darn time, says the first.

What now? says the third.

Send for the padre, says the first.

No need for that, says the musher. I've officiated at many a Klondike burial in my time. Just leave it to me.

Well, says the first onlooker, we've got to thaw him out.

That's right, says the musher. Never get him in the box unless we do.

They pull away the stiffened robes, they haul him out of the sled and drop him. He lies on his side like a toppled statue. He is so heavy that they can do no more than pull him and tug on him all together until he is finally sitting up in the snow, and then half drag, half slide him down the street to an empty snow-covered space behind the saloon.

Boys, says the musher, we need a drink, and off they go, leaving me alone with Uncle Jake.

Sunny, he says, I'm cold.

He is larger than the sled he rode in, and heavier. He is seated bolt upright with his legs outstretched and his mittened hands in his lap. His fur hat looks like a bishop's mitre. No man should be as large as he is. No man should ever sit as he now sits in the snow—unnaturally but at perfect ease. If I touch his shoulder he will topple once again onto his side.

All right! shouts the musher as the rest of them come staggering around the corner of the saloon, let's warm him up!

Can't be done! shouts the first onlooker.

Sure it can! shouts the musher.

Douse him with kerosene! shouts another.

No, no, says the musher. We don't want to burn the body. Just thaw it.

We've got to straighten it out, says the first onlooker.

Stand back there, French Camille, says the musher. Give us room!

The musher tells them where to heap the brush, where to place the logs, and then he leans down and lights the fire.

That ought to do it, says the first onlooker.

Kills two birds with one stone, says the musher. Thaws the ground while thawing the body!

There is no smoke. The flames are invisible. The onlookers hurry to do the musher's bidding and bring more brush, break branches, split chunks of wood. The crescent of heat begins to melt the snow. Somewhere one of them is hammering together heavy boards.

See there, says the musher. Won't be long.

Darned if he isn't dripping, says the first onlooker.

Boys, says the musher, gather round.

The smiling face perspires. The fur is wet. The blue of the eyes is softer.

Sunny, he says, I'm still cold!

Now, says the musher, let's get this business over with. Pile on!

All together! says the first onlooker.

Out of the way, French Camille, says the musher. This is no work for a woman.

Hold his legs, says the first onlooker.

Sit on them, says the musher.

What now?

Well, pull, darn it. Get him around the chest and start pulling.

Unbend him.

It's not as easy as all that!

Let's have another drink.

No, says the musher, it's now or never.

He won't budge!

They are on him like a pack of dogs, grumbling and laughing, half drunk and sobered at the job at hand, and two of them are sitting on the outstretched legs and one is straddling and pushing against his chest and two more are trying to get a grip on him from behind. The hat that is like a bishop's mitre lies in the snow. The musher stands to one side officiating.

What's the matter with him, anyway?

Thawed on the outside, frozen stiff within.

Can't even move the arms.

Can't turn the head.

He's just a darn uncooperative chechaqua. I give up.

Me too.

It's crazy. Plain crazy.

The darn fool doesn't want to be buried. It's his loss, not ours. We've done our best.

Oh hell, says the musher suddenly. I tell you what, boys. It's no use. We'll wait for spring!

That's the spirit! cries the first onlooker.

Back to the saloon! cries someone else. We'll drink to him!

Come on, French Camille, says the musher. Let's go in there and smooch.

Yes, I say, and off we go. But just as I am about to turn the corner of the saloon I hear his voice.

Sunny, he says, I came all this way for you. Don't leave me!

Then it was morning—this morning—and I awoke in Sitka Charley's bed in the loft above the millinery shop that has long since taken the place of Guns & Locks & Clothes. My fists were clenched and my eyes burned, my body ached, I was exhausted. As usual. From down below came the sound of two women laughing. I was goose-pimpled, naked, and no longer partial to women. Quite the contrary. I tried to think of those two below me sitting by mistake on their silly hats, but it didn't help. I tried not to hear them, but their voices were so cheerful that they came up through the floor as unavoidably as the voice of a playing child finds the sufferer of the migraine headache. Feminine frippery, I thought, and hated myself. At the other end of the loft Charley was cooking breakfast on the three-burner hot plate, and I smelled the fat and black coffee.

"Charley," I tried to say.

"Get up," he said.

"I can't do it," I said. "Not this morning."

"I'm tired of you," he said. "Get up."

"I've been dreaming, Charley. I'm sick."

I never awoke in Charley's loft except to the smell of slab bacon on the fire—he always cooked enough to fill the skillet with a half-inch of liquid fat in which he fried our eggs—and the smell of the skookum coffee in the iron pot. This morning the smells of Charley's cooking were as bad as the sounds of the women. And it was February and dark and cold.

"I want to get out of here," I said, still hugging myself under the army blankets and feeling against my cheek the ticking of the hard pillow—Charley would not allow the use of bed linen—and hearing against my will the cheerfulness of the women.

"That's good," said Charley.

One of the women had stopped laughing and was talking about a man named Bob while the other woman continued to laugh. I could not hear what the first was saying but the name kept popping up at me like a little puppet on a finger and it was to spare myself that sound in my ears that I finally managed to push down the covers and to sit up on the edge of the bed. There I sat, nude and shapely, as solid as tinned tuna, but hating poor Bob, whoever he was, while at the same time thanking him for prying me out of Sitka Charley's bed. I shivered, I bit my lip, I squeezed my cold thighs with my spread hands.

"Charley," I said, "what am I going to do?"

"Put some clothes on," he said. "Get dressed."

"I'm not my own woman," I said.

"You're nobody's woman," said Sitka Charley.

I stood up then and, deliberately remaining naked, began to walk around the loft. Here I had often stayed with Charley and Frank Morley in my childhood; here I had understood at last that Uncle Jake was not going to come back; here I had watched as Frank Morley lay curled on his side, dying; here I had been happy enough to share Sitka Charley's hard thin lumpy mattress and blankets. His loft was only a long bare room with the iron bedstead at one end and the hot plate at the other, emptier now than it had been even in Frank Morley's frugal time. But once I had been free to lie in the darkness and run my hands over Sitka Charley's bare ribs that he himself might have carved out of wood or ivory, and with Charley to sleep our uninterrupted sleep. But no more. No more dreamless sleep for Sunny.

"Put your clothes on," he said in his sullen voice.

I walked to one of the front windows and stood peering across at the corresponding window in the Baranof until a man's hairy torso appeared in it—Bob, I thought—and then I went over to the pair of dusty antlers where Sitka Charley keeps the Four-Hundred-and-Five. Carefully, and as I have done repeatedly in these past weeks, I lifted down the cold and heavy Winchester and weighed it, hefted it, cradled it against my nakedness. It was beginning to rust and they had stopped making ammunition for it long ago.

"What's the matter with you?" he said, as I knew he would.

"I've got to get out of here," I said, returning the old rifle to its place across the antlers.

"You can't go like that," he said.

"I can't go at all," I said.

He wiped his hands and walked down the length of the loft, a sinewy sixty-one-year-old man dressed in tight blue denim pants and a khaki shirt; he picked up my wool shirt and trousers and handed them to me.

"You just want to leave old Charley," he said and waited until I took the clothes.

"Just leave," I said.

"No woman sits down to my table naked," he said.

"I'm not going to sit at your table."

When I made no move to put on my shirt and pants, no move to spare poor Charley my nakedness or to ready myself for the return to Gamelands in my customized ex-army jeep, which is all that remains of Hank Laramie except for the greenhouse he built adjoining my log cabin, Charley pulled one of the Hudson Bay blankets off the bed and morosely, without speaking, draped it across my shoulders. Then he took back my shirt and pants and tossed them onto the bed.

Again I wandered around the loft, pausing at the bench where Charley had once made his belts and knives—he had given up his carving and leather working when Frank Morley died—and pausing at the window on the other side of the loft from which I could see the airplane marina and its flotilla of bright new pleasure planes where once, in my childhood and youth, there had been only Rex's Fairchild and Chippy's Curtis and, occasionally, the ragged little Aeronca of some other bush pilot stopping overnight in Juneau. Now there was a whole flotilla of newly bought seaplanes bobbing out there in the drizzle.

I smelled the bacon, the coffee, the sourdough bread that Charley himself still baked in a small portable rusty oven that fit on one of the burners; I heard him crack six eggs into the skillet; I heard him roughly setting the table with the usual tin knives and forks and spoons.

Against my will I joined him, concealing my body in the blanket as insistently as only moments before I had kept it bare, and looked down at the nearly raw bacon and the three fried eggs nuzzling each other on my plate. I thrust a hand out from between the folds of the blanket and raised the heavy cup of scalding coffee halfway to my mouth and then faltered, returned the cup to the saucer with a little anxious clatter. I stared at the grease on Charley's lips, at his hair that was blacker than Uncle Jake's had ever been and as neatly trimmed, at the face that was bony and angular, unlike the faces of other Siwash Indians. But it made no difference to me that Charley was still a handsome man. It made no difference to me to know, as I did know, that on his right forearm he sported a tattoo, and that his tattoo depicted an old-fashioned airplane propeller bisected by a rippling length of ribbon across which in flowing script was written my own name—Sunny. For a good six months his beauty, his prowess, the tattoo of which he had once been shyly proud, had ceased to give me pleasure.

I could not eat. I could hardly bear to watch him eat. I had no one in the world but Charley and I did not want him, no matter the nights I spent in his bed.

"For God's sake," I said suddenly, surprising us both, "I'm not loyal to my Alaskan childhood. I hate it. Haven't you ever felt trapped up here? Haven't you ever wanted to go anywhere? Alaska's just the end of the line, Charley. It's like finding an old rubber boot in a trout stream. I've always hated it. If it weren't for those crazy dreams of mine I'd leave tomorrow."

"You'll never leave," he said, holding the cracked and steaming cup in both hands and staring across the table at me.

"Come on, Charley," I said, "cheer me up."

He shook his head and below us the women were sillier than ever with their laughing and their Bob this and Bob that, though I couldn't understand what they were saying.

"The trouble with you," said Charley all at once, "is no baby."

"Don't start on that," I said.

"When I was a boy—maybe five or six years old—in Sitka," said Charley, "I saw a wonderful thing. White man's magic. I had been taken in by a family of Chilkats—mostly women—and didn't know where I had come from or what was going to happen to me. But I liked living with so many women. There was a young woman and her husband and the young woman's mother and two little sisters and the husband's old mother and me. All of us in a two-room shack—"

"Charley," I said, interrupting him, "are you telling me a story? Here I want nothing more than to get out of Alaska and you're telling me an Alaskan story?"

"Yes," he said.

"Well," I said, "I wish you wouldn't."

"I haven't thought about this part of my life in years," he said. "It's a good story."

"As if I don't have enough stories of my own," I said.

"Well," said Charley as if I had not spoken, "what I especially liked about all those women, was that the young married one had her belly swollen out as big as a house. The mother and mother-in-law and the two little sisters couldn't talk or think of anything except the baby in the young woman's belly. . . ."

"For God's sake," I said, interrupting him again, "I don't like children and can't have any, which you know as well as I do, and I don't want to hear about some Indian woman having a baby."

"Just listen," he said. "I'm telling you something."

"Furthermore," I said, "I don't like you talking like an Indian or condescending to me with a story with some sort of lesson sticking out of it a mile long."

"You could use a lesson or two," he said. "Besides, you asked me to cheer you up."

"Go on," I said, despite myself.

"Well," said Sitka Charley, "everyone except the husband waited for the baby kicking in the woman's belly. The husband was generally off on his boat, but the rest of us spent all our time in the two-room shack with the mother-to-be. The young woman's mother was a fat old creature who daily grew more impatient for the arrival of her first grandchild. The other old woman, the husband's mother, was equally eager for the day of the birth. The little girls never left their sister's side or stopped fondling her belly. I too shared in the joy and mystery that filled that shack, though I was only a small boy and though males were traditionally denied any participation in the rites and preparations that belonged exclusively to women. Anyhow the women went happily about their business, gathering great piles of rags and blankets and readying the little hide-and-wicker basket in which the newborn infant would be hung on the wall. I wanted nothing more than to touch the young woman's belly that became so large that she could hardly walk— but I was only an orphaned boy of five or six and never went so far as to make known my desire, but instead crouched enviously in a corner while the little girls fondled the now gigantic belly and even sprawled across it, laughing and poking at the baby inside.

"At last the labor pains began, and not a moment too soon, judging by the poor young woman's size and the looks of consternation that began to appear on the faces of the two old women. Now, suddenly, the long-awaited event was upon us, and the young mother-to-be, radiant and grimacing by turns, submitted to the ministrations of the old women. The two old women quickly acted on the dictates of their secret knowledge and barred the husband from the shack, admonished the little girls to watch in silence, and, catching sight of me in my corner, shooed me out of the room. However, as soon as their backs were turned, I crept again into the corner where now the little girls themselves were huddling, and in the hours and, as it turned out, even days that followed, came and went as I wished, attentive and privileged and happily unnoticed by the two old women.

"First the old women dressed the mother-to-be in the half-dozen or so additional skirts that were necessary to a successful birth. Then they stretched the young woman out on the floor, raising her knees and bracing her feet against the wooden blocks fastened to the floor for this event, and heaped upon the young woman the numerous blankets that they had gathered. They twisted one of the rags and stuck it between her teeth. They waited, squatting and smiling beside the young woman who would soon produce the infant for which we were all waiting. The young woman groaned, the old women consulted joyously with each other, through the darkness I stared at the great mound that lay in the middle of the bare floor.

"But nothing happened. The two old women began to grumble, to frown, to push on the young woman's belly, all the while urging her to concentrate properly on expelling the child. But nothing happened. The expected glorious moment, I understood, had already come and gone and still there was no baby. The two old women spoke sharply to the mother-to-be. They waited. Then they decided to proceed with the delivery, determined as they were to have their grandchild then and there, despite the recalcitrance of the mother-to-be. On either side of her they pushed, chanting the incantations known only to those who have themselves delivered a living child. Now and again they reached deep inside the mound of skirts and blankets and scowled, shook their heads, lent new fervor to their chanting. After what they deemed a suitable amount of time they drew aside the by now wet mass of skirts and blankets. They wrapped around the young woman's belly the traditional long band of sturdy cloth which they then tied and with the traditional stick of wood, tightened slowly like an immense tourniquet. The young woman screamed, the two old women nodded confidently to each other, the little girls hid their faces, I watched with the bright attentive eyes of a fox cub in his cave. I trusted the old women. I thought that the huge belly would prove no match for the tourniquet. But I was wrong. Around and around they turned the stick, on and on they chanted, and still the child stayed inside and the belly remained as bloated as ever."

"Charley," I said, clutching my own blanket, "for God's sake."

"Wait," he said, "it gets better. It was more than fifty years ago but I see it as clearly as anything that's happened since. No boy was ever luckier than me.

"Well, finally the two old women gave up, as you might expect. They threw aside the stick, removed the broad band of cloth, satisfied themselves that labor was still in progress, then once again buried the poor young woman inside her blankets and sent for the shaman. They were distraught, those old women, and so was I. Never before had their secret knowledge failed them, which was why they now dared to enlist the aid of the shaman despite the taboo against the presence of any male, including even a shaman for all they knew, in the place where a woman was bringing forth a child. He was a cocky old fellow and disdained the poor old women, who were now frightened and humbled by the terrible fate that had befallen them, but devoted himself grandly and wholeheartedly to the moaning female who could not set loose the waters and expel the child. He shook marvelous rattles, he chanted incantations unheard of by the two old women; into the mouth of the mother-to-be he poured a potion, then another potion, then still another. He fed her bits of root and bark and cuds of previously chewed tobacco while the two old women squatted to one side and humbly nodded their encouragement. When he passed the antlers of a female deer back and forth across the belly there was not one of us in that darkened room who was not convinced that the baby's cry would sound immediately beneath the heap of blankets. But there was no cry, no change in the belly, nothing, until finally the shaman accused the poor old women themselves of conspiring to thwart the birth. Angrily he left us once again alone with the shadows, the groaning, the child that remained unborn.

"Now the two old women had no choice. On the third day of anguish there was nothing left to do but send for the young white doctor who had recently arrived in Sitka. This was 1908 or 1910, remember, and Indians were still suspicious of white doctors. Anyhow they sent one of the little sisters to fetch the man who was our only hope.

"At first they refused to allow him into the shack and demanded that he stay outside and work his magic. Then they refused to allow him into the darkened room, but finally did so, grumbling and hugging each other. I remember him well, a tall young white man dressed like anyone else in shirt and pants and boots and carrying a leather satchel. It was difficult to see his face in the shadows but his voice was kind. He asked the two old women numerous questions and allayed their fears. But when he knelt beside the figure bundled up on the floor and made as if to thrust his hand under the blankets, the two old women howled as one and forbade him to so much as touch the blankets or any part of the laboring woman. It was forbidden for any man to touch such a woman, they said. Why, even the shaman had not touched this woman.

"But the young doctor remained kneeling where he was and spoke at length to the two old women. Not only did he convince them with his patience and his kind voice that he must be permitted to save the young woman's life, which was a grave matter that had not yet occurred to the old women, but gradually he restored their faith in an imminent delivery of their grandchild. The ancient taboo was overcome, the doctor smiled, the pleasure of the two old women was mine as well. So the young doctor prepared to raise the skirts and blankets and give us our baby.

"There was not a sound in the room except for the moaning of the young woman whose stamina couldn't last much longer. Then we heard the click of the doctor's satchel. Then we saw him intrude his hand far beneath the blankets, which caused the two old women a moment of dismay, then watched as he withdrew his hand and slowly and gently pulled away layer on layer of skirts and blankets until he had uncovered all he possibly could of the swollen belly. We waited. The old women recovered themselves and rubbed their hands together. Even I understood that the baby inside that bare belly must be immense.

"But where was he?

"Then after only the briefest hesitation, the young doctor made his decision. He reached into his satchel and pulled out a little bottle and a piece of cloth, and then, opening the bottle and pouring some of the liquid it contained onto the cloth, gently he held the wet cloth over the young woman's face. A terrible smell filled the room, like ice that has been saturated in gasoline. Then in terrified amazement we watched as before our eyes the young woman's belly began to deflate. Would you believe it? Down it went, that poor young woman's belly, while those old Chilkat women watched in horror. Before they could move or cry out in alarm, the great naked belly was as flat as any in that room. There was no baby!"

I leaned forward, caught off guard in Charley's triumphant pause, and stared at him. His eyes were dark and golden; outside the engine of one of the private planes was turning over.

"No baby?" I said.

"No baby."

"It was just a fluke?"

"That's right," said Sitka Charley. "The stuff on the cloth was chloroform. The young doctor just knocked out the poor young woman with his chloroform. When she relaxed her muscles her belly went back to normal. She wasn't carrying any child, which is what the doctor had thought. Who knows how long she would have waited for her baby without that chloroform? But the trouble was that the two old women had lost their grandchild. First the shaman had accused them of trying to delay the baby's birth, and now the white doctor had taken away their baby—like that! First one extreme and then the other. They were pop-eyed, those poor old Chilkat women, and furious. They didn't understand what had happened, no matter how kindly and patiently the doctor talked with them, though finally they agreed between them that she who was now sleeping peacefully on the floor would just have to begin again and do a better job next time. And this time there would be no white doctor in the room. As for me, the wonder of what I had seen was almost as good as would have been the baby himself. Also, the doctor noticed me when the whole thing was over and took me off with him. I lived with the white doctor and his pretty wife for two years. Then Frank Morley came along and brought me to Juneau."

Charley paused. He took a sip of his cold coffee.

"So," I said, reaching for my cup, "the woman didn't get her baby but you got your new life."

He nodded.

"Well," I said then, feeling a sudden hunger for my three cold and congealed eggs, "I suppose I have to pay attention to the moral of that story, Charley."

"Yes," he said. "It's a good story but I haven't finished it."

"Go on," I said, eating the cold and rubbery eggs and indifferent to the blanket that was now hanging loose, "what next?"

"You won't believe it," said Charley, "but that young Chilkat woman became a friend of the doctor's wife. They fished together. You see, the doctor and his wife lived in a cabin on a little dock out over the water, and adjoining the cabin was a shed unlike anything I'd ever seen. The doctor was a pretty smart young fellow and believed in sanitation and liked his conveniences. He cut a door from the cabin into the shed, installed windows in the shed, and made a trap door in the floor. Then he built a portable toilet that he kept in a corner. It was just a bottomless pine box with a hole in the top of it, but whenever the doctor or his wife wanted to make use of their toilet, why, they just opened the trap door and set the box over the space in the floor. In bad weather it was easy for the pretty wife to empty her slops down that same open space out in her shed. She put curtains on the windows and installed a stove and a kerosene lantern on a table. It made the biggest difference in winter, of course. The doctor's wife had lined the hole in the box with a piece of fur—would you believe it?—and I'll never forget the luxury of my childhood when I sat out there on the doctor's fur-lined toilet!"

"Charley," I said, laughing and interrupting him, "did you ever tell Frank about that fancy outhouse?"

"I don't know," he said.

"I think you did," I said. "And then Frank told Jake. Because once I saw a pretty good facsimile of that outhouse, except for the fur trimming."

"The fur was the best thing about it," said Charley. "Anyhow that's where the doctor's wife and the young Chilkat woman did their fishing in bad weather."

"They fished through the same hole where they defecated and dumped the slops? That doctor," I said, "had a strange idea of sanitation."

"There was a strong tide," said Charley, "and it was good fishing. Anyhow for two years I lived with them and stayed as close as I could to the doctor's wife, touching her clothes and hanging on to her hand and doing what I could to help her. I was her pet, as she was always telling the young Chilkat woman, and whenever the two of them were together fishing in the shed I was right there with them. I baited their hooks, I cleaned the fish as fast as they hauled them up, it was I who kept the fish biting, as the doctor's wife always told her friend. There were days and weeks when the two young women did nothing but stay in the shed and fish—the doctor's wife for sport, the young Chilkat woman so that she and her husband and her little sisters and the two old women could eat the fish she caught. Day after day at the same hole for different reasons. There's a lesson I learned, all right. And here's the punch line. After about four months of fishing, the young Chilkat woman's belly began to swell, and this time the white doctor verified that there was no mistake. Well, you never saw a happier trio than the three of us out there in the shed when the two young women friends were talking about the event to come and I squatted beside them wielding my knife, though I was still only a small boy, and watching and listening. By the time Frank came across me in the doctor's cabin and took a shine to me and brought me up here to Juneau, the pretty young Chilkat squaw had given birth not to one but to two fat babies and was the pride of everyone concerned, especially the doctor. Well, I guess that young squaw learned her lesson and never disappointed anyone again.

"What do you think of that?"

"I think," I said, laughing and standing up and letting the blanket fall to the floor, "that you're as bad as Jake. But you couldn't have told Jake this boyhood story of yours, eh Charley? Anyhow you've made an unhappy woman glad—I have to admit it."

"If that's all," he said, glancing away from my now comfortably bare body, "then you didn't listen."

"I can read your Indian riddles," I said. "Don't worry."

"Maybe I'll help you," he said, "maybe not."

"Do I need your help?"

"I don't know."

"Charley," I said, "I'm not a Chilkat squaw."

"You'll find out," he said. "No baby."

"I'm leaving," I said, walking around the table and leaning down and pressing against him. "Do you want to come?"

"No."

"I could change my mind and stay."

"No sex," he said and that ended the conversation.

When I reached the bottom of the dark rickety flight of stairs, I paused and listened for the laughing women but heard nothing. Outside I glanced into Millie's Millinery Shoppe, as it was called, and tried the door. But there was no one. Nothing. Gone to Bob's, I said to myself, both of them. Then I got into the jeep and made sure that Charley heard the shriek of my tires, the blast of my horn, the roar of my modified engine with its twin carburetors and overhead cams.

Back here at Gamelands I went into the greenhouse and with hands on hips surveyed the scattered earth, the broken panes of glass, the poor remaining signs of the day when one year ago Hank left and I wrecked the greenhouse, yanked up the whole jungle of flowering marijuana plants and destroyed them all.

Then I returned to the cabin and thought of ridding myself of the skull of His Unholiness and ordering Sitka Charley to chop down our famous totem pole. I thought of Charley taking a chain saw to the base of the totem pole, I saw myself carrying the bear skull in the crook of my arm like a football. I heard the whining of despair, saw the totem pole crashing down, saw myself kneeling on the float beside the Cessna and raising the hammer, bringing it down, smashing the old skull to bits with one blow. Why not?

So here I am on a late mid-May afternoon in 1965 and calmer than I was this morning. I'm alone, in three months I'll turn forty, and I haven't left Alaska and nothing's changed except for the worse. But I'm calmer.

Whatever happened to Uncle Jake?

Where are you, Pascal?

44 —

I came awake—torpid sensual Sunny in bed with Hank—and knew at once that it was morning and that there was a stranger standing in our bedroom doorway. I lay there listening, feeling the sharpness of Hank's hip and the warmth of his body, and was oddly aware of being surprised but not alarmed. Man or woman, I wondered, and was so heavy and comfortable with the night that was past that I hardly cared. A muscle in Hank's shoulder twitched. I sighed. Then I rolled over and raised my head. It was a woman.

A big woman. A woman unlike any I had ever seen. A moose-high woman wearing a slick gray jumpsuit, a pink silk neckerchief, and pearls. A camera in a large black case was slung on a strap from her shoulder. She had enough hair—black and teased and curled and tangled and frizzled and tempestuous—to fill a basket. Her face was as hard and handsome as a man's, and there was something wrong with it.

"Well," I said, lifting myself on my elbow and making no effort to hide my contented flesh, "can I help you?"

"I don't know," she said, looking not at me but at Hank. "Can you?"

"What do you want?" I asked, pleased, though I should not have been, that Hank's face was turned toward me on the pillow and that the stranger was studying his bronzed profile, his auburn hair, his gaunt good looks.

"Why don't you wake him up?" she said at last, glancing at me and twisting a long finger in one of the strands of pearls.

She was a six-foot beauty blocking our doorway, invading our bedroom, disregarding the still lingering atmosphere of the night which anyone could see had been ours. Her wide mouth was beginning to smile—not for my sake, I saw at once, and not for sleeping Hank's—and the faint smile made me see what was wrong with the face. It was formidable, it was classically shaped, it was serene. But it was covered with a crust of scars like crow's feet or tiny scales. Who could have resisted her size, her self-confidence, her clothes, her scars, the very color and mass of all her contradictions? Not I. Not Hank. I began to wonder what the jumpsuit concealed; I liked the crooked narcissistic smile.

"Who are you?" I asked with a light and feathery edge to my voice. "What are you doing in my bedroom?"

"Wrong cabin, I guess. What's his name?"

I laughed, propping myself higher on my elbow, and was conscious of my tight torso, my nudity that was unmarred, the taste of Hank in my mouth. I was smaller than she and younger, but for once in my life uncertain. I felt simultaneously amused, uneasy, ready to do anything I could to please her. I thought that she was a woman of moods and that with a lift of the lip my beautiful shocking visitor might suddenly become no more than a big surly wolfish woman. One glance of those gray eyes and I, tough Sunny, might disappear. But then too I might prove her match. Tough Sunny.

"Listen," I said then, "who are you? Where are you from? Not Alaska, obviously."

She leaned against the doorjamb, crossed her ankles, played with her pearls and the camera dangling in its black leather case. The light beyond the windows was the color of a gray goose in the rain.

"Alaska," she said in her voice that was austere yet not unpleasant, "was known originally as Alaksha. The Great Country. It's one-fifth the size of continental United States. It has a coastline of nearly seven thousand miles. It contains eleven of the twenty highest mountains in North America, including Mount McKinley. The Yukon River is nineteen hundred miles long. The Malaspina Glacier is larger than the state of Rhode Island. Alaska contains forty percent of the fresh water in the United States. It offers the best fishing in the world. The best hunting..."

"All right," I said, trying to interrupt her, "I'm Sunny Deauville." But she was not to be stopped and did not tell me her name as I thought she would.

"A cheechako becomes a sourdough," she continued, looking at Hank's shirt and pants and underpants tossed on the floor, "when she sees the ice freeze in the Yukon, sees the ice melt in the Yukon, shoots a bear, and sleeps with an Eskimo."

"You're no sourdough," I said, laughing. "I'm not either."

"How do you know what I am?" she said, still without looking at me. "You just say the first thing that pops into your head, don't you?"

"No offense," I said quickly.

"I'm not offended," she said. "You're putting words in my mouth."

"What?" I said, blushing—Sunny blushing—but admiring more than ever the voice that was as oddly strong and attractive as the woman herself.

"You probably don't even know how Juneau got its name," she said.

"Good Lord," I said, "it's named after Joe Juneau, of course. Everyone knows how he and Richard Harris found gold around here and named the place after Joe Juneau."

"No," said the woman lounging in our doorway, "you're wrong. Originally Dick Harris named the place Harrisburg after himself. He was a clever egotistical fellow. But as the town grew in size Joe Juneau began to brood about its name, as well he might have, until one day he offered free drinks at Meier's Roadhouse. The entire population of Harrisburg spent the day drinking. Toward sunset Dancut Peterson, who was Juneau's closest companion, mounted an inverted whiskey barrel and proposed a motion to change the name of the town. He said that Joe was actually the father of the town, not Dick Harris, and that Joe's name was more eye-catching, as he put it, than Harris's. The motion carried in one lusty drunken cheer. That was in 1884."

"It's still named after Joe Juneau," I said uncomfortably. "I live here. You don't."

"The men of Alaska," she said, recrossing her ankles and fondling her pearls and scrutinizing the still-sleeping Hank, "have hard hands, smell of burnt wood, and walk in a typically stiff-legged way."

"Hank's not an Alaskan," I said quickly as he began to smile in his sleep—at her, I thought—and to make little whistling snoring sounds while lying with one bare arm stretched across my middle.

"I guess you haven't heard of Cap Lathrop or that heroic bush pilot Carl Ben Eielson," she continued, "or the twenty-three-year-old John Ledyard who was the first American to see Alaska."

"I'm a pilot myself," I said, trying not to lose face entirely.

"If I could still have had children," she said, as I felt myself blushing again and scowling and beginning to perspire, "I might well have been giving my own little half-white, half-Eskimo daughter her Mickinni

Kow-Kow in Top Kick outside of Nome. Mickinni Kow-Kow," she added indifferently, "means warm lunch at all hours."

"I don't have any children either," I said, staring at the square jaw, the pink scarf, the arrogant hair.

"I did not say that I do not have any children," she said. "You're putting words in my mouth again. Can't you listen?"

"It's my town," I said lamely. "My cabin, my bedroom, my boyfriend. Why am I supposed to listen to you?"

"I would happily have borne Lathrop's daughter," she went on, "or Eielson's or George Steller's. Especially George Steller's. They were Alaskan men, as different from each other as they were. Why, Cap Lathrop introduced the motion picture theater into Alaska and made the first Alaskan film, *The Cheechakos,* with wonderful dog-team chases and that inspired scene in which they drive the villain to his death in a deep crevasse of a glacier as large as the Malaspina. The word 'mush,' which the dogsled driver cries to urge on his dogs, is derived from the French *marche,* which is pronounced 'marsh' and is an imperative meaning 'go.' As for Ben Eielson, he was the greatest Alaskan pilot of them all. Noel Wien, Bob Reeve, Sam White—they were excellent flyers. But Ben Eielson was an Alaskan pilot of world renown. The crash that took his life—in Siberia in 1930—was the cause of the first international air search on record."

"I cracked up once," I said, aware of an inexplicable discomfort, "while trying to land on the Kalukna. Trying to land a float plane on a river isn't easy."

"In Alaska," she said, riding over me roughshod and without a pause, "there are one hundred and sixteen times as many commercial aircraft as there are in the sum of the other states, eighty times as many air miles flown, thirty times as many passengers flown, over a thousand times as many pounds of freight carried by air. And this great achievement is thanks to the brave men who fly the planes."

"Well," I said, "I'm a woman."

"In Top Kick," she said in her firm indifferent voice, "when an Eskimo infant has a runny nose, the mother just sucks the mucus from the baby's nostrils and spits it out."

"Good Lord," I said, and laughed, trying to please her.

"Every woman remains a virgin," she said, "until she has borne her first child."

"Now wait a minute," I said, putting my hand on Hank's tawny forearm, "I disagree—"

"If George Steller were alive today," she said, squaring her shoulders and smiling as though Hank could see her in his sleep, "and if I were physically able to do so, I would become a mother all over again, and gladly. Any woman who knows anything at all about Alaska is haunted by George Steller."

"Well," I said glumly, "I've never heard of him."

"One can't extol enough the prowess of the Alaskan male, native or otherwise," she went on. "The stories of their exploits are legion. Why, Ed Peelo, whose fourth wife I became for a brief period in Top Kick, once saved his life and the life of his dog when, marooned in a blizzard, he severed the dog's tail and used it to make a nourishing broth. Ed survived on the broth and the dog survived on the bone from his own tail which Ed gave back to him to gnaw. What woman would not have gladly borne the daughter of such a man?"

"That story," I said, amused despite myself, "dates back to about 1898. It's famous."

"It's true," she said flatly, tightening the pearls around her throat like a choker. "But of all of Alaska's heroes, George Steller stands tallest in the pantheon, I can tell you, the Ed Peelos and Ben Eielsons and Berings and Cooks notwithstanding. No one did more than Steller or even approached his stature. It was Steller," she continued, glancing again at Hank's underpants, "who assured Bering's second trip to our Alaskan coast its place in history. That was in 1741, of course. Anyhow when Bering was near his death, when their crew was disabled to a man by scurvy, it was George Steller who knew the raptures of scientific discovery. Detested by the debilitated crew for his wonderfully arrogant manner, derided by them for his small size and for his totally justified condemnation of their childish gambling, upbraided even by the dying Bering himself, still George Steller faithfully kept his journal of new birds, new plants, mammals then unknown to science, and did all he could to prolong the voyage. It was thanks to Steller's painstaking and loving description of the seal that Russia embarked on what was soon to become the Alaskan Fur Trade. While Bering moaned and the crew pleaded to set sail for home, Steller—George Steller, the German physician and naturalist of worldwide renown—dissected with infinite care a four-ton sea cow—"

"A what?" I exclaimed, and immediately wished that I had not spoken.

"The sea cow, found only in the Commander Islands," she said, "was so delicious that she was hunted ardently for her flesh alone, and was soon extinct. But Steller's brilliant drawings of her survive. You would know nothing of Steller's character unless you had studied them. I have only to glance at Steller's work to want his child."

"Well," I said quickly, "I don't know what you want with poor Hank here."

"You haven't been listening," she said. "You haven't understood what I've been saying."

"I've been listening," I said.

"The point," she said, "is that every Alaskan man—every real Alaskan man—is a legend. It's just that some are more legendary than others."

"The point," I said, "is that this has gone on long enough," which is when Hank awoke.

One moment he was lying beside me deep in his boyishly untroubled sleep, the next he was sitting bolt upright, bare and bronzed, smiling a long slow smile of incredulity and welcome. His auburn hair was tousled, his eyes were fixed on our visitor, his alertness—his no doubt legendary alertness—was unmistakable.

"Good morning, ladies," he said. "What have we here?"

"She just walked in, Hank," I began, but it was no use.

The size of her, the shape of her, and the scars, the camera, the jumpsuit that might have been fashioned from a membrane ripped from the sea cow herself—as if all this were not enough to ruin him for any woman forever, slowly she raised her arms, put her fingers to her temples, and then, with chin raised and elbows out and chest prominently displayed, she pushed her fingers into her great shiny black mass of hair and lifted the hair away from her head and held it there, upswept and wild. It was a gesture of stock theatricality, a shameless ploy. But even I understood that it was an invitation that no man—no legendary man—could refuse. She waited, smiling crookedly at Hank, and then dropped her hands to her sides.

"Well now," he said, "I'm Hank Laramie."

She tilted her head, raised her brows, studied him quizzically, mysteriously, shamelessly.

"Laramie?" she said. "Laramie?"

"Just like the town," he said, laughing and licking his lips and rubbing his unshaven chin and looking at her.

"I know the name of the town," she said, her voice suddenly distant and her face tight. "You don't need to tell me."

I laughed though neither of them heard me, and for that one moment enjoyed the expression on poor Hank's face.

"No offense," he said, and again I laughed and told myself that I was not the only vulnerable person in the room. But the rebuke which he deserved and I awaited did not come, as I was sure it would. Quite the contrary.

"Hank Laramie," she said in her warmest contralto tones, "do you like champagne?"

"Why sure," he said guardedly.

"Then let's drink some champagne together," she said. "Tonight. At the Baranof. At ten o'clock."

"Well fine," he said. "And who am I going to drink this champagne with?"

"Ask for Martha Washington," she said matter-of-factly and no longer smiling.

"Martha..." Hank began, and stopped himself just in time, no matter how much I wanted him to stumble, to fall off the tightrope, to commit the unpardonable act of making light of her name. But he saw the sudden hardness in the handsome face and the look in the gray eyes. He was warned, worse luck for me, and controlled himself. "Ten o'clock," he said. "At the Baranof. Well, I'm glad to know you, Martha Washington."

"You don't know me," she retorted, just to keep him on his toes, I thought, "but call me Marty."

Then Hank was gawking at the empty doorway and she was gone.

"She's some lady," he said after a moment.

"You're not going to the Baranof," I said as cheerfully as I could, "without me."

We asked for her. We were expected. Weren't we though. If we would just have a seat he would ring her room and let her know that we had arrived. No need for that. Sure? Absolutely. Well, then, second floor front. We'd find our way.

For one moment, as we started toward the stairs at the rear of the lobby, I was suddenly convinced that in mere moments she would welcome us—or rather welcome Hank and admit me—to that same room where, as an elated child, I had lain awake savoring my first night in Juneau. Wouldn't they have installed her in that very room?

Wouldn't I recognize it though I had not been upstairs in the Baranof for more than thirty years? The iron bedstead? The cot for me? Just my luck, I thought, smelling the past, looking around for the spittoons and pool table that were no longer there.

Hank started up the stairs ahead of me, and as I hurried after him, I thought that there was never a man, Willie or otherwise, more obviously compelled toward a waiting woman than Hank was now. There was only one purpose in the black silk shirt, the tight jeans, the scalloped boots, the deerskin jacket, the old hat low on his brow—and what was more amusing and also irritating than the sight of a gangling good-looking man with nothing on his mind but sex with a new woman? But then I admitted to myself that I was not amused.

I too had dressed up in clinging shirt and pants for the occasion. I knew what was awaiting him, blunders aside, and would have behaved exactly as he was behaving now had I been a man. And wasn't I, who had been excluded in the morning, coming back for more of the same, or worse, at night? At an unusual time of night? And didn't I still harbor hopes of proving her match, winning her approval, keeping Hank? I did, fool that I was.

I heard her cold voice as I turned the corner and found myself facing the open door of the room that Hank had already entered without me.

"Marty," he said as I trailed in after him, unnoticed, ungreeted, "when you say champagne you sure mean champagne."

"I always mean what I say," she said, true to form.

"So do I," I said, though I might as well have been talking to myself out in the corridor for all they cared. At the sound of my voice Hank made a hasty effort to cover up my intrusion, stepping quickly between Marty Washington and me, while Marty turned her back on us both and pulled shut the door. She was wearing a plum-colored jumpsuit this time, and a lime-green scarf, pink ballet slippers—on feet that were twice the size of mine—and of course the pearls. Her great shimmering head of black hair was prouder and messier than it had been in the morning; her scars, at close range, were livid, fresh-looking, they disfigured not merely her handsome face but the backs of her hands and what I could see of her throat as well. Scarred all over, I began to think, and smelling of deliberately unwashed hair and medicinal soap.

"Well now," said Hank nervously, "here we are."

She merely looked at him once and, without asking either of us to be seated, strode over to the low bed big enough for four and, pushing aside the pillows, arranged herself with back straight and ankles crossed and knees wide, Buddha fashion, at the head of it. There she sat, carelessly dominating ourselves, the room, the hour, and naturally I had never before set foot in this room, as I saw at first glance, and naturally it was the best room in the Baranof and was packed, as poor Hank and I could not have anticipated, with all the paradoxical clutter that represented Marty herself. Her camera of the morning had not promised what we now saw: half a dozen other cameras lying about the room in black cases; one glassy-eyed mechanical beast sitting na-kedly on a tripod; a forest of goose-necked floor lamps, all of them turned on, filling the room with the light of relentless incandescence. And was this the light of seduction? This the light of a woman recently and badly scarred? I grinned inwardly at the sight of poor blinking Hank, and felt relief, discomfort, intimidation as I sidled over to one of the windows fronting the street and found myself staring through the late-night April rain directly at the lighted windows of Sitka Char-ley's loft. Just out of my line of sight bespectacled Charley would be sitting as usual with his adventure story or sportsman's magazine, rock-ing and reading.

I turned back into the light and silence and saw poor Hank glancing first at Marty and her wide-open crotch—and a yawning plum-colored crotch it was—and then at the bottles and cases of champagne that were everywhere strewn and stacked around the carpeted floor between the flood lamps, against the walls. One fat green bottle sat chilling in an ice bucket on the bedside table along with a bevy of glasses, some clean, some not.

Hank finally approached the bedside table and, in a sudden show of determination, took hold of the thick green champagne bottle by its golden neck and pulled it from the ice bucket—too quickly. The drops flew, he stammered, she did not blink or dab at her cheek, and again Hank checked himself—no lighthearted apologies allowed in Marty's room—and drew back, hugging the bottle like a cold wet fat green baby to his chest, and breathed deeply and picked at the golden foil with his fingernails, tore it away. He stared at the bare neck of the bottle and the chubby cork bound in wire; carefully, waiting for the explosion that was sure to come, he untwisted the wire, worked it loose. He glanced at Marty, blushing—despite his outdoor complexion and easygoing nature—and clenched his lean jaws and frowned and buried the cork in his fist. He held his breath, gripped the bottle, struggled against demoralization, and then made a complete turn in the middle of the room and saw as if for the first time the overhead light, the fragile bulbs of the flood lamps, the framed Alaskan scenes behind thin glass on the walls. Where to aim? How to avoid the unforgivable showering of broken glass? The disgrace? But suddenly the bottle began to pull away from him. He clutched it in both hands, arched his back, remembered to clap his hand over the cork, and still the mouth of the bottle swung now here, now there, willfully describing its unpredictable and uncontrollable circles. It aimed itself at Hank's left foot, at the ceiling light, at the tumblers on the bedside table, at the camera gaping helplessly on its tripod. Then it lunged in the opposite direction, dragging Hank around with it, and for one terrible precarious moment aimed its barely stoppered mouth directly at Marty Washington's stern and slightly puzzled, slightly disdainful face.

"No!" he cried and yanked it upward just as the fuse stopped sizzling and the cork let go. There was a bang, Hank's stricken look, and everywhere the furious gushing and foaming and flowing of champagne. It rose high from the mouth of the bottle, spurted between Hank's desperate fingers, soaked his shirtfront, sprayed the room. Marty's eyes grew large, then small and mean. The champagne boiled out of the bottomless bottle. Then it stopped and poor Hank stood holding the dripping thing in his wet hands while Marty stared at him and I laughed to myself in the corner. Unmanned before he had even begun, I thought, as he deserved to be.

"There are more bottles on ice in the bathtub," she said evenly and as if what she was saying were a commonplace.

Hank fled. But hardly had he slammed the bathroom door than the second shot rang out, louder and more echoing than the first, and Hank rushed back to us, the second bottle clumsily swathed in a peach-colored terry cloth towel, and in desperation and before he knew what he was doing, filled all the tumblers, clean or otherwise, on the bedside table. He blanched and shook his head. It was then that Marty unaccountably relented and reached out her hand and smiled her crooked smile and accepted the quickly proffered glass. Weakly Hank returned her smile, shoved the bottle into the ice bucket, and picked up a glass and drank it off.

"Hank," I said, "I'd like some champagne."

He turned, startled at the sound of my voice, and dutifully brought me a glass, though he appeared not to see me or even to know that I had accompanied him to the Baranof, no matter that our fingers touched and that he looked me full in the face. By this time we had not been in Marty's room ten minutes. The late and rainy night was young.

"What you could not know," she said as Hank made his way warily back to the bedside table with two more bottles, "is that I know who you are."

I frowned, she smiled. She accepted another water glass filled with champagne and indicated that Hank should seat himself on a stiff and tottering ladder-back chair beside the bed. They drank together. I resented her suddenly confidential mood, wondered what was coming next. She was a hateful woman.

"That's right," she continued. "I was happily surprised this morning when you told me your name."

"Laramie," he said before he could stop himself, but she only smiled distantly and reached for more champagne, which he quickly gave her.

"To think that here we are, meeting each other in Alaska," she said.

"Pleasure's mine," he said in obvious confusion.

"Who would believe such a coincidence?"

"I don't think I can," he said foolishly.

"The coincidence," she said, resting her free hand on a knee the size of the head of a newborn babe, "is that your Sandy is living with my George."

"George..." he started to say, and stopped himself.

"George Starling," she said coolly. "I kept my maiden name."

"Good Lord," I blurted, though I had promised myself only to drink and listen, and though I knew that trying to reach Hank now was hopeless, "don't believe her, Hank. She couldn't know anything about Sandy."

"Do you mean...?" he faltered.

"That's what I mean," she said. "My husband and your Sandy."

"Hank," I said, my voice slurring, "she's not married. She couldn't be."

For the first time since our arrival she looked at me, turning her massive head and giving me one long affronted glance from across the room.

"I was married at the age of twenty," she said. "I'm still married."

"Well now," said Hank, "so that's who she left me for. Your husband."

"I do not believe that she made the right choice," said Marty, "but I'm afraid I can understand how it could happen. George is an enormously attractive man."

"A teacher," said Hank.

"A specialist in Asian studies," said Marty.

"I remember," said Hank.

"George is not much of a scholar," said Marty, "but he's virile, I can tell you that. Big, blond, and virile."

"Hank's pretty virile himself," I said into the dead white glare of the room, but he wasn't listening.

"They'll never give George tenure," said Marty, clinking glasses with Hank, "but they love him. He's so remarkably virile and yet so modest about his attractiveness to women that his colleagues, lesser men that they are, brag among themselves about his exploits. He sets an example they can admire but don't have to worry about trying to follow. Down to a man they joke about the Asian studies wives—their own wives— as George's girls."

"You put up with that kind of thing?" asked Hank.

"I haven't lived with George for some time. I had my rages, of course, but I was never able to be jealous of his other women for long. That prowess of his. That wonderful nature of his. Where was the woman who could resist him? If I couldn't resist him, who could? Then too he was always pushing me on other men, just to find out if they were as good as he was."

"Hank," I said, surprised at the loudness of my voice, "more champagne!"

"You mean," said Hank, "that he wanted you to go to bed with his friends?"

"Friends. Strangers. 'Check out that big fellow at the other end of the room,' he'd say. Or, 'Marty, check out that big German guy down there on the rocks.' Or, 'Maybe it's time to check out old Stanislaus.' I was never interested in checking them out, to use George's expression, but inevitably I would push my way through the crowd or swim out to some hulking man on a rock—we used to travel a lot, George and I—and then report back to him that this man or that man didn't look like much. Not compared to him, anyway."

"Oh," said Hank. "That's all you did."

"Naturally," said Marty, "I had my moments. How not? Some of them, including Stanislaus, checked out quite well, as a matter of fact."

"I've never had any trouble myself," said Hank.

"I'm not talking about you," said Marty.

"I know," said Hank, wiping his brow.

"There's one thing you better understand right now," said Marty. "I'm a feminist."

"You see," I said, shocked at my lack of pride, "you can't trust her!"

The champagne. His forlorn expression. Her angry face. The two of them looking like wax figures under the intensity of the hot lights. The smell of my perspiration beginning to overpower the scent of my Cachet Noir. And why didn't she get on with it? Why didn't I walk out of the room and out of the hotel and across the street to Charley, and let them do what they wanted? But my presence was no hindrance to either one of them, as I had known from the start, and obviously Marty Washington was not in a hurry. Besides, I admitted to myself, I wanted to stay, to keep them apart if I could, to watch if necessary, to join them if it came to that.

"Anyhow," said Marty, softening, "I know how well you cook and ride horseback—rancho style—and how well you take care of children. I love those children. I also know that for the first time in his life George is jealous—of you."

"Me?" said Hank. "He's stolen Sandy and he's jealous of me?"

"Sandy is not as discreet as I am," said Marty. "So ever since Sandy moved in with him, you've been the one man George can't get out of his mind, though you haven't met."

"Listen," I said, "Hank has all the women he wants, including this woman right here. You're not telling us anything."

"On top of that," she continued, "George is unfamiliar with Alaska's legendary effect on potency. So poor George's situation is worse than he knows."

She laughed, Hank laughed, she waggled her empty glass and told him to bring back not two bottles this time but three. We heard him behind the closed door—splashing endlessly at the toilet, lathering his hands, complimenting himself on what he saw in the mirror, making the ice rattle and clatter in the tub. She turned her head in my direction. I did not allow her to stare me down. Hank was whistling in the bathroom.

"You're an innocent," she said finally. "I'm a feminist."

"Well," I said, "that's a good one. Here I've devoted my life to planes and men and fish and game and you call me innocent."

"An innocent," she said. "There's a difference."

"I like sex as much as you do," I said.

"I don't talk about sex with just anyone," she said.

Another champagne bottle fired off in the bathroom, but she did not look at the door. The whistling stopped.

"An innocent," she said steadily, "is a woman who doesn't suffer.

She has no commitments, no problems. Sex is easy. Her life is without drama and hence without interest to those other than herself."

"Plenty of men are interested in me," I said. "Women too."

"Lots of people are attracted to vulgarity," she said. "That's not what I mean."

"In my experience," I said, "women don't go around insulting other women or stealing their men."

"Your experience," she said coldly, "is contemptible."

"Now just a minute..." I tried to say.

"Contemptible," she repeated. "You are ignorant of the rights of women. You earn your living by exploiting women."

"Gamelands," I said, "is a cooperative."

"A woman who has not borne a child," she said in her detached humiliating way, "does not know anything about being a woman and cannot understand what I mean."

"I don't believe you've got a child," I said. "I don't believe you're married."

"Susanna," she said, "is twenty-one years old. She is not an innocent."

In the bathroom two reports rang out in quick succession, the door opened, and back came Hank carrying by their necks two smoking bottles like a pair of dead geese. He staggered, bounced the bottles up and down, showing off his catch, then crossed the room as if to sit on the edge of Marty's bed but, seeing her face, veered toward the spindly ladder-back chair. Again he filled the water glasses on the bedside table; liberally he slopped her prized champagne into the glasses, onto the table, the carpeting, Marty's nearest knee. He laughed and looked at her slyly, convinced, apparently, that there would be no more rebukes.

"Hank," I said, approaching them and holding out my glass, "it's time to leave."

He filled it, trying, I saw, to keep Marty's face in focus, and drank from his own glass, leaned forward earnestly, whimsically, and licked his lips. I pushed a pile of her lingerie out of an overstuffed chair and sat down.

"Marty," he said, saluting her with his raised glass, "what are you doing up here?"

"There's another thing you should understand," she said, reaching out for a refill. "No direct questions. I do not approve of anyone asking me direct questions."

I snorted, poured myself more champagne, sank into the cushions that smelled of someone else's perfume.

"Why all this stuff?" he said, gesturing at the blinding lamps, the jumble of cameras. "You a photographer?"

There was a new glint in the gray wolfish eyes, I thought, but then, during a long pause, she obviously made up her mind to forgo her principles and humor Hank.

"As a matter of fact," she said, "this trip I'm concentrating on the Alaskan Indian. From the smallest boys to the oldest men. I'm representing the range of males in each of the tribes. Kakes, Chilkats, Thlingets, Stickeens, and so forth."

"Well now," said Hank, and laughed and slapped his knee. I too laughed aloud, thinking that there was one Indian—right across the street—whose portrait Marty Washington would never display in her collection if I could help it.

"Why are you laughing?" she asked Hank.

"No women," he said, happily shifting in his chair and shaking his head.

"Is it necessary that I include women in my study?"

"Guess not."

"Is there some reason I shouldn't limit this study to men?"

"It just struck me, that's all."

"Then you better watch what you say."

Gloom. Glass after glass. Cold bubbles. Bright light. Then Marty underwent another of her changes of mood, visibly, from pink satin ballet slippers to unwashed hair. The shiny purple jumpsuit began rippling; the pearls swung free of her chest as she leaned toward Hank; she stuck the fingers of her free hand into her wide-open crotch, unabashedly. She raised her glass high, curving the enormous arm so that it resembled the horn of a Brahman cow; she smiled a suddenly tender smile, or what passed for one; she breathed as if Hank could feel on his face each warm slow breath she exhaled.

"Let me tell you about Carl Ben Eielson," she said in a sultry confidential tone.

"Tell away," said Hank.

But what familiar sound was this? And didn't they hear it? I looked from Hank to Marty, Marty to Hank, smirking my lewdest smirk, listening happily and attentively to the faint yet unmistakable sound of a bed coming slowly to life above us. How could she fail to hear the creaking? The twang of a spring? A sudden violent lurching sound coming down through the ceiling? Surely she ought to forget Ben Eielson, I thought, and take her cue from what was going on in the darkened room directly above our own. How could she not, I thought, as the random noises became a rhythm.

"Say," said Hank, grinning and looking up at the ceiling, "what's that?"

The ceiling began to shake. The invisible bed frame cracked loudly, held together. The grunts of the man were muffled but distinctly audible, as were the woman's sighs. Still Marty did not acknowledge that anonymous pair and the now pounding bed.

"Ben Eielson," she said, while Hank, clearly torn between listening to Marty or to the anonymous pair, fumbled and brought out his marijuana, "Ben Eielson is the perfect example of Alaska's effect on male potency. Of course I use that word in its broadest sense and on the assumption that it applies equally to women and men."

Hank nodded, filled his pipe, struck the match. "Those folks up there," he said, "have the right idea. Let's smoke."

"No," she said immediately, a slight edge returning to her voice. "We'll smoke your marijuana tomorrow night. Not tonight."

"I'll join you," I said, responding as any ordinary woman would to the situation. But Hank only blew out the match, put away his little plastic sack, worked on another dripping bottle until the cork shot straight up and struck the ceiling.

"Don't worry," he said to the couple above our heads, "it's just a cork."

"They're going faster," I said. "Hear them?"

Something, perhaps an alarm clock, crashed to the floor. The woman moaned.

"Ben Eielson," said Marty, "was the sort of man that gave a dead woman kittens, as his coarser companions liked to say. Why, every woman who flew with Eielson had her snapshot taken with his arm around her in front of the plane—a famous old Lockheed Electra—and many's the child, native or otherwise, that Eielson delivered at ten thousand feet. Alaskan mothers tend to cut such things close, you know. He was a generous parent and faithful husband, though at the time there wasn't an Indian who did not claim that our Alaskan skies were filled with birds fathered by Carl Ben Eielson. He ferried dogs, sleds, mining machinery, sacks of gold, foodstuffs by the half-ton all over Alaska. Numerous little towns depended on Eielson for mail. He was not averse to the occasional corpse, though if its condition of decom-

position happened to be advanced beyond a reasonable degree, he refused the corpse a place in the cabin and carried it outside tied to the
struts. Lone men on ice floes flagged him down; he was daring but not
foolhardy; there were numerous times when, having crashed in some
wilderness spot, he repaired the Electra with rope and saplings. Once,
when he broke an oil line, he shot a moose and rendered the fat into
homemade engine oil—"

"I crashed once," I interrupted, my speech slurred but my head clear.
"It was in the Kalukna River. Engine failure. No water for two hundred
miles except that shallow torrent with its sharp twists and sweeping
bends and not a straight stretch in sight. No wonder I cracked up."

A piece of plaster fell from the ceiling. The woman moaned. Abruptly
the bed stopped its relentless banging and subsided into a gentler, stead-
ier, less urgent rhythm. Breather, I said to myself, and laughed.

"Eielson," she continued, engulfing Hank in her breath, her gaze,
her intimate tone, "was not given to errors in judgment. He never
allowed anyone else to touch the Electra's engine. He was never forced
down because of engine failure. In those days every bush pilot inevitably
died in his plane—if you flew long enough you were bound to suffer
a fatal crash—but Eielson might have lived to die of natural causes had
he not made his one and only error in judgment and had it not been
for Dorblandt, who was the enfant terrible of Alaskan aviation—"

"It wasn't my fault that I crashed," I interrupted again, understanding
that she had finally alluded to something that I had said. "I've always
been my own mechanic. Always. Nothing could have prevented my
engine from konking out that day. It was spring, the skies were clear,
I was on my way back for a couple of fishermen I had left at Purgatory
Lake. I had nothing but smooth flying ahead and was lazily following
the Kalukna that was making its tortured way below me when suddenly
the engine fired off a shot and snarled, choked, gagged, and died. I
pumped the throttle. No use. Air speed down to sixty miles an hour.
So I cut the switch, set the stabilizer, wheeled over, dropped the nose,
and took a new interest in the Kalukna River. Landing a pontoon plane
on a river—especially a river as shallow, turbulent, and crooked as the
Kalukna—isn't an easy job. But I put the Cessna into a steeper glide
and went down to look things over—"

"Carl Ben Eielson," Marty began, but I had gotten under way at
last, had finally begun to talk her down, and I was not going to be
stopped now. The woman above us was emitting little bell-like cries.
The bed sounded like a rock crusher. I pressed my advantage.

"The Cessna," I said, raising my voice and rushing on, "was settling at an even three hundred feet per minute, and I had less than a thousand feet to go with nothing beneath me except heavily timbered slopes, miles of scrub country—no place to land a plane without wheels or with them for that matter—and a lot of scrawny trees standing sentinel along the banks of the river and, of course, the river itself, which was my only hope. At six hundred feet I saw that the Kalukna consisted mainly of rocks, boulders, spray, and sandbars. Everywhere the sandbars were hiding just beneath the rapids. And not a straight stretch of water—even treacherous water—in sight. But I had no choice and so slipped to lose the last of my altitude, dropped the nose for more speed, at fifty feet tried to navigate half a dozen successive twists and turns in the river and then set her down, hard, blinded by those sunstruck frothy waters, pounded by that choppy rock-strewn surface. For a moment I thought I had landed without a hitch, but then the tip of the left pontoon snagged on a sandbar I didn't see and up went the tail, down went the left wing, until after a kind of half-cartwheel, there was the Cessna upended in six inches of water on that sandbar, with me hanging spent but unscathed in my harness. Well, I extricated myself, took a pull on the bottle of Hudson Bay rum I keep under the seat for such occasions, and then ankle deep in the freezing waters surveyed the damage. Broken propeller? Cracked wingtip bow? Staved-in pontoon—"

"Slit open the belly," interrupted Marty in a stentorian monotone, addressing me at last but still staring at Hank, "and if you see any kinked or broken members, don't try to fly it. Check the spars through the inspection plates. If the wingtip is broken, don't try to repair it—"

"Oh," I said with jaunty determination as Hank popped another cork and the man and woman began to moan together, "I followed all the correct procedures, don't worry. I righted the Cessna—luckily there was no wind—and installed the spare propeller, patched the pontoon with a piece of canvas, spent the night in my sleeping bag in the plane. Shortly after sunrise I found the trouble: an exhaust valve stem that had broken between the circlets, causing the valve head to tip, slip, and then lodge itself in the piston head. There was no way of knowing in advance that that valve stem was defective. Could have let go on anyone. Well, I replaced it and two days later, when the Kalukna suddenly rose between its banks, I started up the engine, headed into the wind, and skirting rocks and snags and sandbars and skittering around those twists and turns first on one pontoon and then on the other, at the last gasp I lifted the Cessna safely into the clear air and climbed, circled, and set off for Purgatory Lake, where I met my party—a happier couple of boys you've never seen—and flew them back to Juneau. I never had a more difficult landing or takeoff than that time on the Kalukna River."

Silence. Reluctant silence. Except for the moaning man, the softly singing woman, and the bed that had subsided into another lull.

"Hank!" I said. "Champagne!"

No answer. Half-empty bottle between his knees. Listening to the crooning couple. Ogling Marty.

"Carl Ben Eielson," she said, done with forbearance and once more pursuing Hank with her uncharacteristic smile, "need not have died as he did. He had a handsome shock of red hair, handsome red mustaches—I confess a partiality for red hair—and a potent mind. He need not have listened to Dorblandt, but he did. You see, Eielson in his Electra and Dorblandt in his big Hamilton agreed to rescue an extremely valuable fur cargo from a vessel trapped in the ice off Tin City in the Bering Strait. Eielson and Dorblandt found the frozen ship, landed without mishap on the ice, packed the cabins of their respective planes with furs—there was hardly space enough left in those cabins for the pilots themselves—and readied for takeoff. The crew lined the rail of the icebound ship; the captain watched from the bridge. But before Eielson and Dorblandt could even rev their engines, the ship and ice and waiting planes were all suddenly shrouded in the thickest fog that Eielson had seen in his more than thirty years of flying. The two pilots descended from their cabins and conferred. Eielson said it was impossible to fly in such a fog and urged that they wait until it lifted, but Dorblandt scoffed and said that above five hundred feet they would find clear skies. It was then that Eielson made his fatal error of agreeing with the enfant terrible of Alaskan aviation. They shook hands, waved at the men aboard the stranded vessel, and climbed back into their planes. The engines roared, they released their brakes, Dorblandt led the way up into the fog with Eielson—Carl Ben Eielson—following close behind him.

"Well, the noise of their engines was still audible to those on the ship when one of the planes swung back, emerged from the fog, and landed. It was Dorblandt in his big Hamilton. He cut his engines and sat waiting for Eielson, who never returned. You see, no sooner were they airborne than Dorblandt realized that the fog was just as dangerous as Eielson had said, and so—daredevil or no daredevil—he simply made a circle and landed, thinking that Eielson would follow his lead. But Eielson could not see the Hamilton and flew on—greatest of all heroes of our Alaskan airways—confident that he was safely following a plane he couldn't see and a pilot he knew he couldn't trust.

"Weeks later, when they located the famous old Electra on the Siberian coast, they found Ben Eielson buried in fur. It was a curious sight, as those international rescuers said: the Electra sitting in a spruce grove—its final resting place—intact except for the sheared-off landing gear and a missing wing, and the cabin packed more tightly than ever from rear to front and floor to ceiling with more than a thousand pounds of sealskins, and Carl Ben Eielson himself nowhere to be seen. He was buried inside the half-ton of fur, of course, and when they finally got to him—so went the report—they found him smiling and still warm inside all that fur. As soon as they pulled away the last of the skins and exposed the body, it froze on the spot. He didn't die on impact, you see. There were no broken bones. No bruises. No internal injuries. Not at all. Carl Ben Eielson died by suffocation. But at least he stayed warm in that temperature of sixty degrees below zero, as his smile attested, and died in peace, cushioned as well as warmed by the fur. He was just too much man to go on living and flying, as everyone agreed, and many's the night I've dreamt of giving birth to his daughter at ten thousand feet, with the controls tied and Eielson himself delivering her, and if I could have died in Carl Ben Eielson's arms inside that crushing mass of fur in the old Electra, I surely would have, I can tell you."

A long pause. The empty glass rolling beside her where she sat. The gray and glassy pearls in a heap in her lap. Perspiring. Facial scars glinting in the merciless light. Slowly removing the lime-green silk scarf. Overhead the gentle sound of creaking wood and scratchy springs.

"When I was a girl," I said, licking my lips and wondering how much longer she and Hank could hold out, "I helped to retrieve the body of the man popularly acclaimed as the greatest pilot ever to fly in Alaska. Rex Ainsworth."

Hank lifting himself from his chair and taking a step toward Marty. Bottles rolling beneath his feet. The indefatigable man and grateful woman bouncing suddenly for all they were worth. Again something crashing to the floor—a second alarm clock?—and again the voices soaring as fresh fissures appeared in the ceiling and the plaster fell.

"I've never heard of an Alaskan pilot by that name," said Marty Washington.

Hotly, unsteadily, impatiently, and with all the vulgarity I could muster, I stood up and swayed and grinned at the two of them.

"Time to go," I said. "You're welcome to stay if you want to. But I'm leaving."

Hank started to unbutton his shirt. He laughed and raised his face toward the ceiling and gave a wolflike howl of greeting to the man above. The man howled back. And for nothing more than that—so capricious was Martha Washington—poor Hank was denied.

"Welcome?" she said coldly. "Welcome? The invitation was to drink champagne. Nothing more."

Poor Hank waited, with his boots already off and his trousers already dropped—in his mind at least—and then, displaying more patience and good nature than he had ever before displayed, even to me, he spoke. "Well," he said, with a little rueful smile, "we've done that all right."

"Good Lord," I said, "it's no way to treat an honest man!"

"Tomorrow night," she said. "Ten o'clock."

"Not me," I said.

"Sure thing," said Hank.

On the way to the door I saw that the windows in Sitka Charley's loft were dark. I led Hank out of the room and then turned back for a moment and faced her in the open doorway.

"Sworn to fun," I said. "Loyal to none."

She said nothing. It was obvious that the pair in the room over hers was going to keep right on dogsledding until the crack of dawn. I left her alone with their music.

I awoke to the sound of someone groaning. Myself, I thought. Champagne, I thought. All won, all lost, all over. Buried in fur. Lying there and waiting and then groping a little with a cold foot, a sharp knee, a cold hand. But his side of the bed was empty.

"Hank?" I said thickly, just to sound the silence as painfully as I could. "Hank?"

How, I wondered, had he dragged himself out and off and away? How could the two of them sit happily brunching at the Baranof, if that's what they were doing? Why couldn't I move? Why mine the bitter tongue, the numbness, the head pounding even now to the rhythm of last night's dogsledders when after our return in the dawn hours Hank had been of no more use to me than a length of rotten timber on the floor of a forest?

Wait, I said to myself suddenly. What's wrong? Not merely the champagne. Not Hank. I listened and in the silence and through my affliction there came a small bright needle-sharp barb of alertness: something was wrong. Not just a brunch at the Baranof. Not just the two of them strolling down to the docks in search of photogenic Indians. Something more. Something that had specifically to do with me. What was she up to now? I wondered, and slid from the bed, slowly, and found my pants, a sweatshirt, moccasins.

Out I went into the silence and eye-slitting light, a frantic pasty-complexioned woman staggering in slow motion on urgent business. Uncle Jake was sailing off the top of the totem pole; a seagull was struggling to keep itself balanced on top of his head. I shielded my eyes, hitched up my pants, made my way grimly to the reception lodge. Inside there were Willies—fewer than there should have been—and not one girl or woman except Spooky Ruth, who was drawing beers at the bar. Her hair was tied up in a bandanna, she was wearing a tee shirt that declared in red stenciling across the chest: *We Aim to Please.*

"What's wrong?" I said.

"Sunny," she said, "you ought to look at yourself."

"Ruth," I said, for once indifferent to someone's arm around my shoulder, "what's going on?"

"Short-handed," she said, scooping foam off a glass.

"What?" I said.

"She was just out here, that photographer woman. Frightened away half the Willies—but not Joe here—and persuaded Jenny and those two new girls—Marion and Beth—to go back with her for lunch in town. . . . Wait a minute. Hank's got your jeep. Take the camper."

Spooky Ruth's camper and I rocked and rocketed out of the parking lot—cobwebs, hanging limbs, a startled crow—and down the Glacier Highway and past the airport—limp windsock, blurry rows of light planes as bright as butterflies—and on through the light, the silence, the wet shadows, a second growth of spruce toward Juneau. Behind me lay a fat trail of blue and black exhaust smoke; I straddled the dividing line and squinted, gripped the wheel. Ten minutes from Gamelands I saw him coming—the high-bodied gleaming jeep the color of a ripe pear on top and jet black on the bottom—and swerved, just as he swerved, and managed to stop, put her in reverse, saw that he was doing the same thing and gunned the engine, drove backwards—recklessly, desperately—until I thought better of it and jammed on the brakes, exhaled and shot forward, on my way again, leaving him back there baffled and half off the road.

"She's not up there," the room clerk said defensively, the same disapproving fellow who had been on duty the night before and was still on duty. I believed him.

The Baranof's refurbished dining room. The Baranof's newly added Coffee Shoppe. And Doug's. The Red Dog Saloon. The Two Girls' Luncheonette. The Only Second Class Saloon in Alaska. The Senate Saloon. The Bonanza. Hot griddles. Hot grease. Head. Stomach. No luck.

Finally, as I completed the circle and stood leaning against one of the totem poles across the street from the millinery shop and Charley's loft, finally I understood that of course she had been up there all along and so pushed back into the lobby and once again climbed the stairs that we had climbed the night before and made my way down the corridor, stopped, leaned against the wall. Too late, of course, and from around the corner came her confident academic voice that was as clear and vigorous as cold water. One of them had opened the door. The meeting was over.

"Man in his lust," she was concluding, "has regulated long enough this whole question of sexual intercourse. Now let the mother of mankind, whose right and duty it is to set bounds to his indulgence, rouse up and put an end to the sexual exploitation of women in marriage, in adultery, on dates, and, worst of all, in the long nights of prostitution. Never, never indulge in sex for money, protection, or security. Never have sex if you don't want to. Sometimes it's better to deny yourself in order to deny on principle some insistent male. You too are part of the universal motherhood. Be true to your sisters. Take back the bed. Help put an end to the universal rape. . . ."

The sounds of her advice and encouragement faded. She stopped. I sagged against the wall. I heard their little earnest voices, then their good-bys, then the closing of the door and the whispering of their little feet on the carpeting. They passed me—the three of them—without a glance, without a word. Even Jenny, who nine months before had summoned me to Jimmy and Hank, now hesitated, looked the other way, walked on. I lingered in the silent corridor. I heard footsteps coming down the stairs from the floor above. They found me—lone, ill-kempt, dispirited woman loitering in the corridor of their respectable hotel—and at the sight of me they frowned and quickened their pace, descended to the lobby and the new day beyond.

The drive back was slow, hot, unsteady, precarious. I found Hank on the porch with his chair tipped and his feet on the rail.

"Java," he said, and brought me a cup.

"Do you know what she's doing?" I said, sinking down onto the rustic chaise longue and closing my eyes.

"I do," he said.

"How?" I said.

"Went to her room. Listened outside the door. For as long as I could stand it."

"She wouldn't let you in?"

"No men allowed."

"Well, we're going to lose Marion and Beth. Probably Jenny. And she'll be back for more."

"Not Jenny."

"I give up. That woman can do what she wants. She can have our girls. She can have you. She can chop down Uncle Jake. I'm finished."

He laughed.

"Anyhow," I said, "she's no pilot. I don't care what she pretends or what she tells us about Carl Ben Eielson and the rest of them. She's no pilot."

Silence. Cup in saucer. Scraping chair. Boots clumping.

"Come on," he said, standing there and stretching, "I'll show you."

I followed him. I let him drive. We parked among the half-dozen cars and pickup trucks at the terminal. The windsock was still hanging limp. We heard Bob Stitts, the controller, talking back and forth with an Alaskan Airways pilot due to set down in twenty minutes. Hank led the way. I followed. And there at the far end of the row of flimsy butterflies sat a twin-engine eighteen-place Lockheed Electra with a shiny aluminum fuselage and black tires that would stand, I knew, as high as my waist. It looked like a giant dolphin or a small-scale bomber which a pack of mechanics had spent the morning polishing by hand. Gravely we approached that gleaming Electra, solemnly stood beside it, dwarfed in its fire. How had I missed its steely flash? The terrible reflected light of its menacing opulence?

"Hers?" I said.

He nodded.

"But she doesn't fly it," I said. "She doesn't fly this or any other airplane. She's got some pilot built like her husband. Some handsome pilot who ferries her around in that thing."

"No," said Hank, "she's traveling alone."

"Good Lord," I said. "How do you know?"

"Stitts," he said, matter-of-factly.

Darkness. Depths of sleep. Hank's voice.

"It's ten o'clock," he was saying. "Time to go. If you're coming, that is."

He was somewhere in the darkened room. Had he touched my shoulder? But what had happened? Why was I lying face downward on the unmade bed in my denim pants and sweatshirt and the moccasins that were stiff and cold on my bare feet?

"We should have left ten minutes ago," he was saying. "But maybe you'd rather just stay here and sleep."

He smelled of deerskin, cheap cologne, hair oil, like a man who has enjoyed a long hot shower, a bracing shave. Where was he? Which side of the bed with his hat in his hand, those impatient boots?

"She won't mind if I show up alone," he was saying. "I'll convey your regrets."

The silent shadows were beginning to rumble. The dark shapes were glowering. I was listening, feeling my dead weight, trying to open my eyes, roll over.

She? I thought. Regrets?

I made an angry sound in my throat, I felt that I was wrapped in the dusty fur of some ancient she-bear in a cave, and then Bob Stitts, I thought, and it all came back: the approach of the Alaskan Airways plane, my silence in the returning jeep, the disheveled bed that I climbed back into without a word. There's no shame like the shame of unintended sleep, I thought, and was awake at last.

"Well," he was saying, "old Hank's got to be going. Sure you don't want to come along?"

I heard his insincerity. I sat up in the dark.

"Where are you," I said. "Turn on the light."

"Now Sunny," he said.

"What time is it?" I asked, an arm flung up and across my eyes.

"Pretty late," he said.

"Never mind," I said, "you told me already."

I lowered my arm and squinted, frowned. He had retreated to the doorway and was holding his hat, not wearing it. His auburn hair was pomaded—never before had he put anything on his lovely hair—and his boots were polished, his deerskin jacket was hanging attractively loose on his trim torso. He looked as bright and scrubbed and ready as Uncle Jake atop the totem pole, as I had known he would.

"A fine thing," I said, "letting me sleep like this."

"Well," he said, "I didn't think you wanted to see her tonight anyway. You don't have to."

"Some friend," I said.

"There's still time," he said. "You can turn out, shower, get dressed, fix your hair, have some coffee. No need to hurry. Take all the time you want. She'll wait."

"Hank," I said, as I swung my feet to the floor and he began to grin, "let's go."

"You bet!" he said, and laughed, and the next thing I knew he was warming up the jeep and I was shivering and climbing in beside him. He drove with the window down, one elbow sticking out into the dark night and with only two fingers on the wheel and his other arm across the back of my seat, whistling and now and then cupping my shoulder with his free hand. But reckless? Never had he driven with such head-on speed, such determination, such indifference to the wind, the shrill engine, the way I had to brace myself as he flung us forward and from side to side through the dark night. He wrenched us around a tight black curve, a white owl swooped across the road to safety. Hank laughed. I saw the porcupine, waited for Hank to swerve, felt nothing. Then we were rolling into Juneau and Hank was whistling and squeezing my shoulder and there were streetlights, the sound of a radio, the heavy black smell of the channel.

The lobby was empty. There was no one behind the desk. Hank took long strides toward the stairs, clattered the heels of his western-style boots, and not a woman living could have been fooled by the lightness of his step or the little feminine swing of those narrow hips. For a moment I wanted to catch up with him, hold him around the waist, beg him to leave. But I could only hang my head, keep quiet, follow him up the stairs as if he was the Klondike Kid himself and I the half-white, half-Metlakatla woman he had married, as they say, on the trail.

He knocked. She opened the door.

"Is this your idea of ten o'clock?" she said without preamble and barring our way.

"Sorry," he said, hat in hand. "Sunny here overslept."

"I detest excuses," she said, but stepped back, stood aside, shut the door behind us, walked—if you could call it that—to the enormous bed.

"Well now," poor Hank exclaimed, and I should have known that the bed would be unmade, as indeed it was, and that she would have discarded pearls, ballet slippers, silk neckerchief, and dressed herself in nothing but a black jumpsuit of some sort of tissue-thin material that glittered like mica or fool's gold in the hot lights. There she sat on the rumpled bed naked except for that sinister jumpsuit—black as a raven, black as pitch—and it was obvious that she too had taken a long hot shower and had deliberately left the bed unmade. For Hank.

"Champagne," she said coldly, nostrils flaring, back straight, hands on her knees, white face tilted toward the ceiling, and off he hurried, grinning, dropping his hat, kicking away the empty bottles that lay everywhere underfoot. I looked at her for a moment and then reassured myself that the lights were still on in Sitka Charley's loft. I glanced back at her—I in my sweatshirt and faded blue denim pants—then sat down in the overstuffed chair I had sat in the night before. Her pile of lingerie was still heaped where I had dropped it. Even from across the room she smelled of soap. I began to like my unwashed self, my itching scalp, the taste in my mouth.

"Marty," he called from the bathroom, "where you from?"

"The east," she said, ignoring me and still feigning displeasure.

"From back east?" he called.

"Connecticut," she said impatiently. "I'm from Connecticut."

"So am I," I said.

"I had an idea you're an easterner," he called.

"Another coincidence," I said and laughed.

She was not amused. In fact she looked at me then with such disdain, such flat denial—even for her—that suddenly I thought that I might have gotten it all wrong. Wrong place of birth. Wrong name. Wrong everything. Who was I, anyway? I blushed. I tried to laugh.

"Well," said Hank, emerging from the bathroom, bottle in hand, "I was born in Utah and started out a Mormon."

She smiled. I frowned.

"That's right," he said. "I'm an ex-Mormon. It's where I get my good nature."

The fat green bottle was gently fuming—no popping cork? No spillage? An expert after only one night?—and now he sauntered to the bedside table and, holding the bottle in one hand, deftly filled their glasses. I got up and poured my own. He sat beside her on his spindly chair so that his knees were pushed against the mattress—she smiled, noting the knees—and he hunched forward, produced his pipe, his marijuana, his butane lighter. He puffed, sucked, held his breath, passed her the pipe. The room filled with smoke. She asked for more.

I watched and then went over to him and knelt beside his chair. I intercepted the pipe and kept it to myself, kneeling beside him with a hand on his thigh, until he took back the pipe and reloaded it and puffed and sucked, the smoke drifting across the room, the hot light exaggerating his teeth, his tan, his red-gold hair. I tightened my fingers, they passed the pipe back and forth between them. Drunk last night, high tonight, I thought, and laughed though I felt him pushing away my hand. I tried to rest my head on his thigh but he drew away. Where was the pipe?

I sat back on my heels. The lighter flashed. I couldn't see his face for the smoke, couldn't see hers. No matter how hard and long I listened I heard nothing from the room above us. Checked out this afternoon. No more dogsledding in the Baranof. I giggled.

"You better watch yourself," I said suddenly, nodding, trying to rest my chin on his thigh. "She's going to take back the bed!"

And then I was crawling around the room through the dead and clanking bottles in search of Hank, in search of the pipe, and dragging myself into the overstuffed chair and watching as Marty Washington flourished the missing pipe and puffed on it, admired it, finally relinquished it to Hank.

"... the sinews from the spinal cord of a moose?" Hank was saying.

Sinews? Spinal cord? Is that what he said? I felt a hand inside my sweatshirt and sighed, came awake, discovered that the hand was mine.

"Well," said Hank, "you must be joking."

"You know better than that," she said.

I laughed.

"How else do you think you make the thongs for your snowshoes?" she said. "And I suppose no one has told you how to make butter from the horns of a moose."

"Butter?" he said.

"Is there anything wrong with wanting butter on the trail in winter?"

"Heck no," he said quickly.

"At seventy degrees below zero," she said, "when one has taken refuge from the blizzard in an abandoned cabin—or innie, as the Indians say—and the dogs are buried in the snow outside and the gale is howling, one has only to crack into small pieces the frozen antlers of a bull moose and put them into a pot of water over the fire. The water comes from melted snow, of course. You boil the horns for several days and then take the pot from the fire, remove the horns, and allow the pot to cool. In a short while you will be able to skim off approximately two inches of the best butter you've ever had."

"You don't say," said Hank.

"Why, the best plum duff in the world," she said, staring at him coldly and disdaining the pipe, "is made from the tallow of the bull moose. One always carries along a bottle of Hudson Bay rum to put into the duff."

I listened. She sounded unpleasantly familiar. I heard him begging her to tell him more. I rallied. I opened my eyes. He was coming out of the bathroom, bottle in hand, and asking her about Ed Peelo. She frowned, raised her chin, and then for the first time all night she smiled that crooked smile of hers and deigned to steady Hank's hand while he filled her glass. She looked as if she had just seen fleas on the body of a dead wolf in midwinter, she was that pleased with herself and with the artless purpose of Hank's question.

"When the ice goes out on the Yukon," she said, smiling and staring at the ceiling and confounding Hank, "the first thing one notices is water. Before the breakup begins, the ice on the Yukon stretches as far as one can see and is solid to a depth of ten feet. But then on a cold and silent morning there is a film of still water on top of the ice. Day by day the water rises, climbs the frozen banks of the Yukon, silently floods the great mass of purpling ice below. The ice itself begins to rise under the water. The season has changed, a faint sun illumines acre upon acre of flat water. There is a distant rumbling, a far-off ugly sound, and all the men and boys run down to the banks of the river and watch and listen.

"Now the sound is louder. One thrills to the expectation on the white faces of the men and boys. Upriver an invisible city is collapsing. One hears a sound like the snapping of iron bridges, the colliding of locomotives, the detonations of tall buildings falling to rubble. We listen, something explodes in the invisible city, there are cries on the air. Then up and down the river and from bank to bank the flat water ripples, stirs, grows agitated, then violent, and before our very eyes becomes a vast and rushing current. A cheer goes up from the men and boys which, in the next instant, is drowned in the dreadful roar that sweeps down upon us from around the bend in the river. Cakes of ice as large as city blocks stand on end, crash together, send their splinters flying. Dead caribou appear to be swimming toward the opposite bank and all of us, men and boys and lone woman, are dwarfed and deafened by this wonderful destruction of an icy Alaskan world.

"Then from around the bend comes hurtling toward us a vessel that was moored ill-advisedly to a little dock upriver and held fast in the ice since first it formed. Now the as-yet-unharmed vessel races across our line of vision high in the air, still roped to its little dock. Then it is crushed. Sooner than we can catch our breaths, a cracked wall of ice rises directly in the path of the rusty steamship that has been wrenched free so ignobly and strikes it down.

"'The Emmy Lou,' cries a tall young boy into my ear. 'They've been using her as a cold storage plant all winter. The darn fools.'

"Now she bursts wide open, *The Emmy Lou,* and displays her cargo. Meat. Frozen meat. Shoulders and ribs and haunches and sides of butchered beef brought all the way from Seattle. Dismembered carcasses scattered on the air like shot. Torn limbs. Bloody delectables. Twenty thousand pounds of raw meat shooting and showering across the ice. Then nothing. Not a single life preserver. Not one scrap of its precious cargo. Not one plank or piling of the little dock. Nothing but the roar and contortions of the mighty Yukon disgorging itself of ice on an April day.

"Naturally," she said after a pause, holding the stem of the pipe between her fingers and filling her lungs, exhaling, "naturally not everyone can be as fortunate as I was when I saw the ice go out on the Yukon. The spectacle does not always include a steamship, as it did for me, or a tall young male companion to share the experience. He was a Tena from the Pelly River and much older than his fifteen years first led me to believe. Poor George would have another man to be jealous of, I can tell you, if he knew about Sumdum Billy, though of course he doesn't. I'll show you Sumdum Billy's photograph tomorrow. It's one of the best I've taken."

Hank nodded. I drifted downriver, giggling and lolling in the overstuffed chair and wondering how she could possibly be inexhaustible, as she surely was, and undaunted by the marijuana, as she appeared to be. I felt the trickling of perspiration inside the sweatshirt, kicked off my moccasins.

"The Alaskan Indian," she was saying, "affixes antlers or an animal skull above the door of his cabin in order to guarantee himself continued success in killing that particular kind of game. To the Indian, white men are known as sons of the wolf. From Sumdum Billy's mother I too acquired an appetite for big white owl, as she expressed it."

I awoke and by Marty's silence knew that Hank was in the bathroom and that she and I were alone. One of the flood lamps was lying on its back on the floor, still blazing. I shivered, couldn't bring myself to look at her, waited. Then came her short and final salvo, as it proved to be.

"I hold a commercial airline pilot's license," she said coldly. "I am a mother. I am a professional photographer. I am a sourdough. I have shot the largest and most dangerous of Alaskan animals. My cunt, as Ed Peelo once admiringly exclaimed, is as big as a horse collar—"

"What's that?" said Hank, grinning and stumbling back across the room, "what's that you say?"

"My scars," she said without hesitation and in a suddenly agreeable voice. "I am going to tell you how I got my scars."

"I hadn't noticed," said Hank in confusion.

"I detest having my feelings spared," she said. "I detest embarrassment. Why should you pretend to be unaware of my injuries?"

"Just the way I was brought up," he said.

She smiled.

Owl, I thought. Billy. Connecticut. Horse collar. Now for the scars. And how could I not laugh, wring my hands, mumble to myself in exasperation? How not stiffen, giggle, slide down in my chair, and against my will—oh against my will!—open my eyes and through the smoke stare at her with the awe of a Hank or Ed Peelo or a George Steller, and the rest of them? There she sat, the immense and glistening black-garbed mother of us all, and even as I watched and Hank gurgled she unzipped her jumpsuit far enough to show her handsome cleavage and the broad chest bright with recently healed lacerations, and then spread her thighs still wider and for the last time that night—which I must have known—began again to talk.

"Like any woman who is her own woman," she said, waving away the pipe, "I am not beyond making errors. It's true, don't interrupt! Anyhow, it was natural that I go over to Kodiak Island to shoot my first Alaskan brown bear—"

"Hank!" I cried, but it was too late and I could only listen.

"And yet," she continued, "I need not have refused to be accompanied by a guide, which is what I did. Why, there were any number of excellent men who offered to join me on Kodiak Island. But I refused them all. It was a serious mistake, I can tell you.

"Anyhow, I hired a young man named Matt Hall to fly me to Poverty

Bay on the western side of the island. Matt was no Ben Eielson but he was an adequate pilot and a pleasing young man. At the last minute he implored me to let him stay, though he knew nothing at all about hunting, of course. But I remained firm and, laughing, told him to come back in two days time and sent him off. Poor fellow. Yet as it turned out it would have been better for me—much better—had I allowed Matt Hall to lounge around my camp while I hunted. At least he would have radioed for help when I did not return.

"Who could blame me for wanting solitude? Only in the solitude you find in Alaska does a woman feel truly good in her skin.

"Well, there were still plenty of daylight hours remaining, and after setting up my tent and propane stove I decided that I might as well stroll down the beach and shoot a deer. My brown bear could wait, or so I thought, until the next morning. I put a few shells in my shirt pocket, slung the .375 Magnum from my shoulder—in my opinion that German rifle is superior to any for shooting bear, though it's heavy for deer—and started off. The sun glinted on the water, I smelled the hot dense tangle of deadfalls and towering trees that came down silently and mightily to the very edge of the narrow beach. Several hundred yards from camp fresh droppings appeared and led me on a barely discernible game track through the moist gloom and into a clearing in a thicket where, in a pool of sunlight, a handsome young buck stood waiting. He was a glorious sight, I can tell you, with his proud head turned in my direction and his scut erect. The message in those liquid eyes of his was unmistakable, so after a moment, and with a certain reluctance, I slipped a shell into the Magnum, raised it slowly, settled it comfortably to my shoulder, and fired. I reeled, he fell. My shot reverberated for no other human ears than mine. When I knelt beside him his warm flesh trembled beneath my hand, though of course he was already dead.

"I gutted him reverentially, despite my total unawareness that I was soon to owe my life to this dead creature, and then I tied his legs together and lifted and positioned him across my shoulders, which is the only way to carry a deer in the wilderness if you're alone. He weighed one hundred and fifty pounds, as Matt Hall told me later, but I walked with a light and jaunty step as I set off for camp. I had not been on Kodiak Island an hour, the sun was high, I had already brought down my deer. No woman's contentment could have equaled mine.

"Then I fell. One minute I was walking along thinking how comfortable I felt balancing the Magnum in my left hand and my warm burden on my shoulders, and the next minute I was falling over a thick mossy log which I had failed to see. My shin struck the log, I toppled forward, borne down by the weight of the dead buck, and sprawled in the undergrowth, Magnum flying.

"Well, Hank, I heard a roar, and they were all over me. Bear. A great she-bear and her two devilish cubs. I was pinned beneath the deer, the Magnum was out of reach, the bears were upon me in a terrible blur of light and sound. I had tripped at the very entrance to their den, you see, and the fury of a she-bear surprised with her young is a commonplace. But curiously enough—and this thought occurred to me even in the midst of the din—the cubs were just as vicious as the old she-bear herself. They flung themselves at me, Hank, all three of them, and in the roaring and grunting I smelled them, felt the weight of them, saw the flashing of teeth, claws, the little black eyes hard and wet with anger. Oh they were angry, all right. They were beside themselves with rage. And believe it or not, Hank, in those first few moments of our encounter I could not help telling myself that if I had so foolishly allowed myself to be attacked by Alaskan brown bears, at least it was ironically appropriate that I should suffer the wrath of the female rather than the male bear. The female is a far more dangerous animal, with or without her cubs, and hence is the worthier opponent for a woman.

"Well, there I was—surprised, dazed, yet with enough presence of mind to lie as still as I could, hoping to convince my attackers that the life had already gone out of the body of their victim. It wasn't easy, I can tell you. They cuffed me, they mauled me, and the sound of ripping cloth made me aware of the pain—intellectually, that is, as when the knife slips and you watch the lengthening of the incision. Next I heard the rending of flesh, the crunching of bone, and it was then that I understood what I owed to my young buck. He lay over me so as to protect the back of my head and neck, and now the bears were gorging themselves not on me but on the buck. Fortunate for me that I had shot my deer!

"After a while the snarling abated and just in time. The pain was coming over me in waves and I knew that my right arm was broken. I could not have survived had the she-bear and those murderous cubs of hers continued their initial assault much longer. I waited, listened, and finally dared to open my eyes in a squint. The Magnum was lying about three feet from my left hand, but of course it would have been foolhardy to reach for it, since the old she-bear had stretched herself out in the fading sunlight near the mouth of her den and was watching me. She was growling softly, still ruffled, still not entirely certain that I was lifeless. If I had made the slightest movement she would have killed me on the spot. Despite the pain I had to laugh to myself when the cubs left the safety of the old she-bear and came back to give me a good sniffing. One of them went so far as to lick the blood on my hands and the side of my face, and to nudge my booted foot with its head. Then while the she-bear watched and grumbled and I tried not to breathe, those two cubs began playing together like puppies in the very shadow of my prostrate form.

"For that entire afternoon I did my best not to move and not to lose consciousness, waiting for the opportunity to reach for the Magnum. At dusk I finally thought that I might risk inching forward my left hand unobserved, and tensed myself, waited, and spread wide the fingers of that left hand of mine. That's all. Merely spread my fingers. But that old she-bear let a roar out of her that could have been heard on the other side of Kodiak Island, had there been anyone to hear it, and in a bound was on top of me again, snarling and slavering and raking me with her unsheathed claws. I don't know how I kept from screaming, Hank, but I did, and even managed to prevent myself from passing out just long enough to see that old bear sitting back on her haunches and peering down at me in the absolute conviction that this time she had struck the final blow and that I would move no more. She was the universal mother herself, I thought admiringly, and fainted.

"I awoke once in the middle of that first night and, will you believe it, I found those two malevolent cubs snuggling up innocently not to the old she-bear but to me! They knew I was a woman, Hank, and on that night preferred me for some reason to their mother. She was apparently indifferent to their filial fickleness, since while I was lying in the darkness, grateful for the warmth of her cubs against me, the old creature lumbered over and tore a good bite out of the buck's slender neck, which was only inches from my own neck. Then muttering and wheezing, she took herself back to the mouth of her den, where she lay down alone and fell asleep.

"The next morning it was raining and I was soaking wet and weak from the loss of blood. I listened, heard nothing, and decided that my old female antagonist had surely gone off with her cubs in search of berries or silvery fish in a stream. My task was to disentangle myself from the dead deer and lunge for the Magnum. Then broken arm or no broken arm, I intended to insert three shells in the Magnum and to track down the bear and her cubs and destroy them. Revenge is the better part of a woman, I can tell you.

"But again I was wrong and no sooner did I attempt to shift the burden of the half-eaten buck than one of the cubs squealed in terror and brought back the old she-bear in a bound. Would they never leave? Did the old beast spend all her time lying just out of my line of sight ready to pounce? Anyhow, she gave me a bone-splitting wallop on the side of the head and I fainted. And it was only dawn, Hank, and Matt Hall wouldn't return for another day, by which time, I thought as I went under, I'd be as dead as the deer.

"When I came to, racked and torn in a torment I can only describe as delicious, Hank, I saw immediately that the Magnum had moved and was now only inches from my left hand, as if the ancient matriarch had given it a good shove just to toy with me and increase the frustration of my painful predicament. I could hear the cubs cuffing each other and rolling about in the rain, which meant that the old she-bear could not be far off, and the one thing I knew was that I could not afford to tempt ill fortune any further. Well, somehow I survived my first full day at the mercy of the bears, lying motionless and listening to the old creature muttering to herself at the mouth of her den. Occasionally I thought I heard the droning of Matt Hall's approaching plane, but each time forced the thought from mind and resigned myself anew to the realities of those passing hours. However, by dusk I found the mere thought of a second night intolerable. I was clear-headed, I would meet the challenge, I would have the satisfaction of shooting the bears, no matter that by now it was so dark that I could hardly see the butt of the Magnum.

"Even before I moved, or so it seemed, I heard the snapping of a twig beneath me. Silently I groaned and waited, readying myself as best I could for the final onslaught. Now she would surely crush the life out of me, once and for all. I waited. I became impatient for the unleashing of her fury. I allowed myself a moment of hope. I began to relax. Oh but she was unpredictable, I can tell you. Unpredictable and uncanny. Do you know that she had waddled over to me without a sound? Despite her bulk, her clumsiness, her impetuosity? No snapping twigs for her, I can tell you. To think that a brute of her size and temperament could move like a shadow and with the curiosity of a young girl. To think of it.

"Well, I heard her breathing. That's all. I opened my eyes and found her once again squatting beside me, and this time so close that I could feel her breath as well as hear it. She was puzzled, Hank. Even experiencing the worst fear I have ever known—I admit my fear freely, Hank—I saw by the expression on her evil old face that she suspected that I was not yet dead and that she was considering how best to dispatch this large woman who had intruded into her own domain. But the time for being amused was long past. In another moment or two, I thought, meeting her nasty little eyes with mine, she would be done with her deliberations and treat me to a final display of her death-dealing malignancy.

"But she did not lose control of herself. Not at all. To my surprise she proceeded, in the rain and darkness, to inflict herself on me with matronly calm. Slowly, with a paw as big as the blade of a shovel, she rolled me over, thus freeing me from the deer but also exposing my face and neck and chest to her vengeance. She shifted to all fours and lowered her head and began to chew my shoulder and the arm that was already broken. She experimented with one of her razorlike claws, picking open small wounds on my face and upper body as someone might pluck the strings of a guitar. With the same claw she carefully sliced open my scalp. Like some old beautician she brushed away my hair and found my ear. Finally she could resist no longer the scent and taste of blood and, as I begged her silently to snuff out my breath, and quickly, she flew into one of her familiar frenzies and shredded my shirt and britches and—would you believe it?—caught me up in her two arms and crushed me slowly to that great wet shaggy breast of hers. Needless to say, I fainted—admitting to myself that I had met my match and expecting, at last, never again to regain consciousness.

"Well, I awoke all right, as pained and near dead as anyone could be, but still undaunted. It was dawn, the sun was out, I was alive and, I was certain, alone. Could I move? Could I possibly move? But why had I been spared if not to retaliate? If not to pit the will of a woman against the will of a female bear? So I reached for the Magnum, closed my hand on its cold breech at last, and dragged myself up, staggered, loaded the Magnum, and, bloodied apparition that I was, and relying on my instinctive sense of direction, set off.

"I came upon them not twenty yards away in another and smaller clearing. The old devil was working herself back and forth against her rubbing tree—she had stripped that tree of branches to a height of eight feet, Hank!—and as she swayed in abandon, she gave me no more than a glance of peaceful indifference. I stood there, faint and with my clothes in shreds, my broken arm all but useless, and returned her glance. Then I shot her between the eyes. She fell like

a sad old woman and rolled over. Without a moment's hesitation I
shot the first cub through the shoulders, breaking its spine. The
second, whose squealing had betrayed me the day before, charged.
I waited, admiring the ferocious courage of the little orphaned beast,
and then I raised the Magnum, aimed for the head, and fired. No
sportsman's weapon has a larger bore than the Magnum, Hank, and
it gave me singular pleasure, I can tell you, to see what the old
Magnum did to that bear cub's head.

"Anyhow, Matt Hall returned on schedule the same afternoon and
found me, as he told me in the Indian hospital over in Kake, sprawled
at the entrance to my one-man tent. If he had not flown me to that
hospital—a mere ten minutes away by air—of course I would not have
lived to complete my work on the Alaskan Indian. But Matt Hall was
smarter than I thought and did not panic. His was the first face I saw
when I came to, and it was a nice young handsome face, like yours,
Hank, and a welcome sight."

She stopped. Got off the bed. Put down her half-filled glass. Strode
to the bathroom doorway. Turned. Finished unzipping the jumpsuit.
As easily as someone reaching for a negligee, took it off. Then in the
bathroom doorway, posed with her hands in hair, stark naked.

"Seventy-six puncture wounds," she said, and smiled her crooked
smile as Hank struggled up from his chair. "Sixteen deep lacerations.
Dressing for every wound. From five to eight sutures apiece for the
lacerations. More than two hundred minor cuts and abrasions. The
wounds were infected. It was discovered that one bone in my broken
arm was cracked into fragments. The government nurse—there was
no doctor at Kake—joked about how that she-bear had had a surgeon's
instinct and had all but removed my appendix, and with an incision
any surgeon would have been proud of. But in two weeks I was out
of that little one-room hospital and on my way to Fairbanks with Matt
Hall. In three months I was back at the controls of the Electra and
heading north to become one of Ed Peelo's wives.

"So much for how I got my scars, Hank. And do you know, I still
think of that old she-bear with affection?"

Somehow I found my moccasins and found the door. I turned, and
the last I saw of her, through the smoke and glare, she was holding
out her long naked arms to the ex-Mormon already concealed forever
behind the half-closed door. Then I was gone.

•   •   •

I spent what remained of those dark hours in Sitka Charley's bed. The next morning I doused my face in Charley's basin, drank a cup of his scalding java, went down to the jeep, which was cold and empty where we had left it, and drove out to the airport to confirm what I already knew. Empty tarmac. No Electra. Even the brightly colored light planes had disappeared. Nothing.

A half-hour later I was sitting with Spooky Ruth at the bar in our reception lodge, and we were leaning close to each other and clinking glasses.

"Ruth," I said, "I have just lost a boyfriend to my own father reincarnated in the form of a woman. I've met my match. Your prophecy has been fulfilled. I'm going to leave Alaska."

That afternoon, drunk and cold-sober both, and while Ruth looked on, I smashed the greenhouse and destroyed the marijuana plants. That night the dreams began. Three weeks later, in my presence, Sitka Charley opened the manila envelope that was addressed to him in a bold hand and had been sent airmail from Seattle, and drew forth the ten-by-twelve-inch photograph in which he stands beside one of the totem poles in front of the Baranof. Revenge is the better part of woman, I thought, but then I relented. The photograph, which Charley took to Jack Edwards for framing, still hangs in the loft.

And do I secretly detest Martha Washington, to use one of her favorite words? I do not. It was not because of her that I made my decision, no matter that it took her only two days to abscond with Hank. Even on that afternoon thirteen months ago I listened and nodded in totally drunken agreement when Spooky Ruth lavished her most poetic speech on the only feminist we have ever met. Despite all her orgasmic fireworks, said Ruth, Martha Washington's insights were like the hard click of pool balls and her wisdom was like the ensuing rumble of the pocketed ball. It was Spooky Ruth's ultimate tribute. Would that she might one day say the same of me.

Where are you, Jake?

And you, Pascal?

45 —

I will not visit the Eiffel Tower. In 1892, at the age of twelve, Uncle Jake went to the top of the newest wonder of the world, then only three years old as he was fond of telling me, in the company of his brothers Doc and Granny and their father and the father's favorite maid, while below them his mother strode up and down disapprovingly with the infant Billy Boy in her arms. In my childhood Uncle Jake was fond of evoking the little chimney pots of Paris, as he used to say, spread out far and wide below them in the summer light. But I am not a tourist on my way to a family reunion. I will not go anywhere near the Eiffel Tower. Nor will I make the excursion to Chantilly and to the nearby Deauville chateau, which was the site of the family reunion in 1892. According to Uncle Jake, one entire room in that chateau—and a big room at that—was devoted to stuffed birds and animals, from tiny sparrows to substantial hawks and from rabbits and foxes to deer and wild boars, all hung upside down by thongs from their feet or necks in decorous patterns around the walls. This trophy room was a favorite haunt of the Old Gentleman, Uncle Jake's grandfather, who began each day of the reunion by joining his nine red-coated sons in serenading the assembly with their brass hunting horns, a cacophony worse than anything he had ever heard, said Uncle Jake, while the trophy room frightened him even more than the horns.

But not for me the little chateau near Chantilly. Not for me the offensive evidence of my great-grandfather's artful eye and ignominious treatment of bird and beast, which was the hallmark of that old man's decadence. I am happy to leave the trophy room, if it still exists, to the tourists.

I will go directly to the south of France by train. I will wear my chalky tight-fitting blue denim pants, my white tee shirt decorated with the fleur-de-lis, my aviator's sunglasses. No hat. No coat. Barefooted except for my Alaskan moccasins. A vinyl flight bag for luggage. No wonder that three French soldiers—mere boys—will invite me into their second-class compartment to share their bread, their sausage, their bottles of cheap wine. Old men will stand beside their bicycles and wave to us at country crossings, the great blotchy brown markings on white cows will resemble crudely painted maps of France. I will sate myself on the garlic-tasting sausage. I will drink more paper cupfuls of the cheap red wine than I should. I will laugh more loudly than I need to with those young soldiers. I will even sit on their laps. But nothing more.

Then the all-but-deserted station, the three boys waving to me—heads and shoulders and arms thrust out of the lowered compartment window into the orange light of Provence—and then the disappearing train, the sound of its whistle, an iron cock on a steeple, the rouge-colored village with its weeping willows, town square, war memorial, hotel. I will cross the square to the hotel, my flight bag swinging, my aviator's glasses flushed with the sun, and in front of the hotel there will be a few rickety white metal tables and chairs shaded by peach and sky-blue parasols, and behind a dusty plate-glass window in a little shop adjoining the hotel will be a display of open boxes of chocolate candies and wicker cages filled with birds.

I will sign the blank page of the register. I will go up to my room and hang my flight bag on the end of the brass bedstead. One wooden chair, a mirror, white walls, a fresh rose in a vase, the narrow bed, white bed linen, tall doors opening onto a balcony overlooking the village square—and I will stand on the balcony, look in the mirror, sit on the bed, which will be hard and white enough for a nun. What more do I need? Only a box of the slightly melted chocolates and three birds in a cage.

No shadow moves across the face of the sundial on the wall of the church. The bells are silent. No young girl sings. Nothing stirs the dust of the road that winds between the plane trees out of town. I walk in the fields, watch the swallows, lean on the railing of a small lichen-covered stone bridge at the edge of town. An old man in a black apron serves me earthen pitchers of pink wine. I wear a starched white blouse, a long slate-blue skirt, and spend my evenings alone in the hotel parlor. My narrow bed smells of soap and sunlight. The birds chirp, I lie in bed and eat my chocolates. The breeze that comes to me through the balcony doors, which I never close, is as warm and cool as the surfaces of my darkening skin.

Serenity. Tranquillity. Slumbrous Sunny in the south of France. Not Jacqueline Flowers. Sunny.

But where is Pascal?

Whatever happened to Uncle Jake?

46 —

Sunny, he calls, can you fly this thing?

I awake in the dead light of the dream and it is not Uncle Jake standing in the mouth of the tent where I find myself but an Indian. The tent is large. It is made of gray canvas that sags over a frame of dried-out slender logs. The sun of midsummer is burning through the canvas. I smell the heat, the dust, the flaking bark on the logs. There is an iron stove overturned in a corner, old kettle half filled with sand. I am perspiring, my boots are partially unlaced and as dry and gray as if I have been walking through fields of ashes. There are bugs and twigs in my hair; the boughs I lie upon are dead and brown; I feel the scratchy needles inside my shirt, my pants. I am alone except for the Indian in what I understand at once is an abandoned camp.

No dogs. No smell of woodsmoke. No ring of the ax. No sound of laughter and the clumping of boots. Where are they all?

Sunny, he calls, can you fly this thing?

The Indian makes no sign that he hears the voice. But I hear it, in all its familiar senseless cheerfulness, and I know that there is no one else in the abandoned camp except the Indian and myself, and suddenly my teeth chatter, my skin prickles, I shiver as if I am propping myself on my elbows not in this hot tent but in the deep snow. How can I hear the voice of Uncle Jake and not see him? How can the Indian not hear the voice yet guide me to Uncle Jake, which I know he'll do?

The Indian wears a faded khaki shirt, a pair of torn and threadbare trousers that hang loosely from his hips that are like a child's. He carries a knife in a sheath that hangs from a rope around his waist; his eyes are as bright and menacing as fish hooks.

He says something in a language I do not understand. He turns, I roll over and get to my feet and follow him out of the tent into the hot sun. There are several other tents like mine, bleached and collapsing. In the center of the overgrown clearing a pile of chalky white moose antlers stands as high as my head. A rusty double-handled crosscut saw is propped upright against the pile of bones. A piece of pale blue cloth is snagged on one of the vicious teeth of the saw. Insects are droning inside the skulls from which the great horns sprout like palm fronds of porous bone. I am perspiring again, my skin is prickling.

Sunny, he calls, can you fly this thing?

The Indian leads the way, I follow. There are shadows, rock pools, silent crows, sweating tree trunks in the dark of the woods. The grasses, the leaves, the cobwebs, the hanging branches—nothing moves, and yet I hear the sound of the wind. I am hot and yet the woods are cold and wet. We are in thickets, hidden among high ferns, surrounded by a dense and sulphurous-smelling wilderness in which there are no trails, no paths, no other abandoned camps than the one the Indian and I have left far behind. And yet I smell the sea.

Just in time I stop at the sound of the Indian's voice. There at my feet lies a rusty wolf trap, jaws wide. The Indian waits, I step gingerly around the trap, sweating and shivering, and the smell of the sea is stronger. Then suddenly we emerge again into the light and climb down steep and moss-covered ledges onto the beach of a small and silent cove bounded on three sides by wilderness and on the fourth by the open sea. Not ten yards from the beach is an airplane half submerged in shallow water.

Sunny, he calls, look at the fix I'm in. Can you fly this thing?

No prospectors. No hunters. No camps. No trappers' cabins. Nothing. Yet there at the edge of the beach lies the nearly intact wreckage of an airplane. It is high-winged, single-engined, old fashioned. It is made of some dully gleaming metal that has long since begun to rust. Its fuselage is long and narrow, coffin-shaped, and its great gawky tail assembly rises high into the still air. Windshield, doors, windows—all have been smashed, torn away, destroyed. Long slimy strands of black and yellow kelp hang like snakes from the struts, from the tail assembly, from the big rusty cylinders of the blackened engine. A gull sits on top of the rudder. A crumpled pontoon lies a short distance down the beach.

An airplane in a place like this. A wrecked airplane. And there, sitting bolt upright and as big as life in the seat beside the seat of the missing pilot, is the dark and shadowy figure of Uncle Jake.

I am hot, disheveled, desperate. The sun is flashing and flickering along the length of the wreck; the cabin is half filled with water. The dark figure of Uncle Jake is sitting up to his waist in water. Over my shoulder I see that the Indian is resting himself on a boulder and smoking a cigarette. I speak to him. I try to control my voice. Where are we? Has this hidden cove a name? When did the plane crash? Who found it? Where are the passengers and pilot? Why was there no rescue party? Why no effort to find the bodies and salvage the wrecked plane or at least to remove all signs of it forever from this desolate place? Who was so negligent as to keep the whereabouts of this lost plane unknown to the world?

The Indian says nothing. Either he understands no language other than his own or is indifferent to questions like mine or knows, as even I know, that they cannot be answered. He does not disdain me, slumping on his boulder and smoking; it's merely that he gives me no comfort, no reassurance, no explanations. He is not perplexed by incongruity. Wrecked airplanes and distraught women are no concern of his. Still he watches me as I stare helplessly at the wreck, inspect the shorn pontoon, consider the tops of the trees, attempt to calculate the pilot's error and the sudden downward path of the crashing plane. But it is hopeless. It cannot be done. I am terrified of Uncle Jake in the plane.

Sunny, he calls, can you fly this thing?

Then I notice that the tide is rising. It is visibly higher on the sides of the metal fuselage, is climbing up the struts that brace the wing. It has some terrible significance, this rising water, but what?

Helplessly I step into the black waters, walk stiff-legged toward the plane, sloshing and stumbling until I am shin-deep and then thigh-deep in the waters on which no oil floats. A fish leaps. The gull flaps from the top of the rudder, swoops off and away. Through one of the smashed windows on my side of the plane—I am still not close enough to touch the rusty metal, the rivets, the shards of glass—I am able to see out of the opposite window to a dim and watery horizon. I draw closer. I reach out my hand, touch nothing. The black interior of the cabin is a dank and sodden chaos of seaweed, kelp, empty seats with bloated cushions. I smell the stench, I see a tangle of web straps, and suddenly I am standing nearly to my armpits in the rising tide—I who want only to be back on shore with the Indian—and now I realize at last what is so peculiarly frightening about this wrecked plane. It is this: that soon, in another few minutes, the old salt-encrusted plane that looms before me will be entirely submerged. At every high tide the metal wreckage sinks from view, goes under. That which is meant to fly is beneath the sea. Then as the tide goes out the tip of the rudder appears, the tip of a wing, the tip of the wooden propeller, and slowly the wrecked plane emerges, dripping and covered with fresh barnacles. Day in, day out, with every rising and falling tide the plane must undergo its drowning. It will rust but not disintegrate. No storm will batter it to pieces. It will not disappear.

Go back, I tell myself as against my will I flounder toward the front of the plane. Go back. Don't look. But I cannot help myself.

It's Uncle Jake. Big. Bulky. Dripping. Faceless.

Sunny, he says, can you fly this thing?

Then I am back on shore, sitting on a boulder beside the Indian, drenched and shivering. It's twilight. There is nothing left to see except the long wing, which looks as if it is floating on the high tide, and the tall rudder white with salt. The light fades, the black water laps the edges of the wing, a raven flies out of the woods behind us. Then the ailerons begin to move. The rudder turns. Slowly, clumsily, up and down go the ailerons, back and forth creaks the rudder.

Jake! I cry. Jake!

Then it is gone. Nothing disturbs the now choppy waters of the cove.

Charley? Charley? But he only grunts and turns away.

Sunny, he says, that darn dog...

Somehow I have survived the blizzard and though I have lost my sled, my team, my provisions, still I have no need of fire, gruel, water, dried meat. The blizzard is over. There is no wind. Nothing but the purest snow and brightest light wherever I look, except for a distant grove of willows which is my destination. It is a silent seventy degrees below zero, and yet I feel no burning deep in my lungs. I am bundled up in silky furs, I am gliding swiftly toward the grove of willows on my snowshoes. The light does not pain my eyes. I am safe. I am fit enough to travel the length of the Yukon without stopping for sleep or rest, to cover two thousand miles easily, in the best of humors, should the need arise. To a person of my stamina, what's snowshoeing to a little grove of willows? Nothing at all.

But not everyone is as fortunate a traveler through the northern wastes as I am. Tragedy awaits me—I am convinced of it—in the rapidly approaching stand of wind-bent trees. Someone else's tragedy, not mine. What is it? Who needs my help?

Sunny, he says, that darn dog...

I increase my pace, I am clear-headed, the ominous island of bare and tangled willows looms close. Now I am alerted to the first signs of tragic circumstances.

I arrive. I make one circuit around the perimeter of the grove of willows. Nothing. Not one hint of disorder. Then, expecting the worst, I make my way slowly to the center of the silent grove and there, as I might have known, I find the log cabin buried to the eaves of its sod roof in snow. And behind the cabin I find the sled. Whatever load it hauled has been removed; it has been left in what must have been the lee of the wind behind the cabin; its rawhide harness is empty. Where are the dogs? If some lone and famished and nearly frozen traveler found this grove in the nick of time and took refuge in this log cabin from the fiercest blizzard that ever swept these northern wastes, he would have left his dogs outside and holed himself up in the cabin. No traveler in his right mind would have allowed his dogs to share his cabin. He would have freed them, beaten them back from the open door, left them to burrow deep in the snow and wait out the storm. Where are they? What of the traveler inside the cabin? The empty sled, the silent cabin, the missing dogs are the surest signs of what I have suspected all along: a tragic occurrence.

I circle the cabin, place my shoulder to the low wooden door. It is barred from within. I return to the sled, inspect it with greater care. Why, the poor devil has forgotten his ax! With one blow of it I smash open the door, stand back, remove my snowshoes, peer inside the cabin, then enter.

The glare reflected from the snow behind my back fills the interior of the cabin with bright light. The floor is sod; there is a crude and blackened fireplace, a table on its side; the remnants of two smashed chairs and several wooden crates litter the room. The poor devil tried to burn his furniture and the cargo he dragged off the sled. He was too afraid of the storm or too exhausted, I deduce, to return for the ax. It is a scene of wreckage, and yet I survey it with only one swift glance, which is enough to reveal what even I, familiar as I am with the tragedies of the far north, could not have anticipated. Bones. In a glance I take in the bones that are scattered about the room among the rusty cans, the tin eating utensils, the splintered pieces of wood. But as puzzling and foreboding as are the bones, I am not able to spare them much attention. I have eyes for nothing, or nearly nothing, except the brute beast that faces me from his corner. I am not afraid. I am too self-confident for fear. But I am on my guard.

It is a dog. Mongrel, timber wolf, Siberian husky—it appears to have sprung from all three kinds of animal and from none of them. It is a new breed, the only living example of some terrible new species of Alaskan dog. Its head stands as high as my chest, its ruff is bristling, its eyes are bloodshot. What poor devil would be foolish enough, ignorant enough, sentimental enough to share his refuge from a blizzard with such a brute?

But where did the poor devil go?

I wait, staring at the dog, and gradually I realize that I will not be called upon to wield the ax, which I am still holding in both hands, against this deadly animal. His size and ferocity are undeniable. If he attacked, it would take all my strength to stop him; our battle would be the bloodiest ever waged between dog and woman. But he will not attack. As tall as he stands in his corner, he is weak; for all his size he is gaunt, I see now, and is gently swaying. He looks at me steadily with his bloodshot eyes; his great jaws are calmly closed. His fangs are not visible. His ruff is bristling but he cannot move. He's starving.

I sigh. I lower the ax. I push back the hood of my parka. I allow myself a longer and more careful scrutiny of the evidence of violence that fills the room. Thoughtfully I glance at the overturned table, at the smashed crates and empty gunny sacks that are all that remain of the supplies that the stranded traveler dragged from the sled, and at the bones. My glance lingers on the bones. Large and small, straight and curved, dry and white or darkly stained—they are lying everywhere about the room, licked clean. Bones of some animal shot by the traveler before the storm commenced? But there are too many bones, and too many exactly alike, or nearly so, to have belonged to a single animal. I frown. Then I notice what I haven't noticed before: fur. Small tufts of fur clinging to this bone or that. Why, the poor devil invited his entire team to share his shelter, his fire, what food he had, and this is the result! Not just the lead dog but the entire team! And the lead dog has eaten every last one of the others!

In the silence I hear their howls, their savage cries, their snarling at close quarters, their yelps of pain—just as the stranded traveler must have heard them. I see the leaping bodies, the cringing forms, the victims falling dead one by one—as he must have seen them. What did he do? At the height of the melee did he spring for the door and stagger off into the driving snow? Did he prefer certain death in the blizzard to this chaos of canine carnage?

Slowly I return my gaze to the dog. With new respect I look into the bloodshot eyes. How calm they are. How steady. What tragic intelligence shines from those bloodshot eyes. Sixteen fellow dogs devoured! No wonder!

Then I see the fur mitten.

No, I whisper. No! The poor devil! But the ax forgotten in the sled? The door barred from within? And now the mitten?

I raise the ax. I hold it athwart my chest. I am ready to strike. I look to my either side, take a step to the rear. Another. The second mitten lies not far from the first. I am clear-headed, cautious, my scalp is prickling. All the while I am staring into the gravity—oh what a monstrous gravity it has become!—of those bloodshot eyes.

Slowly, step by step I make my way backwards out of the cabin. Then I fling down the ax, lunge at the door, pull it shut, stand recovering my composure in the sunlit snow.

Sunny, he says, that darn dog...

Then I am briskly snowshoeing across the virgin wastes, off to present the authorities with a full account of this worst of all Alaskan tragedies on record.

Where are you, Charley?

47 —

Between the time of Sissy's death in 1935 and Uncle Jake's disappearance in 1940, Sissy's purse hung undisturbed on the knob of my bedroom door while her lingerie and scant personal effects lay just as she had left them in the three bureau drawers which had been hers and which, in those five years, remained untouched and unopened. Uncle Jake never entirely recovered from Sissy's death. No matter his determination to spare me his gloom; no matter how well he pulled himself together, in Frank Morley's words, in the first weeks and months when he and I first found ourselves alone; no matter his inventiveness, his adventures impulsively undertaken, his long flights of exuberance; no matter the constant efforts of Frank Morley and Hilda Laubenstein to praise him, comfort him, distract him, to lessen his grief in all the ways they could—still Sissy was always somewhere in his thoughts, as he often interrupted their conversations to declare, and still his days of dejection, as he called them, were frequent. Within three months of Sissy's death, and with all his old exactitude and fierce ebullience, he recalled the McGinnises from Olo Island, engaging Rex Ainsworth to fly them to Juneau—Rex said that he had never seen two people so afraid in an airplane as were the McGinnises that day—and using the fare provided by his mother for the purpose, booked their passage to Seattle and sent them back to Connecticut, where, as he said, they belonged. Frank Morley and Hilda Laubenstein attempted unsuccessfully to dissuade Uncle Jake from treating the McGinnises in such a harsh and unreasonable fashion, and were as sorry as I was to see them go. But Uncle Jake held firm and was in the best of spirits until the rainy day we waved them off. Then, as Hilda Laubenstein observed, he began to sink. He refused to have anything more to do with Olo Island; he refused to sell it; he refused even to retrieve the year's harvest of blue fox furs, preferring wrack and ruin, as he said, to accepting the spoils of a deaf and dumb easterner who had had no business in Alaska in the first place. As for the foxes still alive down there, as he told Frank Morley, why, they could just go ahead and starve to death for all he cared. By this time Uncle Jake's melancholy was nearly as severe as it was on the night when Sissy died. Then inexplicably he rallied.

The twice-weekly games of hearts were resumed, with Sissy's place filled by me, and I was careful never again to prevent Uncle Jake from winning, while Hilda, who cooked for the four of us on the nights we played, gave up her cheating. It was Hilda's opinion that the little house on High Ridge Street was part if not all of the reason that Uncle Jake continued off and on to slump. She urged Uncle Jake and me to move down to a recently vacated apartment in the wooden building in which she herself now lived and in which, she reminded us, Doc Haines had long been a resident and still conducted his practice. What better, she argued, than that Uncle Jake and I should have herself and a dentist as well for neighbors? Uncle Jake declined, saying, with a show of agitation that surprised us all and flustered even Hilda, that never as long as he lived would he rob me of the home that Sissy had created for himself and me, which was the end of any thought of our moving.

Prodded by Frank Morley and encouraged by Hilda, Uncle Jake assembled a new crew for *The Prince of Wales*. He replaced French Pete with a ne'er-do-well Polish laborer who had never worked on a boat in his life but who was an expert in the handling and use of dynamite, which, said Uncle Jake, would make him invaluable when they found their mine, as one day they were bound to do. He replaced Wesley Pitts with a man named Densmore—Billy Densmore—who was an exact likeness of the dead cook. Uncle Jake nicknamed his new mate Dynamite Pete after his predecessor and in honor of his calling, while Densmore became our second Belly Burglar. Dynamite Pete, who was soon given the additional nickname of the Bohunk by Uncle Jake, had a habit, as we were all to learn, of biting between his teeth the small bulletlike highly explosive blasting caps used to detonate his sticks of dynamite, which was why Uncle Jake always joked that one day the silly Bohunk was going to blow off his head or at least half his face, a prediction that drew me even more strongly to our new mate than to the original French Pete. Billy Densmore proved a worthier object of Uncle Jake's sentimental derision than had Wesley Pitts; he was, according to Uncle Jake, a better and dirtier cook by far than the dead Belly Burglar.

Though Hilda Laubenstein had joined Frank Morley in encouraging Uncle Jake to assemble his new crew she objected unexpectedly to what Uncle Jake took as a matter of course: my presence aboard *The Prince of Wales* whenever the old boat put to sea in service of some new scheme.

A young girl like myself, said Hilda—I was ten years old—had no business sailing about in an old tub manned only by men, especially by such men as Dynamite Pete and the Belly Burglar, no matter that Uncle Jake was in command and that Frank Morley more often than not would be aboard. The day that Hilda attempted to protect my emerging girlhood from the likes of the inept new mate and the fat little cook was the first of the only two times in his life that Uncle Jake openly acknowledged my gender. He stared at Hilda Laubenstein for a moment, his face working in surprise and anger, and then told her in no uncertain terms that never would any member of his crew think of me as anything but a boy. On *The Prince of Wales* I was for all intents and purposes a boy, he said, and the very idea of my being anything else was preposterous. So from early in 1936 until the spring of 1940, when Uncle Jake finally disappeared, I enjoyed the kindly attentions of Dynamite Pete and the Belly Burglar whenever Uncle Jake and his men built up a head of steam in *The Prince of Wales* and sailed her out of her home port of Juneau. I helped Billy Densmore prepare Uncle Jake's baked beans in the galley, and topside I was a nimbler deckhand than Dynamite Pete. With every trip Hilda, who always managed to wave us off, warned Uncle Jake that he was making a mistake, but Uncle Jake only laughed and said that she should stick to her nursing and leave the fathering to him.

Still he grieved and still he rallied.

In the late spring of 1936, when even Frank Morley, fatalistic as he was, had begun to worry aloud about the unusually relentless rain, there suddenly occurred not one but two mountain slides which, on consecutive days, buried the entire lower third of Juneau beneath tons of nearly liquid mud. This was in the poorer part of town stretching along the water's edge at the base of Mount Roberts between the docks of the Alaska Steamship Company and the high disfiguring heaps of crushed rock dumped into Gastineau Channel by the Alaska-Juneau Mining Company. Here, seven months after Sissy's death, was distraction enough for Uncle Jake. The rains fell, there were roaring and tearing sounds on the air, and the mud that buried shacks to their eaves and the wooden office building of the Alaska-Juneau Mining Company to its second story was as lethal as any bottomless bed of hot lava or mile-long avalanche of snow. In places only the tips of telephone poles showed above the mud; at best the narrow streets were shin-deep in the thickening coffee-colored slime. Rescuers were frantic and exhausted, and among them, caught unaware in the business suit he still customarily wore when not away on *The Prince of Wales*, was Uncle Jake, the boldest and most unflagging of them all. For more than forty-eight hours and despite his inappropriate clothing he defied the elements, as he called them, and went without food or sleep, commandeering any passing car to return him to the disaster area after those brief quarter-hours he spent dripping with mud and hastily drinking Frank Morley's black coffee in Guns & Locks & Clothes. For forty-eight hours he worked like a fiend, as he himself said later, and only once again, when we made our way to the site of Rex Ainsworth's fatal crash, did I ever see his long handsome face happily alight with that expression of alarm and pride so peculiar to him and inspired solely by any event of a catastrophic nature.

The two mud slides carried him along until the following fall, when unaccountably he thought once again of Sissy and began to slump. He spent three dreadful days of dejection from which Frank Morley was able to rouse him only by a last resort: by proposing, that is, that they make another hunting trip to the Kenai Peninsula, a venture that served its purpose though they returned from it empty-handed. In the spring of 1937 we sailed *The Prince of Wales* to William Henry Bay, which Uncle Jake had failed to reach on the maiden voyage of 1930, and there we spent six weeks attempting to salvage two rusted thousand-gallon boilers and the remains of a compressor, the three pieces of machinery having been abandoned years before by other hopefuls who thought there was gold in William Henry Bay. Bearded and unkempt once more, Uncle Jake carried a long-handled double-bitted ax across his shoulder—a dangerous habit as Frank Morley warned—and showed Frank Morley and Dynamite Pete how to rig the blocks and tackle in order to drag the compressor down to the beach on rails made of saplings felled by Uncle Jake himself. The compressor and two boilers stood more than a mile from the beach where *The Prince of Wales* was anchored a hundred yards offshore. The days were long. Each dawn we saw the high grasses flattened by a family of brown bears smart enough, said Uncle Jake, to keep out of his way, since the Four-Hundred-and-Five was always within his reach. We slept in log cabins built and vacated by those other farsighted men and lived on wild strawberries and the Belly Burglar's beans. Uncle Jake was contemptuous of those who had left behind the compressor and boilers in the first place, since, he said, they were worth a fortune, and abandoned mines, where such machinery was sometimes to be found and hence got for nothing, were few and far between, though he himself had already wasted his time on three. He intended to store the machinery in space he planned to rent in one of the warehouses damaged but not destroyed in the mud slides of the previous spring.

When the time came and they had built their raft, the first boiler snapped its moorings, rolled off the raft and sank in five fathoms of black water. They managed to hoist the second boiler to the deck of *The Prince of Wales,* all but capsizing the gallant old boat in the process. It was this boiler that Uncle Jake carried back in triumph to Juneau to await transporting to the mine that he and Frank Morley were still confident of discovering. In disgust they left the compressor behind on the beach, since Uncle Jake mysteriously calculated that it weighed ten times more than the two boilers combined and was, he finally decided, too far gone for repair.

The following spring, in May of 1938, our entire crew set off again, this time for Kuiu (pronounced cue-yew) Island on the trail of zinc. This time, said Uncle Jake, they would find their mine. No one before us had ever searched for zinc or anything else on Kuiu Island; there were no abandoned log cabins for us to inhabit. But Uncle Jake got hold of half a dozen long-outmoded army tents, which were replaced later by three boxlike wooden buildings constructed of green unfinished lumber carried in great stacks on the deck of *The Prince of Wales* to the little cove cut like a notch into the dark shores of Kuiu Island. Foxes were nothing compared with zinc, said Uncle Jake, and Olo Island was nothing compared with Kuiu. The hammers rang, a new gasoline-powered circular ripsaw disturbed the moody silence and in the course of three weeks there arose the naked flat-roofed buildings which, said Uncle Jake, were just the beginning. We would have an entire town, he promised, in six months, and a sizable and sturdy dock stretching far enough from shore to accommodate brand new cargo ships that would travel back and forth directly from the Kuiu Zinc Mine, as he had already named it, to Seattle, where their cargos of ore would be shipped by rail to smelters. He determined that now a permanent gang must remain on the island to raise new buildings as soon as he could find another source of cheap lumber in Juneau, and to stake new claims and develop the claims already staked. Three small shafts were blasted through earth and rock thanks to the exuberant rhythmless detonations of Dynamite Pete's explosives.

Reports from the government laboratory in Juneau regarding samples of rock removed from each of the shafts convinced Uncle Jake that he and Frank Morley had in fact located a deposit of zinc of a size and quality to warrant a mining venture larger than any as yet undertaken in Alaska. The percentage of zinc in the rock was unheard of; the deposit, as far as they could determine from their first three shafts, lay in a thick flat shelf that covered Kuiu Island and probably ran for miles beneath the sea. So Uncle Jake hired three more men—Jim McNear, A. L. Wells, and Fred Stokely—to spend the winter on Kuiu Island with Dynamite Pete and the Belly Burglar, hoping that the rain and snow and freezing weather would not impede their work. He persuaded the local bank to lend him additional funds, as he called them, to replenish the finally diminishing resources of the Deauville-Morley partnership. Periodically Uncle Jake and Frank Morley and I, along with a younger stand-in mate, went down on *The Prince of Wales* to visit the gang—by then an unwashed, unshaven, bad-tempered lot— bringing them fresh supplies and dozens of back copies of *The Midnight Sun,* Juneau's only newspaper. Initially we stayed a mere few days or the time it took Uncle Jake to supervise the unloading of the cloth-wrapped slabs of bacon and new crates of dented cans of beans, and to revive the spirits of his bedraggled gang with long rhetorical promises of wealth which would soon, he said, be theirs.

When funds once again ran low, as indeed they did, Uncle Jake sought out the only honest lawyer in Juneau and had prepared five separate copies of a document providing the holder with fifty shares of stock in the Kuiu Zinc Mine. Thus Uncle Jake made all five members of the gang voting shareholders in the company of which he himself was president. The gang, fired by Uncle Jake's facts and figures and enthu-siasm, and surprised and then pridefully uplifted by his generosity, began to work—more vigorously and cheerfully than even Uncle Jake had expected—for nothing, which in turn extended our visit to the mine for weeks on end so that Uncle Jake might pitch in, as he put it, and do his share of the arduous work at hand. He swung a pick and shoveled muck like the others, heated the tips of steel drills in the white coals of a blacksmith's forge—it was I who turned the iron crank of the forge while Uncle Jake sweated bare-chested over the hot steel. Every night he won again the admiration of his enterprising gang with stories, which hardly half his audience understood, about his privileged boyhood in Connecticut. It was during those weeks and months that Dynamite Pete, who always wore a black and white striped trainman's cap of floppy canvas, showed off his courage by readying his blasting caps between his yellowed teeth, so that Uncle Jake ordered the Bohunk to do his crazy chewing, as Uncle Jake called it, off in the woods at a good safe distance from the rest of us. Many a time, unknown to Uncle Jake, I squatted in the drizzle beside Dynamite Pete and tossed in my cupped hands the little coppery sticks that he kept, also unknown to Uncle Jake, in his pockets.

It was not Dynamite Pete who had an accident, as Uncle Jake had predicted, but Uncle Jake himself. While pounding the glowing tip of a drill on the anvil—he had refused to wear the goggles that always hung from a nail in the smithy—a minuscule chip of hot flying steel lodged in his eye. This episode brought Rex Ainsworth and the Fairchild on the double, as Uncle Jake boasted days later, when wearing his fresh white patch, he also bragged that he would have lost his eye had it not been for Hilda Laubenstein and her magnet. Shortly after his return, the crew hauled ashore the thousand-gallon boiler that had been stored in Juneau.

Uncle Jake might have had his town, his docks, his wealth, which he wanted for the sake of Sissy's memory as well as for my future, had it not turned out that there was a fault, as the geologist from Juneau called it, in the gigantic plate of rock so highly laden with zinc. Uncle Jake and his gang had located only the tip of the iceberg, as the geologist said, nothing more. By the summer of 1939 the shareholders of the Kuiu Zinc Mine had dug and blasted and sunk innumerable new shafts— to no avail. After eleven months they admitted one and all that the main deposit of zinc-bearing rock, miles for all they knew in breadth and length, had cracked in its formation and dropped in such a way as never, they admitted, to be found—at least by them. The small out-cropping that they had originally discovered was worthless.

There was grumbling, anger, disappointment, despair. Much against Frank Morley's advice—the men who had worked on Kuiu Island had been well aware of the risks involved, he said, no matter what Uncle Jake had told them—Uncle Jake went back to the bank and talked the manager into another loan, substantial enough to pay each member of the gang his lost wages. Then he wrote them a formal letter, though Dynamite Pete and two others could not read, stating that he refused to dissolve the Kuiu Mining Company on the eventuality that it might be sold to some well-established firm in the future and that their shares of stock in the company were still in their names and as good as new, so that the wealth they had spent all that year expecting might yet be theirs.

The slump that followed Uncle Jake's final exertions on behalf of his

men and that closed the door as firmly on Kuiu Island as it had long
been closed on that other island in Disillusionment Bay, was the deepest
and longest-lasting of any previous slump that Uncle Jake had known.
It was worse than the aftermath of the murder that had occurred in
1930 in White Eye; it was worse than the days of dejection that had
followed Sissy's death five years after that. This fact alone, casually
mentioned one afternoon by Frank Morley within Uncle Jake's hearing—that Uncle Jake was grieving more for the loss of a mine than
for the death of his own wife—finally pierced the darkness and returned
Uncle Jake once more to Frank, to Hilda, to me, and to his faith in
Alaska.

That night he raised his head, looked into the eyes of each of us in
turn, then he smiled and began to rock the chair in which, for all those
days of dejection, he had sat without one hint of motion. He began to
talk. Animation returned to his face, his voice. He attempted a short
laugh. Another. And then, and despite his weakness and weary looks,
he began, for the first and only time in his life, to speak of Billy Boy,
his beloved younger brother, and of the tragic death that had taken
place on the tennis courts back in Connecticut in 1929. Billy Boy, said
Uncle Jake, grinning and crossing his legs, had been not only the
family's favorite but Sissy's as well. Of course Sissy had been fond of
Doc, though in those days poor Doc had already had a wishbone where
his backbone should have been, as Uncle Jake expressed it, but she had
loved Billy Boy. She had loved him with all the purity of a sister, as
if he had been the brother she had always longed to have instead of
those two sisters of hers.

Why, said Uncle Jake, it was Sissy herself who suggested that poor
Doc be best man at her wedding but that Billy Boy give her away in
marriage, an arrangement to which Uncle Jake's already disapproving
father had readily agreed. So Sissy came down the aisle on Billy Boy's
arm and, in the days to come, was as eagerly Billy Boy's tennis partner
as she was Uncle Jake's, or nearly so. Billy Boy joined Sissy and Uncle
Jake on their evening strolls around the grounds of the Deauville place
in Connecticut. And when I was newly born it was Billy Boy who
attended Uncle Jake on his first visit to the lying-in hospital, and Billy
Boy who watched as Sissy gave me for the first time to Uncle Jake to
hold, and Billy Boy into whose cradling arms Sissy placed me only
moments after taking me back from Uncle Jake. Why, said Uncle Jake,
Billy Boy was as good as my second father, despite his youth, and of
all the Deauville boys was the most tranquil, the most obliging, the

most attentive to his mother's needs and wishes—after Uncle Jake. Uncle Jake said that Billy Boy never did a stroke of work in his life except to push the giant water-filled iron roller across the lawns when they were freshly cut and to drive off in the Stutz Bearcat on endless errands for their unappreciative father. Billy Boy was the most generous person that Uncle Jake had ever known—except for Frank Morley, of course—a brother who had always been ready to lend Uncle Jake the clothes off his own back and who had put the Stutz Bearcat at Uncle Jake's disposal from the time when Uncle Jake had been courting Sissy to the very night before that terrible dawn when they found the white car and its lifeless occupant in the middle of one of the empty and still dew-wet tennis courts.

And here was the point of Uncle Jake's singular story: that Billy Boy's self-inflicted death was not dishonorable. To the contrary, Billy Boy died with gentle strength and deliberation. He drove the car he loved onto the tennis courts he loved and died purely and simply. He had had no reason to do what he did, and it was precisely the mystery of the thing that made the pain of his death bearable and the death itself reflective of a noble spirit. He was found by Uncle Jake and Sissy, who were early risers, only slightly slumped in the seat of the long white gleaming car with the morning sun in his dead eyes and one large hand on the wooden wheel and the other still raised and pointing the revolver at his temple. There was no blood. Why, said Uncle Jake, there wasn't even a bullet hole, at least that he and Sissy ever saw. Only his dearly loved younger brother arrested in an unimaginable tableau that no one but Billy Boy himself could have created and that no member of the family could have thought him capable of creating. The sun, the dew, the silence, the angle of the white machine on the rectangle of red clay, the black revolver held aloft in the deliberately raised hand—it was not just madness as the local paper claimed, it was stunning. It was inexplicable. It was a scene that no one who saw it ever forgot.

By the end of that clear night in late August of 1939, Frank Morley and Hilda Laubenstein, as surprised as they had been that Uncle Jake had begun to speak of the death of his youngest brother—he never did so again—and uneasy as they had shown themselves to have been during parts of the nostalgic narrative, had understood that Uncle Jake had made a double reconciliation with himself that night and were relieved that through the defense of his brother he had once more overcome his grief at the loss of the Kuiu Zinc Mine and Sissy as well. Hilda hugged him, Frank Morley touched his partner's arm. They left.

I prepared the foldaway bed—at fourteen I was a more devoted and efficient housekeeper than Sissy had been—and from behind my closed door listened to Uncle Jake readying himself for sleep.

Several days later Hilda remarked to Frank Morley in my presence that that lugubrious story had certainly done wonders for Uncle Jake, and Frank Morley agreed. Hilda went on, in a reverie rare for her, to say that she did not understand how morbidity could overcome depression, as certainly seemed the case with Uncle Jake, and that she had not liked at all the story that he had told the other night. But, she said, if that's what it took—morbidity—to restore Uncle Jake's largesse of spirit, who was she to complain? Frank Morley nodded and lit up.

We were all at peace.

And so Uncle Jake and I spent our last seven months together in the house on High Ridge Road. Dressed in our woodsmen's clothes we climbed Mount Roberts, hiked out the Silver Bow Basin Road, where I now practiced my target shooting with a six-shot .45-caliber wooden-handled revolver, and sat in the blue shadows around the hot iron stove in Guns & Locks & Clothes, one night a week enjoying Hilda's meals cooked in Sissy's kitchen, and one other night a week enjoying an evening meal at Doug's. We did not comment on Frank Morley's yellowing complexion or loss of weight, together we welcomed the increasing number and diversity of what Uncle Jake took to be Hilda's innocent attentions. We made two more short abortive trips on *The Prince of Wales*. Dynamite Pete did not injure himself or anyone else. Hilda need not have feared for my girlhood. Sissy's purse continued to hang from its doorknob, occasionally causing Uncle Jake to pause and stare. Then he would turn and stand thoughtfully before the bureau containing the three unopened drawers that helped to make the house on High Ridge Street her shrine. We were all at peace.

We were waiting and not waiting. We knew that the day was sure to come when Uncle Jake's inventiveness would once again flare up and all three of us would be forced to submit in our various ways to the future and Uncle Jake's rabid self-inflicted fate. But for now even Uncle Jake was glad to be spared what lay ahead and to enjoy the interim of peace. It lasted for seven months and nothing marred it save one episode involving brief pain for me and considerably odd behavior on the part of Uncle Jake. It was a single episode and short, and it was resolved swiftly enough by Hilda Laubenstein. Yet momentarily it marred our peace.

A toothache. My toothache. An abscessed wisdom tooth, as it turned out, that came in the night like Sissy's and despite the fact that my teeth were and have always been as trouble-free as Sissy's and Uncle Jake's. There it was one morning: half my young girl's face swollen furiously in pain. And again Uncle Jake was suddenly gripped in that odd behavior that unnerved us all. He denied that there was anything the matter with my tooth. He denied my toothache throughout that morning and into the afternoon. He strode down to Guns & Locks & Clothes and canceled the approaching evening's game of hearts. Then he returned to me in anguish and commiseration, begging my forgiveness and setting about with no further delay to cure my tooth himself. I asked him to take me to Doc Haines. He made excuses, he filled the house on High Ridge Street with his loving agitation. He said that both his mother and Sissy had been experts in the matter of aching teeth and that he himself was a master of the remedies that they had known. Compresses, he said. And for the next hours he applied them: hot and cold, interminable, soaking his own Irish linen handkerchiefs in solutions of salt or iodine and water now as hot as I could bear and now as cold as the refrigerator that had replaced our wooden ice chest could make them. Early the next morning he kept Frank Morley out on our porch instead of inviting him in for coffee, saying that I had come down with some sort of fever, and then sent him away.

Oil of wintergreen, he said. For these four years a dusty bottle of Sissy's favorite elixir had stood unopened on our bathroom shelf. Now he held the bottle up to the light and opened it; he tied a makeshift bib around my neck. He swabbed the tooth and surrounding gum with the thick and fiery oil; he waited, and then, sweating and fighting the glaze in his eyes, he cradled my head and gently asked me to open my mouth and tried again. No relief. He saw the tears I had promised myself not to shed. I asked him to take me to Doc Haines. So he gave up at last, shoving aside the washbasin still filled with its soggy mass of ruined handkerchiefs—they were tinted the faint hue of iodine— and left the house and returned with Hilda.

Hilda sniffed the air still heavy with the scent of the oil of wintergreen and frowned. She glanced at me, at the basin, at Uncle Jake and, saying nothing, started out the door. We followed. On our way down the hill Uncle Jake tried once to explain what he called his procrastination, but seeing the way Hilda jerked her shoulders he broke off in mid-sentence and girded himself for the pain he was convinced would stab me once Doc Haines got me into his chair. In the waiting room Uncle Jake once again lost control of himself and tried to persuade Hilda to join me in Doc Haines's office until the job was done, which Hilda naturally refused to do. Once I was safely in Doc Haines's hands, Hilda, as I could tell from the sound of her voice beyond the door, apparently relented enough to comfort Uncle Jake through the long ordeal and did not, I gathered later, make the mistake of offending him as had the unfortunate Nancy on that other similar occasion in the past.

So I was cloistered for my hour or more with Doc Haines, who, unbeknownst to anyone but me, justified in the subtlest possible ways the suspicions that Uncle Jake had not been able to acknowledge or express, at least overtly, then or in the past when he had first harbored them. It was Doc Haines who, without a single touch in any way unprofessional, set me that day in the middle of my fifteenth year on the course of pleasure. Sissy too must have responded to his small and gentle hands, his still coppery beard, his humor, his ageless eyes, the way he had of leaning close to any woman who came to him for help. I hope she did. I hope Doc Haines told her the same stories he told me—about a much older dentist friend of his who, in the friend's early days in Alaska, installed a dentist's chair heavier and more archaic than Doc Haines's own in the cabin of an ancient airplane and flew around the Territory pulling and repairing teeth in all the out-of-the-way places where word of mouth told him he was needed— and I hope that Sissy was as touched as I was by the soothing sound of Doc Haines's voice.

For several days there was constraint between Hilda and Frank Morley and Uncle Jake. There was no discussion of the toothache episode between them. Uncle Jake quickly regained his self-esteem and before long won back the idolatrous affections of his failing partner and his dead wife's best friend. And who is to say that Uncle Jake's brief burst of strange behavior in the middle of my fifteenth year didn't ready me all the more for the suddenly undeniable sensations and erotic schemes that were so late in coming to me but were so swiftly and strongly prompted in Doc Haines's chair? Uncle Jake insisted that there was not another tooth in my head that would ever again send me down, in his words, to that little dentist, and he was right. We were all at peace.

．　　．　　．

Uncle Jake got started on a second search for molybdenite. Then Sitka Charley discovered the whereabouts of the Lincoln totem pole.

So the day came. Inevitably the day came.

48 —

On a drizzly dawn in late March of 1940, we lay at anchor in Rodman Bay. And there we were, the Belly Burglar and I, feeding the men— meaning Uncle Jake and Frank Morley and Dynamite Pete and A. L. (Al) Wells, who had come to Uncle Jake with the rumor of molybdenite up in Rainy Pass above Rodman Bay. That molybdenite, Al Wells had said, was ours for the taking if we could only beat out the party of easterners—just who they were he was not at liberty to say—who thought that they had safeguarded beyond a doubt the recent discovery that had been made in Rainy Pass. Uncle Jake and Frank Morley had conferred, despite Uncle Jake's suspicions about the integrity of A. L. Wells, and had made their decision and, as inconspicuously as possible, had readied *The Prince of Wales* for a three-week exploratory trip to Rodman Bay. Hilda Laubenstein had seen us off; we had slipped out of Gastineau Channel in total darkness and without lights. There was not a person aboard who doubted the good fortune that lay ahead; anticipation had never run so high on *The Prince of Wales* as it did for those long days it took us to reach Rodman Bay.

It was a tricky place to enter, a fact of which every one of us was thoroughly aware, thanks to Uncle Jake's musings on the subject, and far trickier at night. Just as he had expected, Uncle Jake had had no choice but to take us in at 4 A.M.—yet had done so expertly, tensely grinning all the way, and on the wet deck in the cold and drizzly darkness of 4 A.M., the sound of the descending anchor awakened us all to the relief of safe arrival and the first justified pleasure at the possibility of beating out the unsuspecting easterners.

Now, after a mere two hours of damp bunks, tossing and snoring, the sound of water lapping the sides of *The Prince of Wales,* the Belly Burglar and I were serving breakfast and the mood was gone. The fire in the rusty coal-burning stove was at its peak; the pork chops in the two large skillets were sizzling; the java, as even I had come to call it, was already brewed in the two tall chipped enamel pots, and the Belly Burglar, who had roused me out only a few minutes before the men, had made a beautiful batch of golden brown hard sour-tasting biscuits. Still the mood was gone. The two hours of attempted sleep had been enough to destroy it. Uncle Jake and Frank Morley and Dynamite Pete and Al Wells sat around the heavily painted oval table in the dining saloon looking as if they had already climbed to Rainy Pass and had already undergone their usual ordeals and, as usual, had failed. They said nothing. Their eyes were red. They rubbed the backs of their hands against their stubbled cheeks and ran their fingers through their heads of uncombed hair. Uncle Jake did not object, as he usually did, to the sight of Dynamite Pete wearing his trainman's hat at the table. Al Wells, who was from Biloxi, Mississippi, and was the youngest of our men, with a heavy frame and the face of a cherub, had clearly lost what Uncle Jake had called his sparkle. Frank Morley was shivering, despite the heat that filled the dining saloon from the galley, and his shoulders were slumped and his wheezing loud. The kerosene lamp hanging from a davit above the table was motionless but smoking; darkness was giving way to light at the portholes. The dining saloon smelled of bilge water and smoking kerosene and our cooking. And there they sat.

I filled their mugs, brought in the chops and biscuits, the beans and canned apricots, and joined them, while the Belly Burglar stood plate in hand in the doorway as he always did—short and fat and filthy and now worried, obviously, about our men. His face was rounder than Al Wells's face and, like the dead Belly Burglar, he wore black-framed spectacles which he never cleaned and was always afraid of breaking. His eyes were invisible behind the little greasy lenses. I loved him for looking like a fat and scrofulous owl and wished that he were not so worried.

Uncle Jake took a sip of his java, a bite of his chop, a taste of hot beans, and then put down his knife and fork and across the table gave me one of his now rare glances of reproach. I knew what it meant, I had heard him put that particular reproach into words often enough for Sissy. A hair. A hair in his food. If there was anything worse than blood in his meat—especially blood in the joints of a roasted chicken— it was a hair in his food, and though I was better than Sissy had been at keeping the nearly invisible signs of our female selves out of his food, still one occasionally got by. I smiled apologetically and, indifferent to the watching company, he snagged the glistening hair on the edge of his plate and returned to his meal.

Al Wells, in the youthful good-humored southern tones that had exasperated Uncle Jake from the moment the two of them had met, complimented the Belly Burglar on his biscuits. Uncle Jake, who called no man by his nickname unless he, Uncle Jake, had invented it—hence his use of A. L. for Al—and who was offended by any compliment that he himself had not thought to pay, stiffened and raised his chin. The Belly Burglar glanced at Uncle Jake and, on a sleeve stained the moldy green color of spattered grease, wiped the sweat from his face. Dynamite Pete tugged at his floppy cap and, half standing, reached into the center of the table for another chop. Uncle Jake glanced at Frank Morley as if to commiserate with his partner for the way they were saddled, the two of them, with a crew as shabby and forlorn as this one. Frank Morley coughed and pushed away his plate. *The Prince of Wales* was listing more than usual and from above our heads came a pattering sound like that of some small animal running back and forth across our deck. It was then that our row of starboard portholes, which were facing the east, filled suddenly with the unmistakable light of sunrise, drizzle or no drizzle.

"Well, Frank," said Uncle Jake, smiling abruptly and speaking directly to his partner so as to exclude the rest of us, "Rodman Bay is about the worst place anyone could come to."

Frank Morley nodded.

"It's a dead world," said Uncle Jake happily, "as dead as a stone. Why, the glaciers that swept through here killed everything—animals, birds, fish, trees, vegetation—everything but lichen, moss, and a few ferns. I've heard about Rodman Bay ever since I came to Alaska. I've always wanted to visit the place. As for Rainy Pass, why, Rainy Pass is the very devil, or so I've heard. Nothing but peaks and pinnacles and dark gorges and sheer cliffs, and cold and sopping wet the year round when it isn't snowing. You know how it is, Frank, at three thousand feet."

Frank Morley took out his blue bandanna and coughed into it, keeping his sad eyes all the while on Uncle Jake.

"Well," said Uncle Jake, who had already confided to Frank Morley in my hearing that he didn't trust A. L. Wells worth a darn, though the man had earned his keep at Kuiu, "our young friend from Biloxi here just better be right about Rainy Pass. It's going to be a hard job getting up there, I can tell you."

Al Wells said in the voice that made the tips of Uncle Jake's ears turn crimson that his rich easterners could not be wrong.

"Frank," said Uncle Jake, laughing and trying to ignore Al Wells, who was not only the youngest man aboard *The Prince of Wales* this trip but the largest, except for Uncle Jake, and who obviously did not care whether he was ignored or not by the leader of our expedition, "there isn't even any hunting in Rainy Pass. Oh, every once in a while a few mountain goats straggle over from the surrounding country, but they skedaddle fast enough as soon as they get one whiff of that dead atmosphere up there."

"Sounds like a hell of a place," said Dynamite Pete, who caught a quick disapproving glance from Uncle Jake for his language.

"The tides in Rodman Bay," said Uncle Jake, still addressing himself solely to his partner, "are the most treacherous of any place in Alaska. The fogs are famous. The winds are wicked. You'd have a hard time building a city here or bringing cargo vessels into these waters. But we'll do it if we get half a chance."

The pattering sound came again above our heads, the stern of *The Prince of Wales* swung gently, the golden light came in through the portholes, and, as even Dynamite Pete could see, Uncle Jake had finally talked long enough to revive himself if not his crew.

"Well, Frank," he said abruptly, "let's take a look!"

Up the companionway they went, Uncle Jake and Frank Morley, while I followed, as I was meant to, and Al Wells and Dynamite Pete, who had no use for each other and never had, stayed where they were at the table. From below came the sounds of the Belly Burglar rattling about at his clean-up. Uncle Jake and Frank Morley and I emerged into the open air.

We lay in sunlight, silence, still waters. It was dawn but it might have been noon. Not a fish jumped, there was not a bird to be seen, the very deck of *The Prince of Wales* was unfamiliar, foreign, and for a moment the three of us stood together taking deep breaths of the air that smelled of the new day and squinting in the oddly hot light that was reflected everywhere from the wet surfaces of *The Prince of Wales*—from the mast, the stays, the rails, the windows in the pilothouse, the sloping deck. Our anchorage was secure; no other boat but ours, it seemed, had ever lain at rest in the vast crescent of Rodman Bay. Low hills and ledges and spurs rose in broken tiers from the curve of the beach, bare and burnished and sparkling here and there with pockets and patches of lingering snow. There were no shadows. We were close to shore. Here was exactly what Uncle Jake wanted, and part of our pleasure, Frank Morley's and mine, was in seeing how expansively Uncle Jake surveyed the scene and how totally he himself was now a figure of light.

"There it is, Frank," he said proudly, "Rodman Bay."

"Luck's with us so far," said Frank Morley.

"We'll spend the day unloading and setting things in order," said Uncle Jake. "Tomorrow Sunny and Dynamite Pete and A. L. and I will get an early start for Rainy Pass. You and the Belly Burglar can stay aboard in case the weather turns and you have to pull out to a safer distance offshore."

Frank Morley nodded and said that Uncle Jake needn't worry.

Then Uncle Jake's expression changed. His face went blank, turned harsh, deepened in color, grew still brighter, quivered with feeling he hadn't expected and feared to reveal. His wide-open eyes were fixed on the nearly vertical rocky side of the high ridge that dominated the nearest slopes and spurs rising up from the beach.

"Frank," he said, "do you see it?"

Frank Morley shaded his eyes and looked in the direction Uncle Jake was pointing. He shook his head.

"It's green," said Uncle Jake, controlling his voice. "Green."

"Well," said Frank Morley slowly, "I suppose it is. But it's only moss, wouldn't you say?"

"Copper," said Uncle Jake, restraining himself. "Sure signs of copper."

"I doubt it," said Frank Morley, pained that his partner was forcing him to disagree. "I don't think so. It's not the country for copper."

"Frank," said Uncle Jake, "if that's copper up there, we don't have to go another step. Look at the size of it! Why, if that's copper I'll be happy to keep out of Rainy Pass. A. L.'s easterners can have Rainy Pass and all the molybdenite they can find, for all I care. What do you think?"

They turned together and side by side stared across the five or six hundred yards at the wall of rock, Uncle Jake in his black and green checked shirt and woolen pants and leather boots, Frank Morley dressed in his old black hat and canvas duck-hunting coat and pants and rubber boots folded below the knee.

"Sunny," said Uncle Jake without turning around.

"I'll get them," I said quickly and went aft to the pilothouse and took down the heavy leather case containing the binoculars—glasses as

Uncle Jake preferred to say—and returned with the strap of the case over my shoulder. The leather case was as large as the holster for my Smith & Wesson .45-caliber revolver that also hung in the pilothouse.

Uncle Jake reached for the binoculars without a word. He raised them, studied the smear of green on the side of the cliff, then passed them over to Frank Morley, who, after a long moment of adjusting and peering through the eye pieces, passed them back to Uncle Jake.

"It's possible," said Uncle Jake, lowering and then again raising the binoculars for a long steady perusal of the green discoloration high on the rock.

"I still have my doubts," said Frank Morley.

"It's just what happened down at Prince William Sound," said Uncle Jake. "They were convinced that what looked like copper-colored stains was just moss, but they wanted to be sure and so looked for themselves. The largest copper concentrations in the world, Frank. None larger. Bought by the Kennecott Copper Company for a fortune."

"Well," said Frank Morley, "what are you going to do?"

"Take a look!" exclaimed Uncle Jake, handing me back the binoculars and seizing his partner's arm and shaking it.

"You mean you're going to climb up there yourself?" asked Frank Morley, looking askance at Uncle Jake.

"Of course," said Uncle Jake. "How else are we going to find out what we've got up there?"

"Pete," said Frank Morley, "or Al Wells."

"Pete and A. L. couldn't climb a fence and you know it," said Uncle Jake.

"It's dangerous," said Frank Morley. "You've never done any climbing either, Jake. Why risk it at a time like this?"

"I don't give a darn for heights," said Uncle Jake, shading his eyes and grinning at the cliff Frank Morley and I both knew he was going to attempt to scale no matter what Frank Morley said or thought. "When it comes to heights, I'm a regular billy goat. Why, in 1917 I was the envy of officers and men alike on the old *Powhatan* for my fearlessness in going aloft even in the worst weather. I used to be in my glory standing up there in the crow's nest—a hundred feet above the deck, Frank—when the old ship was rolling and pitching to beat the band. I was born for high places, that's the truth. The higher the better."

"I don't like it," said Frank Morley.

"Let me just have a last look through those glasses, Sunny," said

Uncle Jake, and then, when he had finished scanning the cliff and choosing his route, he laughed and said that it was an easy climb and that he and Frank Morley would have their answer—moss or copper— before the day's end. "Up and down in about two hours, Frank," he said. "You'll see."

The Belly Burglar's worry increased as soon as Uncle Jake announced his plan, whereas Dynamite Pete and Al Wells both welcomed the diversion as just what they would expect from Uncle Jake and as an excuse from work. But Uncle Jake insisted that the preparations for the next day's trek to Rainy Pass be completed before he made his investigative climb and ordered Dynamite Pete and Al Wells to get to work at once and to do the job as quickly as they could. The sooner they finished the sooner he started, he said, and the sooner he would bring back the news.

Wasn't it contradictory that like Frank Morley I knew that Uncle Jake should have used his common sense and resisted the impulse to leave us for the sake of doing what no one else would have done, yet silently wished him to do just that? At fourteen—Uncle Jake was sixty and Frank Morley sixty-eight—mightn't I have remembered the broken ribs, the chip of hot steel in the eye, the times he had been reported missing, and admitted to myself that he was forever bent on undergoing personal risk in order to thwart his own plans and to jeopardize the safety and well-being of the few of us who depended on him for love or work? At fourteen, mightn't I have done my best to hold him back? And wasn't it contradictory that I was the willing helper of Dynamite Pete, though Pete, like his predecessor, openly ridiculed Uncle Jake? I was attracted, if anything, to the sinister agreeableness of Al Wells, never once defended Uncle Jake in their presence. How was it that I sided happily with their ill-concealed disloyalty to Uncle Jake yet took for granted that the illiterate Bohunk and deceptive southerner were beneath him? Yes, my behavior at fourteen was contradictory. Yes, I should have seen Uncle Jake for what he was and turned my back on the riffraff, which was how he privately dismissed the Bohunk and the easygoing young catfisherman from Biloxi. But I was no better at fourteen than at five or ten. For Uncle Jake I had long denied to myself my menses though Hilda Laubenstein had done her best to instruct and entice me into young womanhood. At fourteen I was not so different from Sissy despite my boyish ways. Other than Frank Morley and Sitka Charley, I had no one but Uncle Jake. No wonder there was nothing in the world for me but the father-love of that man. But at least I was on the right track with Al Wells and Dynamite Pete, thanks to my first visit to Doc Haines's office.

So I was impatient for the work to be done and Uncle Jake to be off. Frank Morley was in charge of the winch; Dynamite Pete and Al Wells moved quickly. I sat in the stern of the dory and manned the outboard motor while the Belly Burglar helped as much as his health allowed and watched us from the rail approvingly, despite his worry. Uncle Jake joined in, swinging sacks of dried fruit and beans from the deck to the waiting hands of the men in the dory. The sun rose higher. Rodman Bay was ours. Uncle Jake congratulated his first mate and the young southerner on their good work; our supplies accrued in orderly stacks on the beach beneath tarpaulins carefully staked down.

Uncle Jake called time out for lunch. He talked at length about the Kennecott Copper operation in Prince William Sound. Dynamite Pete stretched out for what Uncle Jake called Pete's midday snooze. Al Wells went below for his hand line and began fishing over the side though Uncle Jake told him the only fish in Rodman Bay were fossils. Frank Morley sat hunched over in the sun and smoked, coughing and nursing his fears for Uncle Jake as he told me later. I watched Uncle Jake enter and emerge from the pilothouse and followed him to the bow of *The Prince of Wales,* where we shared the binoculars and Uncle Jake pointed out the treacheries of the ascent he was soon to make.

Back to work. Trouble with the outboard motor. Uncle Jake impatiently reassembling it on the hatch cover. A noticeable strengthening of the tide. A change in the light.

Then Uncle Jake said that it was time to start and that Pete and I would take him over to the beach and join him as far as the base of the cliff. Frank Morley answered emphatically that it was too late for Uncle Jake to make his climb and that it would have to wait until the following morning. But Uncle Jake said there were three hours at least before sundown and that he had waited long enough to satisfy his curiosity about those telltale green stains on the cliff.

"It's a mistake, partner," said Frank Morley.

"Partner," said Uncle Jake with a laugh, "my heart's set on it."

Frank Morley waited, silently giving in to Uncle Jake as he had been doing for nearly a decade, and then, in his hurt and loyal voice, he said that he and I would see him to the beginning of the climb and that Dynamite Pete would remain behind in charge of *The Prince of Wales.* Uncle Jake agreed, after a pause and, with only a modest coil of rope in hand, declared himself ready, whereupon Frank Morley told him to take along my six-shot Smith & Wesson and an extra jacket or sweater of some sort. Uncle Jake laughed and wanted to know whatever for. The climb itself would keep him warm and what possible use could he have for my revolver? There was nothing to shoot in Rodman Bay as he had already said, and even if there were, a knife would afford a man better protection than the side arm. Frank Morley said you never knew and that if Uncle Jake was going we'd better hurry. Uncle Jake donned a faded blue windbreaker stiff with salt, strapped on the Smith & Wesson, holster, and broad cartridge belt turning a dark red-brown in the lowering sun, and swung himself over the side. The Belly Burglar and Al Wells and Dynamite Pete lined the rail to see us off; and Uncle Jake, standing in the bow of the dory, told the Belly Burglar to fix a big feed, as he put it, for supper.

We beached the dory.

"You see," said Uncle Jake, leading us slipping and crunching across the pebbles and onto the solid moraine of the first slope, "it's dead, Frank, stripped bare. Nothing but the scars left behind by ice. Funny thing is that you can still feel the cold breath of those glaciers, can't you? And hear the booming of the ice? And what about the towering firs and the mastodons as big as houses? The destruction of them makes them all the more real, don't you think? It's easier to see what's invisible than what's standing right in front of your face! Nothing like a dead world to teem with life, I've often thought."

Frank Morley made no comment and then, stooping and wheezing, remarked that if anything went wrong Uncle Jake could signal us with the revolver.

"In that case," said Uncle Jake gently, "what would you do? Send Pete and A. L. and Billy Densmore up after me? Some rescuers they'd make, eh Frank?"

Frank Morley said nothing except that the light was fading. The deck of the boat below us was empty. The grade was steep. The rocks and ridges were casting shadows. To our either side the tips of the crescent of Rodman Bay disappeared into the deepening blue of sea and sky. We could go no farther.

There was a gully, a flat rock wall, a ledge wide enough for a man to stand on without having to face inward to the cliff. As Uncle Jake had determined, it was of a length and angle such as to afford him good access up nearly two-thirds of the cliff. Beyond this there was nothing as far as each of us in turn could see through the binoculars but a vertical mass of stone as sheer and smooth as anything we had ever seen. Still higher stretched the immensity of that part of the cliff's face that was, as we now saw, colored the distinct green color of corroded copper. We passed the glasses around again and then Uncle Jake slung the coil of rope over his head and one arm and shoulder and Frank Morley and I sat down side by side on boulders still warm from the sun. Uncle Jake turned toward the gully. Frank Morley hunched forward and held the binoculars in both hands, ready to follow Uncle Jake every step of his way up.

We waited. We watched. Uncle Jake paused once and waved, but even without the binoculars we could see that he had no thoughts of us, really, and that all his attention was fixed on the solid rock and empty light of his climb. We did not wave back. Midway up the ledge he stopped suddenly, leaned casually against the grainy rock, folded his arms, allowed himself to stare off toward the horizon and the setting sun.

"Look at that," said Frank Morley, marveling at Uncle Jake and passing me the binoculars, "he's admiring the view!"

I steadied my breath, propped my elbows on my knees, raised the binoculars, and like some spy or hunter, found him, picked out the butt of the Smith & Wesson, the flashing buckle of the cartridge belt, a mechanical pencil clipped into the breast pocket of the windbreaker, an ear, the black hair, the full face caught in the sun. He was lost in the sight of what no one else had ever seen—from that height, from that exact vantage point above a landscape unfit, as he had said, for bird or beast or man. Then he turned and by the way he did so— slowly, with caution—I could see that the ledge had narrowed and that if the dead panorama he had been looking at was spectacular, his actual situation had become all at once precarious.

We waited, following him with the naked eye—the tiny figure rising now in this direction now in that—and then tracking him once again through the thick greenish lenses of the binoculars. I saw the tips of the fingers of a large waxen hand fixed to a crevice, the toe of a boot in a crack. But the images were becoming smaller, less distinct; he was slipping away from us, working his way up as if the fading light itself were gravity and he some small metal speck hopelessly unable to escape its pull.

Frank Morley and I sighed together when Uncle Jake found an un- expectedly wide rift in the rock and entered it, with sudden ease rose upwards hand over hand. Together we agreed on anxious silence when- ever Uncle Jake was suddenly stopped short in his progress. Once, under his breath and shaking his head, Frank Morley murmured that there was certainly no one like Uncle Jake and that we certainly had to give him credit. Once or twice, by mutual accord, Frank Morley and I forced ourselves to forgo the binoculars and to look away altogether from the cliff, the garden of darkening coppery light near the summit, the suddenly sunstruck figure of the struggling climber. With relief we saw someone smoking on the deck of *The Prince of Wales;* we allowed ourselves respite; we scanned the west where the dying light was still a deceptive gold.

From behind and below us came the faint indistinguishable words of Dynamite Pete's voice raised in obvious anger at Al Wells; the dying light was growing impossibly brighter. Together Frank Morley and I noticed that Uncle Jake had lost his coil of rope. Together we frowned.

Silence, suspended light, and what Frank Morley and I both knew yet could not admit: Uncle Jake was not moving. For long and desperate minutes now he had not moved. High above us he was spread-eagle like a little starfish on the face of the cliff.

"He's stuck," said Frank Morley at last. "Look at him."

Frank Morley's hands were trembling when he gave me the glasses, his long crooked arthritic fingers were cold. We stood up. I put the black eyepieces to my eyes and, without changing the focus, looked. In the dim and wavering circles I saw that Uncle Jake was standing on a lip of rock no wider than his own hand and with his arms over his head, his fingers locked in shallow fissures, his chest and cheek to the wall. He was blurred but I saw him, Uncle Jake, four or five hundred feet above us clinging to nothing at all. His size, his musculature, his energy, inventiveness, impulsiveness, stamina, all were bent to a single purpose: not to move, to stay where he was.

Of course I had seen Uncle Jake grief-stricken; I had seen him hopelessly depressed for days on end; I had seen him rallying against disaster, had seen him afraid. But none of his predicaments had ever been as stark and irrefutable as this one. I had never thought to see Uncle Jake actually singled out by the powers that be, as he sometimes called them, for some imminent and unavoidable accident of a fatal kind. Not once since Sissy's death had I ever expected to find myself a mere witness to the event that none of us believed possible in the first place. Uncle Jake was unable to move, Frank Morley and I were unable to act. He was paralyzed, we were helpless. Our helplessness was the hapless measure of his paralysis. How could Uncle Jake not fall? How long could he hang on before he did? What could we do? For the first and only time in my life I feared for Uncle Jake. Yet even then I believed that he would begin to move, find his way, climb down, save himself, give himself back to Frank Morley and me.

"Look what he's done," Frank Morley groaned. "He's turned around. He's got himself turned around. It's the worst thing he could have done. He'll never get down."

I took the glasses and for the last time found Uncle Jake on his deadly perch on the cliff. There he was, just as Frank Morley had said, standing with his back to the rock and his face to the sky, the sea, the brightening light. Somehow he had reversed his position where there was little enough to stand on and nothing, not so much as a clump of mountain grass, to cling to. He had risked everything and had managed to twist himself around without slipping, without falling, only to find himself precisely in the situation every climber dreads and any child, as Frank Morley said, knows enough to avoid. The toes of his boots protruded into space; he had found faint rocky niches for his hands and with stiffened arms was bracing himself and supporting some of his weight. He was looking into the abyss and grinning.

In the suddenly extinguished light we lost him. The shadows came down the golden face of the cliff, the cliff turned a deep and solid blue. Frank Morley and I stood shivering in the thickening night of Rodman Bay, still craning for a last glimpse of Uncle Jake. We said nothing. But we knew he was up there alone, not daring to move so much as a hand or foot, Frank's partner and my father imprisoned on the edge of emptiness and trying, through fierce inactivity, to survive the night.

We made our way back to the dory, back to *The Prince of Wales*, knowing that Uncle Jake would hear the sound of the outboard motor and see the lights on *The Prince of Wales*. Would those lights be enough? Would he stare down at them and think of Frank and me the night long? Or would he think only of the black night and at some late hour finally jump or fall? As Frank Morley said, there wouldn't even be a moon.

The nose of the dory nudged the side of *The Prince of Wales*. We made fast and went below, where we found all three of them already eating the special supper Uncle Jake had ordered, or rather saw Pete and Al Wells hunched at the grease-filmed oval table and the Belly Burglar in the act of standing and snatching up his plate and hastening toward the galley, since it was the Belly Burglar's habit to join the men at the table only when Uncle Jake was absent and to eat apart from the rest of us and on his feet whenever Uncle Jake was aboard.

We took our places in silence. The Belly Burglar rejoined us, quivering, looking from Frank Morley's face to mine, pushing aside his own large portion of the fish Al Wells had caught despite what Uncle Jake had said about these lifeless waters. It was dark around that table; the smell of fish and fat, kerosene and engine oil, sea scum and salt, was stronger than ever.

"Where is he?" asked the Belly Burglar. "What's wrong?"

"Well," said Frank Morley, "he's in trouble."

"What?" said the Belly Burglar quickly. "What trouble?"

"He's got himself into a fix," said Frank Morley. "He can't climb up and he can't climb down."

"A devil of a thing," said Dynamite Pete.

"The worst of it," said Frank Morley, "is that somehow he got his back to the cliff. If he wasn't afraid of heights before, he is now. I just don't know what got into him. A man with all that experience and that mind of his."

"You mean," said Al Wells, "he's going to stay up there all night?"

"Yes," said Frank Morley after a pause, "if we're lucky."

"Then what?" asked Dynamite Pete.

"Well," said Frank Morley, "there's only one way to get him down. As soon as there's light enough you have to go up after him. You have to get him turned around again. Then you have to chop holes for his hands and feet and take hold of him and slowly move each hand and foot for him until you get him to safe ground. Then we'll probably have to carry him to the dory. I've heard of men frozen in fear on mountainsides. You just have to soothe him and do as I've said."

Dynamite Pete and Al Wells looked at each other, despite their enmity, and saying nothing yet making their meaning clear, returned to their food. The poor Belly Burglar could only stare at Frank Morley and wring his hands.

"If Jake were here," said Frank Morley, "he'd say that we have to do all that's humanly possible to rectify a situation as bad as this one. And that's what we'll do. If he can just hang on until daybreak."

Al Wells and Pete remained silent. After a moment, and having left our food untouched, Frank Morley and I climbed back up on deck to wait out the night. Frank Morley lit the pilothouse with every light and lantern that he could and returned with my .30-30 Winchester, which, along with the Four-Hundred-and-Five, was kept on a wooden rack above the charts. Side by side we sat on a damp hatch cover, huddling in blankets against the chill. A cold mist rose off the water, there were no stars. Frank Morley cradled my rifle across his lap and smoked and coughed. Finally he said that he was going to signal to Uncle Jake every hour so that Uncle Jake would know we were keeping our vigil. A rifle shot, said Frank Morley, was a traditional signal and more personal than a blast on the boat's whistle. We waited, then Frank Morley loaded the Winchester, aimed it off our starboard side, and fired. The sound of the shot rolled into the darkness, abruptly disappeared in silence. We listened. Then through the darkness and from the direction in which our bow was pointed there came at last a feeble answering shot.

"He's hanging on," said Frank Morley, and put his arm around my shoulders, gave me a hug. "There's hope. We're going to get him down."

Twice more Frank Morley fired into that black night, and twice more we heard the faint answering report of the Smith & Wesson. Then around midnight he fired his fourth shot, and as long and hard as we listened there was no reply. Valiantly Frank Morley continued to discharge the Winchester throughout that night as cold and menacing as any of the nights that once darkened Rodman Bay in the glacial epoch that had left us only the ridges and cliffs we knew were there but could not see. Valiantly, since there were no replies. Between his fruitless signals, Frank Morley tried for a while to distract us both with stories: about how as a young man newly come to Alaska he had once had to survive for a week on bannocks, which were cakes made of flour and glacial water and baked on a flat rock facing the fire, and how the bannocks were always thickly filled with a goodly number of what looked like the little brown currants that his mother used to bake in his favorite cake. But they were in fact black flies. About how once on Cleary Creek, under a noon sun, amid the rough surroundings of a new mining camp, in the almost unbroken wilderness, he had helped to bury the first white woman—a young miner's wife—ever to cross the last divide in Alaska. Or about the time a prospector he had known was sent a baby's stocking by his young wife still awaiting his return in Massachusetts, and how, when the poor fellow died soon thereafter, he, Frank Morley, and some of his cronies filled the infant's stocking with gold dust and sent it back to the young widowed mother. Then Frank hugged me to him again in the darkness and said that he was beginning to sound lugubrious and that he better stop talking, which he did.

More shots. More shivering. *The Prince of Wales* was creaking and

listing like an old nautical coffin in those glacial waters. At last Frank
Morley and I peered at the cliff that was faintly emerging beyond our
bow in a dawn light as wet and gray as the dissolving mist. The gray
light suffused the entirety of Rodman Bay. It was dawn, the cliff was
once more the solid and clearly visible mass of rock we had not seen
for nearly ten weary hours. Frank Morley took all the time he could
to wipe the lenses of the binoculars with his blue bandanna. He wiped
his face. He glanced once at me—I could smell his tobacco breath on
the sea air—and then raised the binoculars to his eyes.

Finally Frank Morley said, "He's gone. He's not there."

He did not offer me the glasses. I had not the slightest desire to see
for myself the magnified emptiness of that dead cliff. And yet we had
not given up, Frank Morley and I, despite his dismal stories and the
gloom of Rodman Bay and the uselessness of our night-long vigil. We
stood up, threw off our damp blankets, looked at each other. Frank
Morley declared that Uncle Jake was still alive. Injured and in pain
perhaps but still alive. And I believed him.

Frank Morley told me what to stow in the dory—the first-aid kit
and all the blankets and rope I could find and an ax and hatchet and a
bottle of Hudson's Bay rum—and went below and roused out Dynamite Pete and Al Wells, each of whom grumbled that it was not his
turn to work at such a crazy hour. But Frank Morley forced them both
from their bunks and up on deck and into the dory. Billy Densmore
was left behind to listen for the three shots Frank Morley would fire
from shore if we found Uncle Jake still alive as Frank Morley said we
surely would, and then to radio for help, though Billy had never op-
erated our shortwave radiotelephone and, for that matter, had not once
set foot in the pilothouse of *The Prince of Wales* in all the time he had
served on her.

Rodman Bay was a glassy sweep of dark gray light and twisting
tides and configurations of rock so unfamiliar, suddenly, that midway
between *The Prince of Wales* and the pebbly shore, Frank Morley shook
his head, lowered the binoculars, and in a voice barely strong enough
for me to hear above the sound of our outboard motor, said that now
he couldn't even locate the cliff, let alone the spot on it where Uncle
Jake had last been seen. But as I angled the dory against the current we
saw it again—the high sheer mass of rock in this rising light and on
this fateful day topped by what Frank Morley now called, in language
that was strong for him, that infernal green.

We managed to land despite the current and managed again to drag the dory high onto the beach, though now the dory might have been made of iron, it was that heavy and that hard to move out of the water. And no sooner did we set boots to pebbles than the silence and dawning light of Rodman Bay grew inexplicably cold. There was no wind but we were breathing glacial air, were shivering in canvas and woolen clothes that afforded not the slightest protection against it. Frank Morley had a long fit of coughing, half doubled over and bracing himself on the gunnel of the beached dory. Pete and Al Wells swore as I helped Frank Morley to take a swig of the Hudson's Bay rum which convulsed him in one brief frightening fiery spasm but stopped the coughing. Then we divided the equipment—and I knew as well as the others that the ropes and blankets were intended as much for a dead body as for a man still breathing—and arranged ourselves in pairs: Al Wells and Frank Morley who carried one rifle, Dynamite Pete and I who carried the other. We separated and fanned out. We stumbled, bruised ourselves, were simultaneously eager and afraid to find him. We rendezvoused back at the dory, changed partners—my rifle entrusted, after some hesitation on Frank Morley's part, to the placid southerner rather than to the temperamental Pole. Again we separated.

Did we find him crumpled, face down, between boulders? Did we mistake a distant brownish shape of rock and moraine for Uncle Jake? Did we find him skewed, flat on his back with his blue eyes open, and crushed and dead? Did we at last kneel beside him where he lay wedged at the base of the cliff broken, bleeding, but still alive? Even by midday was there one shot fired by either Frank Morley or Al Wells to call the four of us together for the worst that could have happened in the night? Or three shots signaling that he was still alive?

Nothing. No shots fired. No shred of clothing. No Smith & Wesson lying incongruously in that barrenness as evidence of the hand that had weakened in the night and let it fall. Nothing. Not a trace of him. Swallowed up for good in Rodman Bay.

For a third time—winded, perspiring, white-faced—we rendezvoused at the dory. Even Dynamite Pete and Al Wells appeared to understand the gravity of this day. Pete removed his trainman's cap and in both hands twisted it; for once Al's bland face was serious. Frank Morley climbed into the beached dory and sat on one of the wide board seats and rested himself. In silence I once more handed Frank Morley the Hudson's Bay rum and he raised the solacing bottle, wiped his mouth on his sleeve and sighed, then passed the bottle to Pete and Al, who, surprised at this invitation to share fraternally Frank Morley's grief—and by extension mine—drank as he had, wiped their mouths as he had, sighed as wearily as he had sighed. Frank Morley rolled and smoked one cigarette, hunched on the seat of the dory and fighting for breath. It grew colder. We knew that in the vast gray empty light of Rodman Bay we were merely a handful of intruders singled out for insignificance and suffering.

"What now?" asked Dynamite Pete at last.

"Well," said Frank Morley, climbing slowly out of the dory, "we'll give it one more try. We'll go back to where Sunny and I were yesterday. To that gully where Jake started his climb."

And that's where we found him. In single file we followed Frank Morley up the moraine that was like a frozen mash of crushed bones, around rocks as tall as the vanished mastodons for which Rodman Bay was famous, and straight to the mouth of the gully into which Uncle Jake had disappeared.

Before us was the mouth of the gully, the no longer sun-warmed boulders where Frank Morley and I had sat and watched the climber's progress. And there, pressed against a narrow wall of granite, was Uncle Jake. We stopped. We could not approach the tall stiff figure who, except for the way he stood and the look on his face, might have been readying himself this very moment to start his climb.

"Jake," said Frank Morley softly, staring at the obviously living and unharmed object of our search.

"Uncle Jake," I said, and caught hold of Frank Morley's arm.

"Christ bejesus," said Dynamite Pete, "what's wrong with him?"

"Some kind of shock," said Al Wells.

"Crazy," said Dynamite Pete. "Crazy from this damn place. Twenty damn hours in this crazy place."

"No," said Frank Morley quietly. "He's afraid."

"Petrified, you mean," said Dynamite Pete.

Still we waited. Even I was unable to move, to cross the short distance separating the four of us from my father. Could the legendary Uncle Jake, the Uncle Jake I loved, the man who had never in his life been daunted by anything, have come to this? He was drawn to his full height and was pressing himself from the back of his head to the heels of his boots to the granite wall. His fingers were spread, he was pushing the palms and fingers of both hands against the stone. Every muscle of his great body was contracted; he appeared to be sinking backwards into the granite wall, attempting to fossilize his living remains with all the signs of former life imprinted or buried

in the vast crust of Rodman Bay. His eyes were wide, unseeing. The
holster, still hanging from the cartridge belt around his waist, was
empty.

"What now?" asked Dynamite Pete. "Do we rush him and wrap him
in the damn blankets and tie him up and carry him down to the damn
dory? Not me. It's no job for me. Damn right."

"He's just afraid," said Frank Morley. "He was afraid of falling up
there on the cliff and he still is. But he can walk. He'll walk down to
the dory with Sunny and me."

"Tie him up," said Dynamite Pete. "Damn right."

"Pete," said Frank Morley patiently, "you and Al go back to the
dory and wait for us. We'll be along."

We gave them time to be out of sight and out of earshot, Frank
Morley and I, and then slowly and gently we approached Uncle Jake.
His eyes were wild, he stood as if still on the edge of the six-hundred-
foot abyss in the night. We spoke to him, touched him, gently unstuck
his hands from the rock. Frank Morley took hold of his left arm, I his
right, and though at first he refused to take so much as a step, at last
he came away from the rock wall and between us began to shuffle as
best he could, woodenly, mechanically, all the way down to the beach
and the waiting dory.

The gray and icy light was fading by the time we reached the dory
and maneuvered Uncle Jake until he was seated—still speechless, staring, white-faced—on the dory's center seat, his massive chest and back
draped in one of the khaki-colored blankets.

"You mean," said Dynamite Pete, "we're going to drag this damn
dory into the water with him in it? When we could hardly move the
damn thing when it was empty?"

No one spoke and despite Dynamite Pete we dragged Uncle Jake
like some stunned god down the beach and into the now black and
choppy water so cold it might have been laced with schools of tiny
prehistoric fish turned to ice. The four of us waded up to our shins in
that water, then climbed into the dory. The outboard motor popped
and puffed, we fought the current, we reached *The Prince of Wales* in
the last light. Frank Morley tossed a line to the Belly Burglar. We made
fast.

"Frank," said the Belly Burglar, rubbing his greasy little fat person
in relief, devotion, agitation, "he's alive. . . . He didn't fall."

"How the hell nobody knows," said Dynamite Pete.

Within a mere half-hour, the smells of night and sea rising around us, Uncle Jake lay stretched out flat on his back in his narrow bunk beneath four blankets drawn up to his chin, silently attended by Frank Morley and me. Al Wells and Dynamite Pete were laughing and wolfing down their beans and bacon and calling for the Belly Burglar to join them.

Some time in the middle of that night, when *The Prince of Wales* was silent except for the usual faint noises on an anchored boat at night and except for the snoring of the sleeping trio that was the ship's crew and cook, Frank Morley, who had been sitting in the dark with me on a small upended wooden crate now empty of its tins of bully beef, touched my shoulder once and, in a low voice, said that he had better go up and spend the rest of the night on the army cot where Uncle Jake always slept whenever *The Prince of Wales* was under way. There should always be someone in the pilothouse, even when we were anchored safely, which, as far as he knew, we were.

Then I was alone with Uncle Jake.

He was not asleep—I needed no more than his open eyes to tell me as much—and for all those remaining hours of darkness he was not spared his terror in the release of the sleep he needed. His bunk was narrow but I sat on the edge beside him, every now and again adjusting the blankets, though he did not once move in the course of this my second vigil.

There was a small porthole above the bunk, and without moon, without stars, still a sinister shade of light came to us through that small thick disk of translucent glass in its circle of tarnished brass. I could see the shape of Uncle Jake, the long face, the alertness of the unmoving eyes. Every now and again I adjusted the blankets, felt with a cold hand the steadily beating heart lodged deep in his chest, and wondered if he would ever move or talk again. I wished we had been able to make him comfortable, had at least been able to remove his boots. But Frank Morley had advised against it, saying that it was best to leave him as little disturbed as possible. So there lay Uncle Jake like one of the living dead yet dressed for pressing onward confidently, gallantly, and with all his egotistical force of innocence. At some point I remembered—as Sitka Charley had once told me—how Indians used to wish each other well in the old days: May your totem pole stand long in the land, and may the smoke of your camp rise always. I felt again for Uncle Jake's heart still beating in the depths of his fear. Yet even as I did so, I experienced my first premonition that the smoke would not always rise from Uncle Jake's camp.

Shadow after shadow disappeared. I saw the quick rising and falling of the great chest, saw the gray stubble—at sixty Uncle Jake's hair was still as black as polished coal but his beard, whenever he allowed it to grow to any length, was gray—and saw the painful look in his still-staring eyes. It was dawn. I knew that in only minutes Frank Morley would return to us with Uncle Jake's first cup of coffee. We would raise my father's head and shoulders and force him to take at least a sip of the coffee.

In only minutes Frank Morley did in fact return to us. But without the coffee. Rain had begun to beat down on *The Prince of Wales* like nailheads, so loudly that it all but obliterated the snoring of our still-sleeping cook and crew.

"Jake," said Frank Morley, and ignored my obvious pleasure at seeing him. But why? What was wrong? Why was Frank Morley's face now, when the danger was past, suddenly the color of the rain-sodden ashes of a dead fire? Why was he dressed only in his union suit and woolen trousers—braces dangling—and the hastily donned rubber boots? Why the palsy he was trying to control? Why the eyes more frightened than Uncle Jake's? Why the authority and strength he was trying to summon to his ashen face? And why the wetness in his frightened eyes?

"Jake," said Frank Morley softly, leaning so that Uncle Jake's staring eyes could not avoid Frank Morley's eyes, "I've got some bad news."

Uncle Jake did not move. Frank Morley leaned closer and rested a long thin hand on his shoulder. I thought I could hear barnacles growing in a terrible garden underwater on our hull and hear the cry of a timber wolf far out at sea.

"It's Rex," said Frank Morley, lowering his face still closer to Uncle Jake's. "He's dead, partner. The message just came through from Juneau. He crashed last night on his way to Haines with three passengers. Got completely turned around, partner, and crashed. Rex Ainsworth, right here. Right up in Rainy Pass. At least that's what the Coast Guard thinks. They want us to go up there, Jake. And find them."

I did not expect Uncle Jake to stir, to comprehend Frank Morley's news. How could he? Not even the death of the bush pilot he most admired could find its way to the old Jake through the new Jake's life-in-death paralysis. But if Frank Morley's eyes were wet, why not mine? At fourteen I had my feelings, concealed or not. So why did I not feel grief when I heard what Frank Morley said? Perhaps because Rex's death demanded more than grief. How could ordinary grief be worthy of thousands upon thousands of air miles flown through the Alaskan dream? Or perhaps it was simply that the grief I now felt because of Rex Ainsworth demanded not an ordinary form of expression but some other—some action that would not be recognized as grief at all.

"Partner," Frank Morley said in his gentlest and saddest voice, "they want us to find the wreckage and bring out the bodies. But it can't be done without you. Anyhow, partner, I'll be back."

Again I was alone with Uncle Jake and now alone with Rex as well—dead Rex—in my mind. In 1940 in Alaska, the sound of a single-engined plane heard far from any community of men and women was still unlike that sound heard anywhere else in the world. I heard Rex passing overhead, I saw the yellow Fairchild disappearing into the Alaska of Rex's own intelligence. But why, actually, had we not heard the crash? If it had occurred during my dark hours spent with Uncle Jake, and during Frank Morley's wakeful hours in the pilothouse, and if Rex had crashed up in Rainy Pass, four or five miles at most from *The Prince of Wales,* why had we not heard that loud and awful sound in the night?

The creaking of *The Prince of Wales.* The gray reluctant light of dawn. And still only Uncle Jake and Frank Morley and I were awake and only Frank Morley and I, as far as I knew, were aware of the Coast Guard message that paired these two friends of ten years standing—Uncle Jake and Rex—so that the paralysis of the one was the mirror in which the death of the other shone. Here, I thought, was the end of two adventurers, and an end for those last passengers who had trusted Rex, and an end of sorts for those two of us more loyal than ever to the now unrecognizable Uncle Jake.

I did not know how long Frank Morley would leave us alone or why. I did not know when Billy Densmore would light the galley stove. I did not know what we could do or who among us could climb to the Fairchild or when we would ever get up steam and escape on *The Prince of Wales* from Rodman Bay and Rainy Pass. I thought I heard Frank Morley moving about in the pilothouse without his partner, without a plan, unable to smoke or wipe his eyes, an Alaskan of nearly fifty years sick with grief and, as he told me later, stumped.

Then I heard the voice.

"Sunny," said Uncle Jake so weakly, hoarsely, unexpectedly that I could not believe that he had spoken aloud my name. I shivered, leaned over him as Frank had done, stared into his still-unseeing eyes.

"Sunny," he said again, as if his mouth were filled with silt. I leaned closer, feeling one of his powerful forearms beneath the blankets, waiting for him to tell me what Frank should do.

"Sunny," he said, regaining the voice that was still not quite his own and the first traces of animation in his face, "it was the darnedest thing. One moment I was in my glory climbing up that ledge of white spar—that's what it was, white spar, as it turned out—as nimbly as I used to climb to the crow's nest on the old *Powhatan,* and then I was just standing still with no way to continue climbing, nothing to do. It took me about an hour to get up there, and of course I knew that you and Frank were watching me in the glasses, so when it looked as if I could go no farther, I was mainly worried that you and Frank would worry about me. But do you know, Sunny, that even then the thing that was uppermost in my mind was the fact that a lot of that white spar was covered with moss. It wasn't just bare rock as I had thought. It was moss-covered, and for the first time in my life I was tickled pink that I had been proven wrong.

"Well," he continued, rolling toward me and propping himself on an elbow, "then I got the idea that danger or no danger I wanted more than anything to see the whole uncharted reach of Rodman Bay from where I was, stuck up on the face of that cliff. It was the chance of a lifetime and I couldn't let it go. That's when I turned around. I don't know how I did it, but I did. It took a lot of patience and breath-holding and inching movements for a man my size, but finally there I was, back to the cliff and all of Rodman Bay stretched at my feet. It looked as if the night were rising up out of that black water instead of descending as it should have from the heavens. I've never seen anything like it, Sunny. Never."

He paused. He licked his lips. Blue was showing again in his enlarged and frozen eyes. I thought that now he was beginning to see me through his sightless stare. He cleared his throat. He worked his eyebrows up and down. And smiling? Beginning to smile as he usually did in the face of danger, disaster, disillusionment? I thought he was.

"Well," he said, "that's when I found out that I couldn't descend without eyes in my toes. I knew that if I could turn myself around a second time, a doubly difficult feat under the circumstances, and if I could ascend a mere thirty yards, which I thought impossible, I might be able to lower myself down a draw by the assistance of a scattering of alder bushes, which until that moment I hadn't seen and hadn't believed could even grow in Rodman Bay. By then it was dark. And by then the glamour and purpose had just dropped out of the whole enterprise, I can tell you.

"I don't remember how I got myself turned around again, but I did. And I don't remember how, with only memory to guide me and little else, I did ascend the thirty yards to the draw I'd seen, only to discover a precipice—it was just space I somehow detected in the dark, Sunny—instead of a way down. It had taken me another hour to get there, and all for naught. Of course I had already lost my coil of rope anyway, as you and Frank must have seen. Then through the darkness I heard the report of a rifle, and I knew that old Frank was down there trying, as I might have known he would, to bolster my spirits. So I clung to the precipice with one hand, drew your Smith & Wesson with the other, and managed to get off a reassuring shot to Frank. If I had fired first he would have thought I was calling for help, and of course there was no way by then that help could have been had. It was then that I saw the lights on *The Prince of Wales*. Good old Frank.

"Well, there was only one slim chance left, which was to try for the top of the spur, though I couldn't see it and didn't know where it was. It was getting cold too, I can tell you that. Anyhow, no living man could have clung to the face of that precipice a minute if it had not been for the moss that was rooted like tufts of hair in those small crevices. I was beginning to feel like a blindfolded lizard, Sunny, and a darn fool as well. I don't know what I would have done if Frank hadn't fired his second shot right then, which I answered with a shot intended as a salute to my old partner who was down there waiting the whole thing out with me.

"Somehow—don't ask me how, Sunny—I climbed for another hour. And will you believe it? After all I'd been through, nonetheless I couldn't resist taking a look at those little glimmering lights of *The Prince of Wales*. That's when it came over me, the sickest feeling I've ever known in my life. I don't know why it chose that moment, but it did. Suddenly I was afraid. I was afraid of being up there, and of falling. At least I knew I didn't want to jump. At least I had that much in my favor.

"Well, the powers that be must have changed their minds and hauled me on their invisible lines to within about twelve feet of the summit, where they left me to my own devices. I heard a rifle shot, I fired back, and darned if I didn't drop the Smith & Wesson. I just couldn't return it to the holster—my hand was that numb—and I lost it. I listened but I never heard it hit anything as it fell, never heard it land. Just silence and the climbing sickness verging on pure dread, which was pretty irrational of me as I knew even then.

"I got out my pocketknife. I cut niches for fingers and toe holds. I nerved myself, if you could call it that, and then climbed again, drawing myself up the rock which, under the pressure of each departing foot of mine, crumbled, and in dreadful chunks fell away into space. There I was, Sunny, clinging to my niches and trying to raise each foot before it was too late, with hope and life above me and sure death a thousand feet below. I heard Frank's shots once in a while, but—and I hate to confess it—they no longer mattered.

"There was an alder to hang on to, a narrow shelf, another precipice below, and a jagged wall above. I rubbed my way along that wall, I reached a ridge, descended along another spur—in the darkness, swinging from one alder to another and thinking of only one thing: that no other man could have done what I was doing, if I lived to tell the tale.

"I extricated myself. I climbed up, climbed down. I couldn't see. My sweat was cold. It came to me that I would not be spared, never live to tell this tale. And then I could move no more. I had calculated that I had about two hundred feet left to descend but I could not do it. Not for the life of me, Sunny. There I was, standing with the soles of my boots on something solid and my back to the rock. I braced myself against that rock and waited to fall. I was empty-headed. I thought of nothing, no one. Not even Mother.

"The funny thing is that with the first light—I sensed that gray light rather than saw it—and even with the first sounds of poor Frank's voice, still I did not know I was down.

"But I know it now. And I know something else: that I'll never again climb anything higher than a chair for love or money."

He paused, propped on his elbow and clearly looking at me. He tried to laugh, this large weather-beaten man who might have been trying to rise from the deathbed of his narrow bunk.

"Well, Sunny," he said, "are you glad to have your old father back?"

Before I could answer, before I could kiss his cheek, suddenly he fell back, an exhausted and still-frightened man. But I was glad to have him back. So glad in fact that the occasional strange sensations of dismay I had felt while he talked were buried, at least for the time being, in my adoration of this heroic man.

Then Frank Morley stuck his head in the cabin doorway.

"Frank," said Uncle Jake, again without moving, without turning his head, "we're going after them."

"But Jake," said Frank Morley quickly and obviously delighted at the mere sound of his partner's voice, "you know we couldn't risk

climbing up into Rainy Pass without you to lead the way and to supervise the... work to be done up there."

"Don't worry," said Uncle Jake. "I'll lead the way."

"But Jake," said Frank Morley, "you've been in shock for about
twenty-four hours. You nearly died. And it was the height that did it.
We both know that."

"Frank," said Uncle Jake, "Rainy Pass may be steep but it's a pass,
not a cliff. That's the point: a pass between cliffs but not a cliff itself."

Frank Morley waited.

"Here's what you do," said Uncle Jake. "Radio to Juneau that we're
on our way. Tell them to send a plane down here to fly the bodies back
to Juneau. Tell Pete and A. L. and the Belly Burglar what's happened
and what we're going to do. Tell Pete he has to stay down here aboard
The Prince of Wales. It's going to be strenuous, Frank, but I need you
with me.

"Now, Sunny," he said, laughing and hauling himself once more
onto an elbow, "give me a hand and help me out of here. No more
sick bay for Uncle Jake."

Voices. Commotion. Billy Densmore and pots and pans and pot lids
and ladles. A short elated blast, for some reason, on the whistle of *The
Prince of Wales*.

Frank Morley returned, and while I waited out in the corridor he
helped Uncle Jake to shave, wash off, get himself into a fresh shirt and
fresh pair of pants. Then we helped him to the oval table, where he
sat alone—Billy forbade anyone but Uncle Jake to sit at his, Billy's,
table that morning—and watched Billy Densmore pile the fish and
biscuits and baked beans and half a dozen fried eggs in dishes and bowls
around Uncle Jake, who sat tall at the otherwise empty table and ate
his fill and once more restored himself to life.

Then blankets. Ropes. Some old canvas tarps. And the medicine
chest. Axes. Crowbars. One of the packboards loaded with food and
drink just in case we needed to stay up there longer than Uncle Jake
had estimated that we would.

At the last minute, with Al Wells and Frank Morley already in their
places in the loaded dory and Pete and Billy Densmore standing by to
see us off, at this very moment, at the height of readiness in a cold
drizzle, Uncle Jake suddenly seized my arm as I was starting over the
side for the dory.

"Sunny," he said, frowning and working his eyebrows, "do you think... or wouldn't it be better if you... I mean Pete and Bill could use a third hand aboard. That is, maybe what we're going to see up there and what we're going to have to do just isn't the thing for a... You know that Sissy wouldn't allow it if she were here. You have to draw the line somewhere, she'd say."

Which was the closest that Uncle Jake ever came openly to calling me a girl, and trying to protect me, as a girl, from the horrors intended only for the male. When I didn't answer he looked down at me, and, reassured that for all intents and purposes I was still a boy as he had insisted all along, he smiled and gave me a solemn manly nod. I climbed down into the dory and that was that. My gender, like the great coppery-green discoloration on the face of the cliff that had taken so firm a hold on Uncle Jake's fancy, was not mentioned again.

We beached the dory. We loaded ourselves with the gear that already had the smell and texture and color of dried blood. We followed Uncle Jake into the trickling narrow creek bed that he assumed would take us straight to the top of Rainy Pass. The drizzle turned to heavy rain. On either side of us the sheer walls were wet and glistening and dark. Al Wells's cheerfully expressed complaints began to echo up and down our ascent toward the head of Rainy Pass. Uncle Jake tried to adjust our pace to the labored breathing of his partner.

The pack straps burned our shoulders. The pitch of the creek bed steepened. The rain slackened and was replaced by thin drifts of fog. The creek water sloshed around our boots. Uncle Jake called for a brief halt and rest. We were bareheaded, except for Frank Morley, and wet and colorless except for the checks that patterned our woolen shirts: black and red for Uncle Jake, black and green for Al Wells, black and blue for Frank Morley, green and red for me.

"It won't be long now, Frank," said Uncle Jake, as once more we shouldered our packs and started off.

Then we came to the precipice.

We turned a sudden sharp bend in the narrow pass, at an altitude Uncle Jake estimated at two thousand feet, and there it was. The precipice. A narrow vertical strip of rock that was a good seventy feet high and connected the solid rock facings on either side. The water that had been lubricating our trail, as Uncle Jake had jokingly said, had its source from some invisible mouth at the base of the precipice.

A dead end. Stopped in our tracks three hours from *The Prince of Wales*.

"You know," said Al Wells agreeably, "this crew does a lot of work for nothing."

"Jake," said Frank Morley, wheezing and stooping over and resting his hands on his knees, "it looks as if it can't be done. I know what it means to you, but it can't be done."

"Frank," said Uncle Jake, "there's nothing to it. Why, I just shimmy up that precipice and toss down a rope for Sunny and A. L. You just wait right here to receive... what we lower down."

"Mr. Deauville," said Al Wells, "I'll do practically anything for anyone I work for. And you won't find a more even-tempered man than me, as you know. But Al Wells is not going to break his neck climbing up that rock for nothing but four dead bodies. No, sir. Those dead bodies are just going to have to stay where they are—if they're even there at all—as far as Al Wells is concerned. And while we're at it, I'll tell you something else. No offense intended. But this whole thing is gruesome. Plain gruesome. And no place for a young person. Least of all a girl."

Silence. Rain. Uncle Jake as tall and blackly lit and wet as the high rocks that hemmed us in.

"Besides, partner," said Frank Morley on the only other occasion when he dared to approach outright disloyalty, "you're afraid of heights. You suffered, Jake. If you so much as touch that rock it's going to hit you again: fear of heights. And if you do manage to climb halfway up that precipice and get stuck again, then what? Don't do it. This is a job for the Coast Guard."

We waited. In that wet silence I knew suddenly what Uncle Jake was thinking and who he was thinking of: me. He kept his composure, accepted Al Wells's shocking opinion without anger, as if those words had not been spoken, was careful not to challenge the feelings and logic of his worried partner. He meant to climb, I understood, and with me.

"Sunny," he said, festooning his person with two coils of rope—one around his waist and the other over his head and shoulder—"after I get to the top I'll drop one of these lines down to you. Then you tie the line around your waist, lean back with your feet against the base of the rock, and start walking, so to speak, up the precipice. I'll haul you up. I'll hang on to my end of the rope as if it were looped ten times around a rock or tied to an alder. That solid. That safe. It's easy, Sunny. We'll do the job together."

He smiled, turned away from us, stood at the base of the precipice, raised his head slowly, scanning the entire seventy feet from bottom to top, then drew his pocketknife, opened it, readied himself to cut his niches. Before he began, he glanced once at us over his shoulder and for that one instant there flickered across the clear features of his face the look of terror that had masked him for so many hours only the day before. He wavered. He hated heights, his expression said. He was afraid.

But he turned back to the precipice and with no further hesitation cut his niches, found his crevices and crannies, for forty-five minutes by Frank Morley's railroad watch, scaled those seventy feet without one false move and without looking either up or down. Eyes in his toes, I thought. Unfailing strength. But all of us down below knew what that effort had cost him.

"Sunny!" he called, and there he was, not lying prone at the top of the precipice and peering cautiously over its lip, but standing up there in full view and as precariously close to the edge as any man could get without stepping off. "Sunny!" he called down to me, "here's the rope," and down it swished, my lifeline to Uncle Jake. "All right now," he called, "up you come!"

I tied the rope, I followed Uncle Jake's instructions. Holding on to the rope, attempting to keep the soles of my boots flat to the vertical stone, and leaning back and moving my feet slowly, one after the other, I felt Uncle Jake on the other end of the rope—it was dizzying, but I was not afraid. I was leaning back and looking upwards toward the top of the precipice and into the gray wet sky above us; I swayed, I moved with no feeling of motion, I saw the little niches he had cut into the rock; I knew that I was high in the air and that this effort to obey Uncle Jake—to be worthy, to join him at the top of the precipice that only he and I had climbed—was a risk of the most serious sort and my first. But I was not afraid. I was in my father's hands.

When I swung over the top he caught me, helped me to my feet, laughed, and held me to him with both his arms. Our clothes were wet, the fog was thickening, we were alone on a long narrow walled-in plateau at the highest point of Rainy Pass. Boulders. Crags. Rivulets of icy water. More of the unexpected alders. The strange dignity of what was obviously a never-changing gloom.

"Frank," Uncle Jake called down at last, "we're going to see if we can find them. If we do, I'll lower a rope so we can haul up what we'll need."

We set off, Uncle Jake and I, and there was nothing for us but silence, rain we didn't feel, gloom. Even before we discovered the first signs of the crash, Uncle Jake and I knew that we would find them. The Fairchild and its occupants were ours alone to find. We hadn't walked a hundred yards when we discovered a scrap of yellow fabric fluttering from an alder twig. We said nothing and continued on. A leather glove— man's or woman's we could not tell—lay at our feet. Then one of the yellow doors of the Fairchild, undamaged and leaning against the sheer rock wall.

We made our way around a boulder and saw it: the yellow Fairchild silent, partially intact, partially crushed, the wreckage like a piece of statuary that would remain there among the rock forever. It was canted slightly to one side, its tail raised, the floats still attached. Even from where we stood, Uncle Jake and I could see that the blackened engine was permanently fused to the high black slab of rock that it had struck. And just as we had found one detached door propped against the sheer stone wall, now we saw that the wooden propeller had somehow become separated from the engine before the nose of the plane had struck the eternally unyielding rock and now stood propped upright against the side of the fuselage. It was as if we had not been the first to discover the crash, as if another before us had done his humble best to restore what order he could to the scene.

The smell of high-octane fuel was still heavy on the air. Through the shattered windows we could see dark shapes, hunched and fea- tureless figures, pilot and at least one passenger shrouded in the aura of the flight that would never end, was already over.

"Sunny," said Uncle Jake quietly, "we won't approach any closer for now. We'll go back to the precipice and tell poor Frank we've found them. You'll help me haul up the gear we need."

When we reached the edge of the seventy-foot drop, Uncle Jake leaned over, spoke Frank Morley's name, and lowered one of our ropes. Nothing more was needed. Frank Morley understood. Together Uncle Jake and I pulled up our rope four times until we had collected around us more rope, four tarps, the ax, the crowbar, which we carried back to the wreck.

"Sunny," said Uncle Jake at last, "I want you to stand right where you are. I don't want you to go any closer. Understand? I'll remove them. I'll rope them up in the tarps. Then you can help me drag them back to the edge of the cliff and lower them down."

But when he reached for the ax I reached for the crowbar, and he made no attempt to stop me.

Slowly. Silently. Step by step. As if we had no business intruding, no business being here, no business touching any part of it. With the toe of his boot Uncle Jake nudged aside a newish-looking deerskin purse and then, half visible in its tissue wrappings that had been torn apart, an eight-inch ivory walrus that might have come straight from the Curio Shoppe in Juneau. There we were, standing in the wet darkness under the yellow wing. Forcing ourselves to look inside the cabin of the Fairchild. Shadows. Splinters of glass that had been the windshield glimmering brightly like specks of mica everywhere in that dark cabin.

"Sunny," said Uncle Jake, staring at the business-suited figure strapped in his harness at the dead controls, "there he is. There's Rex. But... don't look at him. Don't look.... There's something wrong—Good Lord, what have they done to Rex?"

We cut away the hard wet yellow fabric of half the cabin, we chopped away half the tubular framework of the fuselage. We used the crowbar to open up the cabin. The Coast Guard message had reported that there were four persons lost in the Fairchild. But Uncle Jake and I found only two.

"Where are they?" asked Uncle Jake, climbing again inside the wreckage, coming back to me, sending me in one direction while he searched in another. We spent as much time as we could afford to, looking for the missing pair, and found nothing, no article of clothing to add to the glove, nothing. The seats in which they should have died—the one beside Rex and the one beside the figure behind him—were empty. The webbed belts that should have held the missing pair in place were instead merely gone. We could not find them or any evidence that they had ever existed.

"We'll have to give up," said Uncle Jake. "The fellow at the Coast Guard station in Juneau must have made a mistake. But it's darn strange, Sunny. And isn't it strange that she never burned? A crash like this one and the Fairchild didn't go up in flames? I wish it had, I can tell you."

Then we had no alternative but to remove Rex Ainsworth's body and the body of the passenger who had flown behind him and who proved, as soon as we commenced our work, to have been a woman. We laid their blanketed figures, still frozen in the sitting positions in which they had died, a good distance from the Fairchild and then wrapped them each in a tarp and bound them at ankles, knees, waist, chest, and neck with rope. We were able to carry the woman back to the edge of the seventy-foot drop but Rex was so heavy that we could do nothing but, using two short lengths of line, drag him to join the body of the person who, said Uncle Jake in a quiet and bitter tone, had been Rex's last companion and a female at that.

White faces staring up at ours. Uncle Jake and I peering down at them. Uncle Jake and I preparing to lower the bodies. Attaching the long ropes. Sitting and bracing ourselves at the edge of the drop. Nudging first one body over the side and, together, playing out the rope and feeling the lumpy bundle swinging, bumping, descending in uneasy haste to Frank Morley and Al Wells. Then doing the same with the other. First the woman and then Rex Ainsworth.

"Frank," called Uncle Jake, standing at the edge of the drop and wiping his face on his sleeve, "we're finished. We're coming down."

Uncle Jake turned to me, and suddenly all his dark mood and shattered hopes—he had expected, actually, to find Rex Ainsworth still alive—were gone, as if once the corpses were out of sight he and I were once again alone together in the privileged aura of special feeling that was always ours.

"Sunny," he said, smiling and proud of me, I knew, for my part in the difficult business that we had just completed, "going down a precipice is very different from climbing it. The only proper way to go down is by what the mountain climbers call rappeling. We'll use two ropes. One of them we'll tie to this alder here, and this is the rope you'll use for your rappeling. You'll pass the rope under your thigh, raise it up your back, and draw it across your opposite shoulder and down your chest. The idea is that you push yourself off from the rock, let the rope slide through your fist so that when the soles of your boots touch the rock you'll have descended five or six feet or so. You have to trust yourself, Sunny. It's not easy but you'll get the hang of it soon enough. Push out, fall, slow your descent by tightening your hold on the rope, swing off again, drop down, slow your descent, push out and fall. That's how you'll do it. With just one hand and a good sense of rhythm. As for the other rope, that one we'll tie around your waist. I'll hold the end of it and play it out while keeping it taut as you go down. That way if you happen to let go of the rappeling rope—which of course you won't—I'll be hanging on to the safety rope to stop your fall so you can collect yourself and start rappeling down again. Do you understand?"

I nodded, we prepared the coils of rope, Uncle Jake knotted the safety rope around my waist, I got myself tangled, as it seemed to me, in the crisscrossing of the rappeling rope, and told Uncle Jake that I was ready. If he meant all this to obliterate the wreck of the Fairchild and to rid my mind entirely of the scene of the crash, he couldn't have been more successful. I thought of nothing but seventy vertical feet of rock and free falling.

"Frank," called Uncle Jake, "Sunny's coming down. She wants a big hug when she reaches the bottom!"

I eased myself over the edge of the precipice, leaned back—into nothingness—and quickly, before I could think, lessened my tight one-handed hold on the rappeling rope and, eyes wide and body cold, flung myself outward and, with sudden exhilaration, made my first arc, fell freely and, like a parachutist remembering to pull the ripcord, squeezed the rope rushing through my closed fist with exactly the tension needed to slow my fall and, briefly, to make contact between the rock and the soles of my boots and, with hardly a pause, to push off again and drop again through space. Down I went. I felt the cold air, with each momentary impact of feet to rock knew the joy of relief, with each submission of myself to space felt the joy of what I knew was groundless fear. The wet sky moved above me. I was the best rappeling pupil—an expert in her first lesson—that Uncle Jake would ever have.

Then in mid-descent something changed. The safety rope. In the midst of my pleasure and concentration I felt that something was different, saw the safety rope dangling loosely beside me, felt my waist suddenly ungirthed. The knot, I realized, had become untied. There was nothing to hold me except my left fist on the rappeling rope. If for even an instant I entertained fear and its attendant confusion, if I lost control of myself and grabbed for the rappeling rope with both hands, if I disturbed in any way the rhythm Uncle Jake had told me to maintain, then I would not be able to hold myself aloft for any more than a minute at most, would lose even the rappeling rope, and plunge down. Now there was no Uncle Jake to save me. Nothing.

But then by willpower, good luck, and the pleasure I was actually taking in my descent, with a sort of blink of the mind's eye, I induced in myself instant amnesia, forgot my father and the other rope, continued down and into Frank Morley's waiting arms.

"I saw what happened," he said softly and wrapped me in the comforting tobacco smell of all the bars and camps and log roadhouses that had ever existed here and there, along rivers and in snowbound passes, in Alaska. Even as I pressed against Frank Morley I saw, to one side, the two tarp-shrouded bodies bent and lying together in the icy water trickling from its secret source beneath the precipice and sloshing around the boots of all four of us.

After a long pause, Uncle Jake appeared in an oddly kneeling position at the edge of the precipice.

"Sunny," he called, "are you all right?"

"She's all right," Frank Morley called up to him.

A still longer pause. Uncle Jake rappeling down in slow motion, a large figure looking, as he undertook each arc, like someone jumping off a bridge. After the first sight of him up there with his rope and his fear, I could not bear to look.

Then he was down.

"Sunny," he said, face white and great frame trembling, "can you imagine what I went through when I felt your safety rope go slack? Why, one minute all was well and I'd never been so proud of you, and in the next instant I felt the tension, all of it, go out of that darn rope. Can you imagine? There I was, knowing that there was nothing at all to prevent your death if, as any beginner might be expected to do, you lost your nerve. And my fault. All my fault. That darn knot, I thought, sitting up there alone and not even daring to look over the edge to see how you were doing. All's I could think of was that darn knot and how I'd tied it wrong or carelessly—your own father, Sunny, and no better man with knots in all Alaska—and how I wanted to have you back up beside me and to have just one more chance—one more—to tie that rope around your waist. Securely. You'll never know, Sunny. But it was torture."

Hanging heads. Hands on chins. Eyes skyward. The corpses soaking up the icy waters. Silence.

"Jake," said Frank Morley gently, "Sunny's the hero. We all understand how you felt. But Sunny managed and that's the important thing."

"I know that, Frank," said Uncle Jake despondently. "You don't need to tell me."

"Well, cheer up then," said Frank Morley. "We've done what we set out to do. And no one was hurt or worse. So come on, partner, we've got to carry these... bodies... down to the beach."

Which is what we did. Uncle Jake held the upper portion of Rex Ainsworth's body, Al Wells the lower; Dynamite Pete hefted the woman's head and shoulders, Frank Morley and I struggled along, out of step with each other and attempting to maintain our grips on her knees and ankles. She was light, and I could have carried her alone with Pete. But we knew that all four of us had a part to play in this last stage of the journey, and neither Frank Morley nor I was willing to trail along uselessly behind this silent stumbling cortege. The drizzle turned back to rain. The fog came down.

We arrived at the beach at 4 P.M. according to Frank Morley's watch, and we had hardly shoved the dory into the water and loaded the bodies into the bottom of it when we heard the engine of an approaching and then circling plane.

"There's timing for you," said Frank Morley.

"But she'll never be able to land," said Uncle Jake. "Not in this soup."

Suddenly the sound of the engine was closer, louder, the plane flying just above our heads, or so it seemed, and swooping down out of Rainy Pass as though the Fairchild we had abandoned for good had come to life and there had been no fatal accident after all.

"Hey," said Al Wells, as out of the fog and not a hundred feet above us the aircraft sent from Juneau came into view, "what kind of plane is that? It's got no floats!"

"Good Lord," said Uncle Jake, "Chippy Smith!"

"It's a flying boat," said Frank Morley to Al Wells. "An old one."

"A time like this," said Uncle Jake, "and they send us Chippy Smith."

"Better than nothing, partner," said Frank Morley.

"Why him?" said Uncle Jake in tones of grief and anger painful for even Al Wells to hear. "Why him, Frank? Don't you see? It ought to be Rex at the controls of that plane and that darn Chippy Smith lying dead in this dory. Chippy's had it coming to him all his life. Not Rex, Frank. Not Rex."

The flying boat made a circle so low and steep and careless that for a moment it looked as if one of its wingtips must catch in the choppy waters and bring the flying boat to an end as final as the Fairchild's end. We expected to see the old flying boat snag on a frothy crest, turn half a dozen cartwheels, and shatter and catch fire and, before our eyes, burn and sink in those freezing waters. Instead it landed, plumed in spray and the familiar bright tongues of flame shooting from its engine nacelle. The engine died, then started up again. The plane turned, aimed toward the shore, drifted to a stop within easy calling distance from where we stood on the beach. Its hatch opened. Chippy Smith climbed out and, standing on the bow of the flying boat, dropped over the side an anchor that would hold the plane in place until we could transfer

our cargo from the dory to the little cabin that would reek, as Uncle
Jake and I both knew, with beer or perhaps on this occasion, whiskey.

Uncle Jake proposed that he and I ferry the bodies to the flying boat.
No one objected. We pushed off, I started the outboard motor, mis-
erably we reached Chippy Smith's old plane and made fast. Chippy,
we saw at once, was not his usual laughing easygoing prankish self.
He was, we saw, half drunk. More than half drunk.

He stood in his shirtsleeves, despite the weather, visible from the
waist up in the open hatchway and smelling, as Uncle Jake said later,
like a brewery flooded with its own undistilled liquors. The plane and
the dory rocked together. The three of us were wet and silent. Chippy
did not greet us nor we him. A short distance to the west of us, poor
Billy Densmore watched helplessly from the deck of *The Prince of Wales*
while from the beach the mournful trio of Frank Morley and Al Wells
and Dynamite Pete looked on. The fog rose, fell, caught all of us in
its wet gray snarls.

It was fitting that Uncle Jake and I, who had dragged these same
bodies from the Fairchild, should now struggle together to lift them
up to Chippy Smith, whose lot it was to pull and tip them back inside
the cabin as best he could. First one and then the other. No matter
what Uncle Jake had said, it was whiskey that Chippy had been drinking
on his flight from Juneau to Rodman Bay, as I saw from one of the
half-filled bottles sitting on his empty seat. The flying boat was in need
of varnish. A boot heel had crushed a hole in the thin wooden skin of
the hull in front of the windshield, and Chippy had not bothered to
repair the hole. It looked as if it was already settling dangerously deeper
into the water, thanks to the terrible weight of its cargo.

We pushed off. Chippy hauled in the anchor, climbed back into his
cold cabin, pulled closed the hatch. Just as the nose of the dory touched
the beach the engine of the flying boat burst into a flaming roar and,
as I turned from my place at the outboard motor to watch, the old
airplane shot across the choppy waters, climbed steeply, and disappeared
in the fog.

"Good luck to him," said Uncle Jake bitterly and giving not so much
as a glance in the direction of the departing plane.

In less than an hour *The Prince of Wales,* with a stricken and silent
Uncle Jake at the helm, was nosing at quarter speed through fog and
rain and darkness out of Rodman Bay.

49 —

Uncle Jake rallied. On High Ridge Street he spent days telling Hilda Laubenstein our adventures in Rodman Bay while Frank Morley and I sat beside the two of them and listened, raptly, as if we ourselves had not been there. All was well.

Still there was something that Uncle Jake could not forget or condone: the two passengers missing from the Fairchild the day we found it. So one afternoon he dressed himself up in business suit, fedora, and a new lightweight topcoat he had treated himself to on our return to Juneau, and went down to the Coast Guard station to investigate, as he said, the facts. Uncle Jake never told us how many Coast Guardsmen he interrogated for those three hours he had spent downtown. But that evening, when once again we were assembled for supper in our house on High Ridge Street, Uncle Jake told us that his nagging thoughts had proved correct. With mounting energy and brightening eye, he told us that what he had learned exceeded by far the worst of his fears. Yes, he said, Rex Ainsworth had carried three passengers on that fatal flight. And who were the two that were missing? None other, he cried, than Jim McNear and Fred Stokely, those fine workers he had taken down to Kuiu and whom, he said, he should have signed onto *The Prince of Wales* instead of the Bohunk and A. L. Wells. If he had exercised better judgment, he said, those two men would not be dead, as presumably they were. He paused. He accepted the tall glass of vanilla ice cream and ginger ale that Hilda handed him at this strategic moment. The ice cream was a recently added touch of Hilda's that made the best drink in the world, as Uncle Jake loved to say. And what, he finally asked, did they think? Wasn't he obligated to return as quickly as possible to Rodman Bay and search until he found those bodies just as he had the others? After all, he said, they couldn't have just been flung into the high heavens and left up there.

Frank Morley looked askance at his partner, and then Hilda Laubenstein, standing and removing Sissy's apron while something began to burn on the stove, told Uncle Jake exactly what he wanted to hear:

that never had she heard anything so infuriatingly foolish in all her life, and that Uncle Jake had had some pretty wild ideas in his time but that this was the worst. Uncle Jake laughed and told Hilda to put on her apron and get back to her cooking. Later he admitted to Frank Morley and me that he regretted the deaths of McNear and Stokely but had told his story and raised his question mainly to get a rise out of Hilda, who had not, unbeknownst to Uncle Jake, believed one word of his proposal to return to Rodman Bay and was learning quickly, as she confided to me still later, how best to please my father.

It was mid-April of 1940. The weather was unseasonably warm and dry. And it was at this time that Uncle Jake declared that there was something new on the air that would again require the services of *The Prince of Wales,* though it was not to sail to within five hundred miles of Rodman Bay. Something extraordinary lay ahead, he declared, and he could feel whatever it was in his bones. The hounds of the future or the powers that be were going to prove for once benevolent. The problem was to ready *The Prince of Wales.* So every morning Uncle Jake donned his office clothes and strode down the hill through the surprisingly sweet air to *The Prince of Wales.* In the pilothouse he changed from business suit and oxfords to overalls and rubber boots and went to work. He allowed no one to join him, no one to help him, not even me. Alone he overhauled the diesel engine, alone he gave the entire interior of the old boat two new coats of thick white paint. He rid the old boat of armfuls, as he said, of useless junk, and tightened fittings, polished brass, surveyed his work with pleasure.

But in fact those last April days were mine. Uncle Jake took more and more to staying away from our house on High Ridge Street which—a fact that he completely ignored—was far more in need of repairs than *The Prince of Wales.* If he was not on the boat, then he was down at Guns & Locks & Clothes or standing alone with Patsy Ann, then still alive, on the docks. In his absence I found myself turning away somewhat from Frank Morley and Sitka Charley to Hilda Laubenstein. I joined her among her sick Indian children; many an afternoon we ate lunch at Doug's; many an evening I visited Hilda's apartment below Doc Haines's office and living quarters until Hilda would look at her watch and say it was time to go back up to High Ridge Street and fix supper for the boys, as she had begun to call them. Between my tenth birthday and my approaching fifteenth, Hilda had changed. With each of her additional five years of age—she was now forty, as Sissy would have been had she lived—Hilda had grown older but younger as well.

She had become a seriously grown woman now showing forth true youth—its energy and freshness and readiness—which in Hilda had all this time been latent. Her youngest years in Alaska had deprived her of youth, as she told me in her apartment, because she was so formidable in build and wielded such power as a government nurse that there was never a man who didn't shy away from her big body, the black bag filled with pills and needles and syringes, the Red Cross pin she always wore on her breast. From the beginning she struck all men as handsome, true enough, but also as matronly, and she had never been able to overcome the image. Now she was a ripe young girl decked out as Juno. The combination, she liked to say at the time, would soon prove irresistible.

Evening after evening Hilda and I talked in her apartment, she with her highball and I with my beer—I needed no word from Hilda to refrain from telling Uncle Jake that I was now a beer drinker of some experience—and in the midst of our conversations hearing occasionally the rise and fall of the music made by Doc Haines's drills. He was up there with his new machines and the old dentist's chair he had not been able to bring himself to replace, and the more Hilda told me about her carnal urges—an expression she used mainly for her own amusement— and about the intimate experiences of other women she had known, as we both blushed and laughed and raised our glasses, the more we paused to listen to the sounds of Doc Haines above our heads, without ac- knowledging our pauses. Then at last Hilda spoke to me directly about Doc Haines and his reputation among women. She made it plain who the now aging Nancy was and why Uncle Jake had such an abhorrence of Doc Haines. She herself had never dated Doc Haines, as she expressed it, but she knew plenty of women who had and did, all under the aegis of the still attractive and still generous Nancy. On and on went Hilda, using such words as petting, disrobing, succumbing, and recreating meetings flagrant or clandestine, and with each of her stories—about grateful women and the nearly feminine prowess of Doc Haines and the articles of underclothing these women wore and the way she had heard that Doc Haines kissed and satisfied each and every one of his women, once only or as many times as they wished—Hilda kindled all the more explicitly her desire and mine. Anything of a passionate nature that a woman did to herself or to a man or allowed a man to do to her was all right by Hilda as she told me one flushed evening after another. Doc Haines, she would say, and we would both sigh and then laugh in each other's faces. But our listening to what was going on above our heads was serious.

In ways that only I could see, Uncle Jake was beginning to detect in some half-conscious fashion this hardly concealed flowering of Hilda's inner life—certainly he never detected mine—which was why he talked incessantly and with ever greater assurance and boisterousness about the new adventure that was fast approaching and that lay just around the bend for all of us. We tried to disguise the feelings we had enjoyed, Hilda and I, and also to disguise our breaths with Dentyne chewing gum as we climbed the hill. But Uncle Jake hung back increasingly from Hilda.

One night she told me with a hug, a kiss on the cheek, and a laugh that Doc Haines was on the lookout for a girl to work for him. He needed a young girl, Hilda said, to run his errands and to do his typing and eventually to acquire the skills of a dental hygienist and even, finally, those of a full-fledged dentist's nursing assistant. Now Doc Haines needed his young girl for only several hours a day, so that I might become that lucky girl with Uncle Jake becoming none the wiser. And so I did. Later, not long after my last trip on *The Prince of Wales,* Hilda told me that it was she herself who, of course, had told Doc Haines that he needed some help and that I was the perfect girl for the job. Naturally Doc Haines agreed. Thus it was that I had already worked for the small and wiry dentist two weeks and had clearly begun to understand from his manner alone what Hilda had been talking about all this while before Uncle Jake heard the best news he had ever heard in his life and had made, more gallantly and enthusiastically than ever before, his announcement.

The announcement was that we were going up to Goodnews Bay immediately. Sitka Charley had told Frank Morley, who in turn had summoned Uncle Jake to Guns & Locks & Clothes to hear from Sitka Charley's own lips the news. After all these years Sitka Charley had finally discovered what Uncle Jake wanted most to know: the whereabouts of the Lincoln totem pole.

50 —

May 1, 1940. Entrance to Goodnews Bay. Early morning. Sunshine. Calm waters. Jake at the wheel. High spirits. The chance of a lifetime, Jake says. What a pleasure to be at his side.

My mother's voice.

But Dynamite Pete, not Uncle Jake, was at the wheel that early morning on the first of May, and it was I, not Sissy, who, along with Frank Morley and Sitka Charley, was standing at my father's side as we passed at less than quarter speed through the narrow entrance to Goodnews Bay. We were grouped near the pilothouse at the starboard rail; the light of the day illumined each of us from within; the heavily wooded and rock-strewn shores between which we were moving were so close that Uncle Jake could have easily tossed an orange, as he said with a laugh, from boat to shore. But there was no danger, he said, because the water at the entrance to Goodnews Bay was fifty fathoms deep, and the port and starboard shores dropped off so abruptly that there was not the slightest chance that we could hit a rock or run aground. We were safe and, by Uncle Jake's unerring calculations, were less than an hour from our destination.

We had already breakfasted. Frank Morley and Uncle Jake and even Sitka Charley were freshly shaven. Our shirts were open at the throat, our sleeves rolled up. The still bright morning air was sweet with the scent of wild flowers buried invisibly deep in the shadows cast by living and rotted trees alike. Shovels, axes, and the special equipment needed for salvaging the Lincoln totem pole—block and tackle, a great and neatly folded rectangular bundle of rope netting, a stack of tools that Uncle Jake had rented from a logging firm in Juneau and that consisted of long wooden handles affixed to large sicklelike curves of iron used to maneuver felled trees—all this special equipment was laid out in an orderly array on our recently scrubbed-down deck, ready for use. Every now and again, from where he stood with one foot resting on a rung of the rail, Uncle Jake, who was generally watching the passing shore or scanning the clear skies even as he spoke quietly to Frank Morley or Sitka Charley, allowed himself one quick and satisfied glance toward all of those physical objects that virtually assured the removal of the Lincoln totem pole from wherever it lay to *The Prince of Wales* and the long wooden cradle that Uncle Jake had ordered custom-made for the one and only example of Indian art inspired by the greatest of all Americans.

"Frank," said Uncle Jake as we emerged into nearly full view of Goodnews Bay, "just look at that, will you? Have you ever seen a grander sight? Why, that water's as smooth and shiny as a silver dollar. And those wooded hills and pink reflections—the whole thing's like a gem in some sort of magic setting. And we've got to bear this in mind: the waters and shores of Goodnews Bay are no different from those of its entrance. Earth and rocks dropping off straight as a die into fifty fathoms, so that we can practically tie up anywhere we want to and just use the boom to lift the netted Mr. Lincoln himself aboard. The situation couldn't be better or the view lovelier." Then, turning his head slightly toward the open pilothouse door behind us, "Just keep bearing to starboard, Pete," said Uncle Jake. "Just keep her steady as she goes and hugging the shore."

Frank Morley and Sitka Charley and I shared his feelings, were as appreciative as he was of the benign and shimmering sight of what we saw. A white ptarmigan flew from one cluster of trees to another; a brief flash far on the water indicated the life of a fish that would never in all this watery beauty be lured to any fisherman's barbed hook.

"The funny thing about ptarmigans," mused Uncle Jake, "is that they have completely feathered feet. Isn't that something, Sunny?"

We cast no shadow. Al Wells, who had long ago apologized for what he had said to Uncle Jake at the climax of our last trip, which was an unmentionable subject for all of us, and who in the interim had somehow become fast friends with the Bohunk, was smoking his pipe in the bow beside the Belly Burglar, who, for his part, and still wearing his apron, was blinking at the vista of Goodnews Bay.

"Now Charley," said Uncle Jake, as he had said periodically since leaving Juneau, "you're really certain about this thing?"

"I am," said Sitka Charley.

"Well, I don't know," said Uncle Jake, partly to indulge his usual inverse sense of humor, since he had believed Sitka Charley from the start, and partly to cause Sitka Charley to tell again what he had repeatedly told Uncle Jake from that first moment in Guns & Locks & Clothes, "those Suslota Indians sound pretty strange to me."

"They're not strange," said Sitka Charley, infinitely capable, it seemed, of providing Uncle Jake with the reassurance he didn't really need, "they're just different."

"Six feet tall," said Uncle Jake, "and bushy-haired and bearded and nearly extinct—that sounds more than just strange to me, Charley. It sounds made up."

"It's not made up," said Sitka Charley. "It's true."

"But whoever heard of a tribe without a history?" asked Uncle Jake. "And descended from the Ainus of Japan? Pretty suspicious, I'd say. It sounds like pure legend to me."

"A wonderful tribe in the olden days," said Sitka Charley. "They were different from other Indians. They were majestic."

"But the peoples of Japan are small," said Uncle Jake, "and these fellows are big. What have you got to say to that?"

Sitka Charley shrugged.

"Maybe they've got some Russian in them too," said Uncle Jake.

"No," said Sitka Charley. "The Ainus were white savages, not dark. That's how the Suslotas got their white man's traits."

"Well, I'm glad they got them one way or another," said Uncle Jake.

Sitka Charley did not reply. For a moment the two of them were silent as *The Prince of Wales* began to round a long irregularity in the shoreline that none of us had anticipated or noticed until now. The bulk of Goodnews Bay lay to our port side; what was now hidden from our view off to our starboard side remained to be seen.

"Now this Suslota John," said Uncle Jake, still wanting to hear again the ending to Sitka Charley's story, "he lives right here in Goodnews Bay?"

Sitka Charley nodded.

"And he and his brother are the last surviving male members of the Suslota tribe?"

"That's what I've heard," said Sitka Charley, staring into the rainbow-invested wilderness we were rounding.

"Just two old men," said Uncle Jake.

"Wonderful men," said Sitka Charley. "And their women. Besides, it's just Suslota John who's old. His brother, Eselota, is only sixty. Your age. All of Suslota John's wives have died, but he lives with his youngest wife's daughter. The husband of the youngest wife's daughter was killed by a bear. Eselota is luckier. He's married. He's married to Suslota John's only granddaughter, who is nearly fifteen years of age, like Sunny."

Uncle Jake refrained from commenting on Eselota's wife and slowly swept his arm toward shore. We saw a deer, another ptarmigan, heard the singing of tiny birds in the trees.

"There's beauty for you, Frank," said Uncle Jake. "What more could we ask?"

Frank Morley smiled and nodded.

"Now Charley," said Uncle Jake, turning once again to the crucial question, "this Suslota John is the one who can lead us to the totem pole? You're sure?"

"Yes," said Sitka Charley. "I never say anything that isn't true."

"Frank," said Uncle Jake, "have you ever heard anything like it? Of course I'd been told by that friend of mine in Washington that such an extraordinary totem pole might exist. But to think that it actually does. Why, I can hardly believe it. And to think that it took these strange birds, the Suslotas, to comprehend the freedom that had been granted to them and to all their kind in Alaska, and then to acknowledge their indebtedness to Mr. Lincoln and honor him the way they did. I tell you, Frank, it seizes the imagination like nothing else I've heard of, that's for sure."

Then we rounded the curve in the shoreline and saw, dead ahead of us, our destination. We were silent. Uncle Jake removed his foot from the rung of the rail, with both hands grasped the rail, and, with both booted feet firmly planted on the deck and his smile fading, stared at the terrain of the little cove we had entered.

"Charley!" he exclaimed without turning his head. "Good Lord, it's burned!"

We waited, Frank Morley and I, as Uncle Jake faced what he took to be his final and most brutal disillusionment.

"Charley!" he cried, "it's burned. We're looking at the ravages of a forest fire. Don't you see? If all that timber burned, then what do you think happened to that darned totem pole—if it was ever there. It was wooden, Charley, wooden. Burned to a crisp!"

Uncle Jake clutched the rail, unable to look at Sitka Charley, unable to look away from the mile or more of charred and twisted stumps and blackened earth that were all that remained in the wake of the flames that had killed everything in sight.

"No," said Sitka Charley in his toneless voice, "it's here. It wasn't burned. It's in a sacred grove of old totem poles. The wind shifted."

"You see," said Frank Morley, "you needn't have worried, Jake. Charley knows what he's doing."

"Well," said Uncle Jake, still unconvinced, "I've had the fright of my life, I can tell you."

"Nothing can harm the sacred grove of the Suslotas' totem poles," said Sitka Charley.

"But according to you they have no family history," said Uncle Jake.

"Just what's told in the sacred grove," said Sitka Charley. "Just a few old totem poles that tell the end of their unknown story. Even Suslota John has forgotten what most of them mean."

"You might have explained this whole thing sooner, Charley," said Uncle Jake, relenting, loosening his grip on the rail and once more raising his right foot to the iron rung. "Anyhow, I hope that Suslota John has not forgotten what Abraham Lincoln did for his people."

"He never knew," said Sitka Charley. "He doesn't care. He's never heard of Lincoln."

"Good Lord," said Uncle Jake. Then after a moment, "I'm sorry you told me that," he said.

"He doesn't understand why you're going to all this trouble," said Sitka Charley, "but he's willing to help."

"Well," said Uncle Jake, "I guess if he takes us to the Lincoln totem pole we'll forgive the poor old fellow's ignorance."

"He's not ignorant," said Sitka Charley.

"Jake," exclaimed Frank Morley with a laugh, "that friend of yours in Washington is in for a surprise!"

"A national monument," said Uncle Jake. "It'll stand forever in the Smithsonian!"

So faith and hope were once more ours as Uncle Jake strode to inspect for a final time the equipment that awaited the moment when at last he would require its use. He tugged at the ropes, he paused at the thirty-foot-long wooden cradle and admired the white pine, the gleaming heads of the bolts that held it together, placed one hand on its edge in reverence as if the cradle already contained its treasure. We shared his happiness, Frank Morley and I, and the light was brighter than ever and the air as yet untainted by the smell of the smoke that would greet us, no matter how long ago the smoldering had ceased, when we went ashore.

"Well, Charley," said Uncle Jake, returning to the rail, "when do we heave to?"

"Right now," said Sitka Charley.

"Here?" asked Uncle Jake. "It all looks the same to me. Are you sure this is the place to drop anchor?"

"This is the place," said Sitka Charley.

Uncle Jake stood tall, raised his voice, called out the orders that brought us to rest in Goodnews Bay. The engine went silent, the anchor chains clattered fore and aft, Uncle Jake declared that he and Frank Morley and I would be the first white people to set eyes on the Lincoln totem pole. Dynamite Pete and Al Wells said that they wanted to go along but Uncle Jake merely laughed and said that they could join us on our second trek to the sacred grove. He told them they would just have to curb their impatience and, until our return, occupy themselves as best they could by taking soundings to confirm the depths of these waters and by readying the smaller pieces of equipment for transferral to the dory.

Our landing site was a granite ledge that rose from the water as high as our chests when we stood up in the dory and Uncle Jake seized the rock and held us steady.

"Charley," he said, "give Sunny a boost."

Then all four of us were standing atop the ledge and turning inland for our first close look at the dark ashen slopes spread before us and covered more thickly than we had thought by the gaunt and tortured forest of burned trees through which we were about to thread our way. The smell of the dead fire was strong, no silence could have been more permanent or more profound. But Uncle Jake was happy enough to break it as we started off with Sitka Charley in the lead.

"Good Lord," he exclaimed, "what do you make of it, Frank? The whole place is teeming with new life! How can it be? Why, just look at that purple-majestied monkshood—that's what it is—growing on those charred twigs like violet-colored butterflies as big as your fist. And all that scattering of dwarf dogwood that's nearly reached its full height of eight inches. And all that mountain cranberry with its icy fruit, and the swarming of caribou-antler lichen. Have you ever seen such a lovely bone-yellowish color, Frank? And you can see how it gets its name, since it looks exactly like tiny replicas of the antlers of a caribou stag. And those flower-laded catkins and all those dashes and streaks of yellow as bright as a daisy. And fireweed. Have you ever seen such acres of fireweed, and isn't it ironic that it should be running rampant through this of all places? Why, nothing I've seen in Alaska touches it for beauty and sheer mystery. It's glorious. There's no other way to describe it."

On and on he talked while we stirred the ashes and unavoidably brushed against the black stumps and leaning skeletal poles of young trees. Unavoidably we too became blackened with soot while Sitka Charley led us onward and Uncle Jake continued marveling aloud at what he now called this post-infernal paradise.

We reached the top of the rise, stopped in our tracks, and there, not twenty feet below us on the downward slope, stood our ancient guide.

"Good Lord," exclaimed Uncle Jake. "Suslota John!"

"Ninety years old if he's a day," said Frank Morley under his breath.

"The king of Indians," said Uncle Jake.

"No," said Sitka Charley, "he's just a Suslota living with his daughter instead of a wife at the end of his days."

"Well," replied Uncle Jake, "I'm glad to see him."

Slowly and wordlessly we descended to the level patch of burnt ground where the old man stood as if he had come from nowhere and would never move or leave. We formed a discreet and silent semicircle facing him; Sitka Charley stepped forward and made a sign which the old man answered with some word or phrase the rest of us could not understand. Of course Uncle Jake and Frank Morley and I had been waiting to see Suslota John, as much for the mystery of the old man as for the way he was going to reward at last Uncle Jake's generally unlucky years in Alaska. Yet not one of us, including Uncle Jake, could have anticipated this first sight of him.

It was the first day in May, warm and clear; Uncle Jake and Frank Morley and I had opened the collars of our shirts and rolled up our sleeves, were wet with perspiration that caused the soot on our forearms and hands and faces to look as if it had been applied by a watercolorist using two colors only, black and purple. And there before us stood Suslota John, taller and heavier of frame than Uncle Jake and calmly dressed for winter. He wore a white man's loosely knitted woolen hat pulled down snugly on his massive head; a long scarf of the same wool and pattern as the hat was wrapped around his neck; and tucked inside pants of rancid sealskin there was a vertically striped shirt sewn from a blanket. The pants were held in place by braces as wide and fiery red as Frank Morley's; his boots were made of heavy cracked translucent skin. His bushy black hair framed his large rectangular face and reached from the edge of the hat to the scarf. His mustache and long square-cut beard were yellowish white. His nose was long and straight, the eyebrows thick and as black as the hair, the eyes as hard and black and unfriendly as those of any youthful Indian ever to murder a white man in the Territory. He clutched between his teeth a small newish-looking clay pipe that sent steady little puffs of living smoke into the ever-present smell of the dead smoke that filled the air.

Even Uncle Jake refrained from commenting on the all-too-solid yet apparitional appearance of Suslota John, who looked like a white man born unmistakably an Indian. Even Uncle Jake, admiring as he did the oldest surviving member of what Sitka Charley had called the most noble tribe of Indians ever to exist in Alaska, was daunted by the look in the old man's eyes.

Sitka Charley faced Suslota John a moment longer, with his right hand made one or two more signs, unanswered as far as we could tell, and then the young Siwash and aged Suslota started off together side by side. Somberly, silently, we followed them down the remainder of the ashy ruined slope to the edge of a vast stand of tall evergreens as healthy as the greenest grass. With rising spirits Uncle Jake murmured to Frank Morley and me that the sight of the growing trees was even more glorious than the paradoxical commingling of death and wild flowers through which we had already passed.

In single file and in descending order with Suslota John followed by Sitka Charley who in turn was followed by Uncle Jake and Frank Morley and finally me, we entered the stand of pine-scented trees on a straight path until at last Sitka Charley raised his arm and the three of us behind him stopped abruptly. Ahead of us shone the sunlight that meant only one thing: a clearing. Suslota John and Sitka Charley stepped into it. Uncle Jake waited and then led Frank Morley and me slowly forward until once again Uncle Jake stopped. Thus Uncle Jake was the first of us to stand at the threshold of the sun-filled clearing.

We were made to wait. Then one by one Sitka Charley summoned us into the sacred grove.

The circular wall of evergreens. High yellow grass. A yellow short-eared owl just visible across the grove in a shadowy pocket in the fanlike branches. Creatures racing invisibly in every direction through the high grass were soon seen and identified by Uncle Jake as brown lemmings, the little mice reputed, he said, to commit mass suicide in the first expanse of open water they could find when summer ended. And last of all the totem poles.

Those of the totem poles that were standing were tall, large of girth, so weathered that the bare gray wood of each might never have worn the thick and shining coats of paint which, at least a hundred years before this day that we gazed on them, had given blue violence to the enormous eyes, brilliant menacing yellow to the great beaks, lightning flashes of red and orange and green to the feathers of the widespread wings. Now only two of these colorless giants stood nearly straight while their brothers tilted this way and that, painfully ready at any time to fall. The few that had already gone down lay flat or nearly flat in the grass, a beak here and a wing there or the belly of some cross-armed monster rising woodenly above the yellow sweet-smelling carpeted floor of the sacred grove. It was on these fallen totem poles that the little brown lemmings were running to and fro before leaping back into the concealing depths of the golden grass.

Silently, without moving, we looked at all that remained of what the Suslota warrior-sculptors had hewn and carved at the height of their powers.

Then in a voice he was hardly able to subdue, "Charley," said Uncle Jake, "Charley..."

"You can talk," said Sitka Charley, "he doesn't care if you talk."

In fact a change had come over Suslota John, who had withdrawn to a short distance from us and had sat down on the largest of the fallen totem poles. He had taken his pipe from his mouth and was watching Uncle Jake closely and smiling at him with a smile as sinister and innocent as a child's. But Uncle Jake failed to notice the old man or to see his smile.

"Charley," said Uncle Jake, scanning the grove once more and turning his all at once strained face toward Sitka Charley, "Where is he? Where is Lincoln?"

"Now partner," said Frank Morley, "he's got to be here."

"I don't see him," said Uncle Jake.

"Look at Suslota John," said Sitka Charley.

"What's he got to do with it?" asked Uncle Jake, glancing at the old Indian. "And what's he grinning about? I don't trust him, Frank. I didn't like his looks from the start."

To Uncle Jake's surprise, Suslota John, who was still watching him with concentrated curiosity and a now much blander smile, raised his free hand and, the hand palm up and its long forefinger extended, began to beckon.

"Well, what do you make of that?" asked Uncle Jake aloud yet to himself. "The old devil."

"Go to him," said Sitka Charley.

"You better do what Charley says," said Frank Morley.

Uncle Jake then looked at each of the three of us in turn and shrugged, walked off through the high yellow grass toward the slowly beckoning Suslota John.

Suddenly, a mere half-dozen strides from the old man who despite his heavy wintry dress appeared ready to take his ease all day in the sun, Uncle Jake stumbled, caught his balance, stopped. Suslota John lowered his hand and, softening the glint in his eyes and opening his mouth so that the smile was so broad that it bared his teeth, he began to nod. A Lapland longspur, a tiny bird of spring colors, flew from one side of the sacred grove to the other and back again to the shadows where the owl stared down at us.

Slowly Uncle Jake leaned over, reached into the high grass, and with arms and hands gently spread wide the grass. He walked several feet to the left, repeated the process. Another several feet. Then he went back to where he had first stumbled and, still slowly, worked his way to his right, pausing, spreading the grass, moving on. Finally he straightened and turned around.

"Frank," he said.

Behind his back Suslota John, no longer smiling, returned his pipe to his mouth, puffed fiercely.

"Frank," said Uncle Jake again, "I guess I owe the old fellow an apology. It wasn't a ruse." And putting his hands on his hips and squaring his shoulders and relaxing, "Come have a look!" he said. Sitka Charley stayed where he was but Frank Morley and I promptly walked forward and joined Uncle Jake. He told us not to touch anything, even the grass, but merely to follow him and see for ourselves what he had to show. He started at the foot of the totem pole—to his right—and proceeded up the length of it toward the head, slowly spreading the grass, patiently allowing Frank Morley and me to lean over and admire each particular section of the totem pole that was lying flat on its back and was more slender but otherwise no different, as far as we could tell, from the rest of the totem poles secluded in the sacred grove.

"You see," Uncle Jake pointed out every time we stopped, "nothing special. Just like the others." This repeated observation seemed to heighten, if anything, his pleasure. "Just the same wings, though more stubby than those on the others—don't trip, Sunny—and the same bloated frogs with those awful faces. The same birds and bears. The same beaks that could have slit the bellies of the very spirits the Suslotas worshipped."

"But we know what's coming," said Frank Morley, his usually sad face reflecting his partner's pleasure.

"Just wait," said Uncle Jake.

As Uncle Jake laughed in triumph, we saw the lower legs and feet. A portion of straight and formal trousers that Frank Morley noted were store-bought, and the two long shoes, resembling the shoes Frank Morley wore back in Juneau, narrow and pointed and sticking up at a perfect ninety-degree angle from the immense beaver's head that the heels were resting on. Then the edge of the frock coat, then the arms, the sleeves that were too short, the long wooden hands pressed to the thin thighs hidden beneath the severe tight skirt of the coat. The narrow waist. The chest, the square-cut beard, the face. And the hat. The famous stovepipe hat with its flat round brim and the long cylinder exactly the circumference of the top of the head and rising three feet beyond the brim. Here the carver's eye had somehow failed since the stovepipe hat was slightly tilted off plumb from the otherwise perfectly greater-than-lifesized figure.

Long and hard we stared at the remarkably recognizable effigy.

"Well," said Uncle Jake, allowing the grass to swing back in place, "there you have it. Mr. Lincoln in Alaska. But what I don't understand, Frank, is the color. How on earth can those shoes, trousers, coat, and hat still retain those faint shades of the coal-black paint with which they clearly gleamed for years after this totem pole was erected? How can the black still show when there's not another sign of paint in the whole grove? It's a physical impossibility, yet there it is. It's the most wonderful touch of all!"

"I don't know," said Frank Morley. "I can't imagine what protected it. Maybe it's just that the darkest color is the only one we're never really rid of."

"Frank," said Uncle Jake, ignoring his partner's rare poetical thought, "I want to shake your hand!"

He did so and we stepped back, grouped tightly together, leaving the Lincoln totem pole to the little brown lemmings. Uncle Jake and Frank Morley immediately conferred.

"Well," said Frank Morley, "what are we going to do?"

"First of all," said Uncle Jake briskly, "under Charley's direction Pete and A. L. are going to have to clear a good wide trail from where we left the dory to the edge of this grove. That'll make them look like a couple of chimney sweeps for sure. Then we'll bring the equipment— a hard job but we can do it. Then we'll chop down one—just one— of the largest of these fine spruces and trim it and saw its lower half into five three-foot logs, the smallest eight or ten inches in diameter, to serve as rollers. Of course we'll trim away just enough grass from around Mr. Lincoln so we can work on him, and cut the grass into a decent path to meet the trail that Pete and A. L. will have widened through the forest. We want to do as little harm as possible to this sacred grove. When we are ready—I think it will take about four days—we'll spread the tarp the length of Mr. Lincoln and work him onto it, on his back, and roll him up in it as best we can—thank goodness the wings are relatively short. Then of course we'll just lift him head and shoulders onto the first roller and push him and slide the next roller under and keep going that way. As each of the tail-end logs slides out from under him we bring it forward and slide it again beneath the shoulders, and so forth until we reach the shore. The actual moving ought to be fairly easy. Just slow. The only thing we'll have to do is be careful. The value of that totem pole can't be measured in money. So Frank..."

But it was here that Uncle Jake stopped in mid-sentence as if to hear something that, through the sounds of his thinking and planning which was what he most enjoyed about his expeditions, he had been conscious of all along. Frank Morley and I looked at him and listened. A quizzical expression joined Uncle Jake's smile. Slowly the three of us, Frank Morley and I taking our cue from Uncle Jake, turned around toward the fallen totem pole on which Suslota John had been sitting. He was no longer there.

"Well," said Uncle Jake, "what do you think of that? Just when I might have thanked him, he disappears. Without so much as a word or sign."

How the old Indian had so silently slipped away we would never know. But the vacancy he left behind was as strong as the glare of unseen eyes. It was as if in his inexplicable departure he had stripped the clearing of everything except the four of us and our fallen totem pole. The brown lemmings had ceased to move. The yellow owl was not to be seen.

"Charley," said Uncle Jake, refusing to allow an old Indian to mar his pleasure or to interfere any longer with his purpose, "it's time to go back. Lead the way."

Uncle Jake did not give up his hopes for a final meeting with Suslota John, no matter how brief. But during our four remaining days in Goodnews Bay—Uncle Jake had accurately predicted the time required for the work—we never again set eyes on the old Indian. Uncle Jake finally said it was probably just as well that we didn't. It was his opinion that Suslota John was still not to be trusted.

• • •

The work began. From dawn to dusk Al Wells and Dynamite Pete chopped and sweated, complained and cursed, and looked more like unwashed coal miners than the chimney sweeps that Uncle Jake had laughingly said they would soon resemble. The trail up and down the infernal slopes was completed, the trail through the stand of green trees widened. Al Wells and Dynamite Pete cared not a hoot in hell as they were quick to say in Uncle Jake's presence, about the damn dwarf dogwood or whatever it was or for all the damn little buds and flowers that so tickled the man who ordered them about all day and didn't lift a finger.

The preliminary equipment was carried to the sacred grove, the spruce chopped down and stripped and sawed into the rollers that Uncle Jake had envisioned, and the grass was cut and neatly trimmed in a nice swath around Mr. Lincoln. All was ready. The day came.

At sunrise of our fourth day in Goodnews Bay, Uncle Jake and Frank Morley and Sitka Charley and Pete and Al—now washed and molli-fied—and I stood together around the oddly naked-looking Lincoln. No brown lemmings. No owl. Silence laden with the highest hopes. The first clear warm light topped the ring of trees and filled the sacred grove.

"Pete and A. L.," said Uncle Jake as soon as the sunlight lit up his face, "spread out the tarp as I showed you. Give it plenty of overlap. Work it as far as you can under the edge of that totem pole from top to bottom."

They did so. On hands and knees they looked up for Uncle Jake's approval.

"Now then, Frank," said Uncle Jake, "we've got to roll him over. Gently. I'll take the head and shoulders, you and Pete and A. L. position yourselves at equal intervals along this priceless totem pole. When I give the word, we'll lift him a little and, in easy stages, roll him over onto his face. Just don't lose your hold on him and let him drop. From the looks of him he must be as solid as an old anchor. But I've got a funny feeling that he's delicate."

Uncle Jake straddled the shoulders, Frank Morley and the other two took their places. The light intensified, the dawn air was fresh with the smell of evergreens and the smell of the distant wild flowers blooming in their beds of ashes. Sitka Charley and I drew closer to watch. Uncle Jake's face was glistening.

"Well," he said, attempting to master his anxiety, "are you ready? Lay hands on him then. Go easy. I don't want the slightest damage done to him. Are you ready? All right then, let's lift him—just a fraction of an inch—and start easing him over. Now."

They leaned to their task. They strained. Agony began to show on the faces of all four of them.

"What the hell," said Dynamite Pete.

Uncle Jake appeared not to hear him. Al Wells sucked in his breath, Frank Morley looked desperately at Uncle Jake.

"All right," said Uncle Jake in a voice verging on a groan, "let go of him."

"Jake..." said Frank Morley, still stooping and peering up in Uncle Jake's direction.

"You too, Frank?" said Uncle Jake.

"I hate to say it," said Frank Morley, "but we've got a problem."

"No," said Uncle Jake, "we'll try again."

"You better think about it, partner," said Frank Morley.

"No," said Uncle Jake. "Get ready. All of you. Now lift."

They tried. They did their best to seize the wood that in its present form was seventy-five years old. They grunted. They lowered their eyes. I caught hold of Sitka Charley's arm. Faint cracking noises came from the totem pole. Again they relaxed their grips, though Uncle Jake had given no order, and straightened up from their work.

"It's no use, Jake," said Frank Morley, wiping his hands on his pants, "it's crumbling, partner. It's breaking apart."

Silence. All four of them, even Uncle Jake, attempting to ignore the chips and flakes of wood they had inadvertently torn from the totem pole. Then my poor stunned father looked from man to man and not one of them could meet his gaze. Then he looked at Sitka Charley and me in mute appeal.

"Partner," said Frank Morley, "he can't be moved. We're going to have to give him up."

"Half the foot of that damn frog came off in my hand," Dynamite Pete confessed.

"Frank," said Uncle Jake in bewilderment, "look what I've done. Look at his shoulder. Some darn wolf might have taken a bite right out of it."

"We've all harmed this totem pole," said Frank Morley. "It wasn't our fault."

"But why?" cried Uncle Jake, unable to accept the obvious, "how can it be?"

"It's punk," said Frank Morley, slowly drawing forth and opening his clasp knife, "it's turned to punk. All of it."

"Wait, Frank," said Uncle Jake, "don't stab that blade into Lincoln."

"Of course I won't," said Frank Morley.

The handle of the knife was a curving six inches of old ivory the color of the elk's tooth Frank Morley wore from the golden chain across his vest. When extended, the blade was also six inches long, a curving narrow piece of steel so polished that it gleamed like sunstruck silver and so sharply honed that Frank Morley could hold between his fingers a human hair and slice it through with ease. Frank Morley stooped over, loosely grasping the handle, and gently touched the point of the knife to the forehead of the beaver supporting the weight—or so was the illusion created by the ancient carver—of Lincoln. We watched as before our eyes the blade sank slowly and easily into the rotted wood until it could go no farther. Frank Morley had exerted no pressure at all on the knife. Easily but unhappily he withdrew the blade and performed this same test at four-foot intervals down the totem pole until he had demonstrated that the entire length of wood could be perforated as readily as soft clay and was so dry that it would immediately disintegrate wherever and no matter how lightly it was touched.

"I'm sorry," said Frank Morley, folding and pocketing his knife, "it can't be moved."

"But the others!" cried Uncle Jake. "Look at them! Great big darn savage things you couldn't even begin to drive a railway spike into with a sledgehammer. Why? Why are they tougher and harder now than were the living trees they came from? Why does the one we're after have to be the only one diseased through and through with rottenness?"

There was a pause.

Then, simply, "I don't know," said Frank Morley.

"That darn Suslota John," said Uncle Jake. "I knew that man wasn't to be trusted."

No one spoke.

"All right," said Uncle Jake at last. "All right. There's only one thing left to do. We'll saw it apart. We'll saw it through the neck of that beaver so as to separate the seven feet of Lincoln and the beaver's head from the rest of it. That way it'll be manageable. We can use a canvas sling to carry him. That way we can at least preserve Lincoln himself."

"Take my advice," said Frank Morley. "Don't mutilate this totem pole any more than we already have. If you try to send any part of it to the Smithsonian, the only thing they'll get is a box of wood dust. There wouldn't even be anything to glue together. Why don't you and Sunny go back to the boat, partner? The rest of us will take care of the equipment. At least you've seen your Lincoln totem pole, Jake. That's pretty good, all things considered."

But Uncle Jake refused to leave. He told Frank Morley just to take the equipment out of his sight. He said he didn't want to hear even the sounds of them moving it once they had dragged it into the trees and didn't want to hear their voices. He said he wanted to stay alone with me in the sacred grove until he felt like moving.

In an hour there was nothing left except the space they had cut in the golden grass around our treasure to reveal that anyone had ever visited the sacred grove. In another half-hour the last of the distant sounds of our workmen had faded and from where we sat on the same totem pole on which Suslota John had sat four days ago and watched us, there was nothing to disturb the original silence of the grove. Occasionally throughout the rest of that morning and well into the afternoon, Uncle Jake stood up and strode half a dozen times across the diameter of the clearing before returning to sit once more beside me. Never did he allow himself to look at the ruin of his last dream.

Shadows joined us. The light turned a color we would not see again.

Finally Uncle Jake stood up and walked to the beginning of the pathway into the trees. He stopped, his back to me, and waited. I followed him until we emerged from the dark life of the green forest and stood looking at the burnt land we had yet to cross. Again he stopped. He turned around to me.

"Well, Sunny," he said, as he searched my face and held my eyes with his and smiled, "Frank was right. At least we found him."

Then we set off for *The Prince of Wales*.

At 11 P.M. that same night, Uncle Jake awoke me and in a whisper told me to come up and join him for a snack and mug of hot coffee—he did not say java—in the pilothouse.

Subdued light cast only by the binnacle lamp and the small tooth-like flame of a kerosene lantern hanging in one corner. The smell of warm dark air coming in through one of the pilothouse doors that he had left ajar. Two high stools on which we perched in the special pleasure of knowing that we were the only ones awake. He had changed into a fresh shirt and fresh pair of pants. He had oiled his boots. His black hair was parted in the middle and shellacked, as he liked to say, with his gel. He had fixed us each a plate of sliced corned beef and thick pieces of bread heavily spread with butter and mustard in alternate layers. The coffee was almost too hot to hold.

"You know," he said in his normally loud and cheerful voice and balancing his plate on a broad thigh, "I haven't thought of Granny in years or of how I discovered his grave in that little cemetery in France. It was a good five months before the end of the Great War. But now it's come back to me, Sunny. Poor Granny and his unpainted wooden cross. It's a good story."

We ate for a few minutes and sipped our coffee. I thought that he was being lugubrious as Hilda Laubenstein had said the last time he talked about one of his brothers, and yet I understood how much he wanted to tell me his story.

Gone were the dreadful hours we had spent on shore. Gone his collapse. Here was my sixty-year-old father once more as ageless as he had always been. Here was I, his only audience at last.

"Well," he said, glancing up into the shadows, "in those days I was just a gob in the U.S. Navy. I could have been an officer but I elected to serve my country as an ordinary sailor. I was no boy, Sunny. I was thirty-seven in 1917. Can you imagine that? I was born in 1880. Anyhow, and as if it wasn't bad enough that I tended to stand out from the rest of the enlisted men on the *Powhatan,* there soon developed a situation that brought me the envy and anger of every officer aboard.

"You see, the *Powhatan* was a troopship that plied back and forth between Hampton Roads, Virginia, and various disembarkation ports on the coast of France. I don't know what I would have done without the storms and the threat of submarines and our games of poker. There was only the smallest possible Navy crew on the *Powhatan.* All the rest of the men packed aboard that old ship were soldiers—three thousand of them and mostly Negroes whom I liked to go down into the holds to visit. They told good stories.

"Anyhow, the first time we docked at Le Havre—it was our third crossing—and even before our gangplank had been lowered, I was summoned by an extremely arrogant young ensign who ordered me to prepare at once to go ashore with my duffel. You can imagine my surprise when I reached the rail and found them lowering the gang-plank—for me. And do you know what was waiting for me at the foot of that gangplank? A limousine. A long black limousine with black shades drawn to conceal its passenger and flying a little French flag from a short staff affixed to its right front fender. Well, that was the beginning of my extraordinary friendship with one of France's youngest women members of the Secret Service. There were not many women in that organization, I can tell you."

The last of the bread. The last of the corned beef. Only coffee dregs in our still warm mugs. The greenish light that turned him into a figure out of a film. The sensation of being quietly afloat at night. The U.S.S. *Powhatan* or *The Prince of Wales*. Which?

"How my French Secret Service agent knew anything about me," he said into the quickening silence of the night around us, "was something I never quite understood. Or why she took such an interest in me. Or how on earth she knew every time exactly where and when we would arrive in France. After all, we sailed under sealed orders and even the captain himself didn't know our destination until the last moment. Yet the black limousine was always on the dock awaiting us, or rather me. You see how powerful that young woman was.

"I won't reveal her name, Sunny. It would be indiscreet, though there was nothing between us of course, except her youth, her laughter, the charming tones of her English, and all the elegance she treated me to in the restaurants of Paris and in little hotel restaurants tightly shuttered in villages that appeared to me to be all but destroyed. I don't know how she knew where those country restaurants were or how those restaurants continued to operate as they did in wartime. I don't know how they did it. Sometimes I thought that my gay young escort wanted something from me, but I never knew what. I still remember her small size, her curly hair, the black dresses she always wore.

"On it went, crossing after crossing, until for the last time—I didn't know it was the last time then—she took me off into the ruined countryside of France. She was as talkative as ever yet different. There was a brightness in her eyes and something oddly hard in her smile. She faced me, her little torso as straight as that of a girl on a horse, from as far away from me as she could get on the leather-covered seat, which was unusual. I asked her if anything was wrong. Certainly not, she said. It was simply that she was going to show me something that she knew, she said, I would appreciate.

"At sundown we stopped at another of the near-empty and half-destroyed villages. I could hear the sounds of distant artillery, she had brought me that close to the front. And do you know where she took me, Sunny? To the village cemetery.

"By then Mother had received the official telegram informing her that Granny was missing in action. That was all we knew. Granny, who was totally unlike the rest of those fliers who often, I regret to say, drank champagne before they went up and were known to fly pieces of female underwear from the wing struts of their airplanes, as if they thought they were knights of old. They desecrated everything, those fliers. But not Granny. He used to live alone in a tent pitched beside his plane on whatever landing field to which his squadron had been temporarily assigned. While the rest of his comrades spent the night carousing, he sat in front of his tent beside his plane and played his violin. Dear Granny. He was thoroughly disliked by every dashing youth in his squadron.

"Well, it was in that cemetery in a dying blaze of sun and surrounded by that distant thunder that I found him. My Secret Service agent led the way. Her high heels wobbled on the gravel of that small wall-enclosed cemetery behind the little church. The few sad monuments to the dead local civilians looked as if they would stand or at worst slightly lean where they were forever, war or no war. Then she stopped. With a flourish of her shapely arm she pointed. And could her smile have been the least bit vindictive? I wasn't sure, and besides, I was already down on one knee at Granny's grave. His rank and our family name were scrawled on the wooden cross from one arm of which they had hung his fur-rimmed flying goggles.

"As I knelt hat in hand for Granny, my escort began to talk. My brother, she said—she was standing just behind my back and speaking in tones that I thought in passing were oddly cheerful for the occasion— was a sweet but curious fellow. What flier, she asked, especially an American, would manage to crash his disabled aircraft in the very center of a poor French village cemetery instead of out in the fields somewhere as all the other young pilots did? But that's what he had done, she said, and in the process he had managed to shear off the marvelous old cock that had stood atop that church spire for five hundred years.

"I listened. I imagined Granny struggling at the dead controls to avoid the village, the steeple, the cemetery. I saw his valiant effort even as the cloth and wooden Spad crashed down and broke apart among the tombstones. I grieved for Granny.

"Her voice came back to me as the last roar of Granny's engine faded.

The villagers had come running, she said, and were amazed at what he had done. Nonetheless they respectfully cleared their cemetery of the wreckage and had honored Granny by burying him with their own family dead. Soon she would inform American Intelligence of what had become of my brother. But she had wanted me to see him first.

"By midnight we were in the most opulent restaurant I had ever visited with her in darkened Paris. I was unable to eat but was happy that she had reverted to her former kind and attractive self. Later she tried to persuade me to dance with her in a typically Parisian dance hall filled with smoke and the high voices of women and girls and the shouts of military officers. I was the only enlisted man in the place. But I was not able to dance with my Secret Service agent. So I sat at a ringside table and watched her twirling and twisting with never the same man twice but all of whom, I noticed, wore wings on their tunics.

"The next morning she drove me back to the ship and I thanked her and never saw her again. Isn't that some story?"

He paused then, stood up and stretched, and went to the open pilothouse door and leaned against the jamb and for a long while breathed deeply and stared off toward where the burned coast lay in darkness. At last he came back to me and tilted my chin and looked down at me with a love I had never seen him express this way before.

"At least I was able to tell Mother that Granny was dead and where he was buried," he said. "At least I relieved her uncertainty. And it helped her to hear the truth from me. The official word was months in coming. And isn't it strange that your old father knew such an interesting French woman in his youth?"

We smiled at each other, my father and I, and unbidden by him I got down from my stool and waited a moment until he took me into his arms and kissed the top of my head. "Well, Sunny," he said, "time for sleep."

51 —

The next morning he did not appear for breakfast. Frank Morley left the table. When he returned he announced as casually as he could that he had looked high and low for Uncle Jake and had not found him. Frank thought that perhaps he had gone back for a last early-morning look at the sacred grove. But the dory, we discovered at once, was still tied to the stern of *The Prince of Wales*. Frank said that anything was possible as far as Uncle Jake was concerned and that he and I would go ashore and see for ourselves. We would probably find him, Frank said, sitting and musing on the same old totem pole where we had last seen Suslota John.

The clearing proved just as empty as when Uncle Jake and I had left it the day before.

Back on *The Prince of Wales* Frank said that Uncle Jake must have decided to take his morning hike in some other direction and that he wanted Pete and Al Wells to join himself and me as they had done in Rodman Bay, and help search for him. It couldn't be serious, Frank said, and yet the day was getting on. It wasn't like Uncle Jake to lose track of time this way. The Belly Burglar had sat down on the edge of his bunk with his head in his hands when Frank had first expressed concern over the whereabouts of Uncle Jake and now refused to speak or move. Frank told him to bear up, but the Belly Burglar was unable to rouse himself and just shook his head.

We went ashore. We fanned out. At the end of two more hours we began to shout for him. But there was no answer and we did not find him.

Late that afternoon Frank radioed for the *Haida,* but as he reported as stoically as possible, it would be at least eight days before she would be able to arrive in Goodnews Bay.

The next morning we searched again and shouted. But there was not a sign of him. Finally Frank decided that we had better head on back to Juneau and let the *Haida* undertake a larger search as soon as she could. Frank told me that Uncle Jake wouldn't be missing for long. That was his promise.

52 —

On August 17, 1940, the day I turned fifteen, Frank and Hilda and Sitka Charley took me to dinner at the Baranof Hotel. Public attitudes toward Indians had begun to change by then and Charley, like Frank, was wearing a white shirt and tie. For the three months since our return to Juneau I had vacillated between spending my nights with Hilda in her now erotically charged apartment and with Frank and Charley in the loft above Guns & Locks & Clothes.

There were candles, fifteen roses, a bottle of champagne that Frank said the occasion called for. He entertained us, or tried to, with stories he said Uncle Jake would have appreciated or with stories about Uncle Jake that none of us had yet heard. Charley told a story or two. Hilda went off on a lengthy spirited tale about the disappointed love that had sent her—too many years ago for a woman to confess—to Alaska, and made hilarious fun of the little westerner who had jilted her without a word. Even Frank laughed at Hilda's story though uncomfortably.

In the midst of the cake, which was hardly the time for intruding into the festivities such a subject, suddenly I found myself voicing unemotionally a decision I had been half-consciously thinking about for weeks. I told them that I wanted to remove our personal effects from the house on High Ridge Street. I said that I wanted to go up to the house—it had remained locked since we had left Juneau for Goodnews Bay—first thing in the morning. After a long silence, Frank said that we could use Charley's new pickup truck and that they would both help. Hilda, knowing that Frank had meant to exclude her, said that she would meet us at 8 A.M. in front of Guns & Locks & Clothes.

A ring set with a tiny nugget of sardonyx, my birthstone, from Frank. A new carved leather belt from Charley. A flat box wrapped in pink tissue and tied with a florid pink bow that Hilda said I would have to wait to open until I was alone with her or in the privacy of my blanketed corner of the loft. The men, she said with a laugh, would understand.

• • •

In the morning Charley was waiting for us behind the wheel of his truck on top of the hill, where he stayed until Frank needed him to lend a hand loading the truck. Hilda and Frank and I stood on the unpainted sagging veranda while Frank turned the key in the rusty lock. Before we entered Frank suggested that Hilda wait in the cab of the truck with Charley, but I told Frank that Hilda and I would take care of Sissy's things and mine alone after he and I had packed up Uncle Jake's belongings, also alone. So Hilda trusted herself to sitting sideways on the veranda railing, one leg swinging, and admiring the summer morning light spreading down the slopes of Mount Roberts while Frank and I went inside the house and put up the shades and opened the windows and kitchen door for air. We found the heavy leather valises that all but filled the closet where Uncle Jake had put them when we had first entered the house on High Ridge Street in 1930. They were moldy, though with a brush of Frank's sleeve the brass locks shone as brightly as when Uncle Jake had bought the valises in the most expensive leather-goods store he could find at the time back east.

We packed the camel's hair coat, the light topcoat, the old stylish fedora. Frank said it was a pity to have to crush Uncle Jake's favorite hat just to jam it into a suitcase, but I insisted. It took us another forty minutes to fill four more valises with all we could find of my father's eastern clothes and Alaskan clothes, leaving the rest of it, including his extra pairs of boots, to be carried to the truck in armfuls and turned over to Charley if he wanted them, which he did. Then Frank carried the valises one by one to the veranda, where he stood smoking while Hilda joined me.

There were two small leather monogrammed valises still standing in the middle of the living-room floor. Sissy's. I opened them. Then as I suddenly understood I had been wanting to do for years, I removed Sissy's dusty purse from the doorknob and placed it, without looking at its contents, into the first valise. Hilda knelt, I brought her Sissy's few articles of wearing apparel—the dresses, her overcoat, the Scottish hat—and her sheet music and modest collection of cosmetics. Then I turned to the bottom three drawers of the bureau. Gently I passed to Hilda Sissy's lingerie, the last old-fashioned signs of her feminine self and still smelling of the lavender scent she had loved. In the last drawer I came upon a stunning find: a pair of ancient fur-rimmed flying goggles. I picked them up and stuffed them into one of the hip pockets in my denim pants. Hilda made no comment. Later the goggles became my good-luck talisman.

At last, on hands and knees before the two valises, Hilda said that she had spent the last five best years of her life waiting for Uncle Jake and that now she could hardly bear what had happened. We hugged each other, she used her handkerchief. I thanked her for helping and asked her to accept the two valises and do with them what she wanted. I said that I had made my choice and had decided to live with Frank and Charley where I belonged. She and Frank and Charley and I would still have our weekly suppers at Doug's though there could be no more games of hearts. She and I would still have our evenings together in her apartment. Nothing would change.

Frank was pleased when I told him I had gone to work for Doc Haines and could now contribute to my keep, which he said was unnecessary. Hilda plied me with nightly questions about our small handsome romantic dentist.

Only weeks after I had accepted my full-time job with Doc Haines, I was working at his side each time he drilled or pulled a tooth and was distracting his male patients from their pain with my female youth, which he told me he had known from the start I'd do. I began to pay attention to the effect I had on the old men with their mouths open and their desperate eyes on me. I began to feel in my own body what those old men were feeling in theirs, despite their shouts and grunts of pain.

It was Doc Haines who showed me who I was—true daughter of the women who used to give so many men such pleasure in the Baranof Hotel in the days of my childhood. And it was Doc Haines who readied me to lose my virginity to Charley that day when he lost his as well while Frank lay napping at the other end of the loft. And finally it was Doc Haines who, four years later, staked me, as the old-timers used to say, to what was eventually to become the fully established Alaska-Yukon Gamelands.

Until the day of his death Frank said that somehow, someday, Uncle Jake would come back to me. How right he was.

53 —

I walk outside, shivering, deep in sleep. I am not surprised to find the Gamelands clearing empty, bereft of mobile homes, reception cabin, the totem pole. There is no wooden gateway to pleasure, no drinking fountain, no sign of Gamelands. The clearing has reverted to ancient days and is frosted over, draped in mist, marked here and there with the prints of deer. It is empty except for a long low smoke-blackened structure made of logs and supporting earthen walls and a roof grown over thickly with wild grasses. The men who are gathered around its entrance are Indians of the Sundown tribe; they are silent, ominous, have come together for some dark purpose that I can almost smell on the cold air. Inside the squat lodge a woman is wailing and I have never heard before such a sound. And yet it is all familiar—the band of men, the wailing, the trickle of wood smoke rising through a hole in the roof, the rack of dried fish near the lodge. I have perhaps seen it in some other dream when the Indians were Kakes or Skoots or Wrangels or Sticks from the Yukon Country. Familiar but only from some earlier and now forgotten dream of Uncle Jake among the Indians.

I approach the silent Indians fearlessly, as I know I must, though I am white and a woman. Stooping low, I enter the squat lodge. Facing me at the far end of the earthen floor with the small fire at his feet and the wailing woman hunched in a near corner, there sits Uncle Jake, bareheaded, cross-legged, bright of eye and smiling. The interior of the lodge is both cold and hot, airless and rancid with a smell of burning fat, close as with the smell of bodies packed together, though there are only the three of us inside this squat lodge. His checked shirt is open at the throat, his boots partially unlaced, his black hair long and matted. There he sits, straight of back, hands on his knees, regal and self-satisfied in the light of the fire. I stand back in the shadows; my eyes are smarting.

Sunny, he says, what do you think? They're preparing me for burial—alive!

He is their adopted son, he explains, the only white man ever adopted by the Sundowns, and for weeks the old Otter, who is chief of the tribe, has been promising him burial alive. According to the Otter it is their highest honor, this ceremonial by which a man is buried into his own death while still alive. Only princes among men are fit for burial alive, as the Otter said, when weeks before he took the white man as his own son and son of the tribe, and, before the assembly and against the advice of the shaman, proclaimed him a prince among men.

Sunny, he says, I want to start the journey!

He looks at me but he does not see me. The wailing of the woman, who is old and hooded in her long black hair, is exactly what he wants to hear. She has been designated his adopted mother, he explains, so her harsh and plaintive grief is to him like flowing waters, like wind over sunlit ice.

I refuse to weep for you, Uncle Jake, I say. He does not hear me, and once again it is the old woman who is wailing, not I, though I would stop my ears to her ugly hopelessness if I could. In all their ceremonials, she seems to say, it is only the women who wail. Without us there would be no wailing. I do not want to become the old woman, yet I too am stricken.

Look, Sunny, he says, they're coming!

Hair-Face enters first, walks in a half-crouch to Uncle Jake on the other side of the fire, leans down, and places a pair of moccasins before the fire.

Sunny, he calls, can you see? I'm going to wear these moccasins through the icy forests of the Wolf to the river of Evil Waters. They're new, Sunny, the old woman has sewn them herself. I'll walk well protected and without noise!

Then comes the Knife, bearing the weapon Uncle Jake will wear on his hip, and carefully lays it before the fire. The buried man will flash it in the frozen night but never will that knife draw blood.

While Hair-Face and the Knife stand aside in the smoky shadows against the sloping walls of sod, and while the old woman scoops up ashes from the death-watch fire and plunges her face into her cupped hands, bathing her wizened face in ashes as if in water, and wails out of her ashen mask, one by one the rest arrive: Ever-Hungry enters with the squirrel-skin parka and the hat made of wolf's fur and the coat sewn from the skin of a seal; and Meat-Killer brings the dead man's spear and bow like a sapling and the arrows straight as the hunter's aim; and Bear-Man holds in his arms the blankets in which they will wrap the dead man for his never-ending nights in the icy forests; and finally the Otter's own two sons carry between them the black canoe to bear him down the everlasting river of Evil Waters. And these Indians too, among the proudest of the Sundown tribe, step into the shadows against the walls.

Sunny! he cries, they don't give a dead man all these things for no reason! Think of the storms! Think of the evil spirits! They know how fiercely I'll have to make my way; they know that I need the best of everything for this journey. Think of it, Sunny: buried alive!

He shovels the air with his great chin, smiling grandly at what he needs for dying arranged in a stark crescent around the fire, turning appreciatively to the old woman and her doleful music. For him? All this for him? There is nothing so terrible but what he must praise it in his childish delight, in his boundless innocence. Dupe of himself, dupe of half a dozen Indians in a dark and suffocating hovel stinking of dead fish. But I am here, whether he sees me or not, and whether or not he speaks to me without acknowledging me. I too am an accomplice to his self-aggrandizement.

Sunny, he whispers happily, the end is near!

Then into this assembly comes the old Otter himself and the disapproving shaman. They stand before the dead man, who looks up at them, face strained in eagerness, and the Otter makes his pronouncement. No white man has ever had this honor, says the Otter, but no white man has ever so deserved it. Even the shaman, he says, has admitted that the man now privileged to be alive in his death, to know the secrets of the soul's journey while still alive, is worthy of this day's event, because he is a white god with the soul of a Sundown warrior. They are proud of him, they envy him, he goes where few living men have ever been. And he shall not return, ever, but live among the shades as long as the Evil Waters flow inside the earth. And now, says the Otter, the journey begins.

He makes a gesture. The old woman howls, the shaman shakes his rattle, and Hair-Face and the Knife and Ever-Hungry and Bear-Man and Meat-Killer and the two royal sons step forth from the shadows and surround the prince among men, hover about him, busy themselves swiftly, slowly, and then are done.

And there he sits, propped at one end of the canoe, tightly bound in blankets from feet to neck and wearing on his head the wolf-fur hat, which I feel that I've seen before, and surrounded by his weapons, his moccasins, his parka. His arms are bound inside the blankets; he cannot move. But he can turn his head and does so, from side to side, slowly, showing off the thick silver fur of the hat and the gleam in his eye.

I'm dead! he exclaims, unable to bear his good fortune. I'm dead!

But then Hair-Face moves. He comes to where I stand outside their circle, hiding myself as best I can in the smoke and shadows, and when he extends to me his hand as brown and rough as bark, I accept what he gives. I am not a Sundown Indian and I am a woman, and yet I accept the little leather sack. They all make way for me, and as the old Otter points and beckons I know that I must do their bidding. The leather sack contains a shard of flint, a piece of steel, tinder. I have been chosen to give him fire. But the fire I give him will not burn, though every night he'll crouch beside it, seeing light where there is no light and warming his hands where there are no flames.

I force myself to pass among the Sundown warriors and to draw near to him, to approach the canoe that will skim the waters but never float, to stand beside the enormous waxenlike figure larger than any man could possibly be, and I have never felt so close to him nor yet so distant. His great head turns and twists, lofty and grinning. The bared teeth shine, the eyes are bright. Slowly I reach down and place the leather sack on his sloping chest; he'll have his fire. I stare at the skin and fur and wood of the paraphernalia they've heaped about him. I hear the rush of the icy waters. And still the great head crowned by the hat fashioned from the thick fur of the wolf turns from side to side as he watches the swift and silent passing of dark shores.

Sunny, he says once into the black night.

But then they are pulling me away from him, the Otter on one side of me and the crafty shaman on the other, and all of us, including the old woman, who no longer wails, are crowding out of the dark and smoke-filled lodge that is his tomb.

54 ——

Three mornings ago—the date was October 17, 1965, exactly two months after my fortieth—Charley shook me awake from that dream roughly, forcibly pulled me out of the night. We were lying between freshly laundered sheets and beneath one of my red and black checked Hudson Bay blankets—the season did not require more—and I was curled up like the fetus I'll never host and with my back to him. It was still dark, he was yanking and hurting my shoulder and even jabbing me anywhere he could with a knee.

"Stop it," I heard him say, "wake up."

Faintly I heard him; without knowing what I was doing I tried to move out of reach of his hand, his knee.

"Now," he said, "right now. No woman makes sounds like that in my bed."

I turned over. I tried to defend myself.

"It's my bed," I was finally able to say, "not yours."

"It's mine when I'm in it," he said.

"Charley," I said, "be reasonable. Lie still for a second."

"You kept me awake all night," he said.

I waited. He was silent, sick of me.

Without thinking, without meaning to, there in the darkness I told him the dream. Not once in all this time had I described a single one of my dreadful dreams to anyone. But now I told Charley about Uncle Jake and the Sundowns. When I finished, surprised at what I had been saying and overcome again with what I had been feeling in my sleep, I smelled the fire that was nearly dead in the fireplace in the other room, smelled the damp wet dawn through the open window, attempted to snuggle close to Charley. Outside it was drizzling.

"All right," he said at last and in a voice that was still harsh, "get up."

He swung himself out of bed, indifferent to his nakedness and the chill in the room, and began to dress. This time I knew enough not to argue, ask for any sort of comforting, and managed to follow his example and shivered, found shirt and pants, socks, boots, sweater, and pulled them on.

"Wear a coat," he said. "It'll be cold."

"Why?" I asked. "Where are we going?"

"Out on the boat," I heard him say as he stalked out of the cabin door and left it open behind him.

He drove the jeep—my jeep—without bothering to turn on the lights and at a reckless speed, faster than even Hank had driven it in pursuit of Marty Washington. We reached the new docks, saw no one, walked far beyond the long rows of pleasure boats and private airplanes. Dawn light was coming down the side of Mount Roberts on our left, the drizzle was finer. Below us the level of black and brackish sea water was changing, measuring as always the time that was always the same, one way or the other.

Our boots echoed on the wet wood. We arrived at the sagging disreputable docks where a few Indians, Charley among them, still moored their gas boats. We climbed down the vertical slimy ladder and jumped the final few feet into the open stern area of Charley's boat where there was hardly room to stand amidst the clutter of tangled nets, bait boxes, coils of rotted rope, tin buckets, an old car battery and tire. Charley tried to start the motor, swore, then scowled when it caught, shrouding us in blue smoke and the smell of gasoline. He cast us off, stepped into the pilothouse that had no door and in which there was just space enough for two, and steered us out into the channel.

We were alone in a small boat sitting low in the choppy water and heading south through the drizzle and gathering light toward Seattle, a thousand miles away. It was cold. There was no dirtier or less safe boat than Charley's. The fumes in the pilothouse, despite the missing door, were as blinding as the waves of spray that periodically struck the dirty glass. Our pace was slow, the motor loud, our rolling and pitching was getting worse. We had had nothing to eat, no coffee, nothing.

"I found him sitting on a crate beside the rail," Charley said suddenly above the noise.

"Who?" I asked, shivering. "What are you talking about?"

"Jake," said Charley. "That time in Goodnews Bay."

"I don't understand," I said.

"When he couldn't do anything with that damn totem pole."

"Do you mean to say," I said, "that you've brought me all the way out here just to remind me of what happened twenty-five years ago?

Why bother? I've thought enough about it already."

"It was still dark," Charley said, ignoring me, "two hours before the light would break. He was sitting on a crate beside the rail with a spare anchor—he was a strong man—and twenty feet of light chain and a coil of fresh line at his feet. 'Charley,' he said, 'I knew you'd come up here and help me.'"

"Wait a minute," I said, "what are you saying?"

I lost my balance, fell against him.

"I knew what he wanted," said Charley, "and I helped him. He always had a plan and he had one then. Infallible, he said. We would just loop the chain around his waist and fasten it securely with U-bolts—he even had the bolts in his pocket—and attach the other end of it in the same way to the anchor. Then we would cut off about twenty feet of the rope and double it so that it would go snugly around his chest up under his armpits and rise up behind him. We would tie both free ends of the rope to the rail and I would lower him over until he was dangling in his sling, as he called it, with just his head above water and the anchor held to his chest where it couldn't be heard when he let it go. As soon as he spoke my name, which would mean that the anchor had stretched the chain full length and was pulling on him, I would cut loose one end—just one end—of the line so that it would slide free through his armpits and down he'd go. Without a sound. Then I would haul in the line and cut it along with its much shorter partner off the rail. I would replace the coil of line—he told me where—and hide the two pieces of line, the long and short, the mostly wet and the thoroughly dry, in the hold. It was ingenious, he said. Infallible. He'd never be found.

"That's what we did, so he wasn't just missing. He was dead. Now you've got something real to cry about."

I stared at him. My eyes burned. I thought I would suffocate in the fumes of burnt gasoline. Again I fell off balance, grabbed one of the spokes of the wretched little iron wheel. He dislodged my hand.

"You're crazy," I said then. "He spent his life making fun of weaklings and ridiculing suicide. It's crazy."

"He wasn't a weakling," said Charley.

"What do you call it then?" I shouted. "He spent his life hurting everyone in sight—he killed my mother—but he wasn't weak. He wasn't weak enough to kill himself and abandon me and not even let us know. And why didn't you tell us? For all those years why did you just keep the whole cowardly thing—and your part in it—to yourself?"

"He told me to," said Charley.

"Then why tell me now? You think this is the way to help me forgive him and to stop my dreams and to let me leave Alaska?"

Another crash of spray. Charley letting go the wheel and looking at me.

"Now you know what happened," he said, the sea becoming rougher and the hot laboring gas motor missing a beat. "It wasn't a matter of strength or weakness. He found he had to make a choice and he made it. He knew what it would mean to you. But he thought he was leaving you Alaska."

"Will you stop?" I shouted. "It's the damnedest thing I've ever heard."

"He was sane," Charley went on, "he was sorry. But he had made his choice. And just as you'd expect he joked about it. 'Charley,' he said while I was rigging him up, 'let me tell you what I once heard an old-timer say. These were his words: *Remember that the axle grease that lubricates your bearings and liberates the crinkles from your brain isn't taken into your nozzle by gulps, but in the form of a sunny and airy stuff that must percolate slowly through your pores by degrees. Take up your gun and rod and send yourself out into it long and often. If you do, it'll be a mighty long time before you go under.* That's what he said. Isn't that something?'"

Somehow I got out of the pilothouse and reached the stern, where I sat huddled with my knees drawn to my chest and my arms over my head. Then I could feel that we were beginning to circle, to turn around. Then we were sailing in a straight line back to Juneau.

We slowed down at last. Charley killed the motor and tied us up and waited for me. Above us on the dock two Indians were talking.

"I'll tell you one thing," said Charley, and helped me up, "when a woman is tired of Alaska she's tired of life. All the life there is is in Alaska."

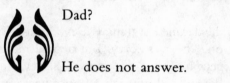 Dad?

He does not answer.

Dad?

No answer.

John Burne Deauville. Cecily Flowers. Sunny.

So here I am, an Alaskan woman feeling good in her skin in Alaska.

About the Author

JOHN HAWKES, the author of over twelve works of fiction, including *The Cannibal, The Lime Twig, Second Skin,* and *The Blood Oranges,* is one of the most distinguished writers of his generation. Mr. Hawkes, who is the director of the Graduate Program in Creative Writing at Brown University, is a member of the American Academy and Institute of Arts and Letters, and the American Academy of Arts and Sciences.